MATHEMATICAL IDEAS
AN INTRODUCTION

CHARLES D. MILLER

VERN E. HEEREN

American River College   Sacramento, California

MATHEMATICAL IDEAS
AN INTRODUCTION

SCOTT, FORESMAN AND COMPANY

Library of Congress Catalog Card Number 79-84980

PREFACE

This book is written mainly for the non-physical science major who desires an introduction to the ideas of contemporary mathematics. It can also be used successfully in courses for prospective elementary and secondary teachers. We presuppose almost no knowledge of previous courses, but a background in algebra and geometry will help to insure success with the reasoning patterns employed as well as with the content itself. Even students who have taken several mathematics courses will usually find the material here to be fresh and challenging.

We believe strongly that mathematics can be very meaningful for the non-physical science major. In an attempt to convince the student of this, we have chosen topics that are interesting; we have attempted, whenever it is appropriate, to point out the practical applications of the ideas; we have included historical material; and we have written in a light and informal manner.

The wide variations in philosophy held by proponents of this type of course can be seen by examining the many available textbooks. Some are essentially historical, with few problems for the student to work; others are almost exclusively concerned with reviewing algebra and geometry; while still others treat only one or two topics in great depth. We have covered an ample number of topics (with historical notes) to a reasonable depth, so that the book offers a full choice of topics and depth of treatment. Thus variation in approach is possible from one class of students to another as well as from one semester to another.

We want the student to come away from this course with the feeling that mathematics is useful and practical. However, it is equally important that he realize that much of modern mathematics is abstract, with practical applications not yet evident.

In writing this book we have been guided by the following objectives:

(1) A broad cross section of topics from modern mathematics should be presented, with perhaps a few topics chosen for historical interest. The topics chosen should be selected on the basis of suitability (for example, we

do not include a watered-down calculus, which would be a disservice both to the student and the subject), interest to the student, and the contribution that each can make toward an appreciation of the types of reasoning used in mathematics.

(2) The student should become familiar with some of the most useful and most dynamic areas of modern mathematics. Almost every field today, whether it be physical science, biology, social science, or business, makes use of either matrices, computers, linear programming, probability, statistics, or group theory. It is not our purpose to provide proficiency in each of these topics, but rather to provide an appropriate introduction.

(3) The book should be written in such a way that the student wants to read it. The student for whom this book is designed quite often excels in verbal reasoning, but is not accustomed to the types of reasoning used in mathematics. In particular, symbols often pose a problem to a student more comfortable with words. We recognize this difficulty and have tried to use special symbols only when they are truly necessary for clarity.

(4) A large number of problems should be included. One of the objectives of a course for the non-physical science major is to give him an appreciation for the mathematical way of working problems. He can obtain this appreciation only by working problems, not by reading about problems.

(5) Examples should be supplied for all new ideas introduced. This book contains around two hundred numbered examples, each chosen to illustrate a new concept or to show the relationship of a new concept to an old idea.

(6) The instructor should have an ample choice of topics. We have treated several topics with reasonable thoroughness; it is an easy matter for the instructor to select those topics which appeal to him and cover them in the depth desired. The book is suitable for courses of varying lengths: four or five chapters would prove ample for a three-quarter hour course, with six to eight chapters proving ample for a three-semester hour course.

The generosity of our publisher permitted us to class test this book with several hundred lower division students. The students in the test were expected to have completed beginning courses in both algebra and geometry, but some of the students had taken these courses many years ago and some students entered the course without a geometry background. The following results were noted in the class testing:

(1) Students who did not have a background in algebra and geometry tended to have trouble with parts of the material. Little actual material from these subjects is useful, but the maturity attained by studying them seems to be very helpful. (A good background in geometry is especially helpful for Chapter 11.)

(2) The topics of the book are reasonably interesting to most students and very interesting to many. Several students expressed a liking for the informal manner of presentation, the numerous examples, and the topics

chosen; "I like and understand math for the first time," was a fairly common remark made by students.

(3) The great majority of problems are workable by most students. A few problems illustrate subtle points and should be explained by the instructor, but the students can work most of the problems with only a minimum of help.

We wish to thank Robert Wesner and Karolyn Tucker of Scott, Foresman who have been a great help to us. Errors seem inevitable in mathematics texts; therefore, each author wishes to take this opportunity to blame the other.

Sacramento, California

Charles D. Miller
Vern E. Heeren

CONTENTS

TO THE INSTRUCTOR

One of the main features of *Mathematical Ideas: An Introduction* is its flexibility. The variety of topics and ideas which are discussed enable the instructor to choose which chapters are best suited to his students, his needs, or his temperament. In order to aid in the selection of subjects, we offer the following guide to the interdependence of the chapters.

CHAPTER 1. This chapter can be skipped with virtually no problem. Chapter 10 mentions base 2, but this could be briefly discussed and then skipped over.

CHAPTER 2. Requires no study of Chapter 1 beyond a definition of counting number and cardinal number (these definitions are also given in Chapter 2.).

CHAPTER 3. The basics of set notation are necessary for this chapter, and ideally it will be preceded by Chapter 2. Some of the problems require the idea of set operations.

CHAPTER 4. This chapter is quite dependent upon Chapter 3.

CHAPTER 5. Again, virtually a self-contained chapter.

CHAPTER 6. Nothing previous is needed for this chapter, but some of the material on graphing is used (and may be skipped) in Chapters 7, 8, and 10.

CHAPTER 7. The basics of set theory are required for this chapter. The last section of the chapter requires a knowledge of the graph of a circle.

CHAPTER 8. Chapter 7 is recommended for this chapter.

CHAPTER 9. No previous work is required, except for the work on group theory, which is needed for section 7.

CHAPTER 10. This chapter is self-contained except for a minor mention of the binary numeration system and a few examples using matrices in section 4.

CHAPTER 11. No previous material is needed, but it is recommended that this chapter not be attempted unless the students have had a course in high school geometry. A very bare knowledge of geometry is presupposed.

Note: a few problems throughout the text depend upon previous chapters. These may be easily skipped or perhaps assigned to better students.

CHAPTER I

NUMERATION METHODS

SECTION 1. THE DEVELOPMENT OF COUNTING NUMBERS

Numbers and Numerals. The idea of number is quite possibly the oldest of all mathematical concepts. It must have been very early in the evolution of man that the need first arose for a method of dealing with and using numbers. Casual observation as well as systematic study by psychologists and other scientists reveal that many animals have the ability to distinguish between different numbers of objects. In lower forms of animal life, however, this innate ability is apparently limited to numbers rarely greater than three or four. Indeed, this limitation is noted even in some existing, primitive, human societies, where the language contains no words for numerical designation other than perhaps *one, two, three,* and *many.*

It is a tribute to man's unique intellectual capacity that he alone has been able to transcend such conceptual limitations of the mind. Early man managed to effectively extend his meager number perception by using the process of *matching* to aid in counting objects. For example, a collection of pebbles might have been matched, one for one, with a group of animals and then, by referring to the pebbles, one could recall and communicate the *number* of animals in the group. All such numbers, including one, two, three, four, etc. are called *counting numbers.* A counting number most often indicates "how many" objects are contained in a particular collection, in which case we refer to it as the *cardinal number* of that collection. If there were twelve animals in the group mentioned above, we would say that its cardinal number (or its cardinality) is twelve. In Chapter 2 we will discuss cardinal numbers of sets in general.

All civilizations throughout history have developed, to some extent, ways of using the idea of a cardinal number. Furthermore, it seems that a second numerical concept has almost always accompanied that of cardinal number, namely the *ordinal number.* As the name implies, this type of number refers to the order, or arrangement, of objects in a collection rather than just to the size of the collection. For example, suppose there are eight teams in a certain football league. At the end of the season, these teams are ranked according to the ordinal numbers *first, second, third,* etc. As a further illustration, consider the days of the week. Tuesday is the *third* (ordinal number) day of the week, Thursday is the *fifth* (ordinal); whereas, the number of days whose names begin with the letter T is *two* (cardinal).

Cardinal and ordinal numbers can usually be distinguished by the form of their names in the language. For example, first, second, third, ninth, and forty-sixth indicate order as opposed to one, two, three, nine, and forty-six which indicate "how many." If you have studied a foreign language, you may recall that cardinal and ordinal numbers are commonly indicated with different forms of the same base word. Nevertheless, one should take care not to depend entirely upon this fact to identify cardinal and ordinal numbers. If we say that our football team is number one in the league or that this is section one of this chapter, we are really using ordinal numbers even though we use the term one rather than first.

Let's return to the development of counting numbers. As we will see, necessity was the impetus for the succeeding steps. After primitive man had learned the process of matching pebbles with animals, he discovered that he must devise a more efficient method to record large numbers. Suppose a primitive hunter encounters a herd of two hundred forty dinosaurs. Realizing that a definite count of heads (or tails) would be advantageous in convincing his fellow tribesmen of the herd's size, he begins gathering pebbles. In a short time though, not only is the collection becoming too heavy to carry, but the hunter starts losing count of the dinosaurs while in the process of searching for pebbles. The most probable solution is to find one long stick and one sharp stone and begin making a series of scratches on the stick, one for each dinosaur. Only two easy-to-handle objects are required, and the scratches can be easily made without losing count.

With this development, man has progressed to the stage of *symbolizing* numbers for the sake of efficiency. Although this is still a process of matching (marks with dinosaurs), the final result (a series of marks) is now a more symbolic and less tangible representation of a number. This process of counting by making a mark for each object in the collection is commonly called *tallying.* For smaller numbers the result might be something like | | | | or | | | | | | |.

Notice that | | | | is a *symbol* which designates the number four. Likewise, | | | | | | | denotes seven. The symbol | | | | is not a number; it only denotes or represents a number. Today we commonly indicate that same number with the symbol 4. Many other symbols have been used by various people to denote this same number, for example, IV, $\cdot\cdot\cdot\cdot$, and ☯. Any symbol that denotes a number is called a *numeral.* Hence there are many different numerals for the number four. The number itself is only an idea conceived in the minds of men. It cannot be seen, touched, or felt. The thing with which we deal directly is the numeral—a written symbol for the number.

In most cases, we need not be unduly concerned with the theoretical distinction between numbers and numerals. In fact, most often we use and speak of numerals as if they were actually numbers. Since we are accustomed to the modern Hindu-Arabic numerals 1, 2, 3, 4, 5, etc., we henceforth use them freely when referring to numbers. We should thoroughly understand, however, that these numerals provide just one of many ways of symbolizing counting numbers. Ancient Greek, Roman, Babylonian, Chinese, Egyptian, and Mayan methods of numeration, as well as others, are equally valid representations of the exact same concept, that of cardinal number.

Let's again consider the hypothetical method of numeration being developed. What we have so far is a set of numerals for representing cardinal numbers according to the scheme in figure 1.1. This method would enable

Number	Numeral
one	|
two	||
three	|||
four	||||
five	|||||
six	|||||| etc.

Figure 1.1

us to symbolize the cardinal number of any conceivable herd of dinosaurs (or of any other collection of objects, for that matter). Obviously though, the numerals for large numbers (such as two hundred forty) would be rather awkward. Even a fairly small number like twenty-five would be written \|\|\|\|\|\|\|\|\|\|\|\|\|\|\|\|\|\|\|\|\|\|\|\|\|. Besides being troublesome to write, it is rather difficult to interpret. Clearly, there must be a better way. The remainder of this section presents a series of modifications of this method, each in turn being more efficient than the last.

A Simple Grouping Method. Consider the collection of squares in figure 1.2. How many are there? Using the method of numeration described above, we would answer that there are \|\|\|\|\|\|\|\|\|\|\|\|\|\|\|\|\|\| squares. To save on space in our notation, we will introduce a new symbol, ⋀, for the number five and divide the set of squares into groups of five as in figure 1.3.

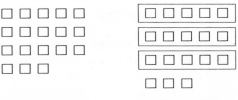

Figure 1.2　　　　　　　　Figure 1.3

There are three groups of five with three squares left over: ΛΛΛ|||. This technique is clearly a space-saver among other things. The number 14 can now be written ΛΛ|||| instead of ||||||||||||||; 23 becomes ΛΛΛΛ|||. Notice that if we had chosen to make use of groups of seven instead of five, the number 23 would be written ΛΛΛ|| (three groups of seven with two left over) and for groupings of nine, we would write 23 as ΛΛ|||||| (two groups of nine and five ones). The size of the groups is arbitrary. In each case the result is a more efficient numeration method than was the tallying technique. This *simple grouping method* constitutes the first step in the quest for ease and efficiency. The size of the basic groups is commonly referred to as the *base*. Hence if we decide on groups of five, we call the system "base 5." If the group size is seven, we are using a "base 7" method.

Let's examine the base 5 simple grouping method a little further. Numerals for a few selected numbers are given in figure 1.4; hopefully, the reader can supply the appropriate numeral for any number not in the table.

Simple Grouping—Base 5

Number*	Numeral
1		
2			
3				
4					
5	Λ
6	Λ|
10	ΛΛ
15	ΛΛΛ
20	ΛΛΛΛ
23	ΛΛΛΛ|||

* Recall that the symbols 1, 2, 3, etc. are really numerals rather than numbers; we use them here merely as the most direct way of identifying the numbers.

Figure 1.4

Suppose we wanted to write a base 5 numeral for the number 67. Would it be thirteen groups of five and two one's like this?

ΛΛΛΛΛΛΛΛΛΛΛΛΛ||

Again, it seems as if the grouping technique should enable us to simplify this long string of symbols. The introduction of the symbol Λ meant that the symbol | would never appear more than four times for a given number. Now let's introduce the symbol Ν, which represents each group of five Λ's, that is, each group of twenty-five. This means the symbol Λ will never be needed more than four times either. (See figure 1.5.)

Simple Grouping—Base 5

Number	Numeral
1	|
2	||
5	Λ
6	Λ|
10	ΛΛ
15	ΛΛΛ
20	ΛΛΛΛ
24	ΛΛΛΛ||||
25	N
26	N|
30	NΛ
31	NΛ|
35	NΛΛ
50	NN
51	NN|
55	NNΛ

Figure 1.5

Since our base is 5, the three symbols \|, Λ, and N are sufficient up to the number NNNNΛΛΛΛ\|\|\|\| (that is, 124). We then introduce a new symbol, M, for five N's. Hence 125 is written M, 126 is M\|, 130 is MΛ, 150 is MN, 155 is MNΛ, and so forth. The next symbol, W, is necessary to represent the number 625 (that is, five M's). Every number has a numeral in which no given symbol is used more than four times. The seven symbols shown in figure 1.6 are sufficient for representing every cardinal number up to 78,124. What would be needed to represent 78,125?

Number	Symbol
1	|
5	Λ
25 ($=5 \cdot 5$)*	N
125 ($=5 \cdot 5 \cdot 5$)	M
625 ($=5 \cdot 5 \cdot 5 \cdot 5$)	W
3125 ($=5 \cdot 5 \cdot 5 \cdot 5 \cdot 5$)	MM
15,625 ($=5 \cdot 5 \cdot 5 \cdot 5 \cdot 5 \cdot 5$)	MW

* Note: the dots here indicate multiplication.

Figure 1.6

Example 1.1.   What counting number is denoted by
$$\mathcal{M}\mathcal{M}\,M\mathcal{N}\mathcal{N}\wedge||||?$$

We see that $\mathcal{M}$ is used twice, which gives $2 \cdot 625 = 1250$. The one M gives 125; the three $\mathcal{N}$'s give $3 \cdot 25$, or 75; the $\wedge$ gives 5; and the four $|$'s give $4 \cdot 1$ or 4. Adding the contributions from the five different symbols used, we have $1250 + 125 + 75 + 5 + 4 = 1459$. Hence the base 5 simple grouping numeral $\mathcal{M}\mathcal{M}\,M\mathcal{N}\mathcal{N}\wedge||||$ denotes the number 1459.

Example 1.2.   Write the base 5 simple grouping numeral for the number 1969.

Observe that 1969 is larger than 625 (at least 1 $\mathcal{M}$ is required) but smaller than 3125 (no symbol above $\mathcal{M}$ is needed). Since $3 \cdot 625 = 1875$, which is less than 1969, we need three $\mathcal{M}$'s. $1969 - 1875 = 94$, so besides the 3 $\mathcal{M}$'s, we need symbols for 94. Three $\mathcal{N}$'s give 75, which leaves 19. Three $\wedge$'s and four $|$'s take care of the 19. Looking back, we need three $\mathcal{M}$'s, three $\mathcal{N}$'s, three $\wedge$'s, and four $|$'s, or $\mathcal{M}\mathcal{M}\mathcal{M}\mathcal{N}\mathcal{N}\mathcal{N}\wedge\wedge\wedge||||$. (Notice that no M was necessary.) The actual procedure can be organized like this:

$$
\begin{array}{rcl}
 & & 1969 \\
3 \cdot 625 = 1875 & \longrightarrow & -1875 \\
\hline
 & & 94 \\
3 \cdot 25 \ = 75 & \longrightarrow & -75 \\
\hline
 & & 19 \\
3 \cdot 5 \ \ = 15 & \longrightarrow & -15 \\
\hline
 & & 4 \\
4 \cdot 1 \ \ = 4 & \longrightarrow & -4 \\
\hline
 & & 0 \\
\end{array}
$$

$$\hookrightarrow \mathcal{M}\mathcal{M}\mathcal{M}\mathcal{N}\mathcal{N}\mathcal{N}\wedge\wedge\wedge||||$$

A Multiplicative Grouping Method.   Simple grouping provides a fairly workable method for symbolizing numbers, but now let's look for another improvement. In example 1.2 we saw that 1969 is denoted by the numeral $\mathcal{M}\mathcal{M}\mathcal{M}\mathcal{N}\mathcal{N}\mathcal{N}\wedge\wedge\wedge||||$. Perhaps we can design a method whereby the need for repetition of symbols is reduced even further. It would help if we had some way to indicate the three $\mathcal{M}$'s without actually writing them all. How about using a *multiplier,* together with the symbol $\mathcal{M}$, to indicate the number of $\mathcal{M}$'s intended. Recall that our simple grouping method gave rise to groups of 1, 2, 3, or 4 of a given symbol; therefore we will need a multiplier for each of these. Let's use the symbols $\odot$, $\odot$, $\odot$, and $\circledcirc$, which are, of course, arbitrary. We choose these particular ones only because they are systematic and easy to remember. Then $\mathcal{M}\mathcal{M}\mathcal{M}\mathcal{N}\mathcal{N}\mathcal{N}\wedge\wedge\wedge||||$ can be written $\odot\mathcal{M}\odot\mathcal{N}\odot\wedge\circledcirc|$, which reduces the number of symbols necessary from thirteen to eight. Sometimes the advantage is even greater. For example, 3124 can now be written $\odot\mathcal{M}\circledcirc M\odot\mathcal{N}\odot\wedge\circledcirc|$ rather than $\mathcal{M}\mathcal{M}\mathcal{M}\mathcal{M}\,M\,M\,M\,M\mathcal{N}\mathcal{N}\mathcal{N}\mathcal{N}\wedge\wedge\wedge\wedge||||$.

Example 1.3.   What number is denoted by ⊙M⊙Λ⊙|?

Taking the symbols in pairs, we have ⊙M which means three 125's, ⊙Λ which means one 5, and ⊙| which means four 1's. We can add these values as follows:

$$
\begin{aligned}
3 \cdot 125 &= 375 \\
1 \cdot 5 &= 5 \\
4 \cdot 1 &= \underline{4} \\
&\ 384
\end{aligned}
$$

Hence the number denoted is 384.

Example 1.4.   Use the new method to write a numeral for the number 1969.

We see from example 1.2 that 1969 was built by using groups of three Ɲ's, three Ν's, three Λ's, and four |'s. Hence the new numeral, using multipliers, would be ⊙Ɲ⊙Ν⊙Λ⊙|.

Our new technique still makes use of groups of ones, fives, twenty-fives, etc., but the number of each is now indicated by the use of a multiplier rather than by repeating the given symbol. That is, the principle of *repetition* of symbols within a group has been replaced by the more efficient principle of *multiplication*. For this reason, we call the new method a *multiplicative grouping method*. We are still using 5 for the base, but remember that this is completely arbitrary. Any counting number except 1 could be used as the base without changing the nature of the method.

Example 1.5.   Design a base 7 multiplicative grouping method and use it to express the number 1969.

We can use the same symbols we have been using, but some take on new values (see figure 1.7). The multipliers themselves are the same as in base 5, except the groups may now be as large as 6. Thus we introduce the new symbols ⊙⊙ and ⊕, as multipliers. Since 1969 is less than 2401, we do

Symbol Values For Base 7

Symbol	Value
|	1
Λ	7
Ν	49 $(=7 \cdot 7)$
M	343 $(=7 \cdot 7 \cdot 7)$
Ɲ	2401 $(=7 \cdot 7 \cdot 7 \cdot 7)$
etc.	etc.

Figure 1.7

not need any /W's. We can use a calculating process analogous to that used in example 1.2:

$$
\begin{array}{rcl}
 & & 1969 \\
5 \cdot 343 = 1715 & \longrightarrow & -1715 \\
 & & \overline{\hphantom{0}254} \\
5 \cdot 49 \ \ = 245 & \longrightarrow & -245 \\
 & & \overline{\hphantom{00}9} \\
1 \cdot 7 \ \ \ = 7 & \longrightarrow & -7 \\
 & & \overline{\hphantom{00}2} \\
2 \cdot 1 \ \ \ = 2 & \longrightarrow & -2 \\
 & & \overline{\hphantom{00}0}
\end{array}
$$

$$\longrightarrow \odot M \odot N \odot \wedge \odot\,|$$

The way in which numbers are broken into grouping units and in which multipliers are used in numerals is summarized in figure 1.8 with a few selected examples.

Multiplicative Grouping—Base 5

Number	Breakdown into Grouping Units	Numeral
3	$3 \cdot 1$	$\odot\,|$
19	$3 \cdot 5 + 4 \cdot 1$	$\odot \wedge \odot\,|$
88	$3 \cdot 25 + 2 \cdot 5 + 3 \cdot 1$	$\odot N \odot \wedge \odot\,|$
342	$2 \cdot 125 + 3 \cdot 25 + 3 \cdot 5 + 2 \cdot 1$	$\odot M \odot N \odot \wedge \odot\,|$
1416	$2 \cdot 625 + 1 \cdot 125 + 1 \cdot 25 + 3 \cdot 5 + 1 \cdot 1$	$\odot N \odot M \odot N \odot \wedge \odot\,|$

Figure 1.8

A Positional Method.   You may have discovered by now that there is a rather natural way to alter the multiplicative grouping method and to save even more space in notation. Notice that in each of the numerals in figure 1.8, there is, starting at the right, a pair of symbols indicating the number of ones intended, then a pair indicating the number of fives, then a pair for twenty-fives, and so on (of course, smaller numbers may require ones only, or perhaps ones and fives as in the case of the number 19). If 7 was the base, the pairs of symbols, reading from the right, would have indicated ones, sevens, forty-nines, three hundred forty-threes, etc. In general, for any base b, the values from right to left are: 1, b, $b \cdot b$, $b \cdot b \cdot b$, $b \cdot b \cdot b \cdot b$, etc. Products like these of one number times itself are often simplified by using *exponential notation*. For example, $5 \cdot 5 \cdot 5$ (which equals 125) can be written (using the exponent 3) as 5^3. The exponential numerals 5, 5^2, 5^3, and 5^4 are called the first, second, third, and fourth *powers* of 5 respectively. Furthermore, 5 itself can be written as 5^1, and 5^0 (the "zeroth" power of 5) is defined as 1. Using this terminology, then, we can say that *in a given numeral* the symbols |, $\wedge$, $\wedge\!\!/$, $\wedge\!\!\wedge\!\!/$, etc. represent ascending powers of the base (| denoting the zeroth power) and that the multiplier with each symbol tells how many of that particular power are intended. Since this pattern always occurs, is it possible to use the multipliers alone and let the power of the base for each multiplier be inferred from the position of the multiplier in the numeral? For example, if 5 is the base, we can denote the number 1416 by ⊙⊙⊙⊙⊙, using multipliers only. The idea of position then allows an automatic interpretation of this numeral:

$$2 \cdot 5^4 + 1 \cdot 5^3 + 1 \cdot 5^2 + 3 \cdot 5^1 + 1 \cdot 5^0$$
$$= 2 \cdot 625 + 1 \cdot 125 + 1 \cdot 25 + 3 \cdot 5 + 1 \cdot 1$$
$$= 1250 + 125 + 25 + 15 + 1$$
$$= 1416.$$

With this *positional method*, the numerals in figure 1.8 can be expressed more simply as shown in figure 1.9.

Number	Multiplicative Grouping Numeral	Positional Numeral
3	⊙|	⊙⊙
19	⊙∧⊙|	⊙⊙
88	⊙∧⁄⊙∧⊙|	⊙⊙⊙
342	⊙∧⁄∧⊙∧⁄⊙∧⊙|	⊙⊙⊙⊙
1416	⊙∧⁄⊙∧⁄∧⊙∧⁄⊙∧⊙|	⊙⊙⊙⊙⊙

Figure 1.9

Perhaps you have already detected a difficulty with this method. How, for example, would we symbolize the number 27 since it consists of one 25 and two 1's, and no 5's. The numeral would involve the zeroth and second powers of 5 but not the first power. We could write ⊙   ⊙, leaving a space in the 5's position, but this could easily be mistaken for ⊙⊙, which denotes seven. The number fifty presents even a greater problem, for here we must leave blank spaces in both the five's and one's positions. The resulting numeral, ⊙   , is barely distinguishable from the one for 10 (⊙   ) or the one for 2 (⊙⊙).

During the historical development of numeration methods, the solution of this problem took various peoples a good many years, perhaps even centuries. Today, with the advantage of hindsight, we sometimes tend to take some historic contributions for granted. One such case is probably the invention of the number 0 (zero). If we add the symbol ◯ to our list of multipliers, we have a perfectly clear positional numeration method. Twenty-seven can be written ⊙◯⊙; fifty is denoted ⊙◯◯. The ◯ is merely a "place-holder" which indicates the absence of certain powers of the base.

In the numeral ⊙○⊙, we say that the ⊙ has a *face value* of 1 and a *place value* of 5^2, or 25. The ⊙ has a face value of 2 and a place value of 5^0, or 1. The ○, in the five's place, has a face value of 0 and makes no contribution to the overall value of the numeral. The face value of a given symbol is always the same, but its place value depends upon the position it occupies in a numeral. The face value is always some number *less than the base* being used (which is 5 in the present case), and the place value is always some *power of the base*. Recall that the last symbol on the right in any positional numeral always has a place value of 1, which is the zeroth power of the base. In summary, we illustrate a few more cardinal (counting) numbers using the positional method in figure 1.10.

Positional—Base 5

Number	Numeral	Number	Numeral
1	⊙	10	⊙○
2	⊙	11	⊙⊙
3	⊙	15	⊙○
4	⊙	24	⊙⊙
5	⊙○	25	⊙○○
6	⊙⊙	26	⊙○⊙
7	⊙⊙	50	⊙○○

Figure 1.10

PROBLEMS

1. Identify each number occurring in the following sentences as either cardinal or ordinal.
   (a) This month has thirty-one days.
   (b) Only one team can be first.
   (c) He is seven feet tall.
   (d) March is the third of the twelve months in a year.
   (e) The number two month is February.
   (f) She is number three in a class of forty.

2. Explain the difference between a number and a numeral.

3. Identify each base 5 numeral as simple grouping, multiplicative grouping, or positional, and determine the number represented:

   (a) ᴺ∧∧I
   (b) ⊙○
   (c) ⊙⊙
   (d) ⊙∧⊙I
   (e) ᴺI I
   (f) ᴺ∧∧∧I I I
   (g) ⊙∧⊙I
   (h) ⊙○⊙

   (i) ᴺᴺM∧ᴺ∧I
   (j) ⊙○○
   (k) ⊙ᴺ○∧
   (l) ⊙M⊙∧
   (m) ᴺᴺᴺᴺ
   (n) ⊙○○○
   (o) ⊙○⊙○
   (p) ⊙ᴺ○I

   (q) ᴺᴺᴺᴺM
   (r) ᴺᴺM∧I I I I
   (s) ⊙M⊙M
   (t) M∧∧I I I
   (u) ⊙⊙⊙○○
   (v) M∧Mᴺᴺᴺᴺᴺ∧
   (w) ⊙⊙⊙⊙⊙⊙○
   (x) ⊙M⊙ᴺ○∧⊙I

4. Supply a base 5 simple grouping numeral for each number given:
   (a) 125   (e) 675   (i) 8000
   (b) 131   (f) 3636   (j) 31,020
   (c) 100   (g) 9827
   (d) 335   (h) 77,234

5. Give base 5 multiplicative grouping numerals for the numbers of problem 4.

6. Give base 5 positional numerals for the numbers of problem 4.

7. Identify the numbers denoted by these base 7 numerals:
   (a) ⊕∨⊙∧⊙I   (b) ⊙∧∨⊙M⊙∧

8. Use base 7 multiplicative grouping numerals to express:
   (a) 1421   (b) 1028

9. If the table of figure 1.7 were extended, what number would the symbol ∧∧∨ represent?

10. If ⊙∧∧⊙∧∨⊙∧∨⊙∧ is a base 6 multiplicative grouping numeral, what number does it represent?

11. The following are base 7 positional numerals. Identify the numbers represented.
    (a) ⊙⊙⊙   (b) ⊙○○○⊙   (c) ○○⊙○○

12. Give base 7 positional numerals for these numbers:
    (a) 135   (b) 697   (c) 7348

13. The first few powers of 5 are 1, 5, 25, 125, 625, 3125, and 15,625. Study the table below and try to discover an easy way to fill in the unknown numerals.

Number	Numeral
4	⊙⊙
5	⊙○
24	⊙⊙ ⊙⊙
25	○○○
124	⊙⊙ ⊙⊙ ⊙⊙
125	?
624	?
625	?
3124	?
3125	?

14. If $7^5 = 16{,}807$, what is the base 7 positional numeral for 16,806?

SECTION 2. HISTORICAL NUMERATION METHODS

In section 1 we introduced a series of related but different methods for writing cardinal numbers, beginning with the very basic technique of tallying and progressing to a simple grouping approach, a multiplicative grouping, and finally a positional method. We chose 5 in each case as a reasonable number to use as a base and followed, overall, what might have been a logical historical development. With this much of a background in these different approaches, let's look briefly at what actually did take place historically.

As with most other inventions of man, numbers and numerals were created as they were needed. As long ago as 5000 years, the keeping of government and business records by Egyptians and Sumerians required the use of large numbers. Ancient inscriptions surviving today tell us a great deal about the methods used by these people as well as those used by the Babylonians, Greeks, Romans, Chinese, Japanese, Central American Indians, and the Hindus of India. To be sure, even within each individual civilization, numbering systems varied from place to place and from time to time. We will investigate just a few of these methods.

We know that at least 5000 years ago the Egyptians were using a simple grouping system. In our earlier discussion 5 was the base, but actually 10 was much more common historically, probably largely because of man's having 10 fingers and his tendency to "count on his fingers." At any rate, the Egyptians used 10 as their base and represented powers of 10 with the set of symbols illustrated in figure 1.11. Of course some of the descriptions

Early Egyptian Symbols

Number	Symbol	Description
1 (or 10^0)	I	straight vertical line
10 (or 10^1)	∩	heel bone
100 (or 10^2)	9	scroll
1000 (or 10^3)	⌡	lotus flower
10,000 (or 10^4)	⟨	bent line
100,000 (or 10^5)	⌔	burbot fish
1,000,000 (or 10^6)	⫸	man in astonishment

Figure 1.11

given in the table are only guesses and some variations of these symbols were evidently used also. For example, sometimes the line for 10,000 was not bent but merely made longer than the line for 1. Also, the scroll for 100 sometimes appeared more like ⓔ or ⌒. Notice that the seven symbols given are sufficient for representing all counting numbers up to 9,999,999.

Since we are more familiar with powers of 10 than with powers of 5, the Egyptian method should be easier than the method in section 1 once we learn the new set of symbols. Notice that now a given symbol can occur in a numeral up to 9 times rather than just 4.

Example 1.6.   Identify the number denoted by

$$\mathrm{ဏ ဏ \ell\ell\ell\ \ell\ \ell\ell\, 9999 \, \frac{\cap\cap\cap\cap\cap\ |||}{\cap\cap\cap\cap\ ||||}}$$

Refer to figure 1.11 for the values of the symbols.

Result.
$$\begin{aligned}
2\cdot 100{,}000 &= 200{,}000 \\
5\cdot 1000 &= \quad 5{,}000 \\
4\cdot 100 &= \quad\ 400 \\
9\cdot 10 &= \quad\ \ 90 \\
7\cdot 1 &= \underline{\quad\ \ \ 7} \\
& \quad\ 205{,}497 \quad \text{answer}
\end{aligned}$$

Example 1.7.   Give an Egyptian numeral for 376,248.

Solution. $\mathrm{ဏ ဏ <<<\ \ell\ell\ell\ \, 99\, \cap\cap\, ||||}$
$\qquad\quad \mathrm{ဏ\ <<<<\ell\ell\ell\ \, 99\, \cap\cap\, ||||}$

Notice that the position or order of the symbols really makes no differ-
ence in a simple grouping numeral. $\mathrm{99\cap\cap\cap\, ||||}$, $\mathrm{||||\cap\cap\cap 99}$, and
$\mathrm{||\cap\cap 99\cap||}$ would each be interpreted as 234. The most common order,
however, was that shown in example 1.7.

For an historical example of the multiplicative grouping technique, we
turn to one of the oldest schemes known, that developed by the Chinese and
later adopted by the Japanese. Recall that a multiplicative grouping system
requires a symbol for each counting number less than the base (the multipliers) and additional symbols for powers of the base. The Chinese-Japanese
method used 10 as the base also. Figure 1.12 gives the symbols.

Traditional Chinese-Japanese Symbols

1	一	6	六	10	十
2	二	7	七	100	百
3	三	8	八	1000	千
4	四	9	九		
5	五				

Figure 1.12

Three peculiarities of this system should be noted. First, a vertical format is used (see example 1.8); second, if only 1 of a certain power of the base
is intended, then the multiplier 1 is omitted; third, the symbol for 1 (10^0)
is also omitted from the "pair" of symbols giving the number of ones. Note:
this omission is a hint of transition toward a positional method.

Example 1.8.   Identify this Chinese-Japanese numeral:

$$
\begin{matrix}
\text{三} \\
\text{千} \\
\text{七} \\
\text{百} \\
\text{六} \\
\text{十} \\
\text{四}
\end{matrix}
$$

The pair at the top is $3 \cdot 1000$, next $7 \cdot 100$, then $6 \cdot 10$, and finally 4 (meaning $4 \cdot 1$). Hence the number is 3764.

Example 1.9.   Give a Chinese-Japanese numeral for 7503.

We need seven 1000's, five 100's, and three. So the numeral is as illustrated here:

$$
\begin{matrix}
\text{七} \\
\text{千} \\
\text{五} \\
\text{百} \\
\text{三}
\end{matrix}
$$

The most obvious example of a positional numeration method is our own Hindu-Arabic system. It had its early beginnings with the Hindus and was later transmitted to Europe by the Arabs, undergoing various changes in the process. The place-holder zero (and indeed even the positional structure) was not included in the earliest forms of the system, and the shapes of the other nine symbols constantly changed. One early version was recorded in Spain near the end of the tenth century:

$$1\ 2\ 3\ 4\ 5\ 6\ 7\ 8\ 9$$

The purely positional form the system finally assumed was introduced to the West mainly by Leonardo Fibonacci of Pisa early in the thirteenth century. But widespread acceptance of standardized symbols and form was not achieved until the invention of printing during the fifteenth century.

Our own method of numeration, of course, uses 10 as its base, and since a positional system needs only the multipliers and the place-holder zero, we have a total of just 10 symbols: 0, 1, 2, 3, 4, 5, 6, 7, 8, 9.

In the numeral 7354, the face value 7 combines with a place value of 1000 to give $7 \cdot 1000$, or 7000. The symbol 3 has face value 3 and place value 100, which gives $3 \cdot 100$, or 300. The 5 in the 10's place and the 4 in the 1's place contribute 50 and 4 respectively. Consequently, we see that the number 7354 really results from the sum of four contributions: 7000, 300, 50, and 4.

The systems mentioned so far in this section have forms very close to the pure simple grouping, multiplicative grouping, and positional systems we designed in section 1 (the bases, of course, are 10 rather than 5). Now let's consider some historical examples that vary more from the pure forms.

Most probably you are familiar with the Roman numeral system, which is still used today, mainly for decorative purposes, on clock faces, for heading numbers in outlines, and for chapter numbers in books. What are the characteristics of the Roman method? Apparently a base of 10 appealed to them also, but in addition they introduced a way to reduce the number of repetitions within a group. Their symbol for 1 was similar to that of the Egyptians and repetitions of this symbol served to denote 2, 3, and 4. Instead of continuing in this same way up to 9 though, they introduced a new symbol for 5. Likewise, the 10 symbol was repeated for 20, 30, and 40, but then a new symbol denoted 50. The same technique was used for 500, 5000, 50,000, and 500,000. This is like a base 10 simple grouping system with a secondary base 5 grouping employed within each of the primary groups. A few more distinct symbols had to be used, but the necessity of repetition was reduced.

The Romans also saved space by utilizing the principle of subtraction. A symbol placed to the left of another of larger value meant that its value was to be subtracted from that of the one on the right. For example, 9 could be written IX (10 minus 1) rather than VIIII (5 plus 4). The same technique was less often applied to denote 4 by IV rather than by IIII. Figure 1.13 gives the most common Roman symbols. Multiples of 1000 were sometimes indicated by placing a bar over the entire numeral, and two such bars meant to multiply by 1,000,000. The use of the basic symbols of figure 1.13 is illustrated by the examples in figure 1.14.

Roman Symbols		Selected Roman Numerals	
Number	Symbol	Number	Numeral
1	I	2	II
5	V	6	VI
10	X	7	VII
50	L	12	XII
100	C	14	XIV
500	D or I⟩	18	XVIII
1000	M or C|⟩	19	XIX
5000	I⟩⟩	30	XXX
10,000	CC|⟩⟩	49	XLIX
50,000	I⟩⟩⟩	85	LXXXV
100,000	CCC|⟩⟩⟩	35,000	$\overline{\text{XXXV}}$
500,000	I⟩⟩⟩⟩	15,510	CC|⟩⟩I⟩⟩DX
1,000,000	CCCC|⟩⟩⟩⟩	15,000,000	$\overline{\overline{\text{XV}}}$

Figure 1.13   Figure 1.14

Classical Greeks employed the letters of their alphabet to denote numbers. One of several ways to indicate that a letter was intended as a numeral was to place a bar over it; but often this distinction was indicated by the context alone. The base of the Greek system was also 10 and the numbers 1 through 9 were symbolized by the first 9 letters of the alphabet. Rather than using repetition or multiplication, the Greeks assigned nine different letters to the multiples of 10 (through 90) and different letters still to each multiple of 100 (through 900). This scheme, usually called a *ciphered system,* suffices for small numbers, but one soon runs out of letters to use. The twenty-seven symbols given in figure 1.15 do not allow the writing of any number greater

Greek Numerals

1	α	10	ι	100	ρ
2	β	20	κ	200	σ
3	γ	30	λ	300	τ
4	δ	40	μ	400	υ
5	ϵ	50	ν	500	ϕ
6	ς	60	ξ	600	χ
7	ζ	70	o	700	ψ
8	η	80	π	800	ω
9	θ	90	$\var<$	900	λ

Figure 1.15

than 999. Numbers less than 1000 are easy to represent by the Greek method. For example, 57 would be $\nu\zeta$; 573 would be $\phi o\gamma$; and 803 would be $\omega\gamma$. For multiples of 1000 (up to 9000), a stroke was used in conjunction with a units symbol, so that, for example, 1000 could be $,\alpha$ or $'\alpha$, 4000 would be $,\delta$ or $'\delta$; and 7777 might be denoted $,\zeta\psi o\zeta$. Tens of thousands were often indicated by the letter M (from the word *myriad* meaning ten thousand) with the multiple shown above the M. For example, 20,000 might be:

$$\overset{\beta}{\text{M}}$$

One of the earliest appearances of a type of positional method of numeration occurred in Babylon following the high point of Sumerian civilization. This was one of the cases in history when the base was not 10; instead, it was 60, thus the place values in a numeral, from right to left, were 1, 60, 3600, 216,000, etc. The Babylonians did not have separate symbols for every counting number less than 60 though. In fact, their method of cuneiform writing on clay tablets with wedge-shaped sticks gave rise to the use of just two symbols in the entire system: $\langle$ and $\mathbb{I}$. In each position of a numeral, the face value was indicated by base 10 simple grouping with $\langle$

denoting 10, ▼ denoting 1. Hence 47 would be written ⟨⟨⟨⟨▼▼▼▼▼▼▼. The symbol for 733 would be ⟨▼▼⟨▼▼▼, that is twelve 60's and thirteen 1's; ⟨⟨⟨⟨⟨▼▼⟨⟨▼▼▼▼▼⟨▼▼▼ would represent $(42 \cdot 3600) + (25 \cdot 60) + (13 \cdot 1)$, or 152,713.

Remember that in section 1, when we set up our positional method, we introduced ◯ (zero) so that we could indicate when a certain position was to have face value zero associated with it. This, of course, is exactly the role that 0 plays in our own Hindu-Arabic system. The Babylonian method, however, suffered for many centuries without the advantage of a zero symbol.

The Mayan Indians of Central America employed a basically positional method (with 20 as the base) but also utilized a secondary simple grouping technique (base 5, as in the Roman system) for indicating the face values in each position. The place values for a base 20 system should be 1, 20, 400, 8000, 160,000, etc., but for some reason the Mayans multiplied 20 by 18 instead of by 20, therefore the place values turn out to be 1, 20, 360, 7200, 144,000, etc. After the 360 value, the others are properly obtained by multiplying by 20. The face values, which might be anything from 0 to 19, are indicated in figure 1.16. Mayan numerals were also written from top to bottom like the Chinese-Japanese. Notice this system does have a placeholder.

Mayan Symbols

0	◯	5	—	10	═	15	≡
1	·	6	ᴗ	11	≐	16	≡
2	··	7	···	12	≏	17	≣
3	···	8	···	13	···	18	≣
4	····	9	····	14	····	19	≣

Figure 1.16

Example 1.10. Represent 1238 in Mayan notation.

Solution.

$$
\begin{array}{rcl}
 & & 1238 \\
3 \cdot 360 = 1080 & \longrightarrow & -\underline{1080} \qquad ··· \\
 & & 158 \qquad ᴗ \\
7 \cdot 20 \ = 140 & \longrightarrow & -\underline{140} \qquad ≣ \\
 & & 18 \\
18 \cdot 1 \ = 18 & \longrightarrow & -\underline{18} \\
 & & 0
\end{array}
$$

PROBLEMS

1. Interpret the following Egyptian numerals:

    (a) ϱϱ∩∩∩|

    (b) ⌒⌒<<⌡∩∩∩||||

    (d)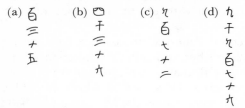

    (c) 𝔛𝔛∩∩∩

    (e) 𝔛𝔛<<<ϱϱϱϱ|||||

2. Interpret these Chinese-Japanese numerals:

    (a) 六
    ≡
    十
    五

    (b) ⌒
    千
    ≡
    十
    九

    (c) 九
    六
    七
    十
    二

    (d) 九
    千
    九
    六
    七
    十
    九

3. Give both Egyptian and Chinese-Japanese numerals for:

    (a) 3   (e) 555   (i) 7060
    (b) 17   (f) 983   (j) 9004
    (c) 87   (g) 2348
    (d) 435   (h) 1000

4. Explain why the Egyptian and Chinese-Japanese systems have no need of a symbol for zero, whereas the Hindu-Arabic system depends heavily upon the symbol 0.

5. Identify each of the following numerals as either Roman, Greek, Babylonian, or Mayan and then give its Hindu-Arabic equivalent.

    (a) ≐   (e) λθ   (i) CC|ƆƆ CMXI

    (b) ψξϵ   (f) ⬯   (j) ,δτμϵ

    (c) LXXIV   (g) <𝐈<𝐈<𝐈   (k) <<<𝐈𝐈<𝐈𝐈𝐈

    (d) <<𝐈𝐈𝐈<<<<𝐈𝐈   (h) ⬯̣   (l) M̷,ϵωπη

6. Give Roman, Greek, Babylonian, and Mayan numerals for each of the following numbers:

    (a) 17   (b) 387   (c) 4695   (d) 9999

7. How is the Roman numeral system different from a pure simple grouping method?

8. Explain what is meant by a "secondary simple grouping" within a positional system.

SECTION 3. COMPUTATION TECHNIQUES

To this point, we have considered several methods of representing or symbolizing counting numbers. The tallying technique, considered first, was improved by making use of the principles of repetitive grouping, multiplication, and place value in that order; the positional type system was apparently the most efficient. It was stated earlier that modifications in numeration methods occurred historically as the direct result of necessity. The earliest methods were needed only for counting and remembering the numbers of objects in certain collections. But as man's endeavors took on a more sophisticated nature, methods of computing (adding, multiplying, subtracting, and dividing) became necessary, and it was the quest for ease in computing which prompted most changes in various numeration methods.

It is not difficult to add two numbers in a simple grouping system such as the Egyptian. For example, ƒ ƒ 99∩∩∩|| and ƒ 999∩|||||| might be added as in figure 1.17. That is, the adding is carried out in the different

$$
\begin{array}{r}
\text{ƒ ƒ} \quad 99 \,\cap\cap\cap \;\; || \\
+ \;\; \text{ƒ} \quad 999 \;\; \cap \;\; |||||| \\
\hline
\text{ƒ ƒ ƒ} \begin{array}{l} 999 \;\cap\cap \;\; |||| \\ 99 \;\;\cap\cap \;\; |||| \end{array}
\end{array}
$$

Figure 1.17

grouping units separately. Sometimes regrouping (or "carrying") is necessary, as in figure 1.18 where the answer contains more than nine heel bones. The regrouping here simply involves eliminating ten of the heel bones from the 10's grouping unit and adding a scroll in the 100's unit.

⟨ ƒ ƒ 99   ∩∩∩∩ / ∩∩∩ || regrouped answer

+ ⟨⟨   999   ∩∩∩ / ∩∩ || / |||

answer   ⟨⟨⟨ƒ ƒ 999∩∩∩∩∩∩|||| / 99 ∩∩∩∩∩∩ ||| →   ⟨⟨⟨ƒ ƒ 999 / 999 ∩∩ ||| / ||||

Figure 1.18

Subtraction is also easy in the Egyptian system. Sometimes "borrowing" (also merely a regrouping process) is used, as in figure 1.19. Note that in this case a heel bone is replaced by ten vertical strokes in the first numeral to provide enough so that the four in the second numeral could be subtracted.

problem   regrouped form

99∩∩∩ || 99∩∩ |||||| / ||||||

− 9 ∩∩ |||| − 9 ∩∩ ||||

                   9 ∩ |||||||| answer

Figure 1.19

Processes like these, for carrying out computations, are called *algorithms*. The Egyptians used an interesting algorithm for multiplying, one which only required a knowledge of addition and of multiplication by 2.

Example 1.11.   Multiply | | | | | by ∩ | | | | / | | | |.

Build two columns of numbers, the first beginning with |, the second with ∩ | | | | / | | | |. See figure 1.20(a). Each column is built downward by doubling the number above. This process proceeds until the first column contains numbers which we can add to get | | | | |, namely | and | | | |. Then, only those numbers in the second column which are adjacent to | and | | | | in the first are added, to get the answer ∩∩∩∩∩ / ∩∩∩∩. Figure 1.20(b) illustrates the same problem (5 times 18) using the Egyptian algorithm but with our own Hindu-Arabic symbols.

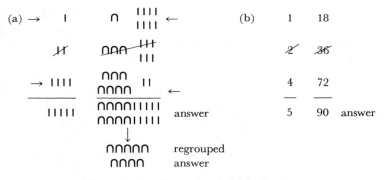

Figure 1.20   Egyptian Multiplication

Obviously, this algorithm becomes lengthy when the numbers involved are large. But we should recall that the ancient Egyptians did not have the computational advantage of the positional method. Consequently, their algorithms were quite ingenious.

Adding and subtracting with Roman numerals is very similar to the Egyptian method, except that the subtraction notation of the Romans sometimes makes the process more involved. For example, the correct sum of the Egyptian numerals |∩ and ∩|| is ∩∩|||, but with Roman numerals we cannot add IV and VII and come up with VVIII. (Even XIII would be incorrect.) The safest method here is to rewrite IV as IIII, then add IIII and VII, getting VIIIIII, which is converted to VVI and then to XI by regrouping. Subtraction is illustrated in the following example.

Example 1.12. Subtract XIV from XXVI.

Set up the problem in terms of simple grouping numerals (i.e. XIV is rewritten as XIIII):

problem:
$$\begin{array}{r} \text{XXVI} \\ -\ \text{XIV} \\ \hline \end{array}$$

problem restated in simple grouping form:
$$\begin{array}{r} \text{XXVI} \\ -\text{XIIII} \\ \hline \end{array}$$

regrouped form:
$$\begin{array}{r} \text{XXIIIIII} \\ -\ \text{XIIII} \\ \hline \text{XII} \end{array}$$ answer

Since four I's cannot be subtracted from 1, we have "borrowed" in the top numeral, writing XXVI as XXIIIIII. The subtraction can then be carried out.

Computation, in early forms, was often aided by mechanical devices just as it is today. The Roman merchants, in particular, did their figuring on a counting board, or *counter*, on which lines or grooves represented 1's, 10's, 100's, etc., and on which the spaces between the lines represented 5's, 50's, 500's, and so on. Discs or beads (called *calculi*, the word for "pebbles") were positioned on the board to denote numbers and computations were carried out by moving the discs around and simplifying. Figure 1.21(a) shows the number 934 represented on a counting board. Figure 1.21(b) shows the additional number 286 entered also, and in 1.21(c) simplification

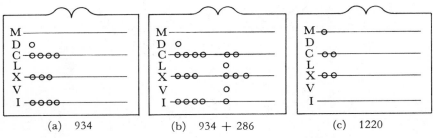

(a)   934   (b)   934 + 286   (c)   1220

Figure 1.21   Addition on a Roman Counting Board

has yielded the sum of the two numbers, 1220. In the process of simplification, five discs on the bottom line were replaced by a single disc in the V space. This made two V's which were replaced by an additional disc on the X line. Five of those on the X line were then replaced by one in the L space and this process continued until the disc on the M line finally appeared.

Although the traditional Chinese-Japanese numeration method did not break groups down into 5's, 50's, and so on, both the Chinese and Japanese used (in fact, still use) devices similar to the Roman counting boards. Any such device is generally referred to as an *abacus*. The Chinese version, the *suan-pan*, consists of a series of rods with sliding beads, as illustrated in figure 1.22. A bar divides five beads below from two above, the ones above having five times the value of those below. Beads positioned toward the dividing bar are in the "active" position; those remaining toward the outside are neutral. The rods, from right to left, have values of 1, 10, 100, 1000, etc. Hence the arrangement in figure 1.22 represents the number 31,706.

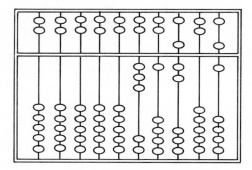

Figure 1.22   Suan-pan

The Japanese version of the abacus, called the *soroban*, usually has just one bead rather than two at the top of each rod and often has four rather than five below. The number denoted in figure 1.23 is 225,149. This type of abacus

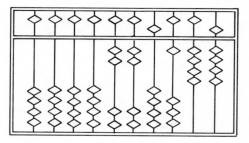

Figure 1.23   Soroban

is sufficient for representing all numbers (the one pictured will go up to 9,999,999,999), but the extra beads of the suan-pan often make computation easier.

Different types of abaci have been used recently in Russia, Turkey, and Armenia, and the device was extremely popular in most of Europe too until the positional method with its computational algorithms was finally perfected. Even today, addition and subtraction can be done more rapidly by skilled abacus users than with our usual pencil and paper methods, but the positional algorithms for multiplying and dividing are much preferred over any techniques used in other numeration methods. We should notice that the abaci used by the Chinese and Japanese are really positional devices since the value of each bead is determined by which rod it is on. As a matter of fact, in addition to the multiplicative grouping system we considered, the Chinese and Japanese employ a separate "scientific" system which is positional and utilizes all the advantages of place value.

PROBLEMS

1. Can you explain the origin of our words *counter* (as a display shelf or table in a store), *calculate*, and *calculus?*
2. Add the following pairs of Egyptian numerals. Then check your answers by converting to Hindu-Arabic notation.

   (a) 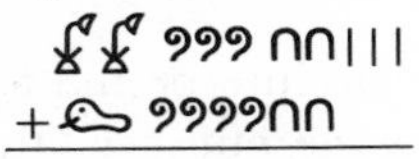 (b) 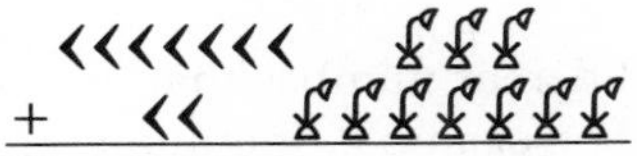

3. Work these subtraction problems in Egyptian and check in Hindu-Arabic:

   (a)  (b) 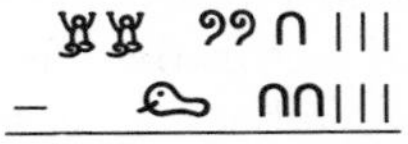

4. Use the Egyptian algorithm for multiplying these pairs of numbers:
   (a) 8 times 27 (b) 5 times 63 (c) 17 times 43
5. Compute these sums in Roman notation and check by converting to Hindu-Arabic:

(a)	(b)	(c)
DCCLIX	LIX	DCCCLX
+ LXXVII	+XLVII	+ CDIV

6. Using the same Roman numerals as in problem 5, subtract instead.

SECTION 4. BASE FIVE ARITHMETIC

In section 1 the positional method of numeration with base 5 was first introduced. It was pointed out that the basic structure of the system was not influenced by the number chosen as base. Starting with this section we discuss bases other than 10 in more detail to show how computation can be performed in other bases and how numbers can be converted from one base to another.

To begin the discussion, let's consider a base 5 positional method where the symbols are the familiar 0, 1, 2, 3, and 4 rather than ○, ·⃝, ··⃝, ∴⃝, and

☺. A base of 5 means only 5 distinct symbols will be used, including the place-holder 0. The table in figure 1.24 gives the base 5 representations of the first 30 counting numbers. Every base 5 numeral except 0, 1, 2, 3, and

Base 10	Base 5	Base 10	Base 5	Base 10	Base 5
1	1	11	21	21	41
2	2	12	22	22	42
3	3	13	23	23	43
4	4	14	24	24	44
5	10	15	30	25	100
6	11	16	31	26	101
7	12	17	32	27	102
8	13	18	33	28	103
9	14	19	34	29	104
10	20	20	40	30	110

Figure 1.24

4 denotes a different number than it would if it were interpreted as a base 10 numeral. For example, the numeral 30 denotes the number "thirty" in base 10 (three 10's and no 1's) but in base 5 it would denote the number "fifteen" (three 5's and no 1's). In base 10, we can write $3 + 4 = 7$. To express this same addition fact in base 5 notation, though, we would have to write $3 + 4 = 12$ (the symbol "7" is meaningless in base 5 and must be replaced by 12—one five and two one's). To avoid confusion, we can use subscripts with numerals to designate the base intended. Thus we could write: $3_{\text{five}} + 4_{\text{five}} = 12_{\text{five}}$ or $3_5 + 4_5 = 12_5$. We will henceforth follow the convention that a numeral without a subscript is base ten unless otherwise stated. The answer obtained when adding in a strange base is likely to be different than you would expect since you are accustomed to working in base 10 only (notice that the numbers *themselves* are no different; they are only written differently in the new notation). As another example, $4_5 + 2_5 = 11_5$. Don't think for a moment that the number four plus the number two equals *eleven*. The above equation is stating the trivial fact that four plus two equals *six*, but in base five the number six must be written 11 rather than 6 (the symbol 6 is not available). In order to insure correct interpretation, we should read the equation $4_5 + 2_5 = 11_5$ as "four plus two equals one-one, base five," rather than saying "four plus two equals eleven, base five," since the word "eleven" is the name of a specific number different than the number six.

  For adding in base 5 it is handy to write down a few reference facts in the form of a base 5 *addition table* (see figure 1.25). Any two one-digit numbers can then be added by checking the table. For example, $4 + 2 = 11$ occurs at the intersection of the row with 4 at the left and the column with

+	0	1	2	3	4
0	0	1	2	3	4
1	1	2	3	4	10
2	2	3	4	10	11
3	3	4	10	11	12
4	4	10	11	12	13

Figure 1.25   Base 5 Addition Table

2 at the top. Other facts apparent from the table are that $3 + 3 = 11$, $2 + 3 = 10$, $4 + 4 = 13$, etc. Notice that the subscripts are omitted here, only because there is no doubt that we are writing base 5 statements. Whenever the situation could be confusing, it is better to use the subscripts.

How would we add the two base 5 numbers, 422 and 243? Arrange the numbers just as you would for base 10 addition. Begin by adding down the column on the right (the 1's column) and carry to successive columns when necessary, just as in base 10 addition. The result:

$$
\begin{array}{r}
422 \\
+243 \\
\hline
1220
\end{array}
$$

Adding three or more numbers in a column is also done just as in base 10, although at first it may be easier to add them two at a time.

Example 1.13.   Carry out this base 5 addition problem:

$$
\begin{array}{r}
1342 \\
221 \\
2142 \\
\hline
\end{array}
$$

Method 1.   First add $\quad \rightarrow \left\{ \begin{array}{r} 1342 \\ + \ \ 221 \end{array} \right.$
1342 and 221

Then add 2142 $\quad \rightarrow \left\{ \begin{array}{r} 2113 \\ +2142 \end{array} \right.$
to the answer

$\qquad\qquad\qquad\qquad \overline{4310} \quad$ final answer

Method 2.   In the 1's column, $2 + 1 + 2 = 10$. Enter 0, carry 1. In the 5's column, $1 + 4 + 2 + 4 = 21$. Enter 1, carry 2. In the 25's column, $2 + 3 + 2 + 1 = 13$. Enter 3, carry 1. In the 125's column, $1 + 1 + 2 = 4$. Enter 4.

$$
\begin{array}{r}
1342 \\
221 \\
2142 \\
\hline
4310
\end{array}
$$

Conveniently, the base 5 addition table in figure 1.25 can be used for performing the operation of subtraction. To find 10 minus 3, for example, we merely locate the number which would be added to 3 to get 10, namely 2. In general, we perform the subtraction column-wise, sometimes having to regroup (borrow) beforehand.

Example 1.14.   Subtract 24301_5 from 42030_5.

Solution.

$$
\begin{array}{r}
3\;\;{}^1 1\;\quad 2 \\
\not{4}\;\;\not{2}\;{}^1 0\;\;\not{3}\;{}^1 0 \\
-2\;\;4\;\;3\;\;0\;\;1 \\
\hline
1\;\;2\;\;2\;\;2\;\;4 \quad \text{answer}
\end{array}
$$

In multiplying and dividing in base 5, we can make use of a *multiplication table* (see figure 1.26). The 31 in the lower right hand corner of the table expresses the product 4 times 4 in base 5, as three 5's and a 1. Other entries are decided in a similar manner, and once we have the table we can merely refer to it when working problems.

Example 1.15.   Multiply 342_5 by 210_5.

Shifting columns and carrying are involved here just as in base 10:

$$
\begin{array}{r}
342 \\
210 \\
\hline
000 \\
342 \\
1234 \\
\hline
132320
\end{array}
$$

answer 132320

Example 1.16.   Divide 2313_5 by 3_5.

We set up the problem just as in base 10 but carry out the steps in base 5:

$$
\begin{array}{r}
421 \\
3\overline{)2313} \\
22 \\
\hline
11 \\
11 \\
\hline
03 \\
3 \\
\hline
0
\end{array}
$$

To check the answer, multiply 421 by 3, obtaining the correct number, 2313:

$$
\begin{array}{r}
421 \\
3 \\
\hline
2313
\end{array}
$$

×	0	1	2	3	4
0	0	0	0	0	0
1	0	1	2	3	4
2	0	2	4	11	13
3	0	3	11	14	22
4	0	4	13	22	31

Figure 1.26   Base 5 Multiplication Table

When first exploring computations in a strange base, one can check his work in the familiar base 10 notation. This means converting the numbers to base 10, working the problem, and checking for consistency. To convert a number from a different base into base 10, it is easiest to expand the given number, using powers of the base as first introduced in section 1. In example 1.13 above we would convert as follows:

$$
\begin{aligned}
1342_5 &= 1 \cdot 5^3 + 3 \cdot 5^2 + 4 \cdot 5^1 + 2 \cdot 5^0 \\
&= 1 \cdot 125 + 3 \cdot 25 + 4 \cdot 5 + 2 \cdot 1 \\
&= 125 + 75 + 20 + 2 \\
&= 222.
\end{aligned}
$$

Similarly, 221_5, 2142_5, and 4310_5 can be converted. Since the answer in base 5 is 4310_5 and since 4310_5 converts to 580, the work in example 1.13 is consistent with its base 10 equivalent, shown here:

$$
\begin{array}{r}
222 \\
61 \\
\underline{297} \\
580
\end{array}
$$

The other examples above can be checked in a similar manner.

PROBLEMS

1. Perform the following base 5 addition problems and check the answers by converting to base 10.

(a)
$$
\begin{array}{r}
32 \\
\underline{14}
\end{array}
$$

(c)
$$
\begin{array}{r}
311 \\
\underline{134}
\end{array}
$$

(e)
$$
\begin{array}{r}
423 \\
24 \\
\underline{2104}
\end{array}
$$

(b)
$$
\begin{array}{r}
423 \\
\underline{102}
\end{array}
$$

(d)
$$
\begin{array}{r}
20 \\
12 \\
\underline{34}
\end{array}
$$

(f)
$$
\begin{array}{r}
43102 \\
22113 \\
\underline{42413}
\end{array}
$$

2. Multiply these base 5 numbers and check in base 10:

(a) 23
      2

(c) 324
     12

(e) 1043
     201

(b) 43
     3

(d) 444
     44

(f) 222
     222

3. Subtract in base 5 and check in base 10:

(a) 234
    111

(c) 32
    23

(e) 222
    44

(b) 42
    22

(d) 1240
    324

(f) 2003
    214

4. Divide in base 5 and check in base 10:

(a) $2\overline{)13}$

(c) $3\overline{)311}$

(e) $12\overline{)144}$

(b) $3\overline{)30}$

(d) $4\overline{)31013}$

(f) $22\overline{)121}$

5. Write the first 50 counting numbers in base 7 notation.

6. Construct addition and multiplication tables for base 7. Remember 1 row (and 1 column) is needed for each symbol to be used.

SECTION 5. OTHER BASES AND BASE CONVERSIONS

In the last section, conversion from base 5 to base 10 was explained. To change from base 7 to base 10, we use the same procedure:

$$
\begin{aligned}
365_7 &= 3 \cdot 7^2 + 6 \cdot 7^1 + 5 \cdot 7^0 \\
&= 3 \cdot 49 + 6 \cdot 7 + 5 \cdot 1 \\
&= 147 + 42 + 5 \\
&= 194
\end{aligned}
$$

All other bases work the same way. For example:

$$
\begin{aligned}
239_{12} &= 2 \cdot 12^2 + 3 \cdot 12^1 + 9 \cdot 12^0 \\
&= 2 \cdot 144 + 3 \cdot 12 + 9 \cdot 1 \\
&= 288 + 36 + 9 \\
&= 333
\end{aligned}
\qquad
\begin{aligned}
101_2 &= 1 \cdot 2^2 + 0 \cdot 2^1 + 1 \cdot 2^0 \\
&= 1 \cdot 4 + 0 \cdot 2 + 1 \cdot 1 \\
&= 4 + 0 + 1 \\
&= 5
\end{aligned}
$$

We simply expand the given number in powers of its base and then simplify the resulting base 10 expression.

If you worked problem 5 in the previous section, you made some conversions *from base 10 into a different base,* 7 in that case. Let's look at a general way of going from base 10 to base 7. Consider the number 1573. What would it be in base 7? To find out, we set up a series of place values for base 7 and enter the appropriate digits, or face values.

Example 1.17.   Convert 1573 to base 7.

We set up the following table:

	(7^4)	(7^3)	(7^2)	(7^1)	(7^0)
place values $\rightarrow$	2401	343	49	7	1
face values $\rightarrow$	?	?	?	?	?

Noting that 2401 is a larger place value than we will need (since it is greater than 1573), we then ask how many 343's are contained in 1573. The answer is 4, thus we subtract $4 \cdot 343$, or 1372, from 1573, leaving 201. Next we can subtract $4 \cdot 49$, or 196, from the 201, leaving 5. Hence no 7's are used but five 1's are needed:

$$
\begin{array}{r}
1573 \\
4 \cdot 343 = 1372 \\
\hline
201 \\
4 \cdot 49 = 196 \\
\hline
5 \\
5 \cdot 1 = 5 \\
\hline
0
\end{array}
$$

This takes care of the original 1573, which we now know is equal to $4 \cdot 343 + 4 \cdot 49 + 0 \cdot 7 + 5 \cdot 1$, or $4 \cdot 7^3 + 4 \cdot 7^2 + 0 \cdot 7^1 + 5 \cdot 7^0$. Therefore we can fill in the face values in the table, and the resulting base 7 number is 4405_7:

343	49	7	1
4	4	0	5

A convenient algorithm is available for shortening the work of the preceding example. It involves dividing the base 10 number successively by the new base and recording the remainders. Working downward, the procedure can be illustrated as in the following example.

Example 1.18.   Convert 1573 to base 7.

Solution.   remainders

$$
\begin{array}{r}
7 \,\underline{|\,1573} \qquad 5 \\
7 \,\underline{|\,224} \qquad 0 \\
7 \,\underline{|\,32} \qquad 4 \\
7 \,\underline{|\,4} \qquad 4 \\
0
\end{array}
$$

The answer is given by the remainders, reading from bottom to top. Hence the number is 4405_7, as before.

This method is good for converting any base 10 number to any other base. Going from a different base to base 10, we use expanded notation as illustrated at the beginning of this section. When conversions are made from one base to another where neither one is 10, it is usually easiest to convert first to base 10 and then to the desired base. Hence, we can now make any base conversions we care to.

Example 1.19.   Convert 5736_8 to base 3.

First we convert to base 10:

$$
\begin{aligned}
5736_8 &= 5 \cdot 8^3 + 7 \cdot 8^2 + 3 \cdot 8^1 + 6 \cdot 8^0 \\
&= 5 \cdot 512 + 7 \cdot 64 + 3 \cdot 8 + 6 \cdot 1 \\
&= 2560 + 448 + 24 + 6 \\
&= 3038
\end{aligned}
$$

Then we convert 3038 to base 3:

$$
\begin{array}{r|r l}
3 & 3038 & 2 \\
3 & 1012 & 1 \\
3 & 337 & 1 \\
3 & 112 & 1 \\
3 & 37 & 1 \\
3 & 12 & 0 \\
3 & 4 & 1 \\
3 & 1 & 1 \\
& 0 &
\end{array}
$$

The final result, read from the remainders, is 11011112_3.

Binary, or base 2, notation has drawn considerable interest, especially in recent times. This is due partly to the fact that it is the lowest possible number that can be used as a positional base (only the two symbols 0 and 1 are used), and partly to several useful applications particularly in the computer field. If we start listing the counting numbers in binary form, we need only make use of 0's and 1's, but the numerals become lengthy very soon, as is evident in figure 1.27.

Since 0 and 1 are the only digits used, binary arithmetic is very easy for mechanical or electronic computing devices. There are only four addition facts necessary in base 2 arithmetic; namely, $0 + 0 = 0$, $0 + 1 = 1$, $1 + 0 = 1$, and $1 + 1 = 10$. Together with the carrying procedure, these facts are sufficient to solve any addition problem. They are commonly expressed in an ordinary addition table, as in figure 1.28.

Base 10	Base 2	Base 10	Base 2
1	1	11	1011
2	10	12	1100
3	11	13	1101
4	100	14	1110
5	101	15	1111
6	110	16	10000
7	111	17	10001
8	1000	18	10010
9	1001	19	10011
10	1010	20	10100

Figure 1.27

Example 1.20. Add the binary numbers 1101011 and 101110, and then check by converting to base 10.

Solution.

$$
\begin{array}{rcl}
 & & \text{check} \\
1101011 & \to & 107 \\
+\ \ 101110 & \to & 46 \\
\hline
10011001 & \to & 153
\end{array}
$$

The real advantage this system has with regard to machines is that each position in a numeral can contain one of just two values. This means that such devices as electric switches (with just two possible conditions, *on* or *off*) can be used nicely to designate the appropriate value in each position.

Since the place values in a binary numeral are 1, 2, 4, 8, 16, etc. (the powers of 2) and all the face values are either 0 or 1, any counting number can be expressed as a sum of distinct powers of 2. For example, $7 = 4 + 2 + 1$ $(2^2 + 2^1 + 2^0)$, $9 = 8 + 1$, $13 = 8 + 4 + 1$, etc. Refer to example 1.11 where the old Egyptian algorithm was used to multiply 5 times 18. Keeping in mind that $5 = 4 + 1$, can you explain why that algorithm worked?

+	0	1
0	0	1
1	1	10

Figure 1.28   Base 2 Addition Table

PROBLEMS

1. Convert 376_8 to base 10.

2. Convert 4203_5 to base 10.

3. Convert 587 to base 4.

4. Convert 6733 to base 9.

5. Convert 4564_7 to base 4.

6. Convert 47 to base 3.

7. Convert 38 to base 2.

8. Convert 110101_2 to base 4.

9. Convert 335 to base 12 (Hint: base 12 notation requires 2 more symbols than base 10. The letters t and e are commonly used for the values ten and eleven.)

10. Construct an addition table for base 12 (see the hint for problem 9).

11. Use the table of problem 10 to work these base 12 addition problems:

    (a) 42*t*   (b) *e*26   (c) 984   (d) *eet*
        357   11*t*   57*t*   *tte*

12. Use the same numbers as in problem 11 but this time subtract.

13. Perform these base 2 addition problems and check in base 10.

    (a) 101   (c) 1001   (e) 10101
         10   111   1011

    (b) 10   (d) 1011   (f) 1011
         1   101   101
        11   11   111
                                             11

14. Construct a base 2 multiplication table.

15. Multiply in base 2 and check in base 10:

    (a) 100   (c) 101   (e) 1110
         11   10   110

    (b) 1111   (d) 10001   (f) 110110
         111   101   1011

16. Why do you suppose we ordinarily use base 10 rather than base 2 even though it requires us to learn 8 more symbols?

17. Subtract in base 2 and check in base 10:

    (a) 1101   (c) 11011   (e) 10
        1001   10   1

    (b) 1110   (d) 101   (f) 10001
         111   11   111

18. Divide in base 2 and check in base 10:

(a) $10\overline{)1100}$ (b) $11\overline{)1100}$ (c) $101\overline{)100011}$

19. Use the ancient Egyptian multiplication algorithm to multiply 14 times 23 and then explain why the algorithm works.

20. Show that $578_9 = 122122_3$. Notice that $9 = 3^2$, $5 = 12_3$, $7 = 21_3$, and $8 = 22_3$. Can you discover a pattern here for converting between bases where one is a power of the other?

SECTION 6. SOME APPLICATIONS OF BINARY NOTATION

If you are a gambler, you may be able to win some money playing an interesting game called Nim, which is closely connected with the binary number system. It is usually played with piles of checkers or similar objects, but for convenience we will use groups of marks to illustrate it. Any number of groups can be used, with each group containing any number of marks desired. Let's start out as in figure 1.29 with 5 groups, containing 6, 3, 5,

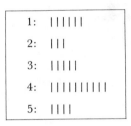

Figure 1.29

10, and 4 marks respectively. Two players make moves alternately, each in his turn being allowed to erase any number (except 0) of marks from any group. That is, he can change just one of the groups, removing anywhere from one to all of the marks in that group. The object of the game is to take the last mark left on the board. A typical sequence, starting with the situation in figure 1.29, might proceed as in figure 1.30, where player A has the first move.

Let's look at this game. At step 5, player B probably knew he had won for all he had to do was to take the remaining one in group 5 to present his opponent with a "balanced" situation. We use this expression to mean that all the remaining marks occur in *pairs* of identical groups. In this particular game, A was presented with just two groups of 5 and was therefore doomed to lose. No matter what he did to one of the groups, B merely did the same thing to the other one. Any time a player can present his opponent with a balanced situation, he has the game wrapped up. For example, if you are

1 — A takes all of group 2

1: | | | | | |
2:
3: | | | | |
4: | | | | | | | | |
5: | | | |

2 — B takes 5 from group 4

1: | | | | | |
2:
3: | | | | |
4: | | | | |
5: | | | |

3 — A takes 3 from group 5

1: | | | | | |
2:
3: | | | | |
4: | | | | |
5: |

4 — B takes all of group 4

1: | | | | | |
2:
3: | | | | |
4:
5: |

5 — A takes 1 from group 1

1: | | | | |
2:
3: | | | | |
4:
5: |

6 — B takes the 1 in group 5

1: | | | | |
2:
3: | | | | |
4:
5:

7 — A takes 3 from group 1

1: | |
2:
3: | | | | |
4:
5:

8 — B takes 3 from group 3

1: | |
2:
3: | |
4:
5:

9 — A takes 1 from group 3

1: | |
2:
3: |
4:
5:

10 — B takes 1 from group 1

1: |
2:
3: |
4:
5:

11 — A takes the 1 in group 1

1:
2:
3: |
4:
5:

12 — B takes the last mark and wins

1:
2:
3:
4:
5:

Figure 1.30

faced with the arrangement shown in figure 1.31, your wisest move would be to take one from group 5, causing that group to balance group 3. The other groups are already balanced in pairs, 1 with 4 and 2 with 6.

```
1:  | | | | |
2:  | |
3:  | | |
4:  | | | | |
5:  | | | |
6:  | |
```

Figure 1.31

All this is very nice, but what if your opponent also knows this much about the game? Then he too will be watching for the first opportunity to "balance the board" against you. Here is where binary notation could give you the edge. In figure 1.29, which shows the opening situation for the game illustrated in figure 1.30, there was no way for the first player, A, to balance the board on his first move, but he still could have guaranteed himself a win at that point had he made the right first move. The technique is explained below.

We first look at the arrangement facing us and write down the number of marks in each group using binary notation as in figure 1.32. Once the numbers are written in base 2, as in figure 1.32(c), we focus our attention

(a) Arrangement	(b) Numbers of Marks in Groups	(c) Numbers of Marks in Binary Notation
1: | | | | | |	6	110
2: | | |	3	11
3: | | | | |	5	101
4: | | | | | | | | | |	10	1010
5: | | | |	4	100

Figure 1.32

on the columns of this set of numbers, that is, the 1's column, the 2's column, the 4's column, etc. If any of these columns contains an odd number of 1's, our move must somehow change it to an even number. In the example at hand (figure 1.33), the 2's, 4's, and 8's columns all have odd numbers of 1's. Therefore we devise a move to change all these without changing the 1's column. Since we can only take marks from one group and since we must change the 8's column, our move will have to involve group 4. The only possible way for us to make a change in all but the 1's column is to change the binary representation from 1010 to 0100. Hence we must take enough marks from group 4 to leave just 4; that is, we take away 6. This presents our opponent with the binary array shown in figure 1.34. His move will

Group	Columns				Group	Columns		
	8	4	2	1		4	2	1
1		1	1	0	1	1	1	0
2			1	1	2		1	1
3		1	0	1	3	1	0	1
4	1	0	1	0	4	1	0	0
5		1	0	0	5	1	0	0

Figure 1.33   Figure 1.34

change at least one of the columns from even back to odd, and we can then devise our second move to change it back to even. Continuing in this way we are sure to win. Of course, if at any time you can see a way to balance the board, then your moves from that point on will be obvious.

Many other games and tricks are based upon the binary number system. As the final item of this section, we offer the following example.

Example 1.21.   Consider the table of figure 1.35.

A	B	C	D	E
1	2	4	8	16
3	3	5	9	17
5	6	6	10	18
7	7	7	11	19
9	10	12	12	20
11	11	13	13	21
13	14	14	14	22
15	15	15	15	23
17	18	20	24	24
19	19	21	25	25
21	22	22	26	26
23	23	23	27	27
25	26	28	28	28
27	27	29	29	29
29	30	30	30	30
31	31	31	31	31

Figure 1.35

This array can be used to quickly ascertain the age of any person 31 years or younger who will just tell you in which of the columns his age appears. For example, if he says his age is in columns B, D, and E only, we merely add 2, 8, and 16, the leading numbers in those columns, to conclude that he is 26.

PROBLEMS

1. What would be the wisest move to make if one were faced with the following situation in a game of Nim?

    1: |||||||||
    2: |||||
    3: |||||||
    4: ||

2. In Nim, when you have adjusted the groups so that each binary place has an even number of 1's in its column, why can your opponent not do the same thing in his turn?

3. If a very sharp Nim player asks you to play a game, and upon investigation you see that the groups are such that all binary columns already contain an even number of 1's, what should you do?

4. (a) Extend the table in figure 1.27 to include all counting numbers through 31.
   (b) Explain how the columns in figure 1.35 were determined (that is, what do the numbers in a given column have in common?).
   (c) How does the "trick" in example 1.21 work?

FOR FURTHER READING

Freitag, A. H., and Freitag, H. T. *The Number Story.* Washington, D.C.: National Council of Teachers of Mathematics, 1960.

Heath, Sir Thomas L. *A Manual of Greek Mathematics.* New York: Dover Publications, Inc., 1931.

Smith, David Eugene, and Ginsburg, Jekuthiel. "From Numbers to Numerals and From Numerals to Computation," (*The World of Mathematics,* ed. James R. Newman, Vol. 1) New York: Simon and Schuster, Inc., 1962.

More detailed discussions of number notions, historical numerations systems, and computation techniques can be found in the references listed above.

CHAPTER 2

SET THEORY

The theory of sets was formulated by the German mathematician Georg Cantor (1845–1918). Before he was thirty, Cantor had begun developing his theory of infinite sets by proving that there are exactly as many algebraic numbers as there are counting numbers. An algebraic number is any number which is a solution of an equation such as

$$3x^2 - 4x + 1 = 0,$$

in which only counting numbers (and negatives of counting numbers) are permitted as numerical coefficients of the variables. Every counting number is an algebraic number: 68 is an algebraic number since it is a solution of the equation

$$x - 68 = 0.$$

Every fraction is an algebraic number: $\frac{3}{4}$ is a solution of the equation

$$4x - 3 = 0.$$

The number $\sqrt{2}$ is a solution of

$$x^2 - 2 = 0,$$

while $\sqrt{-1}$ is a solution of

$$x^2 + 1 = 0.$$

There are many, many algebraic numbers, but Cantor showed that there are just as many as there are counting numbers.

Unexpected results such as this, plus the novel methods used to attain them, made Cantor's mathematics a controversial matter among his colleagues. His principal and most vocal critic was Leopold Kronecker (1823–1891), under whom Cantor had studied at the University of Berlin. Because his theories were so revolutionary, both Cantor and his results came under strong, even bitter, attack from the beginning. The numerous attacks were too great a strain for him to bear; he finally suffered a nervous breakdown and died in a mental hospital.

The modern mathematician finds set theory a very useful tool for introducing rigor and preciseness into his work. According to legend, the Greek mathematician Thales (c. 624–547 B.C.) first recognized the necessity of proving results. The Greeks insisted that all new theorems must be consequences of previous theorems or the basic assumptions (called *axioms* or *postulates*) of the subject under discussion. Definitions of new terms also had to be given carefully in terms of previous definitions. This tradition of rigorous proof was perhaps one of the greatest contributions of Greek mathematics.

This Greek ideal of mathematical rigor received a strong setback with the development of calculus. Although ideas of the calculus can be traced to the Greeks (Archimedes essentially used what are methods of calculus in his work on areas), the basic terminology and theorems were not developed until the seventeenth century, with the work of Isaac Newton (1642–1727) and Gottfried Leibniz (1646–1716).

Isaac Newton, England's greatest mathematician, is unusual among the mathematicians mentioned in this book in that he was not a child prodigy. He was however mechanically adept; he is supposed to have constructed kites containing lanterns in order to scare the superstitious villagers. Newton entered Cambridge University in 1661 and studied under the excellent mathematician Isaac Barrow. In 1664–65 England was ravaged by an epidemic of bubonic plague, which caused the closing of the university. Newton returned home and proceeded to develop the basic ideas of calculus, the law of universal gravitation, and additions to the theory of light (Newton was the first to use a prism to show that light can be broken into its component colors). Newton was only twenty-six when Barrow recognized his great mathematical ability and resigned his professorship in favor of the young Newton.

Newton was reluctant to publish his works because he feared that both his studies and he himself would be attacked by some contemporary scientists for reasons which Newton believed would not be entirely scientific. His friends finally convinced him to publish his main results; his masterpiece the *Principia* appeared in 1687.

Many legends have grown around Newton. Authorities disagree on the apple story; some say that Newton invented the story to satisfy a persistent questioner. Probably false is a legend that says Newton was so absent-minded he cut two holes in his door, a large one for his cat and a smaller one for her kittens.

Gottfried Leibniz (whose life is discussed more fully in Chapter 5) developed the basic ideas of calculus independently from and simultaneously with Newton. A royal battle over the title, "Inventor of Calculus," was fought between continental mathematicians (partisans of Leibniz) and British mathematicians (loyal to Newton). National honor was at stake and charges of "liar" and "thief" were common. Leibniz had introduced a better method of notation for his calculus; in fact his method is the one used today.

Continental mathematicians accepted his notation and began to clarify and to perfect calculus, while the British doggedly insisted on following Newton's cumbersome methods.

Calculus was quite an advanced idea for its time (much as the theory of relativity is an advanced idea for our time) and at first was useful to only top mathematicians. These people were able to produce a wealth of results and conclusions about calculus itself, and with calculus as a tool, about the physical world. They often relied on intuition, a feeling for what is right. Before calculus could become a universal tool, it was necessary to simplify it and eliminate certain shortcomings that had been severely criticized. For example, a basic idea of early calculus was that of an infinitesimal, a quantity greater than zero, but still so small that no multiple of it could be measured. Such fuzzy ideas are lacking from modern calculus. Another basic idea is that of a derivative (which Newton called a fluxion). Many beginning calculus students today can give a reasonable description of a derivative, but in the early days the idea was poorly defined. One critic of Newton's methods (his results were not questioned as much as were his methods) was George Berkeley (1685–1753), an Anglican bishop. In his essay, "The Analyst," the bishop attacked Newton's fuzzy definition of fluxions. ". . . And what are these fluxions? The velocities of evanescent increments. And what are these same evanescent increments? They are neither finite quantities, nor quantities infinitely small, nor yet nothing. May we not call them the ghosts of departed quantities . . .? . . . And of the aforesaid fluxions there be other fluxions, which fluxions of fluxions are called second fluxions. And the fluxions of these second fluxions are called third fluxions: and so on, fourth, fifth, sixth, etc. ad infinitum . . . But he who can digest a second or third fluxion, a second or third difference, need not, methinks, be squeamish about any point in divinity . . ."

Augustin Cauchy (1789–1857) was a leader in the nineteenth-century movement to make calculus precise and rigorous; to replace "ghosts of departed quantities" with carefully written definitions. The standards, which Cauchy insisted be applied to calculus, soon became standard for all mathematics. One tool used to clarify ideas and make them precise is set theory. Sets and set operations are found in a large number of mathematics books published today, simply because of their power to reduce ambiguity and increase clarity.

SECTION 1. BASIC CONCEPTS

We can define the word *square* as a rectangle with all its sides equal, where the word square is defined in terms of the previously understood words rectangle, side, and equal. Such definitions are not always possible in mathematics; for example, how might we define the word *point?* The Greek geometer Euclid defined a point as "that which has no part," a definition so meaningless and vague as to be unacceptable to the modern mathematician. Such words as point and line are undefined basic terms which are used to define other words, but which are not defined themselves. *Set* is also such an undefined word. Sets are familiar: we speak of sets of chairs, sets of stamps, collections of marbles, classes of students, and so on, but we do not attempt to define set in terms of simpler words. Things that belong to a set are called the *elements* of the set. Normally, we use braces to denote a set; thus

$$\{a, b, c, d\}$$

is a set consisting of the four elements a, b, c, d. Sets are usually denoted by capital letters; thus the set above can be written:

$$A = \{a, b, c, d\}.$$

Here the letter A is used as a name for the set. The letter b is an element of set A; this is abbreviated as follows:

$$b \in A.$$

The symbol $\in$ is epsilon, a letter of the Greek alphabet. Read "$b \in A$" as follows: "the letter b is an element of set A," or "b belongs to A." Note that the symbol $\in$ is only used between an element and a set. The symbol $\notin$ means "does not belong."

Two sets are said to be *equal* if they contain exactly the same elements. We can say:

$$\{a, b, c, d\} = \{b, c, d, a\} = \{c, a, b, d\}$$

since all three sets contain exactly the same elements. Note that by this definition the order in which the elements are listed is of no importance.

Example 2.1.   List the elements of the following sets:
   (a) $B = \{$all odd numbers between 6 and 13$\}$.
   (b) $C = \{$all odd numbers between 6 and 1000$\}$.

The list of elements belonging to set B is:

$$B = \{7, 9, 11\}.$$

Note that 13 is not between 6 and 13, just as 13 is not less than 13. Also note that the term "odd" refers to numbers such as 5, 11, -1, -3, and so on, while the term "even" refers to numbers such as 18, 12, 0, -2, -8, and so on; neither term refers to fractions.

Set C contains many elements, and it would be quite a chore to list them all. So we adopt a useful shorthand:

$$C = \{7, 9, 11, 13, \ldots, 997, 999\}.$$

The three dots in the middle, called an *ellipsis,* indicate that the set contains more elements than the ones which are listed. An ellipsis is a signal that some elements have not been listed, but that enough are listed so we can perceive a pattern and know which elements are omitted. The three dots do not mean all numbers between 13 and 997 are elements, only those which also satisfy the condition of being odd.

The sets listed above have a common property: each is a finite set. Later in this chapter, we will define a finite set more precisely, but for now let's just say that a set is finite if the number of elements in the set is either zero or a counting number. Since set A above contains four elements and set B contains three elements, both are finite. It is hard to say off-hand how many elements are in set C, but given sufficient time we could count them; set C is also finite. A set which is not finite is called *infinite*. The set

$$\{1, 2, 3, 4, 5, 6, \ldots\}$$

is infinite since the number of elements in the set is not zero or a counting number. Similarly, the set

$$\{1000, 2000, 3000, 4000, \ldots\}$$

is infinite.

Example 2.2.   Consider the set consisting of all the grains of sand on the earth. Is this set finite or infinite?

How many grains of sand are there on the earth? Certainly it is hard to imagine one person counting them, but there is a limit to them; they do not go on forever. In fact, the Greek mathematician Archimedes (287–212 B.C.) estimated the number of grains of sand it would take to fill the entire universe; that is, the universe as he knew it. (See pages 106–107 in volume I of *The World of Mathematics,* edited by James R. Newman and published by Simon and Schuster in 1956.) This is in contrast to the set

$$\{1, 2, 3, 4, 5, \ldots\},$$

where there is no definite stopping point. It is not possible to even imagine counting all these numbers.

To be useful, a set must be *well defined*. That is, given a particular set and some particular element, it must be possible to determine whether or not the element belongs to the set. Given the set

$$D = \{\text{Mississippi, California, Texas}\}$$

and the element Florida, it is easy to say

$$\text{Florida} \notin D.$$

However, given the set

$$E = \{\text{all lovely women}\}$$

and the element Frieda, it is not possible to say whether

$$\text{Frieda} \notin E \text{ or Frieda} \in E.$$

Even if we knew Frieda it might be possible to get into a dispute concerning her membership in set E; her mother and her sister might have different opinions. Since we cannot necessarily determine whether or not a given element belongs to the set, we say set E is not well defined.

Example 2.3.   Are these sets well defined?
   (a) $F = \{\text{fat chickens}\}$ and
   (b) $G = \{\text{good movies}\}$.

   Suppose Clara Cluck is a little red hen. Does Clara belong to set F? The problem is the ambiguity of the word "fat." It is too general; how fat is fat? Suppose we say instead, "A fat chicken is one that weighs more than four pounds." Then for this set, we would agree on the meaning of the word "fat." After applying the definition to Clara we could determine if she is an element of F. If she weighed more than four pounds she would be in F; if she weighed four pounds or less she would not be. However, without some such agreement upon the meaning of the word "fat" we would have to say set F is not well defined.
   Can we say

$$\textit{How to Stuff a Wild Bikini} \in G?$$

Here again, who is to say? It is well known that disputes arise over the meaning of the word "good" in the expression "a good movie." Again there is no general agreement on the meaning of the phrase "a good movie," and we say this set is not well-defined.

   A common type of set notation is called the *set-builder* notation. For example, the set

$$\{1, 3, 5, 7, 9, \ldots\}$$

can be written

$$\{x \mid x \text{ is an odd number greater than zero}\}.$$

This is read "The set of all x such that x is an odd number greater than zero." The x is a sort of placeholder; we want all possible elements x that have the given property. Set-builder notation is often used to reduce the possibility of ambiguity. For example,

$$\{x \mid x \text{ is an odd number between 13 and 997}\}$$

is preferable to

$$\{15, 17, 19, 21, \ldots, 995\}.$$

The possibility of confusion is reduced here with set-builder notation. Furthermore, set-builder notation is often used because the common property of the elements under discussion is more important than a mere list of the elements. For example,

$$\{x \mid x \text{ is a state that touches the Pacific Ocean}\}$$

quickly shows a common property of the elements, while

$$\{\text{Alaska, Hawaii, Washington, Oregon, California}\}$$

might not.

Example 2.4.   List the elements of these sets:
  (a) $\{x \mid x \text{ is an even number between 3 and 8}\}$
  (b) $\{x \mid x \text{ is a state that touches Mexico}\}$.

The first is "the set of all x with the property that x is an even number between 3 and 8," or $\{4, 6\}$; 8 is not between 3 and 8. Review your geography a little, and the second set becomes

$$\{\text{California, Arizona, New Mexico, Texas}\}.$$

The set of all things under discussion at a given time is called the universal set of discussion or simply the *universal set*. When discussing certain sets of states, the universal set might be the set of all states; when discussing certain sets of numbers, the universal set might be the set of all numbers; and when discussing sets of students, the universal set might be the set of all students or perhaps the set of all people. The universal set depends on the sets under discussion. The letter U is usually reserved for the universal set.

Now look at these two sets:

$$M = \{2, 4, 6, 8, 10\}.$$
$$N = \{2, 4, 6, 8, 10, 12, 14, 16\}.$$

Note that each element of set M is also an element of set N (or, there is no element of M which is not in N); therefore we say M is a *subset* of N, written:

$$M \subset N.$$

To check this, select any element of M and make sure that it is also in N. For example, we have $2 \in N$, $4 \in N$, $6 \in N$, $8 \in N$, and $10 \in N$; every element of M is an element of N, and thus M is a subset of N. We can sketch a situation like this, as in figure 2.1. The circle representing M is completely

$$M \subset N \qquad$$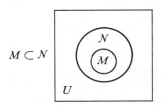

Figure 2.1

inside the circle for *N*. (Why?) The universal set is unspecified; it could be the set of all numbers or perhaps the set of all even numbers less than 50. The symbol ⊂ is used only between two sets; in this book it never appears between an element and a set.

A set containing no elements is called the *empty set*. The set of purple roosters is the empty set. Either of two symbols may be used for the empty set:

$$\text{the empty set} = \varnothing = \{\quad\}.$$

There is only one set that contains no elements; therefore it is proper to speak of *the* empty set.

Example 2.5.   Let $K = \{2, 4, 6, 7\}$.
   (a) Is $K \subset K$?   (b) Is $\varnothing \in K$?   (c) Is $\varnothing \subset K$?

We can use the definition of subset to check these statements.
   (a) Is set *K* a subset of itself? That is, can we say

$$\{2, 4, 6, 7\} \subset \{2, 4, 6, 7\}?$$

Using the definition of subset, we see that every element of $\{2, 4, 6, 7\}$ is also an element of $\{2, 4, 6, 7\}$ (or equivalently, there is no element of $\{2, 4, 6, 7\}$ that is not in $\{2, 4, 6, 7\}$). Thus $K \subset K$.
   (b) Is the empty set an element of set *K*? The empty set by its very name and definition is a set. There are no sets in *K* since the only elements of *K* are the numbers 2, 4, 6, and 7. The empty set does not belong to *K* and is not an element of *K*.
   (c) Is the empty set a subset of *K*? This looks more promising since both $\varnothing$ and *K* are sets, and it is proper to use the symbol ⊂ between two sets. Since there are no elements in $\varnothing$, certainly there are none that are not in *K*. Therefore, $\varnothing \subset K$. In fact, based on the same type of argument used with set *K*, we can say the empty set is a subset of every set.

Example 2.6.   List all the subsets of $\{a, b, c, d\}$.

Is there any way to predict the total number of subsets of this set? A subset of $\{a, b, c, d\}$ either contains or does not contain a given element. Thus the subset $\{a, c\}$ contains *a*, does not contain *b*, contains *c*, and does not contain *d*. This is shown in figure 2.2. Under *a*, there is either a yes or a no; similarly, there are two choices for each of the elements, *b*, *c*, and *d*. With each of the two choices (either yes or no) which can be made for *a*,

{a,	b,	c,	d}
yes	no	yes	no
{a,		c	}

Figure 2.2

there are two possible choices for b; with each of the two choices made for b, there are two possibilities for c; and with each choice made for c, there are two for d. The net result when all these choices are combined is a total of $2 \times 2 \times 2 \times 2 = 2^4 = 16$ possible subsets. Namely,

$\{a, b, c, d\}$	$\{b, c\}$
$\{a, b, c\}$	$\{b, d\}$
$\{a, c, d\}$	$\{c, d\}$
$\{a, b, d\}$	$\{a\}$
$\{b, c, d\}$	$\{b\}$
$\{a, b\}$	$\{c\}$
$\{a, c\}$	$\{d\}$
$\{a, d\}$	$\{\ \ \}$.

A general rule for finding the number of subsets of a given set can be formulated: If a set contains n elements, where n is a counting number, then it has exactly 2^n subsets. Hence a set containing five elements has 2^5, or 32 subsets; a set containing seven elements has 2^7, or 128 subsets; and a set containing one hundred elements has 2^{100}, or 1,267,650,600,228,229,401, 496,703,205,376 subsets.

PROBLEMS

Let $A = \{2, 4, 6, 8, 10, 12\}$, $B = \{2, 4, 8, 10\}$, $C = \{4, 10, 12\}$, and $D = \{2, 10\}$. Let $U = \{$all numbers$\}$. Answer true or false for each of problems 1–29.

1. $6 \in B$.
2. $8 \in C$.
3. $D \in A$.
4. $D \in B$.
5. $D \subset B$.
6. $D \subset A$.
7. $A \subset B$.
8. $B \subset C$.
9. $\varnothing \in C$.
10. $\varnothing \in D$.
11. $\varnothing \subset C$.

12. $\varnothing \subset D$.
13. $\varnothing \subset \varnothing$.
14. $D \subset C$.
15. $A \subset U$.
16. $U \subset A$.
17. $\varnothing \subset U$.
18. $\varnothing \in U$.
19. $8 \notin C$.
20. $8 \notin D$.
21. $8 \notin A$.
22. $6 \notin C$.

23. There are exactly 32 subsets of A.
24. There are exactly 16 subsets of B.
25. There are exactly 6 subsets of C.
26. There are exactly 4 subsets of D.
27. The symbol $\{\varnothing\}$ does not represent the empty set.
28. The drawing of figure 2.3 correctly represents the relationship between sets A, C, and U.

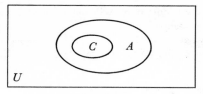

Figure 2.3

29. The drawing of figure 2.4 correctly represents the relationship between sets B, C, and U.

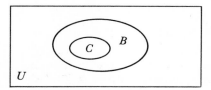

Figure 2.4

List the elements of each of the following sets:

30. $\{x \mid x$ won last year's World Series$\}$.
31. $\{x \mid x$ is a petite purple pigeon on the classroom rafters$\}$.
32. $\{x \mid x$ is an even number between 6 and 13$\}$.
33. $\{x \mid x$ is an even number, and x is an odd number$\}$.
34. $\{x \mid x$ is greater than 11, and x is even$\}$.
35. $\{x \mid x$ is an odd number not less than 11$\}$.

Are the following sets well defined?

36. $\{x \mid x$ is an Easter egg$\}$.
37. $\{x \mid x$ is a green ogre$\}$.
38. $\{x \mid x$ is nice to his mother$\}$.
39. $\{x \mid x$ is a bum$\}$.
40. $\{x \mid x$ is a state of the United States$\}$.
41. $\{x \mid x$ is an odd number between 7 and 9$\}$.

How many elements are there in each of the following sets?

42. $\{2, 3, 4, 5, \ldots, 92\}$.
43. $\{14, 15, 16, \ldots, 76\}$.
44. $\{91, 92, 93, \ldots, 1246\}$.
45. List all the subsets of the set $\{$Tom, Dick, Harry$\}$. How many subsets are there?
46. List all the subsets, if any, of the empty set.
47. Given two sets E and F with $E \subset F$ and $F \subset E$, what further statement can be made about sets E and F?

Write the word finite or infinite for each of the following:

48. $\{x \mid x$ is a counting number greater than 6$\}$.
49. $\{x \mid x$ is a person alive on the earth now$\}$.

50. $\{x \mid x$ is a subset of a set containing 1,000,000 elements$\}$.
51. $\{x \mid x$ is a fraction between 0 and 1$\}$.
52. $\{x \mid x$ is a positive even number$\}$.
53. $\{x \mid x$ either is a person alive on earth today, or else was alive on earth at sometime in the past$\}$.

Find the number of subsets of each of the following sets:

54. $\{x \mid x$ is an even number between 12 and 19$\}$.
55. $\{x \mid x$ is an odd number between 3 and 10$\}$.
56. $\{m, n, p, q, r\}$.
57. $\{a, b, c, d, a, b\}$.
58. $\{$Harry, Sam, John, Harry$\}$.

SECTION 2. OPERATIONS ON SETS

An *operation* is a rule by which one or more objects are used to obtain another (not necessarily different) object. Addition is an operation for which the objects are numbers. For example, the numbers 3 and 7 can be combined according to the rule called addition to obtain the number 10. The numbers 0 and 4 under the same operation yield the number 4. The objects involved in the operations discussed in this chapter are sets.

Consider the set, $A = \{2, 4, 6\}$, and the universal set, $U = \{2, 4, 6, 8, 10\}$. What elements belong to U but not to A? An inspection of U and A leads us to conclude that the set of elements belonging to U but not to A is $\{8, 10\}$. This set $\{8, 10\}$ is called the *complement of A relative to the universal set U,* abbreviated "complement of A" or "A complement." This is an operation because sets A and U were used to determine another set consisting of all the elements of U that are not in A. In set-builder notation, the complement of a set A, written A' and read "A prime," is given by:

$$A' = \{x \mid x \in U \text{ and } x \notin A\}.$$

A' is the set of all the elements of U that are not in A. Two things should be noted at this time. First, A' depends not only on set A but also on the choice of U; if U changes, A' changes. Second, according to the definition, the complement of a set is again a set.

Example 2.7.   With set A drawn as in figure 2.5, shade the set A'.

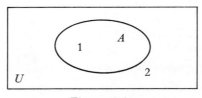

Figure 2.5

This diagram has two regions labeled 1 and 2. Are the elements of region 1 in A'? On the other hand, are the elements of region 2 in set A'? Since only the elements of region 2 are included in A', we shade only that area (see figure 2.6).

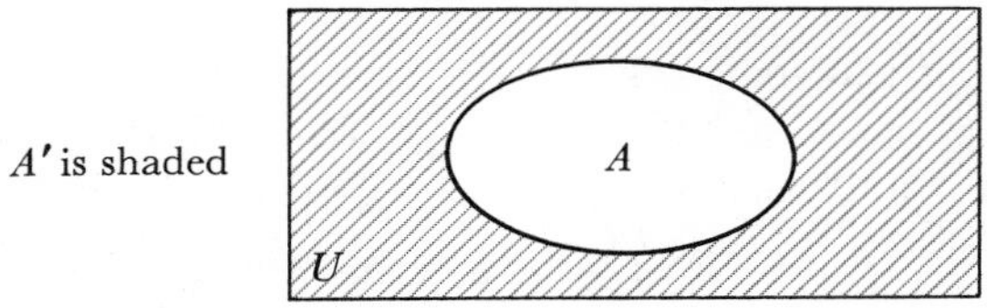

A' is shaded

Figure 2.6

Example 2.8. If $C = \{x \mid x$ is an even number between 6 and 14$\}$ and if $U = \{7, 8, 9, 10, 11, 12, 13\}$, find the complement of C relative to U.

The elements of set C are the following:

$$C = \{8, 10, 12\}.$$

Its complement, C', is the set:

$$C' = \{7, 9, 11, 13\}.$$

Example 2.9. Use set C' from the previous example, and find $(C')'$.

We are looking for the set of all elements of U that are not in C'. Not to be in C' is the same as being in C. Hence $(C')' = C$.

Example 2.10. Given a universal set, U, find $\varnothing'$.

We need the set of all elements in the universal set that are not in the empty set. Since there are no elements in the empty set, we include every element that is in the universal set, so that $\varnothing' = U$.

Example 2.11. Consider a universal set U. If set R is infinite, is set R' infinite?

Let's consider two examples:

$$R = \{2, 4, 6, \ldots\},$$
$$U = \{1, 2, 3, 4, 5, \ldots\}.$$

Set R' is the set of all elements belonging to U but not to R. That is,

$$R' = \{1, 3, 5, 7, \ldots\},$$

which is an infinite set. On the other hand, consider the next example. Assume

$$R = \{6, 7, 8, 9, 10, \ldots\},$$

with U the same as above. In this case,

$$R' = \{1, 2, 3, 4, 5\},$$

which is a finite set. The answer to the question asked must be, "it depends on R."

Now let's look at some other operations which can be applied to sets. The *intersection* of sets A and B, written $A \cap B$, is the set of all elements that belong to both A and B; that is,

$$A \cap B = \{x \mid x \in A \text{ and } x \in B\}.$$

The key word here is "and." We need the set of all elements that at the same time belong to set A and belong to set B.

Example 2.12. Let $A = \{2, 9, 8, 11, 14\}$ and $B = \{1, 7, 8, 9, 10\}$; find $A \cap B$.

The set of elements common to both sets is the set

$$A \cap B = \{8, 9\}.$$

Example 2.13. Let $A = \{2, 9, 8, 11, 14\}$ and $B = \{3, 7, 12\}$; find $A \cap B$.

There are no elements common to both sets, so that

$$A \cap B = \varnothing.$$

Two sets such as these, which have no elements in common, are referred to as *disjoint* sets. In this example, as in the previous one, the intersection of two sets is again a set; by the very definition of intersection this must always be the case.

Example 2.14. Shade $A \cap B$ in the diagram of figure 2.7.

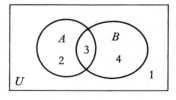

Figure 2.7

The rectangle represents the universal set U, and the circles represent sets A and B. These circles divide the rectangle into four regions, labeled 1, 2, 3, and 4. By the definition of intersection, we take only those elements that belong to both sets. Only region 3 includes elements belonging to both sets; therefore only region 3 is shaded in figure 2.8.

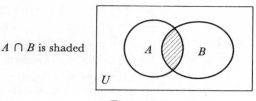

$A \cap B$ is shaded

Figure 2.8

Example 2.15.   Let $A = \{2, 8, 9, 11, 4\}$; find $A \cap A$.

We need the set of all elements that are common to A and A. But since the common elements are simply the elements of set A itself,

$$A \cap A = A.$$

Example 2.16.   Using set A from example 2.15, find $A \cap \varnothing$.

We want to find all the elements that belong to A and also to the empty set. Since no elements belong to the empty set, there are none belonging to both A and the empty set. Therefore,

$$A \cap \varnothing = \varnothing.$$

Example 2.17.   On the diagram of figure 2.7, shade $(A \cap B)'$.

As before, region 3 represents $A \cap B$. The complement of $A \cap B$ is everything that falls outside region 3 and is shaded in the diagram of figure 2.9.

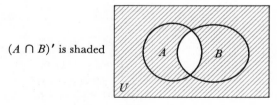

$(A \cap B)'$ is shaded

Figure 2.9

Example 2.18.   On the diagram of figure 2.7, shade the set $A' \cap B'$.

Set A' consists of everything in U that is outside set A. In our diagram, set A is represented by regions 2 and 3, so that A' is represented by regions 1 and 4. Set B', on the other hand, is represented by regions 1 and 2. To find the intersection of these sets, we must find the elements that belong to both, or region 1, which is shaded in figure 2.10 (see p. 52). This figure, together with figure 2.9, demonstrates that $(A \cap B)' \neq A' \cap B'$. Why?

$A' \cap B'$ is shaded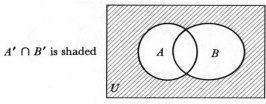

Figure 2.10

Example 2.19.   Using the diagram of figure 2.11, shade set $(A' \cap B') \cap C$.

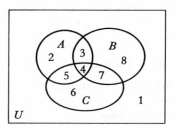

Figure 2.11

There are eight regions for the three sets. $A' \cap B'$ is everything in regions 1 and 6; set C consists of regions 4, 5, 6, and 7. Hence we need the regions common to $A' \cap B'$ and C, or common to 1 and 6 and regions 4, 5, 6 and 7. Therefore region 6 represents the set $(A' \cap B') \cap C$ and is shaded in figure 2.12.

$(A' \cap B') \cap C$ is shaded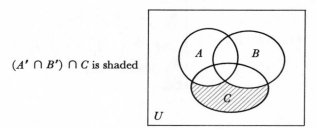

Figure 2.12

The intersection of two sets is the set of all elements that belong to both sets. The *union* of two sets is the set formed by taking all the elements that belong to set A, or to set B, or to both. The union of sets A and B, or $A \cup B$, is

$$\{x \mid x \in A \text{ or } x \in B\}.$$

Example 2.20.   Let $A = \{2, 3, 1, 4\}$ and $B = \{1, 2, 5, 8\}$. Find $A \cup B$.

To find the set of elements that belong to A, or to B, or to both sets, start by listing all the elements of A:

$$\{2, 3, 1, 4\}.$$

Then continue adding the elements of B that have not already been listed, or

$$\{2, 3, 1, 4, 5, 8\} = A \cup B.$$

The elements in this new, larger set belong to A or to B or to both.

Example 2.21.   Shade $A \cup B$ on the diagram of figure 2.7.

We need all the elements belonging to A or to B. This excludes region 1 since those elements belong to neither A nor B. All the elements of region 2 belong to A and therefore to $A \cup B$. The elements of region 3 belong to A and to B, and therefore to $A \cup B$. (Why?) The elements of region 4 belong to B and hence to $A \cup B$. In summary, we must shade everything except region 1, as in figure 2.13.

$A \cup B$ is shaded

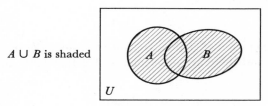

Figure 2.13

Example 2.22.   Shade $(A \cup B)'$ on the diagram of figure 2.7.

In the previous example, we found that $A \cup B$ consists of everything except region 1. This means that $(A \cup B)'$ must consist of region 1, which is shaded in figure 2.14. Exactly the same regions are shaded in figure 2.14, $(A \cup B)'$, and in figure 2.10, $A' \cap B'$. Hence we suspect that:

$$(A \cup B)' = A' \cap B'.$$

Let's work an example to see if this is reasonable.

$(A \cup B)'$ is shaded

Figure 2.14

Example 2.23. Let $U = \{1, 2, 3, 4, 5, 6, 7, 8, 9, 10\}$, $A = \{2, 4, 3, 5\}$, and $B = \{5, 6, 7, 8\}$. Find: $(A \cup B)'$ and $A' \cap B'$.

We have:

(a) A' is the set of elements in U and not in A, or $\{1, 6, 7, 8, 9, 10\}$.

(b) $B' = \{1, 2, 3, 4, 9, 10\}$.

(c) $A' \cap B'$ is the set of common elements in A' and B', or $\{1, 9, 10\}$.

(d) $A \cup B$ is the set of elements in A or in B, or $\{2, 3, 4, 5, 6, 7, 8\}$.

(e) $(A \cup B)'$ is the set of elements in U and not in $(A \cup B)$, or $\{1, 9, 10\}$.

Since the same set results in both statements (c) and (e), we can say that, in this example at least, $(A \cup B)' = A' \cap B'$. This relationship, which is one of *deMorgan's Laws,* turns out to be true for any two sets A and B. (Augustus deMorgan, 1806–1871, was a British mathematician.) We have made the relationship plausible by drawing pictures and giving examples, but a proof can be given.

Example 2.24. Let $A = \{6, 9, 11, 14\}$; find $A \cup A$.

First list the elements of A,

$$\{6, 9, 11, 14\},$$

then add the elements of A that are not yet listed. We have listed all the elements of A, and there are no elements of A that have not already been included. Hence,

$$A \cup A = A.$$

Example 2.25. With A as in the previous example, find $A \cup \varnothing$.

As before, first list the elements of A,

$$\{6, 9, 11, 14\},$$

then list the elements of the empty set not already included. There are, however, no elements in the empty set, which means

$$A \cup \varnothing = A.$$

Example 2.26. Using the diagram from figure 2.7, shade $A' \cup B'$.

Set A' is everything outside A, that is, regions 1 and 4. Set B' includes regions 1 and 2, the regions outside B. To form the union of these two sets, we need the elements either in regions 1 or 4, or in regions 1 or 2. That is, we need regions 1, 2, and 4, as shaded in figure 2.15. This is exactly the same region shaded in figure 2.9 for $(A \cap B)'$, which leads us to believe that

$$A' \cup B' = (A \cap B)'.$$

This relationship is another of deMorgan's laws.

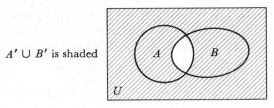

$A' \cup B'$ is shaded

Figure 2.15

Example 2.27.   Are these statements true:
  (a) for any two sets A and B, $A \subset (A \cup B)$,
  (b) for any two sets A and B, $A \subset (A \cap B)$?

We want to know if these statements are true in general for any sets A and B that are chosen. The first statement asserts that A is a subset of $A \cup B$; for this to be true, every element of A must be an element of $A \cup B$, which is the set of all elements that belong to A or to B. Hence statement (a) is true. Sometimes a sketch helps in a problem like this. In figure 2.16, A is shaded horizontally, while $A \cup B$ is shaded vertically. Note that every element of A is also an element of $A \cup B$.

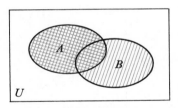

Figure 2.16

The second statement asserts that every element of A is also an element of $A \cap B$; for this to be true, every element of A must also be an element of both A and B, which is not necessarily true, as shown in figure 2.17. Note that A is shaded horizontally and $A \cap B$ vertically. Not all the elements of A need belong to $A \cap B$. Since the statement is not true in general, we mark it false.

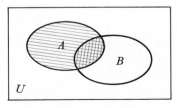

Figure 2.17

We shall discuss one more operation on sets, the operation of set difference, defined as follows: the *difference* of two sets A and B, written $A - B$, is the set of all elements that belong to A and not to B. In set-builder notation,

$$A - B = \{x \mid x \in A \text{ and } x \notin B\}.$$

The symbols A and B are merely placeholders; A stands for the first set under discussion and B for the second. Thus, $B - A$ would be the set of all elements that are in B and not in A.

Example 2.28.   Let $C = \{6, 9, 8, 4, 2\}$ and $D = \{10, 8, 9, 5\}$; find $C - D$ and $D - C$.

To find $C - D$ we need all the elements of C that are not in D: $C - D = \{6, 4, 2\}$. To find $D - C$ we need all the elements of D that are not in C: $D - C = \{5, 10\}$. Note that $C - D \neq D - C$.

Example 2.29.   Use the drawing of figure 2.7 and shade $A - B$.

Set A is composed of regions 2 and 3. Set $A - B$ includes all the elements of A that are not in B. Therefore, we shade only region 2, as shown in figure 2.18.

$A - B$ is shaded

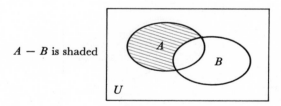

Figure 2.18

Example 2.30.   On the diagram of figure 2.11, shade the set $(A - B) \cap C$.

By checking figure 2.18, we see $A - B$ consists of regions 2 and 5. For the intersection, we need all the elements of $(A - B)$ that are also elements of C. Therefore, we need to shade only region 5, as shown in figure 2.19.

$(A - B) \cap C$ is shaded

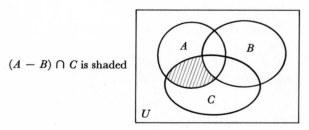

Figure 2.19

PROBLEMS

Let $A = \{2, 3, 4, 5\}$, $B = \{3, 5, 7, 9\}$, and $C = \{2, 4, 5, 7, 9\}$. Let
$$U = \{1, 2, 3, 4, 5, 6, 7, 8, 9, 10\}.$$

Find each of the following sets:

1. $A \cap B$. ~~2~~ 3 ~~4~~ 5 ~~7~~ 9
2. $A \cup B$. 2 3 4 5 7 9
3. $A \cap B'$. 2 4 ~~7~~ 9
4. $B - A$. ~~4~~ 7 7 9
5. $A - B$. 2 4
6. $C - A$. 7 9
7. $C \cup A$. 2 3 4 5 7 9

8. $C \cap B$. 5 7 9
9. $U \cap A$. 2 3 4 5
10. $U \cup C$. 1–10
11. $U - A$. 1 6 7 8 9 10
12. $A - B'$. $\emptyset$
13. $B' \cap A'$. 1 6 8 10
14. $B' \cup C$. 2 4

Make a drawing similar to the one in figure 2.7 for each problem here, and then shade the listed sets:

15. $B - A$.
16. $U - A$.
17. $U - B$.
18. $A - U$.
19. $B - U$.
20. $U - (A \cup B)$.
21. $U - (A \cap B)$.
22. $(A \cap B) \cup B$.
23. $A \cap B'$.
24. $B' \cap A'$.

25. $A' \cup B$.
26. $A' \cap U$.
27. $B' \cap U'$.
28. $A' - B$.
29. $B' - B$.
30. $A' - A'$.
31. $(A - B)'$.
32. $(A - B) \cup (A \cup B)$.
33. $(A - B) \cup (A \cap B)$.
34. $\emptyset'$.

Make a drawing that is similar to the one used in figure 2.11 for each problem, and then shade the sets listed.

35. $(A \cap B) \cap C$.
36. $(A - C) \cup B$.
37. $(A \cap B) \cup C'$.
38. $(A' \cap B) \cap C$.
39. $(A' \cap B') \cap C$.
40. $(A \cup B) \cup C$.

41. $(A - B) \cup C$.
42. $(A - C) \cap B$.
43. $(A - B) - C$.
44. $(A - B) \cap U$.
45. $(A' - B') - C'$.
46. $(A - B')'$.

Answer true or false for each of the following two questions:
47. For any two sets A and B, $(A \cap B) \subset A$. True
48. For any two sets A and B, $A \subset (A - B)$. False

Define a new set operation as follows: the *symmetric difference* of two sets A and B, written $A \triangle B$ ($\triangle$ is the Greek letter delta), is the set $(A - B) \cup (B - A)$, or
$$A \triangle B = \{x \mid x \in A \text{ or } x \in B, \text{ and } x \notin A \cap B\}.$$

49. Let $A = \{2, 4, 6, 8, 10\}$ and $B = \{4, 10, 12\}$; find $A \triangle B$.
50. Find $A \triangle B$ if $A = \{a, k, l, m, n\}$ and $B = \{k, l, m, a, r, p, q\}$.
51. Shade $A \triangle B$ in the sketch of figure 2.7.
52. Shade $A \triangle B'$ in the sketch of figure 2.7.
53. Shade $(A \triangle B) \triangle C$ on the sketch of figure 2.11.
54. Shade $(A' \triangle B') \cap C$ on the sketch of figure 2.11.
55. Shade $[(A \triangle B) \triangle C]'$ on the sketch of figure 2.11.

56. Use sketches to verify that, for any sets A and B,

$$A \triangle B = (A \cup B) - (A \cap B),$$
$$A \triangle B = (A \cup B) \cap (A \cap B)', \quad \text{and}$$
$$A \triangle B = (A \cap B') \cup (B \cap A').$$

57. Let A be any given set. When will $A = A - B$?

58. Let A be any given set. When will $A = B - A$?

59. Is the following statement always true? $A \triangle (B \cap C) = (A \triangle B) \cap (A \triangle C)$.

60. Suppose $A \cap B = A \cap C$. Must $B = C$?

61. Suppose $A \cup B = A \cup C$. Must $B = C$?

SECTION 3.   AN APPLICATION OF SET THEORY

Let's now discuss a use of our set theory.

Example 2.31.   A survey was conducted of a number of college girls, and it was found:

22 like tall men,
25 like handsome men,
39 like rich men,
 9 like men who are handsome and tall,
17 like men who are tall and rich,
20 like men who are handsome and rich,
 6 like men who are all three,
 4 do not like men of any of these types.

How many women were surveyed?

Note first that the statement "9 like men who are handsome and tall" means that when asked the question, "Do you like men who are handsome and tall," 9 girls answered yes. Some of these 9 girls may also like rich men, but we cannot tell from this particular statement. At first glance it might seem reasonable to merely add up all the numbers presented, but this does not work since it leads to overlapping. For example, the 17 girls who like tall and rich men are also counted in the 22 who like tall men and the 39 who like rich men. Let's make a sketch of the situation, as in figure 2.20.

The universal set consists of the set of all girls who were surveyed. From the information given we know that 22 girls like tall men. The set of tall men includes regions b, c, d, and e. Thus these 22 girls are distributed among the four regions. We must decide how to distribute the girls among the various regions in such a manner that we have no overlapping. Note that the smallest total listed above is the 4 girls who do not like men of any of these types. Since these 4 girls are outside any of the circles for tall, rich, or handsome men, they must go in region a. Place the number 4 in region a, as in figure 2.21. There are 6 girls who like men who are all three. Since

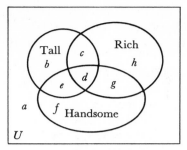

Figure 2.20

region *d* is the intersection of all three circles we place the number 6 in region *d*. The 20 girls who like handsome and rich men are represented by regions *d* and *g*. Thus a total of 20 girls goes in regions *d* and *g*. However, region *d* has 6 girls already, and hence 20 − 6, or 14 girls must be placed in region *g*, which contains the girls who like handsome and rich men who are not tall. By the same method, region *c* contains 11 girls, while region *e* contains 3 girls.

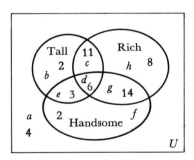

Figure 2.21

A total of 22 girls like tall men. The circle which represents these girls is made up of regions *b*, *c*, *d*, and *e*. As we have already noted, regions *c*, *d*, and *e* account for a total of 11 + 6 + 3 = 20 girls, which means region *b* must contain 22 − 20 = 2 girls. In the same way, region *f* represents 2 girls, while region *h* represents 8. To say, for example, that region *h* contains 8 girls is to say that there are 8 girls who like rich men but do not like tall men and do not like handsome men. All these numbers have been placed in figure 2.21.

No girls are counted twice in this diagram, and we can now add all the numbers from the regions: 4 + 2 + 14 + 6 + 3 + 2 + 11 + 8 = 50. Fifty girls were questioned.

Example 2.32. Miss Bubbles LaRue was employed as an opinion sampler for a nice old man who runs a company which makes products *A*, *B*, and *C*.

She reported the following data, and after analyzing it even the nice old man had to fire the unlucky Miss LaRue. Why?

Her data: Out of 100 men I surveyed, I found:

> 45 like product A,
> 50 like product B,
> 57 like product C,
> 28 like products A and B,
> 20 like products B and C,
> 25 like products A and C,
> 11 like all three products,
> 9 don't like any of the three.

From the data supplied by Bubbles, we can determine the numbers shown in figure 2.22.

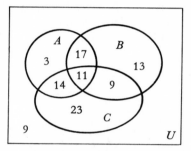

Figure 2.22

By adding all the numbers from the regions, we find the total number questioned: $9 + 3 + 14 + 23 + 11 + 9 + 17 + 13 = 99$. Miss LaRue claimed she questioned 100 people, but her data indicates only 99. No doubt, therefore, she is either incompetent or lazy and must be discharged.

PROBLEMS

1. A survey of 80 freshmen at a certain college found:

> 36 take English,
> 32 take history,
> 32 take political science,
> 16 take political science and history,
> 16 take history and English,
> 14 take political science and English,
> 6 take all three.

(a) How many students are taking English and neither of the other two?
(b) How many students take none of these three courses?

(c) How many students take only history?

(d) How many students take political science and history but not English?

(e) How many students did not take political science?

2. The following data was supplied by a certain fraternity concerning its 102 members:

> 99 like blonds,
> 96 like brunettes,
> 99 like redheads,
> 95 like blonds and brunettes,
> 94 like brunettes and redheads,
> 96 like blonds and redheads,
> 93 like all three.

(a) How many men do not like any of these three types of girls?

(b) How many men like blonds but not brunettes?

(c) How many men like anything but redheads?

(d) How many men like only brunettes?

(e) How many men like exactly two hair colors?

3. Miss LaRue found a second job, reported the following data, and again lost her job. Why this time?

  This survey was taken for the electric company. I checked 117 women in a suburban area, questioned them about their cooking habits, and obtained the following results. I will stake my professional reputation as a surveyor on these results:

> 108 like to bake cookies,
> 109 like to bake pies,
> 103 like to bake cakes,
> 101 like to bake pies and cakes,
> 104 like to bake cakes and cookies,
> 107 like to bake pies and cookies,
> 100 like to bake all three.

4. Toward the middle of the season, peaches for canning tend to come in three types: earlies, lates, and extra lates (there are no middle peaches), depending on the expected date of ripening. During a certain week the following data were recorded at a small peach-receiving station:

> 16 truck loads were dispatched carrying early peaches,
> 36 had late peaches,
> 33 had extra lates,
> 13 had earlies and lates,
> 15 had lates and extra lates,
> 1 had earlies and extra lates,
> 0 had all three.

(a) How many truck loads were dispatched carrying only late variety peaches?

(b) How many had only extra lates?

(c) How many with only one variety?

(d) What was the total number of peach trucks dispatched during the week?

5. Human blood can be one of four types: O, A, B, or AB, depending upon whether it contains no antigen, the A antigen, the B antigen, or both the A and B antigens. A third antigen, called the Rh antigen, is important in human reproduction. Blood is said to be Rh-positive if it contains this Rh antigen, and Rh-negative otherwise. In a certain hospital the following data were recorded:

> 25 patients had the A antigen,
> 17 had the A and B antigens,
> 27 had the B antigen,
> 22 had the B and Rh antigens,
> 30 had the Rh antigen,
> 12 had none of the antigens,
> 16 had the A and Rh antigens,
> 15 had all three antigens.

(a) How many patients are listed here?
(b) How many patients have exactly one antigen?
(c) How many patients have exactly two antigens?

SECTION 4. CARDINAL NUMBER

As explained in the first chapter, a cardinal number answers the question, "how many"; similarly, the *cardinal number of a set* answers the question, "how many elements are in the set?" For example, the set $\{1, 7, 9\}$ contains three elements and has a cardinal number of three. The empty set contains no elements, and its cardinal number is zero. The set of counting numbers is said to have an infinite cardinal number.

Each of the sets $\{1, 7, 9\}$ and $\{41, 62, 37\}$ has the same cardinal number, and we can pair the elements in the following manner:

$$\{ 1 \quad 7 \quad 9 \}$$
$$\updownarrow \quad \updownarrow \quad \updownarrow$$
$$\{41 \quad 62 \quad 37\}.$$

Such pairing is called a *1-to-1 correspondence* between the elements of the two sets. Often this is expressed by saying the two sets are in 1-to-1 correspondence. The "1-to-1" refers to the fact that to each element of the first set is paired just one element of the second set, and to each element of the second set is paired just one element of the first set. The correspondence,

$$\{1 \qquad 8 \qquad 12\}$$
$$\updownarrow \qquad \searrow \quad \nearrow$$
$$\{6 \qquad 11\}$$

is not 1-to-1 since elements 8 and 12 from the first set both correspond to element 11 of the second set. It seems reasonable to say that if two sets have the same cardinal number we can establish a 1-to-1 correspondence between them.

Example 2.33. Is it possible to set up a 1-to-1 correspondence between the sets $\{a, b, c\}$ and $\{1, 2, 3\}$ in more than one way?

Yes, we can establish the correspondence in any of these ways:

$$\begin{array}{ccc} \{1 & 2 & 3\} \\ \updownarrow & \updownarrow & \updownarrow \\ \{a & b & c\}, \end{array} \quad \begin{array}{ccc} \{1 & 2 & 3\} \\ \updownarrow & \updownarrow & \updownarrow \\ \{b & c & a\}, \end{array} \quad \begin{array}{ccc} \{1 & 2 & 3\} \\ \updownarrow & \updownarrow & \updownarrow \\ \{c & b & a\}, \end{array}$$

$$\begin{array}{ccc} \{1 & 2 & 3\} \\ \updownarrow & \updownarrow & \updownarrow \\ \{b & a & c\}, \end{array} \quad \begin{array}{ccc} \{1 & 2 & 3\} \\ \updownarrow & \updownarrow & \updownarrow \\ \{c & a & b\}, \end{array} \quad \begin{array}{ccc} \{1 & 2 & 3\} \\ \updownarrow & \updownarrow & \updownarrow \\ \{a & c & b\}. \end{array}$$

As a rule, there are many ways to set up 1-to-1 correspondences between two sets with the same cardinal number. Usually we do not care how many ways are possible; our main concern is whether or not at least one way is possible.

After a little thought, it should seem permissible to say that if two sets can be placed in a 1-to-1 correspondence, then the two sets have the same cardinal number and hence contain the same number of elements. But let's investigate some of the consequences of this innocent looking assumption.

Example 2.34. How many even counting numbers are there?

At first glance, perhaps the answer might seem to be, "There are half as many even counting numbers as there are counting numbers altogether." But wait; we can set up a 1-to-1 correspondence between the two sets in the following manner:

$$\begin{array}{ccccccccc} \{1 & 2 & 3 & 4 & 5 & 6 & \cdots & n & \cdots\} \\ \updownarrow & \updownarrow & \updownarrow & \updownarrow & \updownarrow & \updownarrow & & \updownarrow & \\ \{2 & 4 & 6 & 8 & 10 & 12 & \cdots & 2n & \cdots\}. \end{array}$$

The matching of n with $2n$ demonstrates the general rule or formula of the correspondence. Since we have established a 1-to-1 correspondence, these two sets must have the same cardinal number and hence contain the same number of elements. We must conclude then that there are just as many even counting numbers as there are counting numbers.

Example 2.35. Can the following two sets be placed in a 1-to-1 correspondence?

$$\{1, 2, 3, 4, 5, \ldots\} \text{ and } \{2, 4, 8, 16, 32, 64, \ldots\}$$

The elements of the second set seem to become sparse; that is, the numbers are increasingly farther apart. But let's attempt a 1-to-1 correspondence anyway. Using exponents, we can write:

$$\{2, 4, 8, 16, 32, 64, \ldots\} = \{2^1, 2^2, 2^3, 2^4, 2^5, 2^6, \ldots\}.$$

Now the desired 1-to-1 correspondence becomes clear:

$$\{1 \quad 2 \quad 3 \quad 4 \quad 5 \quad 6 \quad \cdots \quad n \quad \cdots\}$$
$$\updownarrow \quad \updownarrow \quad \updownarrow \quad \updownarrow \quad \updownarrow \quad \updownarrow \qquad \updownarrow$$
$$\{2^1 \quad 2^2 \quad 2^3 \quad 2^4 \quad 2^5 \quad 2^6 \quad \cdots \quad 2^n \quad \cdots\}$$
$$\updownarrow \quad \updownarrow \quad \updownarrow \quad \updownarrow \quad \updownarrow \quad \updownarrow \qquad \updownarrow$$
$$\{2 \quad 4 \quad 8 \quad 16 \quad 32 \quad 64 \quad \cdots \quad 2^n \quad \cdots\}.$$

According to our assumption, each of these sets contains the same number of elements. It may appear that any two infinite sets can be placed in a 1-to-1 correspondence; however, this is not true, as will be shown in the next chapter.

At this point, we want to establish a more precise definition of the term *infinite set*. First, recall that every set is a subset of itself; given any set A, $A \subset A$. All the subsets of A, except A itself, are called *proper subsets* of A. If $A = \{2, 4, 6, 8\}$, then the subsets $\{2, 6\}$, $\{2, 6, 8\}$, and $\varnothing$ are examples of proper subsets of A; $\{2, 4, 6, 8\}$ is not. Is it possible to put set A in a 1-to-1 correspondence with a proper subset of itself? Set A contains four elements, and the largest possible proper subset of A will contain only three elements (why?). Hence a 1-to-1 correspondence is not possible.

What about an infinite set? Can an infinite set be placed in 1-to-1 correspondence with a proper subset of itself? We already have one such case in example 2.34:

$$\{1 \quad 2 \quad 3 \quad 4 \quad 5 \quad \cdots \quad n \quad \cdots\}$$
$$\updownarrow \quad \updownarrow \quad \updownarrow \quad \updownarrow \quad \updownarrow \qquad \updownarrow$$
$$\{2 \quad 4 \quad 6 \quad 8 \quad 10 \quad \cdots \quad 2n \quad \cdots\}$$

is a 1-to-1 correspondence between the set of counting numbers and a proper subset $\{2, 4, 6, 8, 10, \ldots\}$. (Why is this last set a proper subset?) Example 2.35 established a 1-to-1 correspondence between the set of counting numbers and another proper subset. The same type of thing can apparently be done with all the sets we have called infinite. This is the basis of the following definition: A set is *infinite* if it can be placed in 1-to-1 correspondence with a proper subset of itself. If a set is not infinite it is called *finite*.

Example 2.36. Show that the set of all positive multiples of 50 is an infinite set.

The positive multiples of 50 are the elements of the set:

$$\{50, 100, 150, 200, 250, \ldots\}.$$

To show this set is infinite, we must see if it is possible to put the set in 1-to-1 correspondence with a proper subset of itself. There are many possible ways to do this; here is one:

$$\{\,50 \quad 100 \quad 150 \quad 200 \quad 250 \quad \cdots \quad 50n \quad \cdots\}$$
$$\updownarrow \quad \updownarrow \quad \updownarrow \quad \updownarrow \quad \updownarrow \qquad \updownarrow$$
$$\{100 \quad 200 \quad 300 \quad 400 \quad 500 \quad \cdots \quad 100n \quad \cdots\}.$$

Another is:

$$\{ 50 \quad 100 \quad 150 \quad 200 \quad 250 \quad \cdots \quad 50n \quad \cdots\}$$
$$\updownarrow \quad \updownarrow \quad \updownarrow \quad \updownarrow \quad \updownarrow \qquad \qquad \updownarrow$$
$$\{100 \quad 150 \quad 200 \quad 250 \quad 300 \quad \cdots \quad 50(n+1) \quad \cdots\}.$$

In each case, we have set up a 1-to-1 correspondence between the set of positive multiples of 50 and a proper subset of the set; therefore the set is infinite.

PROBLEMS

Show that each of the following sets is infinite, using the definition of infinite set.

1. $\{x \mid x$ is an odd counting number$\}$.

2. $\{x \mid x$ is the quotient of an odd counting number and 2$\}$. (Hint: This set includes such numbers as $\frac{3}{2}, \frac{7}{2}, \frac{15}{2}, \frac{19}{2}$.)

3. $\{\frac{1}{2}, 1, \frac{3}{2}, 2, \frac{5}{2}, 3, \frac{7}{2}, 4, \ldots\}$.

4. $\{x \mid x$ is the square of an even counting number$\}$.

5. $\{$all positive fractions which have a denominator of 3$\}$.

6. $\{$all negative even numbers$\}$.

7. $\{$all negative fractions with a numerator of 7$\}$.

8. Given three finite sets, A, B, and C, which have the property that $A \cup B = C$, is it true that (cardinal number of A) + (cardinal number of B) = (cardinal number of C)?

9. Suppose in problem 8 that sets A and B are disjoint. Does this affect your answer?

10. Repeat problem 8, with $\cap$ in place of $\cup$.

Define a new operation on two sets as follows: the *cross product* of two sets, written $A \times B$ (read "A cross B") is the new set obtained by forming all possible ordered pairs whose first components are elements of A and whose second components are elements of B. An ordered pair is something like $(-1, 3)$. The word "pair" describes the fact that we have two numbers here, while "ordered" means -1 comes first and 3 comes second. The ordered pair $(-1, 3)$ is not the same as the ordered pair $(3, -1)$. The cross product is the set of all such possible ordered pairs, as described above. For example,

$$\{1, 3, 5\} \times \{2, 4\} = \{(1, 2), (1, 4), (3, 2), (3, 4), (5, 2), (5, 4)\}.$$

The cross product set contains all possible ordered pairs which have first component from $\{1, 3, 5\}$ and second component from $\{2, 4\}$.

11. Calculate: $\{1, 7, 9, 12\} \times \{1, 8\}$.

12. Calculate: $\{2, 4, 8\} \times \{4, 6, 9, 11\}$.

13. Calculate: $\{2, 4\} \times \{1, 3, 5\}$ and compare with $\{1, 3, 5\} \times \{2, 4\}$, as worked out above. In general, is $A \times B = B \times A$?

14. Find: $\{2, 5, 9\} \times \varnothing$.

15. Find: $\{1, 2, 3, 4, \ldots\} \times \{2, 8\}$.

16. Find: $\{1, 5\} \times \{2, 4, 6, 8, 10, \ldots\}$.

17. Find: $\{1, 2, 3, 4, \ldots\} \times \{1\}$.

18. Find: $\{2, 4, 6, 8, \ldots\} \times \{1, 3\}$.

19. If set A is infinite and set B is finite, is $A \times B$ finite or infinite?

20. If both set A and set B are finite, is $A \times B$ always finite?

21. If both set A and set B are infinite, must $A \times B$ be infinite also?

22. If set A contains n elements and set B contains m elements, how many elements are there in $A \times B$?

23. Is the answer to problem 22 changed if sets A and B are disjoint?

24. Suppose $A \times B = A \times C$. Must $B = C$?

SECTION 5. SOME PARADOXES

Consider the following problem:

(1) In a certain village in a faraway land there are two types of men:

(a) Those who do not shave themselves,

(b) Those who do shave themselves.

(2) The village barber shaves all the men who do not shave themselves, and only those men.

Using the two assumptions above, we ask the seemingly innocent question, "Who shaves the barber?"

If he does not shave himself, he is in category (a) above, but (2) states that he is the one who shaves the men in category (a). This means that since he is in category (a), he shaves himself. But if he shaves himself he is in category (b). Hence if we assume the barber is in category (a) we are forced to conclude that he is also in category (b).

This is unacceptable since categories (a) and (b), by their very definition, can have no men in common. Perhaps we will have better luck if we consider the alternative answer to the question asked above. Suppose the barber does shave himself, which means he is in category (b). But he shaves only the men in category (a). Since he is in category (b), he does not shave himself, which places him in category (a). Again we have an unacceptable answer. The assumption that the barber is in category (b) leads to the conclusion that he is also in category (a), which is not possible.

If we assume the barber shaves himself, we have to conclude that he does not shave himself; if he does not shave himself, we have to conclude that he does. This is a paradox.

Let's now obtain a similar paradox in set theory with the following example.

(1) There are two types of sets:

(a) Those sets which are not elements of themselves.

For example, the set $\{2, 3\}$ consists of two elements, the numbers 2 and 3. Certainly the set consisting of the two numbers 2 and 3 is not an element of the set $\{2, 3\}$, that is, $\{2, 3\} \notin \{2, 3\}$. Most sets are of this type. The set of all stars is not a star; the set of all people is not a person; the set of all numbers is not a number. This category consists of all sets A for which it is *false* to write $A \in A$.

      (b) Sets which are elements of themselves.

      For example, $K = \{$all sets which contain more than 1000 elements$\}$. Picture set K as a big box containing all possible sets which have more than one thousand elements. Since all infinite sets have more than one thousand elements, they belong to set K. Surely there are more than one thousand sets, each of which has more than one thousand elements. Hence this big box which we have called set K contains more than one thousand elements. But if set K contains more than one thousand elements, it belongs in set K. So, we may write the true statement: $K \in K$.

      As another example, consider

$J = \{$all sets which may be described by an English phrase of fewer than twenty words$\}$.

      "The set of even numbers between 8 and 20" is a set that may be described by an English phrase of fewer than twenty words; this set belongs in set J. Set J itself can be described in fewer than twenty words, and hence belongs in set J; that is, $J \in J$.

      For our third example, consider set L:

$$L = \{\text{all abstract ideas}\}.$$

      Assume that it is possible to define an abstract idea so that the set is well defined. Certainly the set of all abstract ideas is an abstract idea, and hence L belongs in set L, or $L \in L$.

      Finally, consider set M:

$$M = \{\text{all sets}\}.$$

Because the set of all sets is a set, it is an element of itself, which means we can write $M \in M$.

      In summary, we can characterize the types of sets as follows:

      Set P is of type (a) in case $P \notin P$,
      Set Q is of type (b) in case $Q \in Q$.

    (2) Let

$$R = \{\text{all sets of type (a) above}\}.$$

Set R contains such sets as $\{1, 2, 3\}$, $\{m, n, p, q\}$, $\{1, 2, 3, \ldots\}$, and so on. Set R can be expressed in set-builder notation as follows:

(*) $R = \{A \mid A \notin A\}.$

Here we mean set R consists of all possible sets A, such that A is not an element of itself.

We now consider the question "Is set R of type (a) or type (b)," which is analogous to the previous question "Who shaves the barber?"

What happens if we assume R is a type (a) set? By the definition of a type (a) set, R is not an element of itself, or $R \notin R$. But by equation (*) above, this is precisely the condition which characterizes elements of R; hence R is in R, or R is a type (b) set. In summary, if R is of type (a), then it is also of type (b), which is a contradiction.

On the other hand, what happens if we assume R is a type (b) set? We have $R \in R$, but this means R must satisfy the condition of equation (*), that is, $R \notin R$, hence R is a type (a) set. Here again we have a contradiction since, if we assume R is of type (b), we are also forced to conclude it is of type (a).

Assuming R is either type (a) or type (b) leads to a contradiction. This paradox was discovered in 1902 by the mathematician and philosopher Sir Bertrand Russell, and today is known as *Russell's Paradox*.

As mentioned before, much of the theory of sets, especially that of infinite sets, has its basis in the work of Georg Cantor. The first paradox in set theory was discovered by the Italian mathematician, Burali-Forti, in 1897. His paradox, together with Russell's Paradox and some found by Cantor, led to a reexamination of the basics of set theory and mathematics in general. Partly in an attempt to avoid these difficulties a whole new branch of mathematics was developed. It is called the foundations of mathematics and today is one of the more abstract of the mathematical sciences.

PROBLEMS

Are these paradoxes? Explain why.

1. A Cretan says, "All Cretans always lie." Is he lying?

2. If Zeus can do anything, can he make a stone he cannot lift?

3. A crook steals a child and promises the child's father he will return the child unharmed if, and only if, the father guesses correctly whether or not the child will be returned. What should the crook do if the father guesses that the child will not be returned?

4. An explorer is captured by cannibals. They offer him the opportunity to make a statement with the understanding that if the statement is true they will eat him from his feet up, while if it is false they will eat him from his head down. What should the cannibals do if the explorer says, "I will be eaten from my head down."

5. In lower Yahoo it is declared that every city must have an official hippie. No two cities may have the same official hippie; however, the hippie need not reside in the city where he hips. A new law says that non-resident hippies must live in a new area by themselves. There are so many of them that this new area is declared a city, and hence needs an official hippie. Where should he live?

FOR FURTHER READING

Lipschutz, Seymour. *Finite Mathematics.* ("Schaum's Outline Series.") New York: Schaum Publishing Company, 1964. This is an excellent supplementary text which can aid in understanding some of the topics and concepts covered in this book. It is available at most college bookstores. *Set Theory,* written by the same author for the "Schaum's Outline Series," is more advanced, and little of the material is suitable for this course.

Christian, Robert R. *Introduction to Logic and Sets.* Boston: Ginn and Company, 1958.

Eves, Howard, and Newsom, Carroll. *The Foundations and Fundamental Concepts of Mathematics.* New York: Holt, Rinehart and Winston, Inc., 1965.

Stoll, Robert R. *Sets, Logic, and the Axiomatic Method.* San Francisco: W. H. Freeman and Company, 1961.

Each of the above three books has a very good discussion of set theory.

Kasner, Edward, and Newman, James R. "Paradox Lost and Paradox Regained," *The World of Mathematics,* 3 (1956), 1936–1955. This article contains a storehouse of information on mathematical paradoxes.

CHAPTER 3
MATHEMATICAL SYSTEMS

In the early 1950's, many problems existed in American mathematical education for elementary and high school students. High schools and especially elementary schools could attract few people with college majors in mathematics, and as a result many mathematics teachers had received most of their college training in other fields. Textbooks of the period tended to have little of contemporary interest for students. Of course, there were many excellent teachers working then, but on the whole there was much room for improvement. As one teacher of the period put it, with perhaps some exaggeration, ". . . students were being poorly trained, and, perhaps more important, negative attitudes toward mathematics were being instilled in the minds of countless numbers of American youth."

The mathematical community gradually became more and more concerned about the problem. In the early 1950's, the University of Illinois established the Committee on School Mathematics (UICSM) to write teachers' manuals and sample textbooks for completely new mathematics courses for grades 9–12. Ball State Teacher's College, the University of Maryland, and a few other schools also set up experimental programs.

In 1957, Russia's launching of Sputnik I caused a critical examination and reevaluation of America's program of scientific education, with special attention reserved for mathematics education. Shortly after Sputnik, the federal government bestowed its first grant to what was to become the largest and most influential of the curriculum reform groups in mathematics, the School Mathematics Study Group (SMSG). The textbooks, resulting from the efforts of this group, were experimental and served to stimulate the production of regular commercial texts. Generally, SMSG texts were written by groups of research mathematicians and high school teachers during summer writing sessions and then tested thoroughly in classrooms before being released for widespread use. Teachers who were to use the materials were carefully selected and given special training in the new ideas and methods. This program of in-service training continues today, with the federal government sponsoring summer institutes for junior high and high school teachers each year.

These reform groups tried to discard mathematics that is not relevant to the modern age and to replace it with ideas that are relevant. The material is mathematically correct and sufficiently sophisticated to interest and challenge students who will witness the landing of a man on the moon before they are thirty years old.

"New math" was enthusiastically accepted by many students and teachers because of the great improvement over "old math." Less enthusiasm was encountered on the part of parents, who found they could not help their children with even elementary school homework (however, adults who return to school often find that their children can help them).

The college mathematics curriculum has also been undergoing change in the past decade. The Mathematical Association of America established its Committee on the Undergraduate Program in Mathematics (CUPM) during the 1959–60 school year. CUPM began developing detailed descriptions of recommended courses; the committee was a leader in obtaining more rigorous mathematics courses for prospective elementary school teachers. Today, CUPM is concerned with these large areas: training competent faculty for college mathematics departments, training competent people to teach elementary and secondary school mathematics, and the development of a model curriculum for two-year colleges.

SECTION 1. BASIC CONCEPTS

In the last chapter we studied sets, one of the underlying ideas of contemporary mathematics. Very few areas of mathematics today are divorced from at least the rudiments of set theory. However, as widely used as sets are, there is another concept that is perhaps of greater importance to mathematics, namely the idea of an operation. The most common type of operation is called a *binary operation,* which can be defined as being a rule by which two objects are used to determine a third (not necessarily different) object. For example, if we start with the numbers 3 and 5, then the number 8 can be determined by the binary operation of addition. In a similar way, the binary operation of multiplication can be used to determine the number 24 if we start with the numbers 4 and 6. Other familiar examples of a binary operation are set intersection, set union, and the subtraction and division of numbers.

A less common example is the binary operation of finding the average of two numbers. (Note that finding the average of three numbers is an operation, but not a binary operation.) The familiar symbol $+$, when it appears between two numbers, tells us to add these two numbers. In the same way we can introduce a symbol that will tell us to find the average of two numbers. We could use any symbol that has not already been given another mathematical meaning. Suppose we choose the symbol A; then $3\ A\ 5$ would tell us to find the average of 3 and 5, which is 4. We therefore write

$3\,\mathsf{A}\,5 = 4$. In the same way, $2\,\mathsf{A}\,6 = 4$, $1\,\mathsf{A}\,9 = 5$, $2\,\mathsf{A}\,7 = 4\frac{1}{2}$, and $1\,\mathsf{A}\,1 = 1$.

We are going to study some properties of operations, and for this purpose we are going to introduce some unusual operations. These operations have no particular application but are merely introduced to permit us to investigate some of these properties of operations.

Example 3.1. Define a binary operation, called **B**, by the formula: $a\,\mathsf{B}\,b = a + 2b$. Then find $6\,\mathsf{B}\,4$ and $3\,\mathsf{B}\,5$.

As in algebra, the a and b are placeholders and can be replaced by any number at all that we care to use. According to the formula for this binary operation, we are to add the number a to twice the number b. Following these instructions, $6\,\mathsf{B}\,4$ means to add 6 and (2×4); that is, $6\,\mathsf{B}\,4 = 6 + (2 \times 4) = 14$. Also, $3\,\mathsf{B}\,5 = 3 + 10 = 13$.

Example 3.2. The new binary operation **C** is defined by the rule $a\,\mathsf{C}\,b = (a + b)^2$; evaluate $4\,\mathsf{C}\,2$ and $3\,\mathsf{C}\,5$.

We add a and b and then multiply the sum times itself. Therefore $4\,\mathsf{C}\,2 = (4 + 2)^2 = 6^2 = 36$; and $3\,\mathsf{C}\,5 = (3 + 5)^2 = 8^2 = 64$.

Example 3.3. The new binary operation **D** is defined by the rule, $a\,\mathsf{D}\,b = a$. Find $4\,\mathsf{D}\,3$ and $2\,\mathsf{D}\,7$.

The answer is obtained by simply selecting the first of the two numbers given. Thus $4\,\mathsf{D}\,3 = 4$ since 4 is the first number mentioned; $2\,\mathsf{D}\,7 = 2$.

Recall that
$$\{1, 2, 3, 4, 5, 6, \ldots\}$$
is called the set of *counting numbers*. If we add 0 to the set, we call the elements of the new set *whole numbers:*
$$\{0, 1, 2, 3, 4, 5, 6, \ldots\}.$$
When we include the negatives of the counting numbers we have the set of *integers:*
$$\{\ldots, -4, -3, -2, -1, 0, 1, 2, 3, \ldots\}.$$

A *fraction* is a numeral (see Chapter 1, section 1) of the form $\frac{a}{b}$, where a is a numeral representing an integer, and b is a numeral representing a non-zero integer. Thus, $\frac{3}{4}, \frac{-2}{-1}, \frac{0}{6}, \frac{0}{-9}$, and $\frac{1}{-5}$ are all fractions; $\frac{1}{0}$ and $\frac{\pi}{7}$ are not. A number which can be represented by a fraction numeral is called a *rational number*. We will use some of these sets of numbers in the examples of this chapter.

A *mathematical system* is a set of elements together with one or more binary operations that are rules for combining any two elements of the set. This last phrase is sometimes shortened to read: A mathematical system is a set of elements together with one or more binary operations defined on the set. The set of counting numbers together with the operation of addition forms a mathematical system since the binary operation of addition is defined on the set of counting numbers. The operation of the system must be applicable to the set of the system. It would be meaningless to speak of the system consisting of a set of rabbits together with the binary operation of multiplication since the operation has not yet been defined on the set. We do not know how to multiply two rabbits; two rabbits know how to multiply, but we do not know how to multiply rabbits.

Our definition of mathematical system requires a binary operation; from now on we shall drop the word binary and assume that operation means binary operation.

PROBLEMS

1. Evaluate each of the following:

(a) 2 A 9	(h) −1 B 1	(o) −1 C 8
(b) 3 A 9	(i) 3 B −5	(p) 2 C 6
(c) −2 A −4	(j) $\frac{1}{2}$ B $\frac{1}{2}$	(q) 2 D 5
(d) −3 A −5	(k) 2 C −1	(r) −3 D 4
(e) −3 A 6	(l) 4 C 5	(s) $\frac{1}{2}$ D 3
(f) 2 B 4	(m) −2 C −5	(t) 2 D 2
(g) 0 B 5	(n) 0 C 4	(u) −3 D 5

2. Evaluate each of these; work first inside the parentheses.

(a) 2 A (3 B 4)	(h) 4 D (5 D 3)
(b) −1 C (2 D 5)	(i) −7 C (5 C 3)
(c) 4 B (3 B 5)	(j) 5 C (3 B 5)
(d) 6 C (−2 B 4)	(k) 0 C (0 B 0)
(e) 3 D (−2 B 1)	(l) −1 B (3 A −6)
(f) −4 A (2 A 4)	(m) 2 D (−3 A 6.75)
(g) −$\frac{1}{2}$ C (2 A 6)	(n) −9 A (3 C 7)

3. Define a new operation E by the rule $a \, E \, b = a^2 + ab$. Using this definition, find:

(a) 1 E 0   (b) 2 E 5   (c) −1 E −3   (d) −2 E −4.

4. Define a new operation F by $a \, F \, b = (a + ab)^2$. Using this definition, find:

(a) 0 F 3   (b) −2 F −4   (c) −1 F 4   (d) −2 F 6.

Define a new operation by the following instructions. Select any two counting numbers and find their sum. Divide this sum by 5; disregard the quotient and keep only the remainder. For example, $7 + 9 = 16$. If 16 is divided by 5 a remainder of 1 results, with a quotient of 3. Discard the quotient and write $7 \oplus 9 = 1$, where $\oplus$ is the symbol of this new operation.

5. Find:
   (a) $2 \oplus 6$ (b) $3 \oplus 4$ (c) $3 \oplus 9$.

6. Find:
   (a) $31 \oplus 46$ (b) $21 \oplus 89$ (c) $3 \oplus 2$.

7. Find a rule for an operation **G**, such that: $1\,\textbf{G}\,2 = 3$; $1\,\textbf{G}\,3 = 4$; $2\,\textbf{G}\,3 = 8$; $3\,\textbf{G}\,4 = 15$; $7\,\textbf{G}\,9 = 70$; $2\,\textbf{G}\,11 = 24$.

8. Find a rule for an operation **L** such that: $1\,\textbf{L}\,2 = 3$; $1\,\textbf{L}\,3 = 4$; $2\,\textbf{L}\,3 = 7$; $3\,\textbf{L}\,4 = 13$; $7\,\textbf{L}\,9 = 58$; $2\,\textbf{L}\,11 = 15$; $10\,\textbf{L}\,9 = 109$; $40\,\textbf{L}\,7 = 1607$.

9. Find a rule for an operation **M** such that: $6\,\textbf{M}\,2 = 10$; $1\,\textbf{M}\,4 = -2$; $3\,\textbf{M}\,7 = -1$; $5\,\textbf{M}\,2 = 8$; $-1\,\textbf{M}\,5 = -7$.

10. Answer true or false for each of the following:
   (a) Every integer is a rational number.
   (b) Every integer is a whole number.
   (c) Some rational numbers are not integers.
   (d) Some whole numbers are not counting numbers.
   (e) Some whole numbers are counting numbers.
   (f) Some rational numbers are counting numbers.
   (g) No counting number is not a rational.
   (h) If a number is not a whole number, then it is not a rational number.
   (i) If a number is not a rational number, then it is not an integer.

SECTION 2. THE ASSOCIATIVE PROPERTY

Consider the following problem:

$$12 - 8 - 2.$$

How can we determine the answer? Since subtraction is a binary operation, it can be applied to only two numbers at a time; thus we have two ways of working the problem. We could first associate 12 and 8, subtract to get 4, then subtract 2 to get a final answer of 2, so that:

$$12 - 8 - 2 = 2.$$

Or we could associate 8 and 2, subtract to get 6, and then subtract 6 from 12 for the final answer of 6, so that:

$$12 - 8 - 2 = 6.$$

By performing the subtraction in two different ways, we have obtained two different answers, which means the expression $12 - 8 - 2$ is ambiguous. It is common in a problem of this type to use parentheses as symbols of clarification. If the intent is that the numbers be associated as first described above, parentheses are inserted as follows:

$$(12 - 8) - 2.$$

The meaning here is clear: first, do the work inside the parentheses, and then proceed to the next part, as shown here:

$$(12 - 8) - 2 = 4 - 2 = 2.$$

On the other hand, the second order of subtraction described above is written:

$$12 - (8 - 2).$$

The meaning again is clear: perform the operation inside the parentheses first, then finish.

This example makes it clear that the location of parentheses in a subtraction problem makes a considerable difference. In the expressions $(12 - 8) - 2$ and $12 - (8 - 2)$ the numbers used and the order in which they appear are the same. But the manner of associating these numbers, as indicated by the parentheses, is different in the two expressions and yields two different answers.

Does the same ambiguity arise when adding three numbers? Is it possible to get two different answers for the problem:

$$12 + 8 + 2.$$

Let's see if the answer depends upon the location of the parentheses.

$$(12 + 8) + 2 = 20 + 2 = 22,$$

while

$$12 + (8 + 2) = 12 + 10 = 22,$$

which is the same answer. We can summarize these results by saying that:

$$(12 + 8) + 2 = 12 + (8 + 2),$$

but

$$(12 - 8) - 2 \neq 12 - (8 - 2).$$

These examples tend to make us believe that, in an addition problem involving three numbers, the placement of parentheses is of no importance, while in a subtraction problem it may make a difference. If an operation is such that the location of parentheses makes no difference, we say the operation is associative, or that it has the associative property. This idea may be defined more precisely as follows: an operation $\circ$ defined on some set S has the *associative property* in case:

$$(a \circ b) \circ c = a \circ (b \circ c),$$

for *every* choice of elements a, b, c of S. The $\circ$ is a placeholder which stands for the operation of the system. It may be replaced by the symbol for any operation, such as $+$, $\times$, $-$, **A**, **B**, and so on.

Example 3.4.   In the mathematical system consisting of the rational numbers and operation **A** from the previous section, does **A** have the associative property?

Remember **A** is the operation that determines the average of two numbers. Let's try an example. First notice that:

$$(8 \text{ A } 4) \text{ A } 10 = 6 \text{ A } 10 = 8,$$

while

$$8 \text{ A } (4 \text{ A } 10) = 8 \text{ A } 7 = 7\tfrac{1}{2}.$$

Since the two answers are different, **A** is not an associative operation.

Example 3.5.   Consider the system formed by the set of counting numbers together with operation **D**; does **D** have the associative property?

Operation **D** selects the first of two numbers, which means:

$$6 \text{ D } (9 \text{ D } 4) = 6 \text{ D } 9 = 6,$$

while

$$(6 \text{ D } 9) \text{ D } 4 = 6 \text{ D } 4 = 6.$$

Both answers are the same, but this does not mean we can immediately say **D** is associative. Try several more examples to convince yourself that **D** really is associative.

Example 3.6.   The table of figure 3.1 defines an operation **K** on the set $\{a, b, c, d\}$. Is **K** associative?

To evaluate an expression like $c \text{ K } d$, find c in the column at the left, then read over to the column headed d, which locates the entry b, as shown in figure 3.2. This means that $c \text{ K } d = b$. In the same way, $b \text{ K } c = a$ and $d \text{ K } b = c$. To see if **K** is associative try some examples.

$$(a \text{ K } d) \text{ K } b = d \text{ K } b = c,$$

and

$$a \text{ K } (d \text{ K } b) = a \text{ K } c = c.$$

K	a	b	c	d
a	a	b	c	d
b	b	d	a	c
c	c	a	d	b
d	d	c	b	a

Figure 3.1

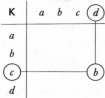

Figure 3.2

Hence

$$a \, \mathbf{K} \, (d \, \mathbf{K} \, b) = (a \, \mathbf{K} \, d) \, \mathbf{K} \, b.$$

In the same way:

$$b \, \mathbf{K} \, (c \, \mathbf{K} \, d) = (b \, \mathbf{K} \, c) \, \mathbf{K} \, d.$$

In the two examples we tried, changing the location of parentheses did not change the answers. Since these two examples worked, we suspect **K** is associative. We cannot be sure of this, however, unless we verify it for every possible choice of three letters from the set.

PROBLEMS

1. Check to see if the following operations have the associative property when defined on the set of rational numbers:
   (a) ÷   (d) **F**
   (b) ×   (e) **C**
   (c) **E**   (f) **L**

2. Insert parentheses to make:
   (a) $100 \div 20 \div 5 = 1.$ (c) $360 \div 18 \div 4 = 5.$
   (b) $100 \div 20 \div 5 = 25.$ (d) $4096 \div 256 \div 4 = 4.$

3. The chart of figure 3.3 defines a new operation **J**. Is **J** associative?

J	m	n	p
m	n	p	n
n	p	m	n
p	n	n	m

Figure 3.3

SECTION 3. THE COMMUTATIVE PROPERTY

It makes a difference whether you put on your socks or your shoes first: the order of doing makes a difference. On the other hand, you can put on either your left shoe or your right shoe first: the order of doing makes no difference. If the order of doing makes no difference we give the name commutative to the situation. The operation ∘ defined on a set S is *commutative* in case:

$$a \circ b = b \circ a,$$

for every two elements a and b of S.

If we look at the operation of addition defined on the set of counting numbers, we see that $3 + 4 = 4 + 3$, $91 + 78 = 78 + 91$, and so on. We can find enough examples of this type to convince ourselves that addition, when defined on the set of counting numbers, has the commutative property.

Example 3.7. Does subtraction, defined on the set of counting numbers, have the commutative property?

Try an example:

$$5 - 4 = 1,$$

while

$$4 - 5 = -1;$$

therefore

$$5 - 4 \neq 4 - 5.$$

The definition of commutative requires that $a \circ b = b \circ a$, for *every* two elements a and b; here we found that $a - b$ is not equal to $b - a$, for every two numbers a and b. Thus subtraction is not commutative.

Example 3.8. In the mathematical system consisting of operation **A** and the rational numbers, is **A** commutative?

Note:

$$8 \text{ A } 12 = 10,$$

while

$$12 \text{ A } 8 = 10,$$

so that

$$8 \text{ A } 12 = 12 \text{ A } 8.$$

It seems reasonable to assert that the average of two numbers can be taken in any order, which means **A** is commutative.

Example 3.9. Consider the mathematical system consisting of the set $\{a, b, c, d\}$ together with operation **K** as defined in example 3.6. Does **K** have the commutative property?

Try examples:

$$c \text{ K } d = b,$$

while

$$d \text{ K } c = b;$$

also

$$b \mathbf{K} c = a,$$

and

$$c \mathbf{K} b = a.$$

There is a useful test which can be employed in a chart like this, when checking for commutativity. Draw a diagonal from the upper left corner to the lower right corner of the chart, as shown in figure 3.4. If it is possible to fold the chart on the diagonal and have the corresponding elements match, then the operation defined by the chart has the commutative property.

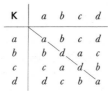

Figure 3.4

PROBLEMS

Replace the word "associative" with the word "commutative" in problems 1 and 3 of the last section and then work them.

SECTION 4. CLOSURE

The operation **A**, as defined earlier, determines the average of any two numbers. Consider the set of counting numbers together with this operation, **A**. We know that $3 \mathbf{A} 9 = 6$, $4 \mathbf{A} 12 = 8$, $10 \mathbf{A} 16 = 13$, and so on. You might wonder whether or not the average of two counting numbers is always a counting number. The answer is no, since, for example, $3 \mathbf{A} 6 = 4\frac{1}{2}$, which is not a counting number. On the other hand, consider operation **B** defined before. (Recall: $a \mathbf{B} b = a + 2b$.) If we select any two counting numbers and apply operation **B**, is the answer always in the set of counting numbers? Try some examples: $2 \mathbf{B} 5 = 12$, $3 \mathbf{B} 9 = 21$, $7 \mathbf{B} 5 = 17$, and so on. It would seem that no matter what two counting numbers *a* and *b* we choose, *a* **B** *b* is always a counting number. We say that such a system is closed, or has the *closure property:* a system consisting of a set *S* and an operation ∘ is *closed* if *a* ∘ *b* is in *S* whenever *a* and *b* are in *S*. We speak of *S* as being closed under, or with respect to, the operation. The definition says, in effect, that if a system is closed, then applying the operation to two elements of the set will result in a third element that is also in the set. If there are any two elements in the set which yield an answer that is not in the set, the system is *not closed.* Above, we found that the system consisting of the counting numbers and operation **A** was not closed because both 3 and 6 are counting numbers, while 3 **A** 6 is not a counting number.

Example 3.10.   Consider the system consisting of the set of even counting numbers and the operation of addition. Is this system closed?

Select any two even counting numbers and find their sum. For example, $12 + 32 = 44$, which is an even counting number. Try other examples: $56 + 88 = 144$, $124 + 46 = 170$, and so on. Each example tried will have an even counting number for an answer. This does not prove that the sum of *every* two even counting numbers is an even counting number, but it does make it sound plausible. Hence we claim this system is closed.

Example 3.11.   Is the set of odd counting numbers closed under the operation of addition? of multiplication?

Select any two odd counting numbers, say 7 and 7. If we add these numbers we have 14, which is not an odd counting number. Therefore this system lacks the closure property.

How about multiplication? Select any two odd counting numbers, such as 7 and 11, and multiply. The product is 77, which again is an odd counting number, as are $23 \times 5 = 115$ and $43 \times 3 = 129$. It would appear that the product of any two odd counting numbers is an odd counting number; this system is closed. We have demonstrated with this example that it is possible for the same set to be closed under one operation and not closed under another operation.

Example 3.12.   Consider the system consisting of the set $\{a, b, c, d\}$ together with operation **K**, defined in example 3.6. Does this system have the closure property?

To determine if the system is closed, we investigate the answers obtained when **K** is applied to the elements in the set. A glance at the chart of figure 3.1 reveals that the answers in the body of the chart are all elements of the set $\{a, b, c, d\}$. If we had found another letter in the body of the chart, the system would not be closed.

PROBLEMS

Are the following systems closed?

1. The set of all odd multiples of 5 under multiplication. (Remember: -15, -5, 15 are multiples of 5.)
2. The set of even multiples of 5 under multiplication.
3. The set of all multiples of 5 under addition.
4. The set of rational numbers and the operation of multiplication; of addition.
5. The set of counting numbers and the operation of subtraction.
6. The set $\{0, 1, 2, 3, 4\}$ and the operation $\oplus$ defined in the first section.
7. The set of all counting numbers which end in zero and the operation of addition; of multiplication.
8. The set $\{0, 1\}$ and the operation of multiplication.
9. The set $\{0, 1\}$ and the operation of addition.
10. The set $\{0\}$ under the operation of addition.
11. The set $\{0\}$ under the operation of multiplication.
12. List all the finite sets of whole numbers that are closed under the operation of addition.
13. List all the finite sets of whole numbers that are closed under multiplication.
14. Is the set of counting numbers closed under the operation of division?

SECTION 5. THE IDENTITY ELEMENT

In the system consisting of the whole numbers and the operation of multiplication, the number 1 has a special property: if a is any counting number, then:

$$a \times 1 = 1 \times a = a.$$

For example, $3 \times 1 = 1 \times 3 = 3$, and so on. Because of this special property of the number 1, we say 1 is the identity element for the set of counting numbers under the operation of multiplication.

Note that 0 plays a similar role in the system of whole numbers under the operation of addition: $5 + 0 = 0 + 5 = 5$, $12 + 0 = 0 + 12 = 12$, and so on. When an element of a system has this special property, it is called the identity element of the system. In general, a system consisting of a set S and an operation $\circ$ has an *identity element*, say e, $(e \in S)$, in case:

$$a \circ e = e \circ a = a,$$

for every element a of set S. This simply means that, when a system has an identity e, it is possible to select any element a of the system, apply the operation of the system to a and e (in any order) and get a as the answer.

Example 3.13.   Consider the system consisting of the set of whole numbers and operation **B**. Does this system have an identity element?

Can we find a whole number e such that $7 \textbf{ B } e = 7$? Try $e = 0$. Certainly, $7 \textbf{ B } 0 = 7 + (2 \times 0) = 7$; you might be tempted to say 0 is the identity element for the system. But study the definition again. It not only requires that $7 \textbf{ B } 0 = 7$, but also that $0 \textbf{ B } 7 = 7$; by the definition of operation $\textbf{B}$, $0 \textbf{ B } 7 = 14$, not 7. This means 0 does not satisfy the definition of identity element for this system. Try other possible candidates for e; you will find that these do not work either.

Example 3.14.   Consider the system consisting of the set of whole numbers and the operation of subtraction. Does this system have an identity element?

By definition, we must find a whole number e such that:

$$a - e = e - a = a,$$

for every whole number a. Again the number 0 satisfies one part; that is, $a - 0 = a$, for every whole number a. However, trouble arises when we consider $0 - a$. For example, $4 - 0 = 4$, but $0 - 4 \neq 4$. Therefore 0 is not an identity element for this system. Again, no other numbers will work either.

Example 3.15.   Does the system consisting of the whole numbers and operation $\textbf{A}$ have an identity element?

Can we find a whole number e, such that $4 \textbf{ A } e = e \textbf{ A } 4 = 4$? If $e = 4$, then $4 \textbf{ A } 4 = 4$. Can we find a whole number e, such that $7 \textbf{ A } e = e \textbf{ A } 7 = 7$? Here $e = 7$ since $7 \textbf{ A } 7 = 7$. But we were forced to use two different values for e. An identity, by definition, must be an element that works in all cases. Thus we must conclude that this system has no identity.

Example 3.16.   Consider the system consisting of the set $\{a, b, c, d\}$ together with operation $\textbf{K}$ as originally defined in the chart of figure 3.1. Does this system have an identity element?

If an element is the identity, then the column appearing directly below it in the body of the chart will be identical with the column at the far left. In this case we see (as illustrated in figure 3.5) that a is the only possible ele-

only possible candidate for identity

K	a	b	c	d
a	a	b	c	d
b	b	d	a	c
c	c	a	d	b
d	d	c	b	a

left column repeated

Figure 3.5

ment which satisfies this condition. We see, in fact, that a actually is the identity since $a \mathrel{\mathsf{K}} a = a$, $b \mathrel{\mathsf{K}} a = a \mathrel{\mathsf{K}} b = b$, $c \mathrel{\mathsf{K}} a = a \mathrel{\mathsf{K}} c = c$, and $d \mathrel{\mathsf{K}} a = a \mathrel{\mathsf{K}} d = d$.

PROBLEMS

Do the following systems have identity elements?

1. The set of odd numbers and the operation of multiplication.
2. The set of rational numbers and the operation of addition.
3. The set of rational numbers and the operation of multiplication.
4. The set of all multiples of 5 under addition.
5. The set $\{0, 1, 2, 3, 4\}$ under the operation $\oplus$.
6. The set $\{0, 1, 2, 3, 78, 5345\}$ under addition.
7. The set $\{1, 2, 3, 4, 78, 1234\}$ under multiplication.
8. The set of counting numbers and division.
9. The set of integers under addition.
10. The set of non-zero rational numbers under multiplication.
11. The set of integers under subtraction.
12. The set of whole numbers under operation C.
13. Define operation T by the chart of figure 3.6. Is a an identity? Why or why not? (Note: the column in the body of the chart directly under element a is the same as the column at the far left.)

T	a	b	c	d
a	a	c	d	b
b	b	a	c	d
c	c	d	b	a
d	d	b	a	c

Figure 3.6

SECTION 6. INVERSE ELEMENTS

The numbers 6 and -6 are often called opposites or inverses of each other under the operation of addition since $6 + (-6) = -6 + 6 = 0$. Also 6 and $\frac{1}{6}$ are inverses of each other under multiplication since $6 \times \frac{1}{6} = \frac{1}{6} \times 6 = 1$. In general, consider a mathematical system consisting of a set S and an operation $\circ$. Elements a and b of S are *inverses* of each other under the operation $\circ$, in case $a \circ b = b \circ a = e$, where e is the identity of the system. Notice that if a system has no identity, then inverses cannot occur.

Example 3.17. Consider the set of all non-zero rational numbers. Does each element of the set have an inverse under multiplication?

Since the system has an identity element, 1, we can continue looking for inverses. Can we find an inverse for $\frac{3}{4}$? We need a number b, such that:

$$\frac{3}{4} \times b = b \times \frac{3}{4} = 1.$$

Verify that the rational number $\frac{4}{3}$ can be used. In fact, if $\frac{m}{n}$ is any non-zero rational number, then

$$\frac{m}{n} \times \frac{n}{m} = \frac{n}{m} \times \frac{m}{n} = 1,$$

so that $\frac{m}{n}$ and $\frac{n}{m}$ are inverses of each other under the operation of multiplication. In a case like this, where the elements of the system are numbers, and the operation is multiplication, inverses are sometimes called *reciprocals*.

The example above shows that every non-zero rational number has a multiplicative inverse. There is no rational number, however, that can be multiplied by 0 to yield the identity 1. Hence 0 itself has no multiplicative inverse. The set of rational numbers together with the operation of multiplication is a system which contains inverses for all its elements except 0.

Example 3.18.   Consider the system of the set of rational numbers and the operation of addition. Does every element of the system have an inverse in the system?

Since we know that the system has an identity element, 0, we can look for inverse elements. Can we find an inverse in the system for $\frac{3}{4}$? That is, can we find a rational number b such that:

$$\frac{3}{4} + b = b + \frac{3}{4} = 0?$$

The desired inverse in this case is $-\frac{3}{4}$; the numbers $\frac{3}{4}$ and $-\frac{3}{4}$ are additive inverses of each other. Note that in this system, 0 is its own inverse since $0 + 0 = 0$.

Example 3.19.   Consider the system composed of the set $\{a, b, c, d\}$ and operation **K** (see figure 3.5). Does each element of the system have an inverse in the system?

In the last section we found that a is the identity element of this system. After an inspection of the chart, we see that b and c are inverses of each other since $b\,\mathbf{K}\,c = c\,\mathbf{K}\,b = a$. Note that d is its own inverse, since $d\,\mathbf{K}\,d = a$. Also, a is its own inverse. To find the inverses when a chart, such as this, is given, inspect each row of the body of the chart for the identity element. If it does not appear in a particular row, then the element at the left in that row has no inverse.

PROBLEMS

Consider the following systems. Does every element in the system have an inverse in the system?

1. The set of counting numbers and the operation of addition.
2. The set of counting numbers and multiplication.
3. The set of integers and addition.
4. The set of rational numbers and multiplication.
5. The set of integers and operation **A**.
6. The set of all odd integers and addition.
7. The set $\{0, 1, 2, 3, 4\}$ and the operation $\oplus$.

SECTION 7. THE DISTRIBUTIVE PROPERTY

Let us now investigate a property that concerns two operations defined on the same set. Let $\circ$ and $\&$ be any two operations defined on the same set S; we say $\circ$ is *distributive* with respect to (or over) $\&$ in case

$$a \circ (b \, \& \, c) = (a \circ b) \, \& \, (a \circ c),$$

for all elements a, b, and c of S.

Example 3.20.   Is addition distributive over multiplication on the set of counting numbers?

We replace $\circ$ with $+$ and $\&$ with $\times$; we want to know if

$$a + (b \times c) = (a + b) \times (a + c),$$

for all counting numbers a, b, and c. We can try an example:

$$3 + (4 \times 5) = 3 + 20 = 23,$$

while

$$(3 + 4) \times (3 + 5) = 7 \times 8 = 56.$$

This is enough to allow our saying that addition is not distributive over multiplication on the set of counting numbers.

Example 3.21.   Is multiplication distributive over addition on the set of counting numbers?

We replace $\circ$ with $\times$ and $\&$ with $+$; we want to know if

$$a \times (b + c) = (a \times b) + (a \times c),$$

for all counting numbers a, b, and c. We can try an example:

$$5 \times (3 + 4) = 5 \times 7 = 35,$$

while

$$(5 \times 3) + (5 \times 4) = 15 + 20 = 35.$$

Other examples would also work; multiplication is distributive over addition on the set of counting numbers.

Example 3.22. Is operation **B** distributive over operation **D** on the set of counting numbers?

Again we try examples:

$$7 \textbf{ B } (4 \textbf{ D } 8) = 7 \textbf{ B } 4 = 7 + (2 \times 4) = 15,$$

and

$$(7 \textbf{ B } 4) \textbf{ D } (7 \textbf{ B } 8) = 15 \textbf{ D } 23 = 15.$$

Let's try another example:

$$9 \textbf{ B } (3 \textbf{ D } 6) = 9 \textbf{ B } 3 = 15,$$

and

$$(9 \textbf{ B } 3) \textbf{ D } (9 \textbf{ B } 6) = 15 \textbf{ D } 21 = 15.$$

These and other examples should convince you that **B** is indeed distributive over **D**.

PROBLEMS

1. Is multiplication distributive over subtraction on the set of rational numbers?
2. Is multiplication distributive over division on the set of rational numbers?
3. Is addition distributive over subtraction on the set of integers?
4. Is operation **D** distributive over operation **B** on the set of counting numbers?
5. Is operation **C** distributive over operation **A** on the set of whole numbers?

SECTION 8. A REVIEW

Both as a review and as a handy reference, we are going to list the six basic properties which we have been studying. If a system consists of a set S together with the operation $\circ$ defined on S, we can say that:

(1) Operation $\circ$ has the *associative property* in case:

$$a \circ (b \circ c) = (a \circ b) \circ c,$$

for all choices of a, b, and c in S.

(2) Operation $\circ$ has the *commutative property* in case:

$$a \circ b = b \circ a,$$

for all elements a and b in S.

(3) The system has an *identity element, e,* in case:

$$a \circ e = e \circ a = a,$$

for every *a* in *S*.

(4) Elements *a* and *b* in the system are *inverses* of each other with respect to $\circ$ in case:

$$a \circ b = b \circ a = e,$$

where *e* is the identity of the system.

(5) The system is *closed* with respect to $\circ$ if, for every two elements *a* and *b* in *S*, $a \circ b$ is in *S*.

(6) In addition to $\circ$, if a second operation & is defined on *S*, then $\circ$ is *distributive* over & in case:

$$a \circ (b \,\&\, c) = (a \circ b) \,\&\, (a \circ c),$$

for all elements *a*, *b*, and *c* in *S*.

PROBLEMS

1. Does $(A \cap B) \cap C = A \cap (B \cap C)$, for all sets *A*, *B*, and *C*?

2. Does $(A \cup B) \cup C = A \cup (B \cup C)$, for all sets *A*, *B*, and *C*?

3. Define a universal set *U* as the set of counting numbers. Form a new set which consists of all possible subsets of *U*. This new set of subsets together with the operation of set intersection forms a mathematical system. Which of the above six properties are satisfied by this system?

4. Replace the word *intersection* with the word *union* in problem 3; then answer the above question.

5. Is $\cap$ distributive over $\cup$ on the set of subsets of problem 3?

6. Is $\cup$ distributive over $\cap$ on the set of subsets of problem 3?

7. Consider the system consisting of the set $\{m, n, p\}$ and operation **J**, as defined by the chart of figure 3.7.

J	m	n	p
m	n	p	n
n	p	m	n
p	n	n	m

Figure 3.7

Which of the properties listed above hold here?

8. Consider the system consisting of the set $\{A, B, F\}$ with the operation * defined by figure 3.8.

*	A	B	F
A	B	F	A
B	F	A	B
F	A	B	F

Figure 3.8

Which properties hold here?

9. Consider the system consisting of the set $\{A, J, T, U\}$ together with operation # defined by figure 3.9.

#	A	J	T	U
A	A	J	T	U
J	J	T	U	A
T	T	U	A	J
U	U	A	J	T

Figure 3.9

Which properties hold here?

10. Consider the system composed of the set $\{1, 2, 3, 4, 5\}$ with an operation T defined by the chart of figure 3.10.

T	1	2	3	4	5
1	1	2	3	4	5
2	2	4	0	2	4
3	3	0	3	0	3
4	4	2	0	4	2
5	5	4	3	2	1

Figure 3.10

Which properties hold?

11. The chart of figure 3.11 defines an operation Z on the set $\{r, s, t, u\}$. Which properties hold in this system?

Z	r	s	t	u
r	u	t	r	s
s	t	u	s	r
t	r	s	t	u
u	s	r	u	t

Figure 3.11

12. State the property that applies in each of the following:
  (a) $3 + 4 = 4 + 3$.
  (b) $-2 + (3 + 4) = (3 + 4) + -2$.
  (c) $5 \times (3 \times 7) = (5 \times 3) \times 7$.
  (d) $17 \times (\frac{5}{5}) = 17$.
  (e) $7 \times (5 + 4) = (5 + 4) \times 7$.
  (f) $13 \times (\frac{1}{13}) = 1$.
  (g) $5 + 7$ has an answer which is a counting number.
  (h) $(2 + 5) + 7 = 7 + (2 + 5)$.
  (i) $14 + -14 = 0$.
  (j) $11 \times (-4) = (-4) \times 11$.

SECTION 9. DECIMALS

We have studied fraction numerals (a numeral having the form $\dfrac{a}{b}$, where a represents an integer and b a non-zero integer); now let's discuss decimal numerals. Consider a straight line; select any point on it and label it 0. Next select any point to the right of the one labeled 0 and label it 1. These two points, 0 and 1, give a scale by which all other numbers may be represented by points on the *number line* (see figure 3.12). A rational number can also be

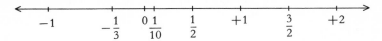

Figure 3.12

expressed as a decimal as follows: we use the rational number $\frac{4}{11}$ as an example. Consider the interval of the number line from 0 to 1, and divide it into ten parts, each part labeled as in figure 3.13.

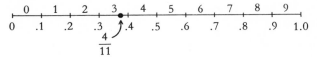

Figure 3.13

The rational number $\frac{4}{11}$ is in the interval labeled 3; thus we begin the decimal representation of $\frac{4}{11}$ by writing

$$\frac{4}{11} = .3\cdots.$$

Next we divide the interval from .3 to .4, which contains $\frac{4}{11}$, into ten equal parts, as labeled in figure 3.14 (see p. 90). Here $\frac{4}{11}$ is in the interval labeled 6, so that we may write:

$$\frac{4}{11} = .36\cdots.$$

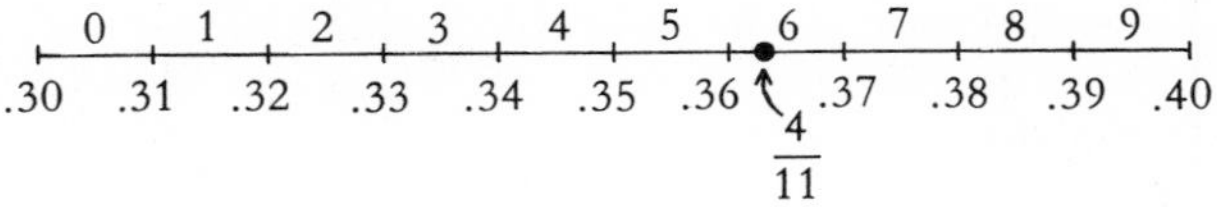

Figure 3.14

Divide the interval from .36 to .37 into ten equal parts, labeled in figure 3.15. Now we have:

$$\frac{4}{11} = .363\cdots.$$

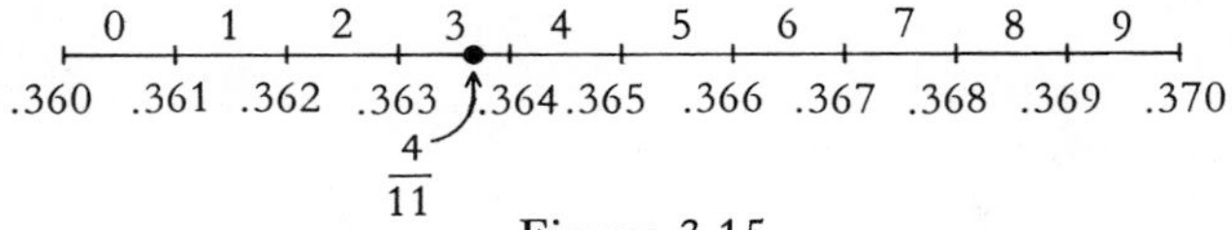

Figure 3.15

By continuing this process we can obtain as many decimal digits as desired; it will be found

$$\frac{4}{11} = .363636\cdots,$$

where the block of digits, 36, repeats indefinitely. (Note: in the process above, if one of the division points lands on the number, choose the interval to the right.)

To simplify notation, we write

$$\frac{4}{11} = .\overline{36},$$

where the bar indicates that the block of digits, 36, repeats indefinitely. Here are other examples of this notation:

$$\frac{1}{11} = .090909\cdots = .\overline{09}$$

$$\frac{1}{3} = .333333\cdots = .\overline{3}$$

$$\frac{1}{6} = .166666\cdots = .1\overline{6}$$

$$\frac{1}{13} = .076923076923\cdots = .\overline{076923}$$

$$\frac{9}{5} = 1.8 = 1.80000\cdots = 1.8\overline{0}$$

$$\frac{1}{4} = .25 = .2500000\cdots = .25\overline{0}$$

Each time the bar is used to indicate an unending repetition of a given block of digits; numbers which have such decimal representations are called repeating decimal numbers or simply *repeating decimals*. All other decimals are called *non-repeating decimals*.

Example 3.23.   Determine whether the rational number $\frac{1}{7}$ is represented by a repeating or a non-repeating decimal.

To determine the decimal equivalent of a rational number, the procedure explained above could be used. However, there is an easier method: simply divide the denominator into the numerator.

$$
\begin{array}{r}
.142857 \\
7\overline{)1.00000000} \\
\underline{7} \\
30 \\
\underline{28} \\
20 \\
\underline{14} \\
60 \\
\underline{56} \\
40 \\
\underline{35} \\
50 \\
\underline{49} \\
10
\end{array}
$$

The next step is to divide 10 by 7, which is exactly where we began. Hence the digits of the quotient start repeating, and we can write:

$$\frac{1}{7} = .142857142857\cdots = .\overline{142857}$$

By understanding this example, we can convince ourselves that any rational number can be represented by a repeating decimal. Each step of the division process produces a remainder which must be less than the divisor (7 in the above example). Since there are a finite number of such remainders possible, they must eventually begin to repeat, which in turn makes the digits of the quotient repeat.

We know then that every rational number can be represented by a repeating decimal. Is it also true that every repeating decimal represents a rational number? The answer is yes. An easy case occurs when only zeros repeat: for example, $.789\overline{0}$ is the same as $789/1000$, while $6.3578\overline{0}$ is the same as $63,578/10,000$.

In case digits other than 0 repeat, as in $.\overline{85}$, we can employ the following procedure.

(1) Let $x = .\overline{85}$, that is: $x = .85858585\ldots$

(2) Multiply both sides of the statement in (1) by 100 (since there are two digits in the part that repeats), which results in:

$$100x = 100(.85858585\cdots) = 85.85858585\cdots,$$

or $100x = 85.\overline{85858585}\cdots.$

(3) Subtract the statement in (1) from the final statement in (2):

$$100x = 85.85858585\cdots$$
$$\underline{x = \quad .85858585\cdots}$$
$$99x = 85$$

(4) Solve the equation from (3):

$$x = \frac{85}{99}.$$

Since we defined x to be $.\overline{85}$, we now have:

$$.\overline{85} = \frac{85}{99}.$$

As a check, we can convert 85/99 into decimal form by the procedure of example 3.23.

$$
\begin{array}{r}
.85 \\
99{\overline{\smash{)}\,85.00}} \\
\underline{79\ 2} \\
5\ 80 \\
\underline{4\ 95} \\
850\cdots
\end{array}
$$

Example 3.24.   Write $.0\overline{6}$ as the quotient of two integers.

Follow the steps outlined above: let $x = .0\overline{6} = .066666\cdots$. Then we have:

$$10x = .66666\cdots$$
$$\underline{x = .06666\cdots}$$
$$9x = .6,$$
$$x = \frac{.6}{9}.$$

Since .6 is not an integer as required, we multiply both numerator and denominator by 10.

$$x = \frac{.6}{9} = \frac{.6 \times 10}{9 \times 10} = \frac{6}{90} = \frac{1}{15}.$$

Therefore $.0\overline{6} = \frac{1}{15}$.

The following example may seem a little strange or unusual, but its purpose is to demonstrate how ordinary things done in an "unordinary" way can produce "unordinary" results.

Example 3.25.   Which rational number is represented by $.\overline{9}$?

Proceed as above:

$$
\begin{aligned}
10x &= 9.999999\cdots \\
x &= .999999\cdots \\
\hline
9x &= 9 \\
x &= 1.
\end{aligned}
$$

Hence $.\overline{9} = 1$.

This is not merely an approximation—these two numbers are equal. Perhaps this will make it seem more plausible:

$$\frac{1}{3} = .3333333\cdots = .\overline{3}$$

$$1 = \frac{3}{3} = 3\left(\frac{1}{3}\right) = 3(.33333\cdots) = .99999\cdots = .\overline{9}.$$

Or what about this unorthodox way of dividing 9 by 9:

$$
\begin{array}{r}
.9999 \\
9\overline{)9.00000} \\
8\,1 \\
\hline
90 \\
81 \\
\hline
90 \\
81 \\
\hline
90\cdots \\
\end{array}
$$

In this section we have seen that every rational number can be represented by a repeating decimal, and that every repeating decimal represents a rational number. In the next section, we shall discuss numbers that have non-repeating decimal representations.

PROBLEMS

1. Express as a repeating decimal:
   (a) $\frac{1}{19}$ (d) $\frac{2}{7}$ (g) $\frac{1}{4}$
   (b) $\frac{2}{11}$ (e) $4\frac{5}{9}$ (h) $-2\frac{3}{7}$
   (c) $6\frac{2}{3}$ (f) $-\frac{11}{15}$ (i) $\frac{11}{7}$.

2. Find the rational numbers represented by the following repeating decimals:
   (a) $.3\overline{5}$ (d) $.14\overline{9}$ (g) $.15\overline{0}$
   (b) $.\overline{142857}$ (e) $.0\overline{99}$ (h) $.1414\overline{14}$
   (c) $.70\overline{7070}$ (f) $.339\overline{99}$ (i) $1.2\overline{45}$.

3. Does the decimal .101001000100001··· represent a rational number?

4. The process of constructing decimals described in this section uses ten subdivisions at each step, producing decimals in base 10. A similar process, using only two subdivisions at each step, produces decimals in base 2. Write the following numbers as base 2 decimals:

(a) $\frac{1}{2}$ (c) $\frac{1}{4}$ (e) $\frac{2}{3}$

(b) $\frac{1}{3}$ (d) $\frac{1}{8}$

SECTION 10. REAL NUMBERS

We have seen that every rational number can be expressed as a repeating decimal and every repeating decimal represents a rational number. In the problems at the end of the last section, we found that the number .10100100010000··· is not a repeating decimal (no single block of digits repeats) and hence does not represent a rational number. A number which is represented by a non-repeating decimal is called an *irrational number*. Examples of irrational numbers include:

$$\sqrt{2} = 1.414214\cdots$$
$$\sqrt{3} = 1.732051\cdots$$
$$\pi = 3.141592653589793\cdots$$
$$\frac{1}{\sqrt{2}} = .707107\cdots$$
$$\frac{1}{\pi} = .318309886\cdots$$
$$\pi^2 = 9.8696044036667637\cdots.$$

In the problem set below, you are asked to prove that $\sqrt{2}$ is irrational.

A *real number* is one that can be represented by a decimal, either repeating or non-repeating. In other words, the set of real numbers is composed of the set of rational numbers and the set of irrational numbers. We may summarize the names we have used for numbers as in figure 3.16:

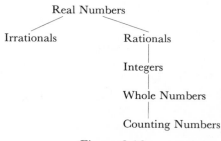

Figure 3.16

PROBLEMS

1. Below is a proof that $\sqrt{2}$ is irrational. Give a reason for each step preceded by an asterisk.

   There are two possibilities:

   (1) there is a rational number $\frac{a}{b}$ such that
   $$\left(\frac{a}{b}\right)^2 = 2.$$

   (2) there is no such rational number.

   We work with (1); if it leads to a contradiction, or false statement, then we know (2) must be the correct choice. We assume there exists a rational number $\frac{a}{b}$ such that $\left(\frac{a}{b}\right)^2 = 2$; we can also assume $\frac{a}{b}$ is in lowest terms.

   Since $\left(\frac{a}{b}\right)^2 = 2$, we also have:
   $$\frac{a^2}{b^2} = 2,$$

   * so that
   $$a^2 = 2b^2.$$

   * $2b^2$ is an even number.
   * Therefore, a^2 is an even number,
   * and a must be even.

   Since a is an even number, it must be a multiple of 2; that is, we can find a counting number c such that $a = 2c$. (For example, 14 is an even number and $14 = 2 \times 7$.) Hence, $a^2 = 2b^2$ becomes $(2c)^2 = 2b^2$.

   * Therefore, $4c^2 = 2b^2,$
   * or $2c^2 = b^2.$

   * $2c^2$ is an even number.
   * b^2, and hence b, are even numbers.
   * A contradiction has been reached. (Hint: we have shown that both a and b are even numbers.)

   * We must accept assumption (2) from above.

2. In the problem above, we proved that $\sqrt{2}$ is irrational. Modify the proof to show $\sqrt{3}$ is irrational.

3. Notice that $2^2 = 4$, so that $\sqrt{4} = 2$. We know that 2 is a rational number; hence it is not possible to modify the proof that $\sqrt{2}$ is irrational in order to prove $\sqrt{4}$ is irrational. Go through the steps of the proof presented in problem 1, replacing 2 with 4, and find where the proof fails.

Although the set of real numbers is a large set, it does not contain all the numbers. For example, the equation $x^2 + 1 = 0$ can be solved for x, giving $x = \sqrt{-1}$. There is no real number whose square is -1 since the square of any real number is positive or zero: $(-4)^2 = 16$; $(-1)^2 = 1$; $0^2 = 0$; and so on. Hence $\sqrt{-1}$ is not a real number. We introduce the special symbol $i = \sqrt{-1}$, making $i^2 = -1$. Numbers such as i, $3i$, $-4i$, and so on are called *imaginary numbers*. Note that $\sqrt{-4} = \sqrt{-1 \cdot 4} = \sqrt{-1} \cdot \sqrt{4} = 2i$. Also note $i^3 = (i \cdot i)i = (-1)i = -i$. A sum of a real and an imaginary number, such as $2 + 3i$, is called a *complex number*. Note that every real number is a complex number since, for example, $3 = 3 + 0i$.

4. Evaluate i^7.

5. Evaluate i^9.

6. Evaluate i^4.

7. Evaluate i^{11}.

8. Find a number equal to $\sqrt{-9}$.

9. Find a number equal to $\sqrt{-16}$.

10. Find a number equal to $\sqrt{-\frac{1}{4}}$.

11. Find all solutions of the equation $x^2 + 100 = 0$.

12. Find all solutions of the equation $x^2 = -144$.

13. Place the complex numbers and the imaginary numbers on the chart of figure 3.16.

SECTION 11. CARDINAL NUMBERS OF SETS

There is an infinite number of counting numbers, there is an infinite number of rational numbers, and there is an infinite number of real numbers. Intuitively, it seems there are "more" rational numbers than counting numbers, and "more" real numbers than rational numbers (there are "more" decimals that do not repeat than decimals that do). In this section we are going to investigate more completely the cardinal numbers of these sets. The "smallest" set listed is the set of counting numbers, which is part of our basic definition.

A set of elements is called *denumerable* or *denumerably infinite* or is said to have cardinal number d if it can be placed in one-to-one correspondence with the counting numbers. Think of d as being the "smallest" infinite number. The number d is a cardinal number of a set; to the question, "How many counting numbers are there," we would answer, "There are d of them."

Recall from the last chapter that two sets have the same cardinal number if they can be placed in one-to-one correspondence with each other. This fact is basic to this section.

Example 3.26.   What is the cardinal number of the set of whole numbers?

The set of whole numbers contains one more element than the set of counting numbers, and hence should have a cardinal number, $d + 1$. However, consider the following correspondence:

$$\{1, 2, 3, 4, 5, 6, \cdots, \quad n, \quad \ldots\}$$
$$\updownarrow \updownarrow \updownarrow \updownarrow \updownarrow \updownarrow \qquad \updownarrow$$
$$\{0, 1, 2, 3, 4, 5, \cdots, n - 1, \ldots\},$$

which is a one-to-one correspondence between the set of counting numbers and the set of whole numbers. Here $n \leftrightarrow (n - 1)$ is the general term or rule of the correspondence. Since we have a one-to-one correspondence, we conclude that the cardinal number of the set of counting numbers is the same as the cardinal number of the set of whole numbers, or

$$d + 1 = d.$$

Example 3.27.   What is the cardinal number of the set of integers?

Every counting number has a negative, therefore we might expect the cardinal number of the set of integers to be $d + d$, or $2d$. However, we can set up a one-to-one correspondence between the set of integers and the set of counting numbers:

$$\{1, 2, \quad 3, 4, \quad 5, 6, \quad 7, \cdots, 2n, \quad 2n + 1, \ldots\}$$
$$\updownarrow \updownarrow \quad \updownarrow \updownarrow \quad \updownarrow \updownarrow \quad \updownarrow \qquad \updownarrow \qquad \updownarrow$$
$$\{0, 1, -1, 2, -2, 3, -3, \cdots, \quad n, \qquad -n, \ldots\}.$$

Since we have this one-to-one correspondence, the cardinal number of the set of integers equals the cardinal number of the set of counting numbers, or

$$d = 2d.$$

We agreed that two sets have the same cardinal number if they can be placed in one-to-one correspondence. But when we applied this agreement to certain infinite sets, we obtained some strange results. But wait, a stranger example is coming. We know that there is an infinite number of rational numbers between the counting numbers 1 and 2, and therefore there must be more rational numbers than counting numbers. Let's see.

Example 3.28.   What is the cardinal number of the set of rational numbers?

A rational number can be represented as the quotient of two integers. There are d possible integers that could be numerators and $d - 1$ possible integers that could be denominators (0 cannot be a denominator) for a maximum of $d(d - 1)$ possible rational numbers. Look now at the chart of figure 3.17. The non-negative rational numbers whose denominator is 1 are written in the first row; those whose denominator is 2 are written in the second row, and so on.

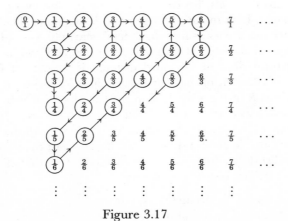

Figure 3.17

Notice that every non-negative rational number appears in the list sooner or later. For example, $\frac{327}{189}$ is in row 189 and column 327. Follow the arrow drawn in figure 3.17, and let $\frac{0}{1}$ correspond to 1, $\frac{1}{1}$ to 2, $\frac{2}{1}$ to 3, $\frac{1}{2}$ to 4, (since $\frac{2}{2} = \frac{1}{1}$, we do not use it), $\frac{1}{3}$ to 5, $\frac{1}{4}$ to 6, and so on. In this way we have set up a one-to-one correspondence between the set of non-negative rationals and the set of counting numbers. By using the method of example 3.27, we could extend this correspondence to include the negative rational numbers as well. Hence we can assert that the set of rational numbers has cardinal number d.

Do all infinite sets have cardinal number d? We have only one set left, the set of real numbers. Surely there are more real than rational numbers. Let's see.

Example 3.29.   Does the set of reals have cardinal number d?

There are two possibilities:
(1) The set of reals has cardinal number d.
(2) The set of reals does not have cardinal number d.

For the time being, let's assume that (1) is true. If (1) is true, we can set up a one-to-one correspondence between the set of reals and the set of counting numbers. We do not know what sort of correspondence we might have, but we assume it can be done. Thus, some decimal (all real numbers can be represented as decimals) corresponds to 1, some decimal corresponds to 2, and so on. As an example, suppose

$$1 \leftrightarrow .68458429006\cdots$$
$$2 \leftrightarrow .13479201038\cdots$$
$$3 \leftrightarrow .37291568341\cdots$$
$$4 \leftrightarrow .985223671611\cdots$$
$$\vdots \qquad \vdots$$

We assume the existence of a one-to-one correspondence between the counting numbers and the reals; hence we are claiming that every decimal is in the list at the right. Let's make a new decimal K as follows. The first decimal in the list above has a 6 as its first digit; let K start off $.4\cdots$ ($4 \neq 6$). Since the second digit of the second decimal in the list is 3, we let $K = .45\cdots$ ($5 \neq 3$). The third digit of the third decimal is 2, and let $K = .457\cdots$ ($7 \neq 2$). The fourth digit of the fourth decimal is 2, and let $K = .4573\cdots$ ($3 \neq 2$). Continue K in this way. Is K in the list which we assumed contains all decimals and hence all real numbers? The first decimal differs from K in at least the first spot, the second differs from K in at least the second spot, and the n-th decimal in the list differs from K in at least the n-th spot. Every number in the list differs from K in at least one spot, so that K cannot be in the list. We can summarize this by saying:

(1) We assume every decimal is in our list.
(2) The decimal K is not in our list.

Since both of these cannot be true, our original assumption has led to a contradiction. By the method of indirect proof, we must accept the only possible alternative to our original assumption: the cardinal number of the set of reals is not equal to d.

The set of counting numbers is a subset of the set of real numbers, thus it would seem reasonable to say the cardinal number of the set of reals, which is commonly denoted by the letter c, is greater than d. Is there a cardinal number between d and c? Cantor himself did not think so, but he was unable to prove his guess. Cantor's *Hypothesis of the Continuum* was long considered one of the major unsolved problems of mathematics—until the early 1960's when the American mathematician Paul J. Cohen showed that the assumption that no such cardinal number exists leads to correct results, and also that if it is assumed such a cardinal number really does exist, correct results will still be obtained.

PROBLEMS

Prove that each of the following sets has cardinal number d.
1. {multiples of 5}.
2. {multiples of 1,000,000,000,000}.
3. {even numbers}.
4. {odd counting numbers}.
5. {odd numbers}.
6. {1000, 1001, 1002, 1003, 1004, . . .}.
7. {negatives of counting numbers}.
8. $\{\frac{1}{2}, \frac{1}{4}, \frac{1}{8}, \frac{1}{16}, \frac{1}{32}, \frac{1}{64}, \ldots\}$.
9. Consider a line segment of length 1 inch. Show that it is possible to set up a one-to-one correspondence between the points of this segment and a line. (Hint: bend the segment.)
10. Refer to figure 3.17. In setting up the one-to-one correspondence, why did we skip numbers such as $\frac{2}{2}$, $\frac{4}{2}$, and so on?

FOR FURTHER READING

Dantzig, Tobais. *Number, The Language of Science.* New York: The Macmillan Company, 1954. Also available in paperback published by Doubleday Anchor.

Gamow, George. *One, Two, Three, Infinity.* New York: Viking Press, 1947. Also available in paperback published by Mentor.

Keedy, Mervin. *Number Systems: A Modern Introduction.* Reading, Massachusetts: Addison-Wesley Publishing Co., Inc., 1965.

Parker, Frances. *The Structure of Number Systems.* Englewood Cliffs, New Jersey: Prentice-Hall, Inc.

Further discussions of many of the ideas of this chapter are presented in the books mentioned above. For additional information on cardinal numbers see the references listed at the end of Chapter 2.

CHAPTER 4

GROUP THEORY

Many ideas of mathematics are considered highly esoteric when first introduced, and yet these same ideas are later found to have valuable practical applications. Thus square roots of negative numbers were considered highly esoteric and abstract when first introduced; these numbers are now used very extensively in the study of electricity. Group theory provides another example. When introduced in the early 1800's, groups were considered a very advanced idea; the ideas and concepts of group theory were understood only by the top mathematicians. Gradually, however, practical applications have been found for group theory: groups are used in the study of crystal structure; groups are used in the study of the configuration of molecules; groups are used in studying the structure of human genes; groups were found necessary by Albert Einstein for his special theory of relativity. In this chapter we shall first discuss the history of group theory, and then consider some examples.

The study of group theory began with the work of Augustin-Louis Cauchy (1789–1857); shortly after Cauchy's first works on groups came new discoveries by Niels Henrik Abel (1802–1829) and Evariste Galois (1811–1832).

Cauchy was born in Paris shortly after the end of the French Revolution. Political turmoil and unrest made life extremely difficult for the Cauchy family. Food was indeed scarce during this period and the malnutrition Cauchy suffered as a child caused him to be sickly all his life. Cauchy's talent in mathematics was encouraged by mathematical friends of the family. He did quite well scholastically at the university, but his personal-social life was apparently miserable. (Cauchy, we are told, was strongly religious and continually tried to convert his fellow students.) By the time he was 27, he was acclaimed as one of the world's great mathematicians; one word from him could make the career of an aspiring young mathematician. Unfortunately for mathematics and for Cauchy's rating in mathematical history, he declined, for one reason or another, to give a word of encouragement to either Abel or Galois.

Niels Henrik Abel was the greatest mathematician Norway ever produced. The mathematicians of Norway, quickly recognizing the genius of Abel, were able to persuade the government to send him on a tour of the leading mathematical centers of Europe. He had a very difficult time working with the leading mathematicians because the merit of his discoveries was not always apparent. To his dismay, he found himself unable to secure a teaching position at any university. He was responsible for maintaining his mother and a number of younger brothers and sisters, and this responsibility, together with overwork on mathematics, led to tuberculosis and death when he was 26. Two days after he died word reached his home that he had been appointed professor at the University of Berlin, one of the major universities of the time.

One of Abel's major discoveries concerns the conditions under which certain equations may be solved. For example, the equation $ax^2 + bx + c = 0$ is called a quadratic and is solved by the quadratic formula:

$$x = \frac{-b \pm \sqrt{b^2 - 4ac}}{2a}.$$

Similar, longer formulas are known for equations containing x^3 or x^4 as the highest power of x. Abel proved, using group theory, that no such formula is possible for an equation containing x^5.

Evariste Galois was born just outside Paris in 1811. Sent off to school at age 12, he soon developed a strong dislike for the institution and its methods. The educated people of the time felt that a study of the classics was the key to a good education. Therefore, the young Galois spent many hours on Greek and Latin and won several academic prizes for his proficiency. Mathematics as taught in the school consisted of a little algebra and a little geometry introduced into the curriculum whenever time could be found. Galois was intrigued by geometry and quickly mastered a book which took most students two years. His growing awareness of his mathematical powers made him contemptuous of his pedantic instructors, and they in turn began to dislike him and his attitude. Galois wanted greatly to be admitted to the Polytechnique, the leading French university for mathematics, but he did not pass the entrance examination. When he realized his failure, he threw a blackboard eraser into the face of one of his examiners. He felt, perhaps with justification, that his mathematical attainments were so great that his examiners were not competent to judge him. Galois submitted several scientific papers in competitions, but they always seemed to be mislaid, or not understood, or returned for more work. He became increasingly disillusioned with the scientific community and gradually gave vent to his frustrations by becoming a political radical against the monarchy. He was imprisoned for his political activities, and as soon as he was released, his political enemies tricked him into a duel. He sat up the night before the duel and wrote out his masterpiece, a work using group theory to give conditions under which algebraic equations may be solved. He was killed in the duel at age 21 and buried in a common, unmarked grave. The totality of his collected works fill a book of only 60 pages.

Had the leading mathematicians of the time been more receptive to the work of these young mathematicians, perhaps they might have enjoyed a longer and more productive life. The debate on this question continues. With this discussion in mind, we now ask the question, *"What is a group?"* To begin to answer this question, we are going to construct an example of a group.

SECTION 1. TRIANGLE SYMMETRIES

Cut an equilateral triangle out of a piece of light cardboard; make the triangle about three inches on a side. Label the triangle as shown in figure 4.1. Make sure 1′ is behind 1, 2′ is behind 2, and 3′ is behind 3. We will study certain *symmetries* of this triangle, that is, the results that are obtained when the triangle is moved according to certain rules that will be established.

Front   Back

Figure 4.1

Hold the triangle with the front facing you and the 1 on top; this is the *basic position.* Rotate the triangle clockwise 120° so that the 1 moves into the position formerly held by the 2, and the 3 ends up on top. We use the letter A to denote this rotation of the triangle. See figure 4.2. The letter A indicates a clockwise rotation of 120° from the previous position.

Basic Position: Apply A: Result:

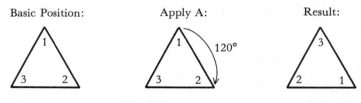

Figure 4.2

Example 4.1.   Assume the triangle is in the position shown in figure 4.3. Apply rotation A to the triangle.

We apply a clockwise rotation of 120°, which moves 3′ into the position occupied by 2′. The result is shown in figure 4.4.

Figure 4.3   Figure 4.4

The second rotation, or symmetry, denoted by B, is a clockwise rotation through 240°, as shown in figure 4.5.

Basic Position: Apply B: Result:

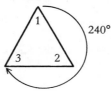

240°

Figure 4.5

Example 4.2. Apply rotation B to the triangle of figure 4.6.

A clockwise rotation of 240° places the triangle in the position shown in figure 4.7.

Figure 4.6   Figure 4.7

To perform the third rotation, called C, flip the triangle about an imaginary vertical line drawn through the top of the triangle, as shown in figure 4.8.

Basic Position: Flip about a   Result:
                        vertical line:

Figure 4.8

Example 4.3. Apply C to the triangle of figure 4.9 (see p. 104).

Imagine a vertical line drawn through the top of the triangle, and flip the triangle about that line (figure 4.10) (see p. 104).

Figure 4.9

Figure 4.10

Now imagine a line drawn from the lower left corner of the triangle to the middle of the opposite side; a flip about this line is denoted by D. To apply D to the triangle, place one hand at the lower left corner and the other hand at the middle of the opposite side. Then flip the triangle so that the back side comes to face you.

Basic Position: Imagine the diagonal   Result:
                     line, and flip about
                     that line:

Figure 4.11

Example 4.4.   Apply symmetry D to the triangle of figure 4.12:

Imagine a diagonal line drawn from the lower left corner to the middle of the opposite side, and flip the triangle about that line. The result is shown in Figure 4.13.

Figure 4.12

Figure 4.13

The letter E represents a flip of the triangle about an imaginary line drawn from the lower right corner to the midpoint of the opposite side, as shown in figure 4.14.

Basic Position: Flip about a line   Result:
                     drawn from lower right
                     to the middle of the
                     opposite side:

Figure 4.14

Lastly we define F: F means to leave the triangle alone. We will see that F is the identity element for the system we are constructing from these triangle symmetries.

The chart of figure 4.15 is a summary of the symmetries we have defined.

LETTER	DESCRIPTION	RESULT*
A	Rotation through 120°	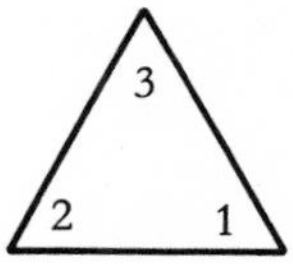
B	Rotation through 240°	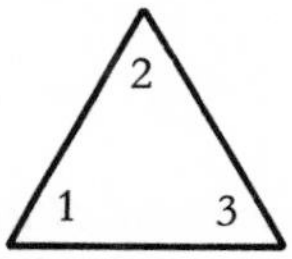
C	Flip about a vertical line	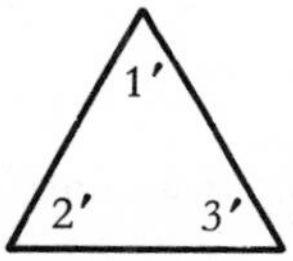
D	Flip about a line drawn from lower left to the middle of the opposite side	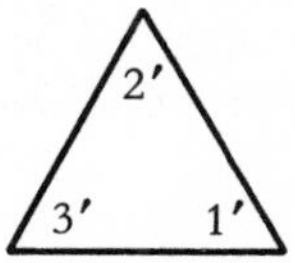
E	Flip about a line drawn from lower right to the middle of the opposite side	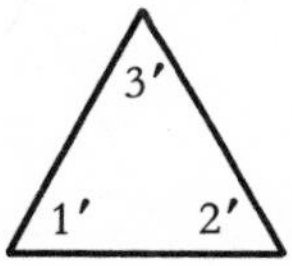
F	Leave the triangle alone	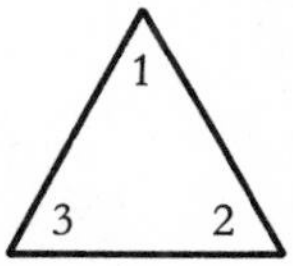

*When applied to the basic position

Figure 4.15

We now have half of a mathematical system: a set of elements, $\{A, B, C, D, E, F\}$. We must define an operation that combines two of these triangle symmetries to obtain a third. Let us agree that AC means the following: begin with the triangle in basic position, apply A, then apply C to the result (figure 4.16) (see p. 106).

Basic position:

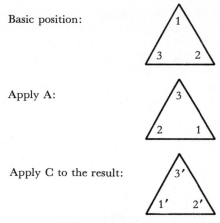

Apply A:

Apply C to the result:

Figure 4.16

The sequence of A followed by C gives the same result as applying only E to the triangle in basic position; hence:

$$AC = E.$$

Example 4.5. Evaluate BE.

Using the definition given above, we begin with the triangle in the basic position and apply B to it, figure 4.17. We then apply E to the result, figure 4.18. Since C alone would have given the same result, we say

$$BE = C.$$

Figure 4.17

Figure 4.18

PROBLEMS

Consider the triangle of figure 4.19. For each question below, rotate and flip the triangle according to the instructions presented. The result will place the triangle in one of the positions of figure 4.15; write the letter of that position.

Figure 4.19

1. Apply A.
2. Apply B.
3. Apply C.
7. Apply A, and then apply B to the result.
8. Apply C, and then D.
9. Do E twice.
10. Apply D and then C.
11. Apply C twice.
12. Complete this chart:

4. Apply D.
5. Apply E.
6. Apply F.

	A	B	C	D	E	F
A	B	F	E	C	D	A
B	F	A				
C				A	B	C
D		C				
E			A			
F	A				E	

13. Does this system, composed of {A, B, C, D, E, F} and the operation defined above, have the commutative property?
14. Does the system have the associative property?
15. Does the system have an inverse for A? for C? If so, what are they?

SECTION 2. THE DEFINITION OF A GROUP

Consider now a mathematical system consisting of a set S and an operation $\circ$ defined on S. This system is a *group* (S is a group under $\circ$) in case:
(1) The system is closed.
(2) The system has the associative property.
(3) The system has an identity element.
(4) Every element in the system has an inverse in the system.

It does not matter what other properties are satisfied by the system; a group requires only those four properties mentioned above. Now let's check to see if the system of symmetries of a triangle forms a group. Check each requirement:

(1) Closure. Any two symmetries may be combined to yield a third symmetry and so the system is closed.

(2) Associative property. To see if the system has the associative property we try some examples. First notice:

$$D(BE) = DC = B,$$
while
$$(DB)E = CE = B,$$
so that
$$D(BE) = (DB)E.$$
Also,
$$(AC)D = ED = B,$$
and
$$A(CD) = AA = B,$$
which means $A(CD) = (AC)D.$

Other examples should also work; this system has the associative property.

(3) Identity element. As mentioned earlier, F is the identity element for the system. That is, if x represents any of the six symmetries in the set, $\{A, B, C, D, E, F\}$, then $xF = Fx = x$.

(4) Inverse elements. Suppose A is applied to the triangle in basic position. Symmetry B, applied to the result, will return the triangle to basic position. Hence AB = F. Similarly, BA = F, which means A and B are the inverses of each other. If C is applied to the triangle in basic position, another application of C will return the triangle to basic position. Therefore CC = F and C is its own inverse. In the same way, D, E, and F are each their own inverses. Every element in the system has an inverse in the system.

Our system of six symmetries together with the operation of combination defined on them satisfies the four requirements and hence is a group.

The next two examples illustrate some groups that are perhaps more familiar.

Example 4.6.   Is the set of integers a group under addition?

We check each of the four requirements:
(1) Closure. The sum of any two integers is an integer.
(2) Associative property. The addition of integers, as mentioned in the last chapter, is associative.
(3) Identity element. The number 0 is the identity for this system.
(4) Inverse elements. Every integer has an integer inverse under addition; 6 and −6 are inverses of each other, −10 and 10, and so on.
Hence the set of integers forms a group under addition.

Example 4.7.   Does $\{1, -1\}$ form a group under multiplication?

Again we check the four requirements:
(1) Closure. Note $(-1)(-1) = 1$, $(-1)(1) = -1$, and $(1)(1) = 1$. The system is closed.
(2) Associative property. Multiplication of integers is associative.
(3) Identity element. The identity element for multiplication is 1, which is in the set.
(4) Inverse elements. The number 1 is its own inverse under multiplication, as is −1.

PROBLEMS

This problem set presents an opportunity to develop another group similar to that of triangle symmetries. Cut out a small square and label it as in figure 4.20. Be sure that 1 is in front of 1′, 2 is in front of 2′, 3 is in front of 3′, and 4 is in front of 4′. Figure 4.21 lists the symmetries of a square.

Front   Back

Figure 4.20

LETTER	DESCRIPTION	RESULT*
M	Rotation through 90°	3 4 / 2 1
N	Rotation through 180°	2 3 / 1 4
P	Rotation through 270°	1 2 / 4 3
Q	Leave the square alone	4 1 / 3 2
R	Flip about a horizontal line through the middle of the square	3′ 2′ / 4′ 1′
S	Flip about a vertical line through the middle of the square	1′ 4′ / 2′ 3′
T	Flip along a line drawn from upper left to lower right	4′ 3′ / 1′ 2′
V	Flip along a line drawn from lower left to upper right	2′ 1′ / 3′ 4′

*When applied to the basic position, Q.

Figure 4.21

The first eight problems refer to these symmetries.
1. Complete a chart of combinations of symmetries.
2. Does the system have the closure property?
3. (a) Does (MR)S = M(RS)?
   (b) Does (TS)T = T(ST)?
   (c) Does (QN)R = Q(NR)?
   (d) Do you think the system has the associative property?
4. Does the system have an identity element?
5. Find the inverse of each element, if possible.
6. Is this system a group?
7. Is {M, N, P, Q} a group under the operation of combination?
8. Is {R, S, T, V} a group under the operation of combination?

Are the following systems groups?
9. The odd counting numbers under addition.
10. The counting numbers under addition.
11. The integers under multiplication.
12. The integers under subtraction.
13. The rationals under addition.
14. The rationals under multiplication.
15. The rationals under division.
16. The prime numbers under addition.
17. {0, 1} under addition.
18. {0, 1} under multiplication.
19. {1, −1} under addition.
20. {1, −1} under division.

SECTION 3. A GROUP OF REARRANGEMENTS

In this section we investigate another example of a group. Consider the symbols 1-2-3 in that order. There are several ways in which the order could be changed, for example, 2-3-1. This rearrangement is written:

$$1\text{-}2\text{-}3$$
$$2\text{-}3\text{-}1$$

Replace 1 with 2, replace 2 with 3, and 3 with 1. In the same way,

$$1\text{-}2\text{-}3$$
$$3\text{-}1\text{-}2$$

means replace 1 with 3, 2 with 1, and 3 with 2, while

$$1\text{-}2\text{-}3$$
$$3\text{-}2\text{-}1$$

tells us to replace 1 with 3, leave the 2 unchanged, and replace 3 with 1. All possible rearrangements of the symbols 1-2-3 are listed in figure 4.22 where, for convenience, a name has been given to each rearrangement.

We can combine two rearrangements as with the triangle symmetries: thus, by B*F* we mean first apply B* to 1-2-3 and then apply F* to the

A*: 1-2-3   B*: 1-2-3   C*: 1-2-3   D*: 1-2-3
    2-3-1   2-1-3   1-2-3   1-3-2

          E*: 1-2-3   F*: 1-2-3
              3-1-2   3-2-1

Figure 4.22

result. Rearrangement B* changes 1-2-3 into 2-1-3. Then apply F* to this result, 1 becomes 3, 2 is unchanged, and 3 becomes 1. In summary:

> 1-2-3
> 2-1-3   Rearrange according to B*.
>   3   By F*, 1 is replaced by 3.
> 2-3   Next, 2 remains unchanged.
> 2-3-1   As a last step, 3 changes into 1.

The net result of B*F* is to change 1-2-3 into 2-3-1, which is exactly what A* does to 1-2-3. Hence

$$B*F* = A*.$$

Example 4.8.   Find D*E*.

We use the procedure described above.

> 1-2-3
> 1-3-2
> 3
> 3   1
> 3-2-1

Apply D*. To apply E*, first replace 1 with 3. Next, replace 2 with 1. The last step is to replace 3 with 2. The result: D*E* converts 1-2-3 into 3-2-1, as does F*. Hence

$$D*E* = F*.$$

As further examples note A*B* = D* and F*E* = B*.

Again we have a mathematical system: the set $\{A*, B*, C*, D*, E*, F*\}$ and the operation of combination of two rearrangements. Is this system a group? We check the requirements.

(1) Closure. Combine any two rearrangements and the result is another rearrangement. Hence the system is closed.

(2) Associative property. Try an example:

First,   (B*D*)A* = E*A* = C*,
while   B*(D*A*) = B*B* = C*,
so that   (B*D*)A* = B*(D*A*).

Since other examples will work out similarly, the system is associative.

(3) Identity element. The identity element is C*. If *x* is any rearrangement, then *x*C* = C*x = *x*.

(4) Inverses. Does each rearrangement have an inverse rearrangement? Begin with the basic order 1-2-3 and then apply, say B*, resulting in 2-1-3. The inverse of B* must convert this 2-1-3 back into 1-2-3, by changing 2 into 1 and 1 into 2. But note B* itself will do this. Hence B*B* = C* and B* is its own inverse. By the same process, E* and A* are inverses of each other. Also, each of C*, D*, and F* is its own inverse.

Since all four requirements are satisfied, the system is a group. Rearrangements are also referred to as *permutations,* and this group is sometimes called the *permutation group on three symbols.*

PROBLEMS

1. Make a chart of combinations for the group of rearrangements of three symbols.
2. Is {A*, B*, C*} a group under the operation of combination?
3. Is {C*, D*} a group under the operation of combination?
4. Is {C*} a group under the operation of combination?

There are 24 different rearrangements of four symbols, as shown in figure 4.23. Form the mathematical system consisting of these 24 rearrangements together with the operation of combination.

A	1-2-3-4 1-2-3-4	G	1-2-3-4 2-1-3-4	N	1-2-3-4 3-2-1-4	U	1-2-3-4 4-1-2-3
B	1-2-3-4 1-2-4-3	H	1-2-3-4 2-1-4-3	P	1-2-3-4 3-2-4-1	V	1-2-3-4 4-1-3-2
C	1-2-3-4 1-3-2-4	J	1-2-3-4 2-3-4-1	Q	1-2-3-4 3-1-4-2	W	1-2-3-4 4-2-1-3
D	1-2-3-4 1-3-4-2	K	1-2-3-4 2-3-1-4	R	1-2-3-4 3-1-2-4	X	1-2-3-4 4-2-3-1
E	1-2-3-4 1-4-2-3	L	1-2-3-4 2-4-3-1	S	1-2-3-4 3-4-2-1	Y	1-2-3-4 4-3-1-2
F	1-2-3-4 1-4-3-2	M	1-2-3-4 2-4-1-3	T	1-2-3-4 3-4-1-2	Z	1-2-3-4 4-3-2-1

Figure 4.23

5. Do you think the system is closed?
6. Is the system associative?
7. Does the system have an identity element? If so, what is it?
8. Does every element in the system have an inverse in the system? If so, what is it?
9. Is the system a group?
10. Is {A, G} a group under the operation of combination?
11. Is {A, B, G, H} a group under the operation of combination?

12. Is {*A, Z*} a group under the operation of the system?
13. Is {*A, B, C,* · · · , *M* } a group under the operation of combination?

SECTION 4. REMAINDER ARITHMETIC

Let's construct another mathematical system which forms a group. We say

$$a = b(\text{mod } m),$$

in case both *a* and *b* leave the same remainder when divided by *m*; *a* and *b* are integers, and *m* is a counting number greater than 1.

Example 4.9.   Which of the following statements are true?
(a) 6 = 11(mod 5).
(b) 92 = 47(mod 8).
(c) 63 = 27(mod 9).
(d) 2 = 52(mod 5).

We use the definition of *a* = *b*(mod *m*) in order to answer the question.
(a) Divide 5 into 6 and the remainder is 1. Divide 5 into 11 and the remainder is 1. The remainders are the same; the statement is true.
(b) Eight into 92 leaves a remainder of 4, while 8 into 47 leaves a remainder of 7. The remainders are not the same; the statement is false.
(c) Nine goes into 63 with remainder 0, and 9 goes into 27 with remainder 0. The statement is true.
(d) Divide 5 into 2, and the quotient is 0 with remainder 2, which is the same remainder obtained when dividing 5 into 52. The statement is true.

Example 4.10.   Evaluate:
(a) (4 + 3)(mod 5).
(b) (2 + 3)(mod 5).

Again we use the definition.
(a) Note 4 + 3 = 7 = 2(mod 5). Hence 4 + 3 = 2(mod 5).
(b) Since 2 + 3 = 5 = 0(mod 5), we have 2 + 3 = 0(mod 5).
Using the methods of example 4.10 we can write a mod 5 addition table.

+	0	1	2	3	4
0	0	1	2	3	4
1	1	2	3	4	0
2	2	3	4	0	1
3	3	4	0	1	2
4	4	0	1	2	3

Addition mod 5

Figure 4.24

Example 4.11. Construct a mod 5 multiplication table.

As a sample, note that $(3 \times 4)(\mathrm{mod}\ 5)$ may be evaluated as follows: $3 \times 4 = 12 = 2(\mathrm{mod}\ 5)$. Using this process we may write the table.

×	1	2	3	4
1	1	2	3	4
2	2	4	1	3
3	3	1	4	2
4	4	3	2	1

Multiplication mod 5

Figure 4.25

Do not confuse a mod 5 system with base 5 representation of numbers. Mod 5 is involved with remainders only; it is not possible to count in mod 5. The number 2 represents the number of x's here: *xx*, while the number 7 represents the number of x's here: *xxxxxxx*. However, $7 = 2(\mathrm{mod}\ 5)$ so that the same number of x's appear each time. Hence we state that it is not possible to count in a mod 5 system. On the other hand, base 5 is a very good way to count. There are 2_5 x's here: *xx*, and 12_5 x's here: *xxxxxxx*.

Let us consider the system consisting of the set $\{0, 1, 2, 3, 4\}$ and the operation of addition mod 5. Does this system form a group? We check each of the four group requirements.

(1) Closure. The table of figure 4.24 shows that the system is closed.

(2) Associative property. Try an example.

$$2 + (4 + 3) = 2 + 2 = 4,$$
while
$$(2 + 4) + 3 = 1 + 3 = 4,$$
and
$$2 + (4 + 3) = (2 + 4) + 3.$$

Any other examples you try will also work.

(3) Identity element. The identity element for addition mod 5 is 0. Check that $x + 0 = 0 + x = x$ for all numbers x of the system.

(4) Inverse elements. Can we find an inverse for 2 in this system? We must find a number y such that $2 + y = y + 2 = 0$. By inspection of figure 4.24, we find $y = 3$ since $2 + 3 = 3 + 2 = 0$. Hence 2 and 3 are the inverses of each other in this system. Every element of the system has an inverse in the system:

$$0 + 0 = 0,$$
$$1 + 4 = 4 + 1 = 0,$$
$$2 + 3 = 3 + 2 = 0.$$

We conclude that the set $\{0, 1, 2, 3, 4\}$ is a group under the operation of addition modulo 5. It can also be shown that the set $\{1, 2, 3, 4\}$ is a group under the operation of multiplication modulo 5 (why is zero omitted?).

Example 4.12.   Does the set $\{1, 2, 3, 4, 5\}$ form a group under the operation of multiplication mod 6?

First, we should construct a multiplication table for mod 6, as has been done in figure 4.26. To determine if this is a group, begin by checking the requirements.

×	1	2	3	4	5
1	1	2	3	4	5
2	2	4	0	2	4
3	3	0	3	0	3
4	4	2	0	4	2
5	5	4	3	2	1

Multiplication mod 6

Figure 4.26

(1) Closure. The body of the table contains a 0, but 0 is not an element of the given set. Therefore, the system is not closed. Note, for example, that $2 \times 3 = 0$, and $3 \times 4 = 0$.

If we were to continue checking the requirements, we would find that the system is associative, that it has an identity element, and that there are no inverses for 2, 3, or 4. Since not all of the requirements are satisfied, the system is not a group.

We have found that the mod 6 system is not a group under multiplication, while the mod 5 system is. We might then ask the question: when is the set $\{1, 2, 3, \cdots, n - 1\}$ a group under the operation of multiplication mod n? Perhaps the system is a group only if n is odd and never if n is even. But this guess might be a little too hasty. Let's consider another example.

Example 4.13.   Does the set $\{1, 2, 3, 4, 5, 6, 7, 8\}$ form a group under the operation of multiplication mod 9?

First, the requirements:
(1) Closure. Note $3 \times 3 = 9 = 0 \pmod 9$, which means the system is not closed and thus is not a group.

Clearly, our odd or even guess is wrong. Let's see what else might work. Note that neither mod 6 nor mod 9 under the operation of multiplication formed groups; also note that both 6 and 9 are divisible by numbers other than themselves and 1. Perhaps this is the key. Mod 21 could not form a group for example, since $3 \times 7 = 21 = 0 \pmod{21}$. The following result seems correct: the set of numbers $\{1, 2, 3, 4, \cdots, n - 1\}$ is a group under the operation of multiplication mod n, if n is a *prime* (a number divisible only by itself and 1).

PROBLEMS

1. Which of these are true:
   (a) $6 = 7(\text{mod } 2)$
   (b) $48 = 1{,}345{,}673{,}421(\text{mod } 2)$
   (c) $132 = 13(\text{mod } 7)$
   (d) $46 = 11(\text{mod } 5)$
   (e) $3 = 9(\text{mod } 3)$
   (f) $0 = 1551(\text{mod } 3)$
   (g) $234 = 102(\text{mod } 6)$
   (h) $99 = 132(\text{mod } 11)$

2. Make an addition table for mod 7.

3. Make a multiplication table for mod 7.

4. Verify that the set $\{1, 2, 3, 4\}$ is a group under the operation of multiplication mod 5.

5. The odometer (dial that records total distance traveled by the car) in an ordinary car can be considered an example of a mod system. Mileage totals are recorded mod what number?

Are the following systems groups?

6. $\{0, 1, 2, 3, 4, 5, 6\}$ under addition mod 7.

7. $\{1, 2, 3, 4, 5, 6\}$ under multiplication mod 7.

8. $\{1\}$ under multiplication mod 2.

9. $\{2, 4, 6, 8, 10, 12, 14\}$ under multiplication mod 8. (Hint: note that $8 = 0(\text{mod } 8)$ and hence any 0 may be replaced with an 8.)

10. $\{2, 4, 6, 8, 10, 12\}$ under multiplication mod 7. (Hint: note that $12 = 5(\text{mod } 7)$ so that 5 can be replaced with 12.)

11. $\{0, 1\}$ under addition mod 2.

12. $\{28, 131\}$ under addition mod 2. (Hint: see the hint for problem 10.)

13. Try enough examples to decide upon the truth or falsity of the following statement: if n is any counting number greater than 1, then $\{0, 1, 2, \cdots, n - 1\}$ is a group under the operation of addition mod n.

SECTION 5.   EQUATIONS IN MOD SYSTEMS

Now let us investigate some equations that involve mod systems. For example, let us find all whole number solutions to the equation: $x = 5(\text{mod } 8)$.

We want to find the set of all whole numbers which, when divided by 8, leave a remainder of 5. The first such number is 5 since $5 = 5(\text{mod } 8)$; the next is 13 since $13 = 5(\text{mod } 8)$, and so on. That is, if $x \in \{5, 13, 21, 29, 37, \ldots\}$, then $x = 5(\text{mod } 8)$. The solution set can also be written this way:

$$\{5, 5 + 8, 5 + 8 + 8, 5 + 8 + 8 + 8, \ldots\}.$$

The latter method of writing the solution set illustrates the pattern that can be used to obtain solutions of equations such as these.

Example 4.14.   Find the set of all whole number solutions of the equation: $x = 7(\text{mod } 11)$.

Using the previous example as a model, we write the solution set:

$$\{7, 7 + 11, 7 + 11 + 11, 7 + 11 + 11 + 11, \therefore .\},$$

or

$$\{7, 18, 29, 40, \ldots\}.$$

Example 4.15.   Find all whole number solutions of the equation: $3x = 2(\text{mod } 5)$.

Begin by trying various whole numbers:

$$
\begin{aligned}
0: \quad & 3 \times 0 \neq 2(\text{mod } 5), \\
1: \quad & 3 \times 1 \neq 2(\text{mod } 5), \\
2: \quad & 3 \times 2 \neq 2(\text{mod } 5), \\
3: \quad & 3 \times 3 \neq 2(\text{mod } 5), \\
4: \quad & 3 \times 4 = 2(\text{mod } 5).
\end{aligned}
$$

There is no reason to try larger numbers since any larger number will equal, in our mod 5 system, one of the numbers 0, 1, 2, 3, or 4. Hence $x = 4$ is the smallest solution, which means either:

$$\{4, 4 + 5, 4 + 5 + 5, \ldots\},$$

or

$$\{4, 9, 14, 19, \ldots\}$$

is the solution set of the equation. As an example, let's verify that 19 is a solution: $3 \times 19 = 57 = 2(\text{mod } 5)$.

Example 4.16.   Find all whole number solutions to the equation: $6x = 3(\text{mod } 8)$.

Begin by trying various whole numbers:

$$
\begin{aligned}
0: \quad & 6 \times 0 \neq 3(\text{mod } 8), \\
1: \quad & 6 \times 1 \neq 3(\text{mod } 8).
\end{aligned}
$$

By the same process, it will be found that the numbers 2, 3, 4, 5, 6, and 7 are not solutions either. As before, there is no need to try larger numbers. Hence we must say that this equation has no solutions. This result is plausible since $6x$ must always be an even number no matter what whole number is used for x, and hence cannot leave a remainder of 3 when divided by 8.

Example 4.17.   Find all whole number solutions for the equation: $48x = 8(\text{mod } 8)$.

By trying various whole numbers we see that all whole numbers are solutions for the equation; such an equation is called an *identity*. More common identities include $x + x = 2x$ and $x^3 \cdot x^5 = x^8$.

Example 4.18. Solve the equation: $48x = 8(\mathrm{mod}\ 8)$.

To simplify the work, let's divide both sides of the equation by 8, obtaining $6x = 1(\mathrm{mod}\ 8)$. The second equation has no solutions since $6x$ is even and cannot have a remainder of 1 when divided by 8.

Something is wrong somewhere. In example 4.17 the equation had all whole numbers as solution set, while in example 4.18 the same equation has no solutions. We went wrong when we divided both sides of the equation by 8; some of the common rules of algebra are not valid in mod systems.

Example 4.19. George is a clerk in a shoe store. Lady 1 comes in and looks at all the shoes George has in stock. As he shows her the shoes, he stacks the boxes in stacks of 7 boxes each, with 2 boxes left over. After George returns all the boxes to the shelf, Lady 2 enters to look at all his shoes. This time he puts the boxes in stacks of 5 each, with 4 boxes left over. The last customer, Lady 3, looks at the shoes while George places them in stacks of 3 each, with 2 left over. George knows there are less than 200 boxes of shoes, and none of the ladies bought any. How many boxes of shoes does he have?

We are told nothing about the number of stacks at each showing of the shoes, but we do have some information on the number of boxes in each stack, and the number left over each time. Let s stand for the number of boxes of shoes. If the boxes are stacked 7 high there are 2 left over; that is, if 7 is divided into s a remainder of 2 is obtained. Hence

$$s = 2(\mathrm{mod}\ 7).$$

In the same way

$$s = 4(\mathrm{mod}\ 5),$$

and

$$s = 2(\mathrm{mod}\ 3).$$

We must find a value for s that satisfies all three equations.

Consider the first equation. If we solve it by the methods used above we find the solution set to be:

$$\{2, 9, 16, 23, 30, 37, 44, 51, 58, 65, 72,$$
$$79, 86, 93, 100, 107, 114, 121, 128, 135, 142,$$
$$149, 156, 163, 170, 177, 184, 191, 198\}.$$

(We stop at 198 since the answer is less than 200.) The answer must also satisfy the second equation, $s = 4(\mathrm{mod}\ 5)$. Hence in the set above, we find all the numbers that leave a remainder of 4 when divided by 5:

$$\{9, 44, 79, 114, 149, 184\}.$$

The answer must also satisfy the last equation, $s = 2(\mathrm{mod}\ 3)$. The numbers 44 and 149 are the only elements of this last set that leave a remainder of 2 when divided by 3. Hence

$$\{44, 149\}$$

is the solution set for this problem. Either one of these two numbers satisfies the conditions for s, and without futher information we can only say that George has either 44 or 149 boxes of shoes. However, even George should be able to distinguish between the two answers just by looking at his stack of boxes.

PROBLEMS

Find all whole number solutions for the equations below.
1. $4x = 2 \pmod 6$.
2. $4x = 2 \pmod 8$.
3. $2x = 6 \pmod 9$.
4. $6x = 6 \pmod{12}$.
5. $5x = 1 \pmod 5$.
6. $11x = 5 \pmod{12}$.

7. Find all whole numbers x which satisfy:

$$x = 1 \pmod{10}.$$
$$x = 2 \pmod 3.$$
$$x = 0 \pmod 7.$$
$$100 \leq x \leq 200.$$

8. Find all whole numbers x which satisfy:

$$x = 1 \pmod 2.$$
$$x = 2 \pmod 3.$$
$$x = 4 \pmod 5.$$
$$x \leq 100.$$

9. Fritz runs a sightseeing bus in Haight-Ashbury. On a recent trip he noticed that his tourists lined up 7 deep at a stall selling flowers, with 1 tourist left over. When listening to a lecture on the effects of work on the psyche, the visitors filled rows of 5 seats each, with 3 taking pictures in the back and not sitting. On the bus, the tourists sat 4 abreast, with 3 left over. Fritz knows his bus holds only 50 people. How many were on the tour?

10. Ronald is a miser who counts his \$100 bills every night before putting them back in his mattress. He can put them in stacks of 7, 5, or 2 with none left over. If he has between 100 and 200 bills, how much wealth does he sleep on?

11. Charles shows his superb color slides upon request (and even sometimes when not requested). At the March meeting of the Woman's Club, the seating was arranged so that the ladies saw his marvelous slides of Death Valley while sitting in rows of 4, with 2 left over. The April meeting had the same number of women for his excellent Yosemite slides, this time in rows of 5, with 1 member standing. In May the ladies were privileged to view the outstanding slides of Lassen National Park. This time the seating was arranged in rows of 11 with 9 in the last row. If fewer than 100 ladies could see the slides, how many were there?

SECTION 6. CYCLIC GROUPS

Consider the set $\{1, 2, 3, 4\}$ and the operation of multiplication mod 5. We have found that this system forms a group. Now notice that we can write:

$$2^1 = 2(\text{mod } 5).$$
$$2^2 = 4(\text{mod } 5).$$
$$2^3 = 8 = 3(\text{mod } 5).$$
$$2^4 = 16 = 1(\text{mod } 5).$$
$$2^5 = 32 = 2(\text{mod } 5).$$

In summary: $2^1 = 2$, $2^2 = 4$, $2^3 = 3$, and $2^4 = 1$.

Since all the elements of the group can be expressed as powers of 2, we say that 2 *generates* the elements of the group, or that 2 is a *generator* of the group. Notice also that:

$$3^1 = 3(\text{mod } 5).$$
$$3^2 = 9 = 4(\text{mod } 5).$$
$$3^3 = 27 = 2(\text{mod } 5).$$
$$3^4 = 81 = 1(\text{mod } 5).$$

Hence 3 is also a generator of the group. On the other hand,

$$4^1 = 4(\text{mod } 5).$$
$$4^2 = 16 = 1(\text{mod } 5).$$
$$4^3 = 64 = 4(\text{mod } 5).$$
$$4^4 = 256 = 1(\text{mod } 5).$$

Therefore, 4 is not a generator of the group. A group which contains at least one generator is called a *cyclic group*. Note that the identity element cannot be a generator of any group containing a minimum of two elements (why?).

Example 4.20. Consider the group consisting of the set $\{A, J, T, U\}$ of the rearrangements on four symbols and the operation of combination. Is this group cyclic? If it is, find all the possible generators.

Since the identity element A cannot be a generator, we might try J:

$$J^1 = J.$$
$$J^2 = JJ = T.$$
$$J^3 = JJJ = U.$$
$$J^4 = JJJJ = A.$$

Since J is a generator of the group, the group is cyclic. Is T a generator?

$$T^1 = T.$$
$$T^2 = TT = A.$$
$$T^3 = TTT = T.$$
$$T^4 = TTTT = A.$$

Rearrangement T is not a generator. In the problem set at the end of the section, you have the opportunity to show that U is a generator.

Example 4.21.   Is the group of symmetries of the equilateral triangle a cyclic group?

Look for a generator:

$A^1 = A$	$B^1 = B$	$C^1 = C$	$D^1 = D$	$E^1 = E$
$A^2 = B$	$B^2 = A$	$C^2 = F$	$D^2 = F$	$E^2 = F$
$A^3 = F$	$B^3 = F$			

There are no generators; the group is not cyclic.

PROBLEMS

1. In example 4.20, verify that U is a generator.
2. Is the set of integers a cyclic group under the operation of multiplication?
3. Is the set $\{1, -1\}$ a cyclic group under the operation of multiplication?
4. Is the set $\{1, 2, 3, 4, 5, 6\}$ a cyclic group under the operation of multiplication mod 7?
5. Is the set $\{A, G, H, B\}$ of rearrangements on four symbols a group under the operation of combination? Is it a cyclic group?

SECTION 7. SUBGROUPS AND ISOMORPHISMS

At this time, recall the set $\{A, B, F\}$ of symmetries of an equilateral triangle, defined in figure 4.15. Is this set a group under the operation of combination? We must check the four requirements necessary for a group.

(1) Closure. Figure 4.27 is a table showing the combinations of the elements of the system. Note that the system is closed.

	A	B	F
A	B	F	A
B	F	A	B
F	A	B	F

Figure 4.27

(2) Associative property. We know from section 2 that the entire system of triangle symmetries has the associative property; hence this smaller system must also have the associative property.

(3) Identity element. The identity for the set of symmetries is F.

(4) Inverse elements. The chart (figure 4.27) shows that

$$AB = BA = F$$
$$FF = F.$$

The system is a group; it is a subgroup of the group of symmetries of the triangle. That is, if we consider two groups:

(a) a group composed of set S and operation ∘
(b) a group composed of set T and the same operation ∘,

then we say group (b) is a *subgroup* of group (a) in case $T \subset S$.

Example 4.22.   Consider the system formed by the set $\{C, F\}$ of symmetries of the triangle, together with the operation of combination. Is this system a subgroup of the group of symmetries?

First, we make a chart of combinations, as in figure 4.28. From the chart, we see that the system is closed; we also see that C and F are their

	C	F
C	F	C
F	C	F

Figure 4.28

own inverses. The identity element F is in the system. (Is it necessary to check the associative property?) The system, therefore, is a subgroup of the group of triangle symmetries.

We have now studied many mathematical systems which are groups. These systems have been quite varied: triangle and square symmetries, symbol rearrangements, mod systems, and number systems. Yet a close examination of these systems indicates they have at least four things in common: (1) they are closed, (2) they have the associative property, (3) they have an identity element, and (4) every element in the system has an inverse in the system. Let us now discuss some groups which have more in common than just these four properties.

First look at the group consisting of the set $\{0, 1, 2, 3\}$ and the operation of addition mod 4, and the subgroup $\{A, J, T, U\}$ of the group of rearrangements on four symbols. Figure 4.29 shows the tables of combination

	0	1	2	3
0	0	1	2	3
1	1	2	3	0
2	2	3	0	1
3	3	0	1	2

	A	J	T	U
A	A	J	T	U
J	J	T	U	A
T	T	U	A	J
U	U	A	J	T

Figure 4.29

for these two groups. We can establish the following 1-to-1 correspondence between the elements of these groups:

$$0 \leftrightarrow A$$
$$1 \leftrightarrow J$$
$$2 \leftrightarrow T$$
$$3 \leftrightarrow U.$$

Note that $J \leftrightarrow 1$, $T \leftrightarrow 2$, and $JT = U$ while $1 + 2 = 3$; also $U \leftrightarrow 3$. Try another example:

$$2 + 3 = 1$$
$$\updownarrow \quad \updownarrow \quad \updownarrow$$
$$T \quad U = J.$$

And another example:

$$3 + 1 = 0$$
$$\updownarrow \quad \updownarrow \quad \updownarrow$$
$$U \quad J = A.$$

In each case the answers match under the 1-to-1 correspondence specified above. In fact, a close examination of figure 4.29 shows that the entire charts correspond. This means the rule of correspondence has a special property: when two elements from one set are chosen, and the corresponding two elements are selected from the other set, the answer obtained for the first two corresponds to the answer obtained for the second two. A correspondence of this type is called an *isomorphism*, which, translated from the Greek roots, means *same structure*. If it is possible to set up an isomorphism between two groups, the groups are said to be *isomorphic*. Isomorphic groups are essentially identical; the basic structures are the same, with the only differences being in the names of the elements.

Example 4.23. Is it possible to find an isomorphism between the subgroup $\{A, B, F\}$ of the group of symmetries of the triangle and the subgroup $\{C^*, E^*, A^*\}$ of the group of rearrangements on three symbols?

	F	A	B			C*	E*	A*
F	F	A	B		C*	C*	E*	A*
A	A	B	F		E*	E*	A*	C*
B	B	F	A		A*	A*	C*	E*

Figure 4.30

Figure 4.30 shows charts for these groups. Through trial and error, the order has been changed so that the charts will match under the following 1-to-1 correspondence:

$$C^* \leftrightarrow F$$
$$E^* \leftrightarrow A$$
$$A^* \leftrightarrow B.$$

Since the charts of figure 4.30 match under this correspondence, the groups are isomorphic. Therefore, if we select any two elements from the first group, and the corresponding two elements from the second group, the answer for the first two will match the answer for the second two. For example,

$$
\begin{array}{ccc}
\text{E*} & \text{A*} & = \text{C*} \\
\updownarrow & \updownarrow & \updownarrow \\
\text{A} & \text{B} & = \text{F.}
\end{array}
$$

In both the examples, an isomorphism was established between the elements of a group and a subgroup of a rearrangement group. While the first example established an isomorphism between a group of four elements and a subgroup of the rearrangement group on four symbols, the second example had a group of three elements isomorphic to a subgroup of the rearrangement group on three symbols. There is a good reason for this. A theorem proved by Arthur Cayley (see Chapter 9) asserts that any group containing n elements (where n is a counting number) is isomorphic to some subgroup of the rearrangement group on n symbols. Thus the group of six symmetries of the equilateral triangle will be isomorphic to a subgroup of the rearrangement group on 6 symbols. (To find this isomorphism, relabel the back of the triangle, changing 1' into 4, 2' into 5, and 3' into 6.) Isomorphisms are discussed in greater detail in the books mentioned at the end of this chapter, and most of them contain proofs of Cayley's Theorem.

PROBLEMS

Consider the mathematical systems formed by each of the sets listed below and the operation of combination. Do these systems form subgroups of the group of symmetries of the square? (see figure 4.21).

1. $\{M, N, P, Q\}$.
2. $\{Q, N\}$.
3. $\{Q, R\}$.
4. $\{Q, S\}$.
5. $\{Q\}$.
6. $\{Q, M\}$.
7. List five subgroups of the group of integers under addition.
8. Find a subgroup of the group of rearrangements on four symbols that is isomorphic to the subgroup $\{M, N, P, Q\}$ of the group of symmetries of the square.
9. Find a group isomorphic to $\{1, 2\}$ under multiplication mod 3.
10. Consider the group $\{1, 2, 3, 4\}$ under multiplication mod 5 and $\{0, 1, 2, 3\}$ under addition mod 4. Are these groups isomorphic?
11. Find two groups, each containing four elements, that are not isomorphic.
12. Find a subgroup of the group of rearrangements on four symbols that is isomorphic to the group $\{1, 2, 3, 4\}$ under multiplication mod 5.
13. Find the subgroup of the group of rearrangements on six symbols which is isomorphic to the group of symmetries of the triangle.

FOR FURTHER READING

Birkhoff, G., and MacLane, S. *A Survey of Modern Algebra.* New York: The Macmillan Company, 1965.

Eddington, Arthur S. "The Theory of Groups," (*The World of Mathematics,* ed. James R. Newman, Vol. 3) New York: Simon and Schuster, Inc., 1956.

Fang, Joong. *Theory and Problems of Abstract Algebra.* New York: Schaum Publishing Company, 1963.

McCoy, Neal H. *Introduction to Modern Algebra.* Boston: Allyn and Bacon, Inc., 1960.

Niven, Ivan, and Zuckerman, H. *Introduction to the Theory of Numbers.* New York: John Wiley and Sons, Inc., 1966.

Weiss, M. J., and Dubisch, R. *Higher Algebra for the Undergraduate.* New York: John Wiley and Sons, Inc., 1962.

CHAPTER 5
SYMBOLIC LOGIC

The study of logic was systematized by Aristotle (384 B.C.–322 B.C.) well over two thousand years ago and carried to great depths (or heights) of subtlety by medieval scholars. An attempt by Gottfried Wilhelm von Leibniz (1646–1716) and his successors to simplify and expand traditional logic led to symbolic or mathematical logic. Symbolic logic uses a special set of symbols to represent ideas, rather than words like Aristotelean logic. The use of symbols and mathematical procedures tends to increase clarity of thought and preciseness of expression.

Leibniz, one of the first mathematicians to suggest the possibility of symbolic logic, is often referred to as a universal genius because of his work in law, religion, diplomacy, logic, history, and philosophy, as well as mathematics. He hoped that symbolic logic would become a *universal characteristic* and unify all of mathematics. His search for a universal language in which all errors of thought would appear as computational errors led him not only to the discovery of symbolic logic, but also to calculus. As mentioned before, Leibniz developed the basic ideas of calculus about the same time as Isaac Newton, with a violent argument erupting over whom should receive the credit. He taught himself Latin and Greek, and when he was only twenty-one years old, he had studied enough to earn a Doctor of Law degree and an offer of a university professorship. Leibniz declined the offer and instead became a lawyer for the Elector of Mainz. He proved himself an effective diplomat and backroom wheeler-dealer. He has been credited with being at least partly responsible for the concept of balance of power. He fathered an abortive scheme to reunite the Catholic and Protestant Churches, with a second failure coming from his attempt to reunite two Protestant sects.

Mathematicians following Leibniz had no interest in his universal characteristic, and, in fact, no further substantial work was done in symbolic logic until George Boole (1815–1864) began his studies. Boole was determined to raise himself out of the extreme poverty of London into which he was born. He planned to accomplish this feat through self-education, mainly in the classics. He became an "usher," an assistant teacher, in an elementary school, in a day when teaching elementary students was not considered a respectable trade. At the age of twenty, he opened a school of his own, while studying mathematics on the side. In 1849, Boole became a professor of mathematics at an Irish university and finally had ample time to devote to his mathematical research. It was during this time, in 1854, that he completed his masterwork, *An Investigation of the Laws of Thought.*

Bertrand Russell (1872–   ) and Alfred North Whitehead (1861– 1947) considerably advanced mathematical logic with their *Principia Mathematica,* a 2000-page, three-volume work which appeared between 1910 and 1913. The book begins with a small number of basic assumptions and undefined terms of logic, upon which is built the complete development of symbolic logic. The authors then turn their attention to arithmetic and define all the ideas of arithmetic (such ideas as number, the successor number of, addition, multiplication) in terms of the definitions and assumptions of logic. They show the lack of need for further assumptions; the few made for logic suffice for all of arithmetic.

Now we turn our attention to the study of symbolic logic.

SECTION 1. BASIC CONCEPTS

In symbolic or mathematical logic, a *sentence* is a statement which is either true or false, but not both true and false. For example,

> The sky is blue.
> Water runs uphill.
> $3 + 1 = 6$.

are all sentences. Each one is either true or false. On the other hand,

> Close the door.
> Eat your spinach.

are not sentences by our definition; we cannot say they are either true or false. A statement such as

$$x + 4 = 9.$$

is an *open sentence* since it becomes true or false whenever a number is put in place of x.

A sentence containing a *connective,* such as *and, or, not, if* . . . , *then* . . . , is called a *compound sentence,* while a sentence containing no connective is called a *simple sentence.* Thus

> Death Valley is in New York.

is a simple sentence, while

> *If* I go fly a kite, *then* I will discover electricity.
> *No* man is an island.

are compound sentences. The *truth-value* of a compound sentence (that is, the truth or falsity of the sentence) depends on the connectives used and the truth-values of the component simple sentences. In this chapter, we want to determine the truth-values of given compound sentences based on the truth-values of the component simple sentences.

To simplify our work with logic, we introduce a certain notational shorthand. We denote simple sentences with letters such as p, q, r, s, with the following symbols used for connectives:

$$and \ \wedge$$
$$or \ \vee$$
$$not \ \sim$$

For example, if p represents the simple sentence "It is raining" and q stands for "It is cloudy," then $p \wedge q$ means "It is raining *and* it is cloudy," while $p \vee \sim q$ represents "It is raining *or* it is *not* cloudy." The compound sentence "It is *not* true that it is raining" could be written $\sim p$.

The compound sentence $p \wedge q$ is called the *conjunction* of the simple sentences p and q; $p \wedge q$ is true only if both simple sentences are true, otherwise $p \wedge q$ is false. We summarize this by means of a *truth table* (see figure 5.1), which shows all four of the possible combinations of truth-values for the simple sentences p and q.

p	q	$p \wedge q$
T	T	T
T	F	F
F	T	F
F	F	F

Figure 5.1

We may use this truth table to determine the truth-value of conjunctions. For example:

North America is an island, and $3 - 2 = 1$.

is false since the first simple sentence is false and the second true. This same conjunction illustrates another important property of mathematical logic: the simple sentences forming a compound sentence need not be related. Thus:

The aardvark is a mammal, and Harry Truman was President.

is a perfectly good compound sentence which happens to be true. (Why?) Normally, sentences connected by $\wedge$ are related to each other. However, to avoid the problems of trying to define "related sentences" we do not require that the sentences comprising a conjunction be related.

In ordinary discourse, the connective *or* is ambiguous in meaning: the sentence *p or q* can mean either "*p or q* or both," or "*p or q* but not both." The sentence:

To graduate, you must take Math 20 or Winetasting 7A–B.

has the following meaning: "You will graduate only if you take Math 20, or Winetasting 7A–B, or both of these courses." On the other hand, the sentence

I will take Lucretia or Frieda to the prom.

means, "I will take Lucretia, or I will take Frieda, but I shall not take both beauties."

We shall agree that $\vee$ represents the first *or* described, that is, $p \vee q$ means *p or q* or both. With this meaning of *or*, $p \vee q$ is called the *disjunction* of the sentences *p* and *q*. The disjunction "I have a quarter, or I have a dime" means "I have a quarter, or I have a dime, or I have both a quarter and a dime," and is true in case I have at least one of the two coins. Following this example, we may write the truth table for disjunction:

p	q	$p \vee q$
T	T	T
T	F	T
F	T	T
F	F	F

Figure 5.2

A disjunction is false only if both simple sentences are false.

Example 5.1.   Consider the sentence: $(p \vee q) \wedge (r \vee p)$, where *p* is false, and *q* and *r* are true. Find the truth-value of the entire sentence.

Work first inside the parentheses. From the *or* truth table, when the first sentence is false and the second true the entire sentence is true:

$$(p \vee q) \wedge (r \vee p)$$
$$\text{F}\quad\text{T}$$
$$\text{T}$$

Similarly, $r \vee p$ is true; all that remains is to check the *and* truth table for the row that has both sentences true.

$$(p \vee q) \wedge (r \vee p)$$
$$\text{T}\qquad\qquad\text{T}$$
$$\text{T}$$

The sentence is true.

The symbols p and q in the basic truth tables are placeholders without a specified meaning. Think of the symbol p as representing the first simple sentence under discussion, with q representing the second simple sentence. Hence when checking the truth-value of a sentence, such as "$r \lor p$," where r is true and p false, find that row of the *or* table which has T in the first column and F in the second, disregarding the labels at the top of the truth table.

The connective *not*, usually called the *negation*, has the following truth table:

p	$\sim p$
T	F
F	T

Figure 5.3

The negation of the sentence:

I like pretzels.

is given by:

I do not like pretzels,

or

It is false that I like pretzels.

Be careful when forming the negations of sentences containing the words "all," "some," or "none." For example, write the negation of

All dogs have fleas.

The sentence is false, which means its negation must be true.

No dogs have fleas.

is again false and cannot be the negation of the original false sentence. A correct negation would be

Not all dogs have fleas.

or

It is not the case that all dogs have fleas.

The negation of:

Some numbers are less than 10.

("some" means the same as "at least one") would be

No numbers are less than 10,

or

It is not the case that some numbers are less than 10.

The negation of

No man is over six feet tall.

is either

Some men are over six feet tall,

or

It is not the case that no men are over six feet tall.

PROBLEMS

1. Classify each of the following as (a) sentence, (b) open sentence, (c) neither.
   (a) Today is Thursday.
   (b) Yes.
   (c) 3 + 1.
   (d) Bring the paper.
   (e) Washington D.C. is a state.
   (f) Not all blonds have more fun.
   (g) $9 - 2 = 12$.
   (h) Hello.
   (i) $x + 4$.
   (j) $y + 2 = 7$.
   (k) $3 + s$ is larger than 9.
   (l) Not all numbers are equal to zero.
   (m) Study mathematics to put hair on your chest.
   (n) x is an articulate aardvark.
   (o) x is a puppy.
   (p) I like person H.

2. Classify each of the following sentences as simple or compound. State the connective used in each compound sentence.
   (a) I like Joyce, or I like Fred.
   (b) Not all men are immortal.
   (c) Today is Saturday, or today is Sunday.
   (d) $3 + 1 \neq 4 - 2$.
   (e) $7 - 6 = 1$.
   (f) Joyce is nice, and Sam is too.

3. Lawyers sometimes use the phrase "and/or." This phrase corresponds to which usage of the word *or* as mentioned in the text?

4. Let p represent the sentence "I am a nice boy" and q represent "I like girls." Convert each of the following compound sentences into words.
   (a) $p \wedge q$
   (b) $\sim(\sim p \wedge q)$
   (c) $(\sim\sim p) \wedge \sim q$
   (d) $\sim(q \wedge p)$
   (e) $(\sim p) \vee q$
   (f) $(\sim p) \vee (\sim q)$
   (g) $\sim p \vee \sim q$
   (h) $\sim(q \vee \sim p)$

5. Let p represent the sentence "Oliphant is cute," with q representing "Fred is cute." Convert each of the following compound sentences into symbols. Assume "ugly" and "cute" are opposites; that is, to be "not ugly" is to be "cute."
   (a) Both Fred and Oliphant are cute.
   (b) Oliphant is cute, and Fred is ugly.
   (c) Neither Oliphant nor Fred is cute.
   (d) Oliphant is cute, or Fred is ugly.
   (e) Either Oliphant is cute, or Fred is cute, but not both.

(f) It is not the case that both are cute.

(g) Both are not cute.

6. For each of the following compound sentences, let p represent a sentence having truth-value **T** and q and r represent sentences having truth-values **F**. Find the truth-value of the entire sentence.

   (a) $(\sim p \wedge q) \vee (r \wedge \sim q)$.

   (b) $(\sim p) \wedge (q \vee \sim r)$.

   (c) $(r \wedge p) \vee (q \wedge p)$.

   (d) $(\sim r) \wedge (q \vee \sim q)$.

   (e) $(p \wedge \sim p) \vee p$.

   (f) $(r \wedge \sim q) \vee (p \wedge q) \vee (r \wedge \sim p) \vee q$.

7. In problem 5 above, assume Oliphant is cute and Fred is ugly. Under these assumptions, which of the sentences are true?

8. Construct a truth table for the connective "not-not," symbolized $\sim\sim$.

9. Write the negation of each of the following.

   (a) His mother is tall.

   (b) All cows were once calves.

   (c) No dew forms in the desert.

   (d) All stars are yellow.

   (e) Some men eat pancakes.

   (f) Some sentences have stupid negations.

   (g) All rioters riot.

SECTION 2. MORE CONNECTIVES

The sentence "if p, then q," called the *conditional* or *implication*, is commonly symbolized $p \rightarrow q$, read "p arrow q." The arrow truth table is somewhat more difficult to obtain than the others we have determined; we use the following sentence as an example to show how to find the arrow truth table.

Senator Sellavote, while running for re-election, says

> If I am elected, then taxes will go down.

As before, there are four possible combinations of truth-values for the component simple sentences:

> He was elected, and taxes go down.
> He was elected, and taxes did not go down.
> He was defeated, and taxes went down.
> He was defeated, and taxes did not go down.

For the first possibility, we assume the Senator was elected and taxes subsequently did go down; since he told the truth, we place **T** in the first row of the arrow truth table. We do not say that taxes went down because he was elected since perhaps he had nothing to do with it at all. Next, if the Senator was elected and taxes did not go down, he did not tell the truth and we place **F** in the second row of the truth table. In the third situation, we assume the Senator was defeated, but taxes subsequently went down anyway. Senator Sellavote did not lie since he only promised to reduce taxes if elected. He made no claim about what would happen if he were not elected, and in fact, his campaign promise gives no information about what would happen if he lost. Since we cannot say the Senator lied, we place **T** in the third row of the truth table. Similarly, if the Senator is defeated and taxes do not go down we cannot blame him since he only promised that taxes would decrease if he were elected. Hence we place a **T** in the last row also. We now have:

p	q	$p \to q$
T	T	T
T	F	F
F	T	T
F	F	T

Figure 5.4

By checking this truth table, the sentence:

$$\text{If } 3 + 1 = 6, \text{ then Lassie is a cow.}$$

is seen to be true since both component simple sentences are false.

It is important to notice that the use of the connective $\to$ in no way implies a cause and effect relation. Any two sentences may have an arrow placed between them to create a compound sentence. For example, the sentence:

$$\text{If George gets up in the morning, then the sun will rise.}$$

is true since the second part is true (why does that make the entire sentence true?). Certainly there is no connection between George's getting up and the sun rising; the sun will rise whether or not George gets up.

Example 5.2.   Find the truth-value of the sentence

$$q \to p,$$

where q represents a true sentence and p a false one.

The first sentence (q) is true and the second (p) false. Locate the row of the truth table that corresponds to first sentence true and second false— the second row. The sentence is false.

Example 5.3.   Evaluate the truth-value of the sentence:

$$(p \to \sim q) \to (\sim r \to q),$$

where p, q, and r are all false.

As before, begin work inside the parentheses. Since q is false, $\sim q$ is true:

$$p \to \sim q$$
$$\text{F} \qquad \text{T}$$
$$\text{T}$$

In the same way, $\sim r \to q$ is false. Finally:

$$(p \to \sim q) \to (\sim r \to q)$$
$$\text{T} \qquad\qquad \text{F}$$
$$\text{F}$$

The connectives *unless* and *either* . . . , *or* . . . are common in everyday language. A new symbol could be introduced for each of these connectives, but it is not necessary. Instead, both of these connectives will be defined in terms of our previous connectives.

Thus, *unless* is defined in the following manner: "p unless q" is the same as "$\sim q \to p$" (if q does not occur then p will). Verify the entries in the "unless" truth table:

p	q	p, unless q
T	T	T
T	F	T
F	T	T
F	F	F

Figure 5.5

"Either p, or q" means "p or q, and not both p and q"; that is, "either p, or q" can be written:

$$(p \lor q) \land \sim(p \land q).$$

Using the definition of "either p, or q," verify the entries in the following truth table:

p	q	either p, or q
T	T	F
T	F	T
F	T	T
F	F	F

Figure 5.6

Example 5.4.   Find the truth-value of the sentence:

$$3 + 1 = 6, \text{ unless the sky is pink.}$$

Since both component simple sentences are false, the last row of the *unless* truth table gives the answer: the sentence is false.

Example 5.5.   Find the truth-value of the sentence:

$$\text{Either } 9 + 3 = 14, \text{ or } 6 \times 7 = 42.$$

The first simple sentence is false and the second true. Here, the answer is found in the third row of the *either* . . . , *or* . . . truth table: the sentence is true.

Example 5.6. Find the truth-value of the sentence:

> Either I will not go to town unless it rains, or
> I will go to town and it will not rain.

Assume I do go to town, but it does not rain.

Let p represent "I will go to town" and q represent "it will rain." Then p is true and q false. The sentence of the example may be symbolized

$$\text{either } (\sim p \text{ unless } q) \text{ or } (p \wedge \sim q).$$

(Note: there may be more than one way to write such a sentence in symbols.) The sentence "$\sim p$ unless q" is false, while "$p \wedge \sim q$" is true; thus the entire sentence is true.

PROBLEMS

1. Write each of the following sentences using the *if* . . . , *then* . . . connective.
   (a) It is a bird, if it flies.
   (b) All men have heads.
   (c) He goes to town on Saturday.
   (d) Anything that has fleas is a dog.
   (e) Any dog has fleas.
   (f) Europe trembles when Napoleon snorts.
   (g) No dogs are cats.

2. Let p represent the sentence "I study hard" and q represent "I pass this lousy course." Express each of the following in words.
   (a) $p \rightarrow q$.
   (b) $q \rightarrow \sim p$.
   (c) $\sim(p \rightarrow \sim q)$.
   (d) p unless q.
   (e) q unless p.
   (f) $p \rightarrow \sim q$.
   (g) $\sim q \rightarrow p$.
   (h) $(\sim p) \wedge (p \rightarrow q)$.
   (i) either p, or q.
   (j) $p \wedge (\text{either } \sim q \text{ or } \sim p)$.

3. Let p represent the sentence "I go to town" while q represents "It rains." Express each of the following symbolically.
   (a) If it rains, I will not go to town.
   (b) Either I go to town, or it rains.
   (c) I will go to town unless it rains.
   (d) It will rain unless I do not go to town.
   (e) I will go to town, and it will rain.
   (f) It will not rain unless I go to town.
   (g) Either it will rain, or I will go to town, unless it rains and I do not go to town.

4. Assume, in problem 3, that p is true and q false. Which of the sentences are true?

5. Find the truth-value of each of the following sentences. Assume p and r are true, with q false.
  (a) $(p \rightarrow q) \rightarrow q$.
  (b) $q \wedge (r \rightarrow q)$.
  (c) either $(p \rightarrow q)$ or $(r \rightarrow \sim q)$.
  (d) either $(p$ unless $r)$ or $(q \wedge \sim r)$.
  (e) either $(p$ unless $[q \rightarrow r])$ or $(p \wedge \sim p)$.
  (f) $[\sim(p \wedge \sim r)$ unless (either $\sim p$ or $\sim q)] \rightarrow (p$ unless $r)$.

6. Define the connective *neither . . . , nor . . .* by saying *"neither p, nor q"* means the same as *"not p and not q."* Write a truth table for *"neither . . . , nor . . . ."*

7. Define a new connective, *because,* by saying *"p because q"* means the same as *"q → p."* Write the *because* truth table.

8. Translate into symbolic statements. Indicate the letters used for each simple sentence. There may be more than one way to do each problem.
  (a) Either he will not do it, or I will go to town.
  (b) Leslie does not like Fred, because either Fred is fat, or Leslie is not pretty.
  (c) Neither I will go nor George will stay, unless Alicia does not buy a coat, and Sam will not go.
  (d) If neither Sam likes apples nor Albert likes figs, then Sam will be a farmer if Albert goes to New York.
  (e) Because I like raisins, Hortense will not go.
  (f) Either neither A nor B is a hippopotamus, or Joseph cannot work because Sam will not go unless Fred is a barber.

We have defined the connectives *unless* and *either . . . , or . . .* in terms of previous connectives. In fact, all the connectives we have used can be defined in terms of just two: $\sim$ and $\vee$. For example, $p \wedge q$ can be written $\sim(\sim p \vee \sim q)$. (Check the truth tables.) Also, $p \rightarrow q$ can be written $\sim p \vee q$.

9. Write $\vee$ and $\rightarrow$ in terms of $\sim$ and $\wedge$.

10. It is also possible to write our connectives in terms of $\sim$ and $\rightarrow$. Decide which connective is expressed by
  (a) $\sim p \rightarrow q$.   (b) $\sim(p \rightarrow \sim q)$.

11. In fact, it is possible to write all our connectives in terms of one connective. Define a new connective *stroke* (written $\mid$) by the chart of figure 5.7. Decide which connective is expressed by
  (a) $p \mid p$.   (c) $(p \mid q) \mid (p \mid q)$.
  (b) $(p \mid p) \mid (q \mid q)$.   (d) $p \mid (q \mid q)$.
  (The stroke connective was developed by the American mathematician C. S. Pierce, 1839–1914).

p	q	$p \mid q$
T	T	F
T	F	T
F	T	T
F	F	T

Figure 5.7

12. Another connective which can define all our connectives is the *dagger* (written ↓) which is defined by

p	q	$p \downarrow q$
T	T	F
T	F	F
F	T	F
F	F	T

Figure 5.8

Decide which connective is expressed by

(a) $p \downarrow p$. (c) $(p \downarrow p) \downarrow (q \downarrow q)$.

(b) $(p \downarrow q) \downarrow (p \downarrow q)$. (d) $[(p \downarrow p) \downarrow q] \downarrow [(p \downarrow p) \downarrow q]$.

13. Both | and ↓ may be defined in terms of each other. Show that:

(a) $p \downarrow q$ has the same truth table as $[(p \,|\, p) \,|\, (q \,|\, q)] \,|\, [(p \,|\, p) \,|\, (q \,|\, q)]$.

(b) $p \,|\, q$ has the same truth table as $[(p \downarrow p) \downarrow (q \downarrow q)] \downarrow [(p \downarrow p) \downarrow (q \downarrow q)]$.

SECTION 3. TRUTH TABLES

A truth table is a chart which shows how the truth-values for a particular compound sentence depend on the connectives used and the truth-values of the component simple sentences. In this section, we discuss a method for obtaining truth tables of more complicated expressions.

For example, let's construct the truth table of

$$(\sim p \wedge q) \vee \sim q.$$

To begin, list all the possible combinations of truth-values for the simple sentences p and q:

p	q	$(\sim p \wedge q) \vee \sim q$
T	T	
T	F	
F	T	
F	F	

Figure 5.9

Insert the truth-values of $\sim p$ and q:

p	q	$(\sim p \wedge q) \vee \sim q$	
T	T	F	T
T	F	F	F
F	T	T	T
F	F	T	F

Figure 5.10

Next, use the connective $\wedge$ to obtain the truth-values of "$\sim p \wedge q$."

p	q	$(\sim p \wedge q) \vee \sim q$
T	T	F F T
T	F	F F F
F	T	T T T
F	F	T F F

Figure 5.11

We may disregard the two columns of truth-values that were used to find the truth-values of "$\sim p \wedge q$." Now write the truth-values of $\sim q$:

p	q	$(\sim p \wedge q) \vee \sim q$
T	T	F F
T	F	F T
F	T	T F
F	F	F T

Figure 5.12

To obtain the final truth table, use the connective $\vee$:

p	q	$(\sim p \wedge q) \vee \sim q$
T	T	F F F
T	F	F T T
F	T	T T F
F	F	F T T

Figure 5.13

Example 5.7.   Write the truth table for the sentence:

$$(\sim p \wedge r) \vee (\sim q \wedge \sim p).$$

The sentence has three letters: p, q, and r. How many lines may we expect in its truth table? As we have seen, there is a total of four possible combinations of truth-values for p and q. For each of these four, there are two possibilities for r (T or F), with a total of eight combinations of truth-values for the three sentences. The truth table must, therefore, contain eight lines.

p	q	r	(~p ∧ r) ∨ (~q ∧ ~p)
T	T	T	F F T **F** F F F
T	T	F	F F F F F F F
T	F	T	F F T F T F F
T	F	F	F F F F T F F
F	T	T	T T T **T** F F T
F	T	F	T F F F F F T
F	F	T	T T T **T** T T T
F	F	F	T F F **T** T T T

Figure 5.14

Example 5.8. Find the truth table for:

$$(p \rightarrow q) \rightarrow (\sim p \lor q).$$

Work as before:

p	q	(p → q) → (~p ∨ q)
T	T	T **T** F T T
T	F	F **T** F F F
F	T	T **T** T T T
F	F	T **T** T T F

Figure 5.15

Notice that the sentence is always true, irrespective of the truth-values of the simple sentences; such a sentence is called a *tautology*. Other examples of tautologies include "$p \lor \sim p$," "$p \rightarrow p$," "$(\sim p \lor \sim q) \rightarrow \sim (q \land p)$," and so on.

PROBLEMS

Construct the truth tables for each of the following sentences. Identify any which are tautologies.

1. $\sim p \lor \sim q$.
2. $(\sim p \land \sim q) \lor (p \lor q)$.
3. $\sim p \rightarrow \sim q$.
4. $\sim p$ unless $\sim q$.
5. either $\sim p$ or q.
6. $p \rightarrow (q$ unless $p)$.
7. $(\sim p \lor \sim q) \land (\sim p \rightarrow \sim q)$.
8. $(p \rightarrow q) \rightarrow (\sim q \rightarrow \sim p)$.
9. $(\sim p \rightarrow \sim q) \rightarrow (q \rightarrow p)$.
10. $(\sim p \rightarrow \sim q) \rightarrow (p \rightarrow q)$.
11. $(p \lor q) \rightarrow (q \lor p)$.
12. $(q \rightarrow p) \lor (\sim q \lor \sim p)$.
13. $[(r \lor p) \land \sim q] \rightarrow p$.
14. $r \rightarrow (p \land \sim q)$.
15. $(\sim r \rightarrow s) \lor (p \rightarrow \sim q)$.

16. Consider the sentence $(\sim p \vee r) \wedge [s \rightarrow (t \vee u)]$. How many lines will be in its truth table?

17. Suppose a sentence contains the simple sentences p, q, r, s, t, u, and v. How many lines will appear in its truth table?

18. Use truth tables to show that each of the following have the same truth-values for *any* combination of truth-values of the simple sentences p and q.
    (a) $p \rightarrow q$.   (b) $\sim p \vee q$.   (c) $\sim(p \wedge \sim q)$.

19. Consider the set of elements $\{T, F\}$ and the connective $\vee$. Show how $\vee$ may be used to define an operation on the set, and then see if the resulting mathematical system is a group.

SECTION 4. MORE ON THE CONDITIONAL

Three new sentences may be obtained from the *direct statement* $p \rightarrow q$:
(1) The *converse:* $q \rightarrow p$.
(2) The *inverse:* $\sim p \rightarrow \sim q$.
(3) The *contrapositive:* $\sim q \rightarrow \sim p$.

Example 5.9. Write the converse, inverse, and contrapositive of the sentence:

If I have a dollar, then I can buy a six-cent stamp.

If we let p represent "I have a dollar" with q representing "I can afford a six-cent stamp," the sentence may be written "$p \rightarrow q$." The converse, "$q \rightarrow p$," becomes:

If I can buy a six-cent stamp, then I have a dollar.

which, notice, is not necessarily true. The inverse, "$\sim p \rightarrow \sim q$" is written:

If I do not have a dollar, then I cannot afford a six-cent stamp.

which again is not necessarily true. The contrapositive, "$\sim q \rightarrow \sim p$" is given by:

If I cannot buy a six-cent stamp, then I do not have a dollar.

which is a true sentence.

This example shows that the converse of a true sentence need not be true. It can be, but it need not be.

Example 5.10. Construct the truth tables of the sentences "$p \rightarrow q$," "$q \rightarrow p$," "$\sim p \rightarrow \sim q$," and "$\sim q \rightarrow \sim p$."

Using the method of the last section, we have:

		Direct	Converse	Inverse	Contrapositive
p	q	$p \rightarrow q$	$q \rightarrow p$	$\sim p \rightarrow \sim q$	$\sim q \rightarrow \sim p$
T	T	T	T	T	T
T	F	F	T	T	F
F	T	T	F	F	T
F	F	T	T	T	T

Figure 5.16

The contrapositive and the direct statement (see figure 5.16) always have the same truth-values, as do the converse and the inverse. Hence a statement may always be replaced by its contrapositive without affecting its meaning.

Example 5.11. Write the converse, inverse, and contrapositive of the sentence:

$$\sim p \rightarrow \sim q.$$

The converse: "$\sim q \rightarrow \sim p$," the inverse: "$p \rightarrow q$," and the contrapositive: "$q \rightarrow p$."

There are several ways of translating "$p \rightarrow q$" into words; "if p, then q" is one. For example,

> If you marry the boss' daughter, then
> you will get ahead in the company.

can also be written

> Marrying the boss' daughter is sufficient for
> you to get ahead in the company.

According to this sentence, marrying the daughter is enough to assure getting ahead. Other things, such as being hardworking and industrious, might also assure getting ahead, but at least we know marrying the daughter will do it.

> Marrying the boss' daughter is a necessary
> condition for getting ahead.

is a sentence with a different meaning: one condition that is necessary in order to get ahead is that you marry the boss' daughter. Other things might also be required, such as being the son of the largest stockholder, but being the boss' son-in-law is one requirement. Hence we may write:

> If you get ahead, then you married the boss' daughter.

This last sentence can also be written:

> You can get ahead only if you marry the boss' daughter.

that is, marrying the boss' daughter is one requirement for getting ahead.
In summary, "$p \rightarrow q$" can be translated into words as follows:

> if p, then q.
> q, if p.
> p, only if q.
> p is sufficient for q.
> q is necessary for p.

For example, the sentence:

> An isosceles triangle has two equal sides.

can be written in any of the following ways (among others):

> If a triangle is isosceles, then it has two equal sides.
> A triangle has two equal sides, if it is isosceles.
> A triangle is isosceles only if it has two equal sides.
> Being isosceles is sufficient for a triangle to have two equal sides.
> Having two equal sides is necessary to make a triangle isosceles.

Example 5.12.   Let p represent "A triangle is equilateral" and q "A triangle has three equal sides." Write in symbols:
   (a) A triangle is equilateral, if it has three equal sides.
   (b) A triangle is equilateral, only if it has three equal sides.
   (c) Being equilateral is a sufficient condition for a triangle to have three equal sides.
   (d) Being equilateral is a necessary condition for a triangle to have three equal sides.

Sentences (a) and (d) become $q \rightarrow p$, while (b) and (c) are $p \rightarrow q$. The conjunction of (a) and (b) is "p, if q, and p, only if q," which is often written, "*p if, and only if, q*," [symbolized: $(p \rightarrow q) \wedge (q \rightarrow p)$]. The conjunction of (c) and (d) is "p is *sufficient* for q and p is *necessary* for q," written "*p is necessary and sufficient for q*." [Again symbolized $(p \rightarrow q) \wedge (q \rightarrow p)$].

The sentence $(p \rightarrow q) \wedge (q \rightarrow p)$ is so common in mathematics that it is given a special name and a special symbol: $(p \rightarrow q) \wedge (q \rightarrow p)$ is called the *biconditional* and written $p \leftrightarrow q$.

Example 5.13.   Construct the truth table for $\leftrightarrow$.

Using the definition of the biconditional, we have:

p	q	$(p \rightarrow q)$	$\wedge$	$(q \rightarrow p)$
T	T	T	T	T
T	F	F	F	T
F	T	T	F	F
F	F	T	T	T

Figure 5.17

Example 5.14.   What is the meaning of the sentence:

You like mathematics ↔ you are strange.

We may write this sentence in any of three ways:
(a) If you like mathematics you are strange, and if you are strange then you like mathematics.
(b) You like mathematics if, and only if, you are strange.
(c) Liking mathematics is a necessary and sufficient condition for being strange.

PROBLEMS

Translate each of the following into the form "$p \rightarrow q$."
1. I will go to town if it rains.
2. I will go to town only if it rains.
3. Doing homework is a necessary condition for passing the class.
4. Kissing Lolita is sufficient to get me into trouble with her father.
5. I drive fast only if my father is the traffic judge.
6. An order from my wife is a sufficient condition to get me to cut the lawn.
7. Long grass is necessary before I will cut the lawn.
8. I will cut the grass only if it is not a hot summer afternoon.
9. The temperature goes over 100° in Sacramento only if it is summer.
10. Writing a book is a necessary condition for boring students.
11. I feel bad only if I lose on the slot machine.

Write the converse, inverse, and contrapositive of each of the following.
12. Blonds have more fun.
13. Cigarette smoking endangers health.
14. Those who take part in the student riots will miss a lecture on Early Miocene Fossils.
15. All that glitters is not gold. (Is this old saying true?)
16. All dogs have fleas.
17. People who live in mansions are rich.

Find the truth-value of each of the following:
18. $3 + 1 = 6$ if, and only if, the sky is red.
19. $3 - 2 \neq 3$ if, and only if, Pythagoras was a Turk.
20. $3 - 5 = -2$ is a necessary and sufficient condition for $2 - 1 = 1$.
21. A triangle is a polygon is a necessary and sufficient condition for a snake to be a fish.

Two sentences which can both be true of the same object are called *consistent*. For example, "it is green" and "it is small" are consistent sentences. Sentences which cannot both be true about the same object are called *contrary;* "it is a Ford" and "it is a Chevrolet" are contrary. Label the following pairs of sentences as contrary or consistent.
22. That is Tom Jones. That is Harry Smith.
23. That is an animal. That is a cow.
24. That is a pig. That is a bacterium.
25. She is rich. She is poor.

26. He has power. He has wealth.

27. Let d represent "direct statement," c, "converse," p, "contrapositive," and i, "inverse." The chart of figure 5.18 shows a method of combining two of these letters. Explain the method used.

	d	c	p	i
d	d	c	p	i
c	c	d	i	p
p	p	i	d	c
i	i	p	c	d

Figure 5.18

28. Show that the chart of figure 5.18 represents a group.

29. Show that $\{d, p\}$ with the same operation as above is a group.

30. Is the group of problem 28 cyclic? If so, name a generator.

31. Is the group of problem 29 cyclic? If so, name a generator.

32. Find a group from Chapter 4 that is isomorphic to the one of problem 28.

33. Are there any groups of four elements from Chapter 4 that are not isomorphic to the group of problem 28?

SECTION 5. VALID ARGUMENTS

We may use the ideas developed in this chapter to study the validity of reasoning. For example, consider:

If I pick strawberries, then my fingers get red.	$p \to q$
I pick strawberries.	p
$\therefore$ My fingers get red.	$\therefore q$

Recall from geometry that $\therefore$ means "therefore." This argument consists of two *premises*, or *hypotheses*, and a *conclusion;* the argument is *valid* if:

$$[(p \to q) \wedge p] \to q$$

is a tautology. (That is, the argument is valid if the sentence "the conjunction of the premises implies the conclusion" is a tautology.) By means of truth tables, it can be shown that the argument is valid. The pattern of argument illustrated above:

$$\begin{array}{c} p \to q \\ p \\ \hline \therefore q \end{array}$$

is called *modus ponens*, or the *law of detachment*.

Example 5.15.   Is the following argument valid?

> If diamonds are expensive, then coal is expensive.
> Coal is not expensive.
> _____
> Diamonds are not expensive.

If p represents "diamonds are expensive" and q represents "coal is expensive," the argument may be written

$$p \to q$$
$$\frac{\sim q}{\therefore \sim p}$$

Form the sentence:

$$[(p \to q) \wedge \sim q] \to \sim p;$$

the argument is valid if the sentence is a tautology. Construct a truth table:

p	q	$[(p \to q)$	$\wedge$	$\sim q]$	$\to$	$\sim p$
T	T	T	F	F	T	F
T	F	F	F	T	T	F
F	T	T	F	F	T	T
F	F	T	T	T	T	T

Figure 5.19

The valid argument:

$$p \to q$$
$$\frac{\sim q}{\therefore \sim p}$$

is called *modus tollens*, or the *law of contraposition.*

The argument is valid even though the conclusion of the example is false. A valid argument can have either a true conclusion or a false conclusion, depending on the truth-values of the premises. If the premises are all true, and if the argument is valid, then the conclusion is true.

Example 5.16.   Is the following argument valid:

> If she buys a coat, she will buy a hat.
> She buys a hat.
> _____
> She buys a coat.

The argument can be written in the form

$$p \to q$$
$$\frac{q}{\therefore p} \qquad \text{FALLACY}$$

A truth table shows that the sentence:

$$[(p \to q) \land q] \to p$$

is not a tautology; therefore the argument is invalid. If "$p \to q$" is replaced by "$q \to p$," the argument becomes valid. The argument would therefore be valid if the direct statement and converse had the same truth-values, which they do not. For this reason, this argument is sometimes called the *fallacy of the converse*.

In the same way,

$$\begin{array}{r} p \to q \\ \underline{\sim p} \\ \therefore \sim q \end{array} \qquad \text{FALLACY}$$

is sometimes called the *fallacy of the inverse*.

Testing for the validity of arguments by truth tables can at times be a laborious, rather dull procedure. The following pictorial method, although not as exact, is often a good substitute.

Example 5.17.   Test the validity of the argument:

> If you like Hortense, then you will like Fred.
> You do not like Hortense.
> ─────────────────────────
> You do not like Fred.

The rectangle of figure 5.20 represents the universal set of all people. Following the first premise of the argument, the circle representing people who like Hortense is placed completely inside the circle representing the set of people who like Fred. By the second premise, there are two possible locations for the element "you." "You" inside the "like Fred" circle satisfies both premises but not the conclusion. Since we are not forced to accept the conclusion the argument is invalid.

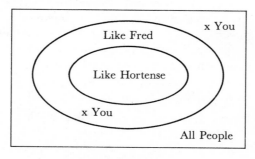

Figure 5.20

Example 5.18.   Test the following argument for validity.

> All people who eat a lot get fat.
> All beautiful women are fat.
> ─────────────────────────
> All beautiful women eat a lot.

Certainly the conclusion is false, but is the argument valid? From the premises, the circle representing the set of all people who eat a lot must be completely inside the circle representing the set of fat people, as must the circle representing the set of beautiful women. However, there are several ways to combine the "eat a lot" and "beautiful" circles, as shown in figure 5.21. Since the conclusion is not true in all cases, we are not forced to accept it, which means the argument is invalid.

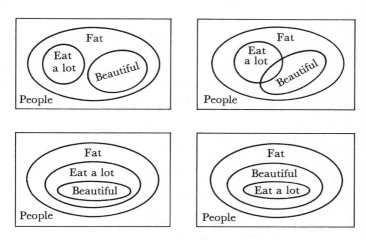

Figure 5.21

Example 5.19. List two different valid conclusions for the following premises.

> Everything that costs a lot of money is desirable.
> Some things that cost a lot of money are healthful.

Figure 5.22 shows a possible diagram of the situation described by the premises. From the diagram, it is possible to produce at least two valid conclusions: "Some things that are healthful are desirable" and "some things that are healthful cost a lot of money."

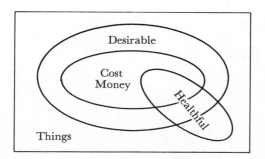

Figure 5.22

PROBLEMS

Use truth tables to test the validity of each of the following:

1. $p \rightarrow q$
$\underline{q \rightarrow r}$
$p \rightarrow r$

4. $\underline{p \wedge q}$
p

2. $p \vee q$
$\underline{p \quad\quad}$
$\sim q$

5. p
$\underline{q \quad}$
$p \wedge q$

3. $p \rightarrow q$
$\underline{q \rightarrow p}$
$p \wedge q$

6. $(p \rightarrow q) \wedge (q \rightarrow p)$
$\underline{p \quad\quad\quad\quad\quad\quad}$
$p \vee q$

Test the validity of the following arguments:

7. If I buy a new car, then I will have to make payments.
I bought a new car.
I have to make payments.

8. If I buy a new car, I have to make payments.
I did not buy a new car.
I do not have to make payments.

9. If George goes to town, he will need a new hat.
If he needs a new hat, he will need a new coat.
If he needs a new coat, he will want new shoes.
If George goes to town, he will want new shoes.

10. If Sandra buys a new purse, she will not need a key ring.
If she needs a key ring, she will need another key.
If she needs another key, she will need another lock.
If Sandra buys a new purse, she will need another lock.

11. If Hortense does not pass this course, she will not be able to catch a husband who makes $15,000 a year.
She passed the course.
She caught her husband.

12. If Herbert gets tired of textbook authors who try unsuccessfully to be funny, then he will not like math.
He likes math.
He does not get tired of such authors.

13. All cars are black.
Some cars have power steering.
Some cars with power steering are black.

14. All chickens love to scratch on the ground.
Roger Rooster is a chicken.
Roger loves to scratch on the ground.

15. All boring people have bad breath.
Some boring people eat turnips.
All people who eat turnips have bad breath.

16. All people who love wine have a red nose.
    Some people who love wine also love bourbon.
    Some people who love bourbon have a red nose.

17. All people who drive little red sports cars have long hair.
    All people who have long hair are sweet.
    Some pawnbrokers are not sweet.
    (a) Some pawnbrokers drive a little red sports car.
    (b) Some pawnbrokers are sweet.
    (c) Some pawnbrokers do not have long hair.
    (d) Some people who are sweet are not pawnbrokers.
    (e) All people who drive little red sports cars are sweet.

18. All college students love a good time.
    All happy people love a good time.
    Some happy people wear wigs.
    (a) Some happy people are college students.
    (b) Some college students are happy.
    (c) Some people who wear wigs are happy.
    (d) All people who like a good time are not college students.
    (e) All people who wear wigs love a good time.
    (f) No college student wears a wig.
    (g) Unhappy people do not wear wigs.

SECTION 6. PROBLEMS FROM LEWIS CARROLL

Lewis Carroll, author of *Alice's Adventures in Wonderland,* was really the Reverend Charles Lutwidge Dodgson, a mathematical lecturer at Cambridge University in England. Queen Victoria told Dodgson how much she enjoyed *Alice* and how much she wanted to read his next book; he is said to have sent her *Symbolic Logic,* his most famous mathematical work. In his *Symbolic Logic* Dodgson makes some strong claims for the subject: "It [symbolic logic] will give you clearness of thought—the ability to *see your way* through a puzzle—the habit of arranging your ideas in an orderly and get-at-able form—and, more valuable than all, the power to detect *fallacies,* and to tear to pieces the flimsy illogical arguments, which you will so continually encounter in books, in newspapers, in speeches, and even in sermons, and which so easily delude those who have never taken the trouble to master this fascinating Art." All the problems in this section come from Dodgson's book.

Consider now the following three premises.

> Babies are illogical,
> Nobody is despised who can manage a crocodile,
> Illogical persons are despised.

We want to obtain a valid conclusion from these premises. First, convert the premises into conditional sentences.

If you are a baby, then you are illogical.
If you can manage a crocodile, then you are not despised.
If you are illogical, then you are despised.

Let p be "You are a baby," q be "You are logical," r be "You can manage a crocodile," and s be "You are despised." The sentences may then be written:

$$p \to \sim q$$
$$r \to \sim s$$
$$\sim q \to s.$$

Since the letter p appears only once, we begin with it. Using the contrapositive of "$r \to \sim s$," we rearrange the three sentences as follows:

$$p \to \sim q$$
$$\sim q \to s$$
$$s \to \sim r.$$

from which we obtain a valid conclusion, "$p \to \sim r$." (Truth tables can be used to verify the validity of the argument. See, for example, problem 1, section 5.) In words, the conclusion becomes, "If you are a baby you cannot manage a crocodile," or as Lewis Carroll would have written it, "Babies cannot manage crocodiles."

Example 5.20.   Supply a conclusion for the following premises.

No one takes in the *Times* unless he is well-educated.
No hedgehogs can read.
Those who cannot read are not well-educated.

Let p be "One takes the *Times*," with q "One is well-educated," r as "One is a hedgehog," and s "One can read." The three premises may then be written:

$$p \to q$$
$$r \to \sim s$$
$$\sim s \to \sim q.$$

Note that since r appears only once, we can begin by writing a sentence which has r on the left.

$$r \to \sim s.$$

We need a sentence with $\sim s$ on the left (why?).

$$r \to \sim s$$
$$\sim s \to \sim q.$$

To get $\sim q$ on the left we take the contrapositive of the remaining sentence.

$$r \rightarrow \sim s$$
$$\sim s \rightarrow \sim q$$
$$\sim q \rightarrow \sim p$$

The valid conclusion: "No hedgehog takes the *Times*."

Example 5.21.   Supply a valid conclusion for the premises:

> No kitten, that loves fish, is unteachable.
> No kitten without a tail will play with a gorilla.
> Kittens with whiskers always love fish.
> No teachable kitten has green eyes.
> No kittens have tails unless they have whiskers.

Symbolize the phrases as follows: p: "The kitten loves fish," q: "The kitten has green eyes," r: "The kitten has a tail," s: "The kitten is teachable," t: "The kitten has whiskers," and u: "The kitten is willing to play with a gorilla." The premises may be written:

$$p \rightarrow s$$
$$\sim r \rightarrow \sim u$$
$$t \rightarrow p$$
$$s \rightarrow \sim q$$
$$\sim t \rightarrow \sim r.$$

Letter u appears only once, therefore we begin with it. We need the contrapositives of "$\sim t \rightarrow \sim r$" and "$\sim r \rightarrow \sim u$"; after rearranging the order of the sentences we have:

$$u \rightarrow r$$
$$r \rightarrow t$$
$$t \rightarrow p$$
$$p \rightarrow s$$
$$s \rightarrow \sim q$$

A valid conclusion is given by "$u \rightarrow \sim q$." In this example the translation back into English is easier if we take the contrapositive: "$q \rightarrow \sim u$," or, "A kitten with green eyes will not play with a gorilla."

PROBLEMS

Supply a valid conclusion, in words and in symbols, for each of the following.
 1. No ducks waltz.
    No officers ever decline to waltz.
    All my poultry are ducks.
    Let p: "ducks," q: "my poultry," r: "officers," and s: "willing to waltz."

2. Every one who is sane can do logic.
No lunatics are fit to serve on a jury.
None of your sons can do logic.
Let *p*: "able to do logic," *q*: "fit to serve on a jury," *r*: "sane," and *s*: "your sons."

3. No experienced person is incompetent.
Jenkins is always blundering.
No competent person is always blundering.
Let *p*: "always blundering," *q*: "competent," *r*: "experienced," and *s*: "Jenkins."

4. All unripe fruit is unwholesome.
All these apples are wholesome.
No fruit, grown in the shade, is ripe.
Let *p*: "grown in the shade," *q*: "ripe," *r*: "these apples," and *s*: "wholesome."

5. No name in this list is unsuitable for the hero of a romance.
Names beginning with a vowel are always melodious.
No name is suitable for the hero of a romance if it begins with a consonant.
Let *p*: "begin with a vowel," *q*: "in this list," *r*: "melodious," and *s*: "suitable for the hero of a romance."

6. Nobody, who really appreciates Beethoven, fails to keep silent while the Moonlight Sonata is being played.
Guinea pigs are hopelessly ignorant of music.
No one, who is hopelessly ignorant of music, ever keeps silent while the Moonlight Sonata is being played.
Let *p*: "guinea pigs," *q*: "hopelessly ignorant," *r*: "keep silent," and *s*: "appreciate Beethoven."

7. Promise-breakers are untrustworthy.
Wine-drinkers are very communicative.
A man who keeps his promises is honest.
No teetotalers are pawnbrokers.
One can always trust a very communicative person.
Let *p*: "honest," *q*: "pawnbrokers," *r*: "promise-breakers," *s*: "trustworthy," *t*: "very communicative," and *u*: "wine-drinkers."

8. No one, who is going to a party, ever fails to brush his hair.
No one looks fascinating if he is untidy.
Opium-eaters have no self-command.
Every one, who has brushed his hair, looks fascinating.
No one wears white kid gloves, unless he is going to a party.
A man is always untidy, if he has no self-command.
Let *p*: "going to a party," *q*: "brushed hair," *r*: "self-command," *s*: "looks fascinating," *t*: "opium-eaters," *u*: "tidy," and *v*: "wears white kid gloves."

9. No shark ever doubts that it is well fitted out.
A fish, that cannot dance a minuet, is contemptible.
No fish is quite certain that it is well fitted out, unless it has three rows of teeth.
All fishes, except sharks, are kind to children.
No heavy fish can dance a minuet.
A fish with three rows of teeth is not to be despised.
Let *p*: "dance a minuet," *q*: "certain that he is well fitted out," *r*: "contemptible," *s*: "having three rows of teeth," *t*: "heavy," *u*: "kind to children," and *v*: "sharks."

10. All the dated letters in this room are written on blue paper.

None of them are in black ink, except those that are written in the third person.

I have not filed any of them that I can read.

None of them, that are written on one sheet, are undated.

All of them, that are not crossed, are in black ink.

All of them, written by Brown, begin with "Dear Sir."

All of them, written on blue paper, are filed.

None of them, written on more than one sheet, are crossed.

None of them, that begin with "Dear Sir," are written in the third person.

Let p: "begin with 'Dear Sir'," q: "crossed," r: "dated," s: "filed," t: "in black ink," u: "in third person," v: "I can read," w: "on blue paper," x: "on one sheet," and y: "written by Brown."

FOR FURTHER READING

Carroll, Lewis (Charles L. Dodgson). *Symbolic Logic and the Game of Logic.* New York: Dover Publications, 1958.

Copi, Irving. *Symbolic Logic.* New York: The Macmillan Company, 1965.

Suppes, Patrick, and Hill, Shirley. *First Course in Mathematical Logic.* New York: Blaisdell Publishing Company, 1964.

CHAPTER 6

ANALYTIC GEOMETRY

Analytic geometry is the branch of mathematics that applies algebraic methods to the study of geometrical figures. By means of its methods, many kinds of lines, curves, and surfaces can be described through the use of algebraic equations. The development of the subject is customarily attributed to René Descartes, the French philosopher-mathematician (1596–1650). Besides the invention of analytic geometry, Descartes made a tremendous number of contributions to the fields of astronomy, physics, philosophy, and theology.

Descartes would not publish his works on theology and science because he feared the power of the Inquisition, which had forced Galileo to recant his belief that the earth revolved around the sun, a fact central to Descartes' work. His peaceful life of writing and meditating was shattered when the Queen of Sweden, the nineteen-year-old Christine, commissioned him to be her tutor. Unfortunately, the intense cold of the winter in Stockholm was too much for him, and he died within the year.

The Bernoulli family of Switzerland, who had fled the religious persecution of their native Belgium, expanded and continued the work of Descartes. They were as serious about mathematics as most families are about money. In three generations this remarkable family produced eight well-known mathematicians, four of whom are of the first rank. Competition was keen among the family members; in fact, competition frequently resulted in bitter rivalry. Two brothers, Jacob I (1654–1705) and Johannes I (1667–1748), worked primarily on the same types of problems, which gave rise to jealousy and even violent public feuds. Johannes I even threw his son out of the house when the son won a mathematical prize for which the father had also competed.

SECTION 1. BASIC CONCEPTS

To begin our study of analytic geometry, let's consider an example of an *ordered pair* of numbers, $(3, -2)$; the word "pair" is used because there are two numbers, while the word "ordered" means that 3 is to be considered the first number and -2 the second. Because of this requirement of order, we can write: $(3, -2) \neq (-2, 3)$. This is not the same as with sets, where $\{3, -2\}$ is the same as $\{-2, 3\}$ since both sets contain exactly the same elements. Usually the first component of the ordered pair is the *x value*, and the second component is the *y value*.

A *relation* is defined as a set of ordered pairs. Thus

$$\{(3, -2), (4, 7), (2, 1)\}$$

is a relation. Such simple relations are of little interest; normally we shall state a rule that shows how to obtain a *y* value from a given *x* value. For example, this is a typical relation:

$$\{(x, y) \mid x + y = 2, x \text{ is an integer}\}.$$

We want to find the set of all ordered pairs (x, y) (x and y integers), such that $x + y = 2$. The ordered pair $(1, 1)$ belongs to this relation since $1 + 1 = 2$. Other examples of ordered pairs belonging to this relation are $(2, 0)$, $(5, -3)$, and $(7, -5)$. (We can use the phrase, "belonging to this relation," since a relation is a *set* of ordered pairs.) In fact, this relation contains an infinite number of ordered pairs.

Consider this relation

$$\{(x, y) \mid x = y^2, y \text{ is a real number}\}.$$

Note: *y* can have any value since it is to be squared, and *any* number can be squared. On the other hand, *x* can never be negative since y^2 is always positive or zero. Therefore

the set of possible *x* values is $\{x \mid x \geq 0\}$,
the set of possible *y* values is $\{y \mid y \text{ is a real number}\}$.

The set of all possible *x* values is called the *domain* of the relation, and the set of all possible *y* values forms the *range* of the relation.

Example 6.1. Find the domain and the range of the relation

$$\{(x, y) \mid 2x = y, 1 \leq x \leq 4\}.$$

The relation contains such ordered pairs as $(1, 2)$, $(\frac{3}{2}, 3)$, $(4, 8)$, and so on. The ordered pair $(5, 10)$ does not belong to the relation. (Why?) Any number between 1 and 4, inclusive, can be an *x* value, while the *y* values lie between 2 and 8 inclusive. Hence:

the domain is $\{x \mid 1 \leq x \leq 4\}$;
the range is $\{y \mid 2 \leq y \leq 8\}$.

Let us now investigate a method of pictorially representing a relation. In figure 6.1, the horizontal line is called the *x axis*, and the vertical line is called the *y axis*. Together both axes form a *Cartesian coordinate system* (named after René Descartes), which can be used to find points corresponding to ordered pairs of numbers. The point of intersection of the two axes is the *origin* of the coordinate system. To the right of the origin is a scale of positive values of x; the negative values are to the left. The positive values of y lie above the origin, negative values below. The origin itself is the zero point of both the x axis and the y axis. The origin is labeled $(0, 0)$, expressing the fact that it is the zero point of both axes. To locate the point $(3, 6)$, count 3 units to the right on the x axis, then count 6 units up parallel to the y axis. Figure 6.2 illustrates the points $(3, 6)$, $(-1, 3)$, $(4, -2)$, $(-3, 0)$, and $(0, -1)$.

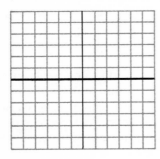
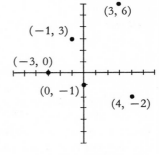

Figure 6.1   Figure 6.2

In this coordinate system, any point in the plane may be located with an ordered pair, and any ordered pair represents some point in the plane. Note: in this context, the x value of an ordered pair is often called the *abscissa*, and the y value is referred to as the *ordinate*.

Example 6.2. Locate on a coordinate system all the ordered pairs that belong to the relation

$$\{(x, y) \mid x = y + 3, x \text{ is a counting number between 3 and 9}\}.$$

If $x = 4$, then $y = 1$. Therefore the ordered pair $(4, 1)$ belongs to the relation, as do $(5, 2)$, $(6, 3)$, $(7, 4)$, and $(8, 5)$. Note that no other ordered pairs are possible because of the restriction on x. These points have been plotted in figure 6.3.

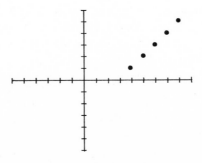

Figure 6.3

Example 6.3.   Plot all the points that belong to the relation

$$\{(x,y) \mid x + 2 \le y; x = 1, 2, 3, \text{ or } 4; y = 2, 3, 4, \text{ or } 5\}.$$

Note that the domain and range of this relation are each restricted to a relatively few numbers. No ordered pair in the relation has $x = 4$ since none of the listed y values are large enough; that is, using the y values listed, the sentence, "$4 + 2 \le y$," cannot be true. The ordered pairs that belong to the relation are plotted in figure 6.4.

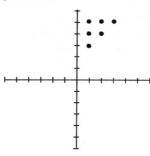

Figure 6.4

A *function* is a particular type of relation in which no two ordered pairs can have the same x value but different y values. For example, the relation $\{(x,y) \mid x = y^2\}$ is not a function since the ordered pairs $(16, 4)$ and $(16, -4)$ both belong to the relation; the ordered pairs have the same x values but different y values. On the other hand, $\{(x,y) \mid x = 2y\}$ is a function: if two ordered pairs have the same x value they also have the same y value.

Another special type of relation is called an *equivalence relation*. A relation R is an equivalence relation if it satisfies the following three requirements:

(1) R must be *reflexive*. If r is an element of the domain of R, then (r, r) must belong to R.

(2) R must be *symmetric*. If (r, s) is an element of R, then (s, r) must also belong to R.

(3) R must be *transitive*. If (r, s) and (s, t) belong to R, then (r, t) must also belong to R.

Perhaps the simplest example of an equivalence relation is

$$R = \{(x,y) \mid x = y, x \text{ is a counting number}\}.$$

To prove that R is really an equivalence relation we must show that R satisfies the three requirements listed above.

(1) Suppose r is any counting number. Is $r = r$? Since it is, we can write $(r, r) \in R$, and the first requirement is satisfied.

(2) Suppose we know $(r, s) \in R$. Then we have $r = s$ and hence $s = r$, so that $(s, r) \in R$, which satisfies the second requirement.

(3) Suppose both $(r, s) \in R$ and $(s, t) \in R$. Then $r = s$ and $s = t$, so that $r = t$ and $(r, t) \in R$.

Relation R satisfies all three requirements; it is an equivalence relation.

Example 6.4.   Consider a set of children's blocks of various colors. We can define a relation R on these blocks by saying $(x, y) \in R$, if x and y are blocks of the same color. Is R an equivalence relation?

We again check the three requirements:

(1) Reflexive. Given a block x, is $(x, x) \in R$? That is, is a block the same color as itself? Yes, and therefore R is reflexive.

(2) Symmetric. If a block x is the same color as block y, that is, if $(x, y) \in R$, can we say block y is the same color as block x? Again yes, so that $(y, x) \in R$ and R is symmetric.

(3) Transitive. If block x is the same color as block y, and block y is the same color as block z, is block x the same color as block z? Yes, and R is transitive.

Since relation R satisfies all three requirements, it is an equivalence relation.

Example 6.5.   Let:

$$R = \{(x, y) \mid x < y, \ x \text{ is a counting number}\}.$$

Is R an equivalence relation?

We begin to check the requirements:

(1) Reflexive. Is $(x, x) \in R$? That is, if x is a counting number, is $x < x$? It is not, and so R is not an equivalence relation. Verify that R is transitive but not symmetric.

PROBLEMS

Find all ordered pairs that belong to the following relations. Graph each relation, state the domain and range of each, and identify those which are functions.

1. $\{(x, y) \mid x = y; \ x \text{ is an integer between 3 and 8}\}$.
2. $\{(x, y) \mid 2x + 1 = y; \ x \text{ is an integer between 2 and 5}\}$.
3. $\{(x, y) \mid 2x - y = 4; \ x \text{ is a counting number between 1 and 7}\}$.
4. $\{(x, y) \mid x + y^2 = 6; \ x = 2\}$.
5. $\{(x, y) \mid y^2 = x; \ x = 0, 1, 4, 9, \text{ or } 16\}$.
6. $\{(x, y) \mid x = y^2; \ y = -3, -2, 0, 1, 3\}$.
7. $\{(x, y) \mid x \leq 2y; \ x = 1, 2, \text{ or } 3; \ y = 0, 1, \text{ or } 2\}$.
8. $\{(x, y) \mid 2x + 1 \geq y; \ x = 0, 1, 2, 3; \ y = -1, 3, 5\}$.
9. $\{(x, y) \mid y - x \geq 2; \ x = -1, 0, 1; \ y = -1, 3, 5\}$.
10. $\{(x, y) \mid x = 3; \ y = -1, 0, 4, 7\}$.
11. $\{(x, y) \mid y = -3; \ x = -4, -3, 0, 1, 6\}$.

Which of the following relations are equivalence relations? If a given relation is an equivalence relation, give examples to show that each requirement is satisfied; if a relation is not an equivalence relation, give examples to show why it is not.

12. Consider the set $\{1, 2, 3, \ldots, 9999\}$ and the relation R defined as follows: $(x, y) \in R$ if x and y contain the same number of digits. For example, $(3, 9) \in R$ since each is a one-digit number. Similarly, $(56, 31)$ and $(1234, 5678)$ are elements of R.

13. Consider the set of all people and the relation R defined by: $(x, y) \in R$ if x and y weigh the same.

14. Consider the set of all people and the relation R defined by: $(x, y) \in R$ if x and y are not the same weight.

15. Consider the set of all people and the relation R defined by: $(x, y) \in R$ if x and y weigh within two pounds of each other.

16. Consider the set of all people and the relation R defined by: $(x, y) \in R$ if both x and y have the same parents.

17. Consider the set of counting numbers and the relation R defined by: $(x, y) \in R$ in case x and y leave the same remainder when divided by 5.

18. Consider the set of all boys and the relation R defined by: $(x, y) \in R$ in case x is the brother of y.

19. Look at the graph of figure 6.5. A vertical line has been drawn, cutting the graph at more than one point. The fact that the line cuts the graph at more than one point means the graph does not represent a function. Why?

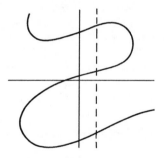

Figure 6.5

20. Problem 18 shows that a relation can be symmetric and transitive but not reflexive. Thus something must be wrong with the following "demonstration" that a relation which is symmetric and transitive, is also reflexive. Point out the flaw in the argument.

    Let R be a relation, which we can assume is symmetric and transitive; show R is also reflexive. Because R is symmetric, $(r, s) \in R$ implies $(s, r) \in R$. However, since R is transitive, (r, s) and (s, r) in R imply $(r, r) \in R$. Thus R is also reflexive.

SECTION 2. LINEAR RELATIONS

A relation such as

$$\{(x, y) \mid 2x + y = 4\},$$

which contains no squared or higher powers and no products such as xy, is called a *linear relation*. This relation defines a certain set of ordered pairs,

(x, y), where the y value may be obtained from the x value by the rule, $2x + y = 4$. For example, $(0, 4)$ belongs to this set of ordered pairs since $2(0) + 4 = 4$. Also $(-3, 10)$ belongs to this relation since $2(-3) + 10 = 4$. For each number we select for the x value, we can always find the corresponding y value. Hence the relation is an infinite set of ordered pairs. (If no domain is specified we assume it to be the set of real numbers.) Let's see how we can draw the graph of this relation.

To begin, we select a few x values and find the corresponding y values. For example,

$$\text{if } x = 3, \text{ then } 2(3) + y = 4, \text{ or } y = -2$$
$$\text{if } x = 2, \text{ then } 2(2) + y = 4, \text{ or } y = 0$$
$$\text{if } x = -1, \text{ then } 2(-1) + y = 4, \text{ or } y = 6.$$

The ordered pairs $(0, 4)$, $(3, -2)$, $(2, 0)$, $(-1, 6)$, and many others, belong to the relation. These points are plotted in figure 6.6. Note the pattern that results. A straight line can be drawn through all the points plotted on the graph. Select any other x value and find the corresponding y value. The point determined by the resulting ordered pair will lie on the same straight line. It can be proven (see the book by Taylor and Wade mentioned at the end of the chapter) that any linear relation has a graph which is a straight line.

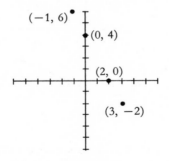

Figure 6.6

Example 6.6.   Draw the graph of the straight line which results from

$$\{(x, y) \mid 4x - 5y = 20\}.$$

Since this is a linear relation, its graph is a straight line. Two points completely determine a straight line; hence two points would suffice to locate the graph. However, it is often best to plot three points of the graph, the third point acting as a check. Any three values of x may be chosen, and the corresponding y values found. Some x values are often simpler to work with than others; here for example, it is perhaps easiest to let $x = 0$, $x = 5$, and $x = 2\frac{1}{2}$. We can then find the corresponding y values:

$$\text{if } x = 0, \text{ then } 4(0) - 5y = 20, \text{ and } y = -4,$$

if $x = 5$, then $4(5) - 5y = 20$, and $y = 0$,
if $x = 2\frac{1}{2}$, then $4(2\frac{1}{2}) - 5y = 20$, and $y = -2$.

These values give the ordered pairs $(0, -4)$, $(5, 0)$, and $(2\frac{1}{2}, -2)$ which are plotted in figure 6.7. The line which has been drawn through the resulting points is the graph of $\{(x, y) \mid 4x - 5y = 20\}$.

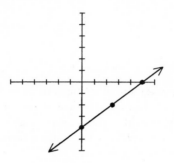

Figure 6.7

Example 6.7.   Draw the graph of the linear relation

$$\{(x, y) \mid y = 3\}.$$

As in the previous example, select three values of x and find the corresponding y values. But note: no matter which x values are picked the y value is always the same, that is, $y = 3$. Hence we have ordered pairs such as $(7, 3)$, $(-3, 3)$, $(4, 3)$, and so on. The graph of these points is a horizontal line, as shown in figure 6.8. Any relation such as $\{(x, y) \mid y = k, k$ a real number$\}$ has a graph which is a horizontal line.

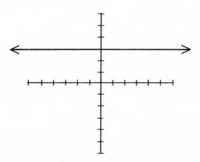

Figure 6.8

In the same way, it can be shown that the graph of the relation

$$\{(x, y) \mid x = k, k \text{ is a real number}\}$$

is a vertical line.

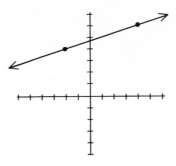

Figure 6.9

An important characteristic of a line is its *slope*. Figure 6.9 shows a line containing the points $(-2, 4)$ and $(4, 6)$; the slope of this line is the difference of the y values divided by the difference of the x values, or $(4-6)/(-2-4)=(-2)/(-6) = 1/3$. In general, if a line passes through points (x_1, y_1) and (x_2, y_2), the slope of the line is given by

$$\frac{y_2 - y_1}{x_2 - x_1}.$$

Think of the slope as being a vertical change divided by a horizontal change; it is a measure of the steepness of a line.

Example 6.8.   What is the slope of the line passing through the points $(4, 4)$ and $(11, 11)$?

Assume that $(4, 4)$ is (x_1, y_1) so that the slope is:

$$\frac{y_2 - y_1}{x_2 - x_1} = \frac{11 - 4}{11 - 4} = \frac{7}{7} = 1.$$

Example 6.9.   What is the slope of the line:

$$\{(x, y) \mid 2x - y = 5\}?$$

To find the slope we need two points that lie on the line. Hence we select two x values and find the corresponding y values. Verify that $(0, -5)$ and $(5, 5)$ are two points of the line; the slope then is:

$$\frac{5 - (-5)}{5 - 0} = \frac{10}{5} = 2.$$

Example 6.10.   Find the slope of the horizontal line:

$$\{(x, y) \mid y = 2\}.$$

Find two ordered pairs, such as $(3, 2)$ and $(5, 2)$, which belong to the relation. The slope is given by

$$\frac{2 - 2}{5 - 3} = \frac{0}{2} = 0.$$

Every horizontal line has a slope of zero.

Example 6.11.   Find the slope of the vertical line:

$$\{(x, y) \mid x = -3\}.$$

We find two ordered pairs that belong to the relation: $(-3, 5)$ and $(-3, 8)$. The slope is given by the quotient $\frac{3}{0}$, which is not a number since division by zero is impossible. Hence a vertical line has no slope. The slope of a horizontal line is the number zero; a vertical line has no slope.

PROBLEMS

Draw the graphs of the following linear relations.

1. $\{(x, y) \mid x + y = 4\}$
2. $\{(x, y) \mid 2x - y = -3\}$
3. $\{(x, y) \mid 2x = y + 4\}$
4. $\{(x, y) \mid 4 - y = \frac{1}{2}x\}$
5. $\{(x, y) \mid y = 0\}$
6. $\{(x, y) \mid x = -2\}$

7. $\{(x, y) \mid x - y = 3\}$
8. $\{(x, y) \mid 4x - 2y = 5\}$
9. $\{(x, y) \mid y = 3x - 1\}$
10. $\{(x, y) \mid 2y = \frac{1}{2}x - 3\}$
11. $\{(x, y) \mid x = 4\}$
12. $\{(x, y) \mid 2x = 6\}$

Find the slope of each of the following lines.

13. $\{(x, y) \mid x + 4 = y\}$
14. $\{(x, y) \mid 2x - y = 7\}$
15. $\{(x, y) \mid 2y = 4x\}$
16. $\{(x, y) \mid 4y = 2x + 1\}$

17. $\{(x, y) \mid y - x = 6\}$
18. $\{(x, y) \mid y - 3x = 8\}$
19. $\{(x, y) \mid y = 5\}$
20. $\{(x, y) \mid 2y = 6\}$

Each of the problems below consists of two relations. For each problem graph both lines on the same set of axes, and find the point (if any) where they cross.

21. $\{(x, y) \mid x + y = 3\}, \{(x, y) \mid x - y = 3\}$
22. $\{(x, y) \mid 2x - y = 6\}, \{(x, y) \mid 2x + y = 6\}$
23. $\{(x, y) \mid 2x + y = 8\}, \{(x, y) \mid 2x = -5 - y\}$
24. $\{(x, y) \mid 2x - y = -1\}, \{(x, y) \mid x + 2y = 17\}$
25. $\{(x, y) \mid x + y = 3\}, \{(x, y) \mid 3y + 2x = 10\}$
26. $\{(x, y) \mid 2x + 3y = -5\}, \{(x, y) \mid 3x - y = 9\}$

27. Find the slope of each line in figure 6.10. (Hint: locate two points the lines pass through.)

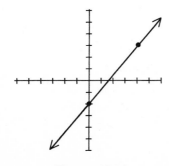

Figure 6.10A

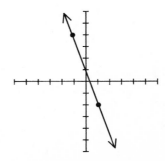

Figure 6.10B

28. Graph the lines having the following slope and going through the point listed:

(a) $(6, 2)$ slope 0.   (d) $(-1, 5)$ slope $\frac{3}{2}$.

(b) $(-1, 5)$ no slope.   (e) $(2, 0)$ slope $-\frac{4}{3}$.

(c) $(3, -4)$ slope 1.

SECTION 3. LINEAR INEQUALITIES

A line divides a plane into three parts: the line itself and two *half-planes*, one on either side of the line. In figure 6.11, the line divides the plane into half-planes A and B, and the line itself. Note: the line belongs to neither half-plane and the half-planes are disjoint; that is, they have no points in common. The idea of a half-plane is useful in graphing linear inequalities.

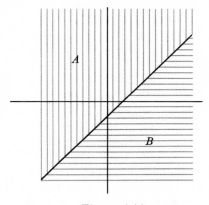

Figure 6.11

A *linear inequality* is a relation such as

$$\{(x, y) \mid 2x - y \leq 4\}.$$

We already know how to graph the straight line $\{(x, y) \mid 2x - y = 4\}$; its graph is shown in figure 6.12. However, in this relation we are also dealing with an inequality, and we must determine the set of ordered pairs which

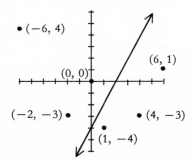

Figure 6.12

satisfy the inequality. Figure 6.12 shows our straight line plus six selected points, three on each side of the line. By inspection, we see that $(-6, 4)$, $(-2, -3)$, and $(0, 0)$ satisfy the inequality, while the other three points do not.

Since the three ordered pairs which satisfy the relation all lie in the same half-plane, we try other points in this half-plane. For example, if we try $(-8, -2)$ and $(-3, 2)$, we find that both satisfy the inequality and belong to the relation; in fact all the points of this same half-plane belong to the relation, as shown in the graph of figure 6.13.

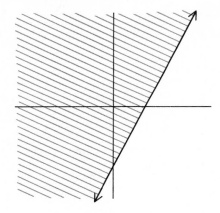

Figure 6.13

Example 6.12   Draw the graph of the linear inequality

$$\{(x, y) \mid 2x - y < 4\}.$$

The only difference between this relation and the previous one is that here the points of the straight line are not included; a common way to indicate this is to have the line dotted, as in figure 6.14.

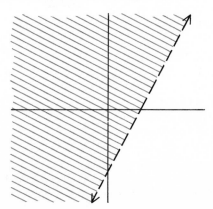

Figure 6.14

Example 6.13   Draw the graph of the linear inequality

$$\{(x,y) \mid 4x - 2y \geq 5\}.$$

As before, we first draw the graph of the line determined by the relation

$$\{(x,y) \mid 4x - 2y = 5\}.$$

We know from the work above that we need one of the half-planes determined by the line. To determine which half-plane is needed, select any point not on the line and see if it belongs to the original relation. Often, a good choice is the point $(0, 0)$. Does $(0, 0)$ satisfy the inequality? In other words, can we say $4(0) - 2(0) \geq 5$? Since the answer is no, the half-plane containing $(0, 0)$ is not the one we want. The half-plane we need has been shaded in figure 6.15.

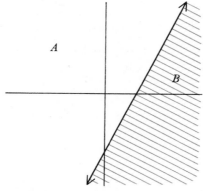

Figure 6.15

PROBLEMS

Draw the graphs of each of the following linear inequalities.

1. $\{(x,y) \mid 2x - y \geq 4\}$.   5. $\{(x,y) \mid 3x + y \leq 2\}$.
2. $\{(x,y) \mid x \leq 5\}$.   6. $\{(x,y) \mid y \geq -3\}$.
3. $\{(x,y) \mid x - y \geq 6\}$.   7. $\{(x,y) \mid y - 3x < -1\}$.
4. $\{(x,y) \mid 2x + 3y \geq 6\}$.   8. $\{(x,y) \mid x - 2y \geq -5\}$.

In problems 9–14, shade the intersection of the relations listed.

9. $\{(x,y) \mid 2x - 2y \geq 5\}\{(x,y) \mid x + y \leq 4\}$.
10. $\{(x,y) \mid 3x - 2y < 6\}\{(x,y) \mid 3x - y = 4\}$.
11. $\{(x,y) \mid x = 5\}\{(x,y) \mid y < 4\}$.
12. $\{(x,y) \mid x + y > 6\}\{(x,y) \mid 2x - y < 4\}$.
13. $\{(x,y) \mid x \geq 0\}\{(x,y) \mid y \geq 0\}\{(x,y) \mid x + 2y = 4\}$.
14. $\{(x,y) \mid x \geq 0\}\{(x,y) \mid y \geq 0\}\{(x,y) \mid x + 2y \leq 4\}$.

Draw a square in the plane. Select any two points inside the square. Label one point A and the other point B. Draw line segment AB. Is all of AB inside the square? Are there any possible circumstances that could make part of AB lie outside the square? Repeat the same thing with a circle, a triangle, and figure 6.16. A figure is said to be *convex* if, for any two points A and B inside the figure, the line segment AB is always completely inside the figure. A square, circle, and triangle are convex; figure 6.16 is not. A convex figure, together with the points of its interior, is often called a *convex set.*

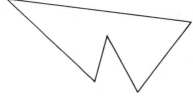

Figure 6.16

15. Draw three different convex figures.
16. Draw three different non-convex figures.
17. Is the intersection of two convex sets always convex?
18. Is the union of two convex sets always convex?

SECTION 4. LINEAR PROGRAMMING

The Smith Manufacturing and Distributing Company makes two products, potrezebies and zotyls. Each potrezebie yields a profit of $3, while each zotyl earns $7. The company must manufacture at least one potrezebie per day (Mr. Smith's son is in charge of packaging and must be given some work to do), but no more than five (Junior does not want to pack too many potrezebies). Production problems limit the number of zotyls to six per day (Mrs. Smith, who runs the zotyl stuffer, likes to quit early). As a further complication, the number of potrezebies cannot exceed the number of zotyls. How many of each should the company manufacture in order to obtain the maximum profit?

This problem is an example of a large group of problems which may be solved by the methods of *linear programming.* The mathematician G. B. Dantzig developed linear programming in 1947 to aid in solving problems of allocating supplies for the Air Force. Today linear programming is used extensively in business and social science. The problems we solve in this section give only a hint of the many uses to which linear programming may be directed.

Let's return to the problem of the Smith Company. To begin, we translate the statements of the problem into symbols. To do this, assume

x = number of potrezebies to be produced per day
y = number of zotyls to be produced per day.

The company must produce at least one potrezebie,

$$x \geq 1,$$

but no more than five:

$$x \leq 5.$$

No more than six zotyls may be made in one day:

$$y \le 6.$$

The number of potrezebies may not exceed the number of zotyls:

$$x \le y.$$

The number of potrezebies and zotyls produced cannot be negative:

$$x \ge 0, \quad y \ge 0.$$

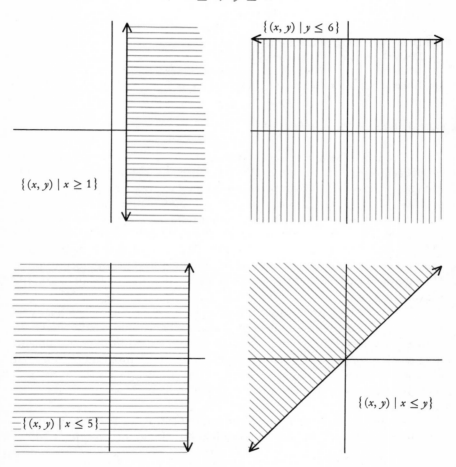

Figure 6.17

Let's now consider the restrictions, or *constraints*, placed on production:

$$x \ge 1, \quad y \le 6, \quad x \le 5, \quad x \le y, \quad x \ge 0, \quad y \ge 0.$$

To determine the maximum profit subject to these constraints, first sketch the graph of each constraint. The graphs of four of the constraints are shown in figure 6.17. The only feasible values of x and y are those that satisfy all constraints; that is, the values which lie inside the intersection of the graphs of the constraints, as shown in figure 6.18. Any point lying inside the shaded area of figure 6.18 satisfies the restrictions as to the number of potrezebies and zotyls that may be produced.

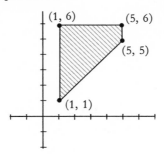

Figure 6.18

Since each potrezebie yields a profit of $3, the daily profit is $3x$ dollars. Similarly, the profit from zotyls will be $7y$ dollars per day, with the total profit given by

$$3x + 7y.$$

The problem may now be stated thus: find x and y from the shaded region of figure 6.18 that will produce the maximum possible value of $3x + 7y$. A basic theorem of linear programming states that in a case such as ours the maximum profit will be obtained at a corner of the graph. By referring to figure 6.18, we see that the corner points are $(1, 1)$, $(1, 6)$, $(5, 5)$, and $(5, 6)$. We now check these corner points to determine the profit produced at each:

Point	Profit
$(1, 1)$	$3(1) + 7(1) = 10$
$(1, 6)$	$3(1) + 7(6) = 45$
$(5, 5)$	$3(5) + 7(5) = 50$
$(5, 6)$	$3(5) + 7(6) = 57$

Hence the maximum profit of $57 per day will be obtained if five potrezebies and six zotyls are manufactured each day.

Example 6.14.   George, who is ill, takes vitamin pills. Each day he must have at least 16 units of vitamin A, 5 units of vitamin B, and 20 units of vitamin C. He can choose between pill #1 which costs 10 cents and contains 8 units of A, 1 of B, and 2 of C, and pill #2 which costs 20 cents and contains 2 units of A, 1 of B, and 7 of C. How many of each pill should he buy in order to minimize his cost?

Let: x = number of pill #1 to buy.
        y = number of pill #2 to buy.

The cost in pennies per day is given by:

$$10x + 20y$$

since George buys x 10¢ pills and y 20¢ pills. George gets his vitamin A supply as follows: 8 units from pill #1 and 2 units from pill #2. Altogether, he receives $8x + 2y$ units of vitamin A per day. Since he must get at least 16 units we may write:

$$8x + 2y \geq 16.$$

Pill #1 and pill #2 each supply 1 unit of vitamin B. George needs at least 5 units per day, which means:

$$x + y \geq 5.$$

We obtain a similar inequality for vitamin C:

$$2x + 7y \geq 20.$$

Note also that:

$$x \geq 0, \text{ and } y \geq 0,$$

since George cannot buy negative quantities of his pills.

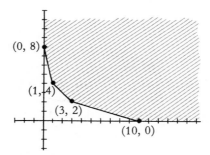

Figure 6.19

Again to minimize the total cost of the pills we need the intersection of the graphs of the constraints, as shown in figure 6.19. We check the corners to find the lowest cost. (The coordinates of the corners can be obtained, in many cases, by inspection of carefully drawn graphs. Various algebraic techniques are available for use when the graphs do not cross in "nice" places. One such method is described in Chapter 9.)

Point	Cost
$(10, 0)$	$10(10) + 20(0) = 100$
$(3, 2)$	$10(3) + 20(2) = 70$
$(1, 4)$	$10(1) + 20(4) = 90$
$(0, 8)$	$10(0) + 20(8) = 160.$

Hence George's best bet is to buy 3 of pill #1 and 2 of pill #2 each day, bringing the total cost to 70¢ per day. He receives the minimum amounts of vitamins B and C, but an excess of vitamin A. Even though he has an excess of vitamin A, this is still his best buy.

PROBLEMS

1. Find the minimum value of the expression, $x + 3y$, subject to the constraints:

$$x + 2y \geq 12,$$
$$x \geq 6,$$
$$y \geq 0.$$

2. Find the minimum value of $3x - 2y$, subject to the restrictions:

$$x + y \geq 1,$$
$$x - y \geq -1,$$
$$x + 2y \leq 4,$$
$$y \geq 0.$$

3. Farmer Jones raises only pigs and geese. He wants to raise no more than 16 animals with no more than 12 geese. He spends $5 to raise a pig and $2 to raise a goose. He has available $50 for this purpose. Find the maximum profit he can make, if he makes a profit of $8 per goose and $4 per pig.

4. A wholesaler of party goods wishes to display his products at a convention of party goods buyers in such a manner that he gets the maximum number of inquiries about his potrezebies and zotyls. His booth at the convention has 12 square feet of floor space which may be used for display purposes. A display unit for zotyls requires 2 square feet, and for potrezebies 4 square feet. Experience has told the wholesaler that he should never have more than a total of five units of potrezebies and zotyls on display at one time. If he receives three inquiries for each unit of zotyls and two inquiries for each unit of potrezebies on display, how many of each should be displayed in order to get the maximum number of inquiries?

5. An office manager is considering the purchase of filing cabinets. He knows that cabinet #1 costs $10 each, requires 6 square feet of floor space, and holds 8 cubic feet of files. On the other hand, each cabinet #2 costs $20, requires 8 square feet of floor space, and holds 12 cubic feet. He can spend no more than $140 due to budgetary limitations, while his office has room for no more than 72 square feet of cabinets. Cabinets may not be stacked on top of each other. He desires the maximum storage capacity within the limitations imposed by funds and space. How many of each type should he buy?

6. The local Boy Scouts decide to go into business in order to earn money to buy "able-to-leap-tall-buildings-at-a-single-bound" He-man pills. They decide to manufacture "Smokey the Bear" ashtrays and "Susan Spotless" cuff links. They have two machines that may be used for this purpose, a drill and a saw. Each ashtray needs one minute on the drill and two minutes on the saw; each cuff link set needs two minutes on the drill and one minute on the saw. The drill is available at most for 12 minutes per day, and the saw is available no more than 15 minutes per day. Each

product provides a profit of $1. How many of each should they manufacture in order to maximize profit?

7. Work problem 6 if the profit per ashtray is $2, with the profit per cuff link set $1.

SECTION 5. THE DISTANCE FORMULA

As we have studied, linear equalities have graphs that are straight lines; let's consider some equalities that are non-linear. But before we can discuss these more complicated relations, we need a formula for calculating the distance between two points.

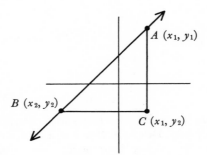

Figure 6.20

The Distance Formula. The distance between the point (x_1, y_1) and (x_2, y_2) is given by:

$$\sqrt{(x_1 - x_2)^2 + (y_1 - y_2)^2}.$$

Figure 6.20 shows a right triangle ABC; the length of AC is $y_1 - y_2$ and the length of BC is $x_1 - x_2$. According to the Pythagorean theorem, therefore, the length of AB is:

$$\sqrt{(x_1 - x_2)^2 + (y_1 - y_2)^2},$$

which is what we wanted to prove.

Example 6.15.   Find the distance between the points $(3, -5)$ and $(-1, 2)$.

Using the distance formula we have:

$$\sqrt{[3 - (-1)]^2 + [-5 - (-2)]^2},$$

or $\sqrt{4^2 + -3^2} = \sqrt{16 + 9} = \sqrt{25} = 5.$

The points $(3, -5)$ and $(-1, -2)$ are 5 units apart.

Example 6.16.   Find the distance between the points $(-1, 7)$ and $(1, 5)$.

Using the distance formula again, we find:

$$\sqrt{(-1-1)^2 + (7-5)^2},$$

or

$$\sqrt{(-2)^2 + 2^2} = \sqrt{4+4} = \sqrt{8}.$$

PROBLEMS

In each problem below, find the distance between the points listed.

1. $(3, 2), (-1, -1)$ 4. $(-2, 13), (-3, 1)$
2. $(6, 1), (3, -3)$ 5. $(1, 1), (2, 1)$
3. $(3, 2), (1, 7)$ 6. $(4, 3), (7, -12)$

7. Use the distance formula to prove that the points $(1, 3)$, $(5, 6)$, and $(9, 9)$ all lie on the same line. (Hint: The sum of two sides of a triangle is always greater than the third side. Assume that the three points are not on the same line and that they are the vertices of a triangle.)

SECTION 6. CONIC SECTIONS

Now let us consider the circle shown in figure 6.21 with center at the origin and radius equal to 5. The point (x, y) has been labeled in figure 6.21 and represents the coordinates of a point lying on the circle. Our object is to

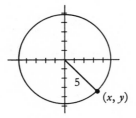

Figure 6.21

find the relation that identifies all such points (x, y) on the circle. We can determine this relation by first finding the distance between (x, y) and the center, $(0, 0)$, using the distance formula:

$$\sqrt{(x-0)^2 + (y-0)^2} = \sqrt{x^2 + y^2}.$$

Since this distance is equal to the radius 5, we have:

$$5 = \sqrt{x^2 + y^2},$$

or, upon squaring both sides,

$$25 = x^2 + y^2.$$

Therefore our circle is identified by the relation

$$\{(x,y) \mid x^2 + y^2 = 25\}.$$

Any ordered pair which belongs to this relation lies on the circle, and any point on the circle belongs to the relation.

Example 6.17.   Draw the graph of the relation

$$\{(x,y) \mid x^2 + y^2 = 81\}.$$

As above, this relation represents a circle with center at the origin and radius $\sqrt{81}$, or 9.

Example 6.18.   Sketch the graph of the relation

$$\{(x,y) \mid x^2 + y^2 \leq 36\}.$$

A circle divides a plane into three disjoint parts: the circle itself, the interior of the circle, and the exterior. We might guess that this relation represents the circle itself, together with either the interior or the exterior of the circle. To decide which, select a point, such as $(0, 0)$, that is not on the circle. Since $0^2 + 0^2 \leq 36$, the point $(0, 0)$ belongs to the relation; the relation represents the circle together with its interior, as shown in figure 6.22.

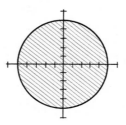

Figure 6.22

Example 6.19.   Find the intersection of the relations

$$\{(x,y) \mid x^2 + y^2 \leq 49\} \text{ and } \{(x,y) \mid x^2 + y^2 \geq 9\}.$$

The first relation is a circle with center at the origin and radius 7, together with the interior of the circle. The second relation is a circle with center at the origin and radius 3, together with all points in the exterior of the circle. The intersection of these two graphs, as shown in figure 6.23, is a ring or doughnut.

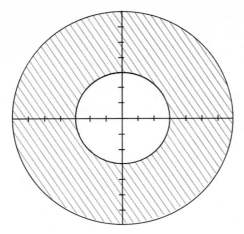

Figure 6.23

Another common graph which is not a straight line is the *parabola*. A parabola is the set of points in a plane that are equally distant from a given line and a given point not on the given line. In figure 6.24, AB is the given line while P is the given point. Note that every point of the parabola is equally distant from point P and line AB (recall that the distance from a point to a line is measured on the perpendicular from the point to the line).

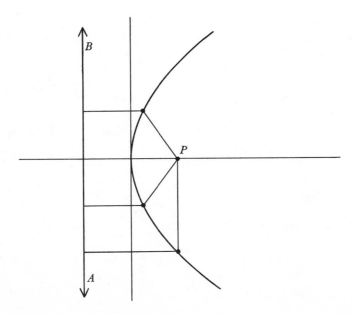

Figure 6.24

It is possible to use the distance formula, as we did for the circle, to obtain the equation of a parabola, but the details of such an approach are unnecessarily complicated for this course. The derivation of the equation of a parabola, together with proofs of all equations mentioned in this section, is given in the book by Taylor and Wade listed at the end of the chapter. It is sufficient to say that the parabola of figure 6.24 can be expressed as

$$\{(x, y) \mid y^2 = 16x\},$$

while the parabola of figure 6.25 can be expressed as

$$\{(x, y) \mid y = x^2\}.$$

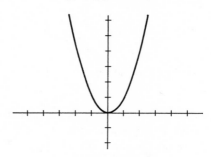

Figure 6.25

Example 6.20.   Draw the graph of the relation

$$\{(x, y) \mid x = -4y^2\}.$$

The relation is a parabola since one variable is squared and one is not. Since the equation represents a parabola we know the basic shape of the graph; all we need do is plot a few points to see how it is situated. Note first that no x value can be positive (why?). If $x = 0$, then $y = 0$; thus the point $(0, 0)$ belongs to the relation. If $x = -4$, then $y = 1$ or $y = -1$. Thus $(-4, 1)$ and $(-4, -1)$ lie on the graph. These three points, together with our knowledge of the basic shape of parabolas, enable us to sketch the graph of our relation (see figure 6.26).

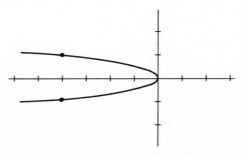

Figure 6.26

The parabola is a very useful curve. For example, a vertical cross section of a spotlight forms a parabola. An object thrown into the air will approximately follow a parabolic path.

In figure 6.27 we have selected two points, $(4, 0)$ and $(-4, 0)$; an *ellipse*, in this case, is the set of all points whose distances from these two points $(4, 0)$ and $(-4, 0)$ add up to a fixed number, such as 10. In figure 6.27, we

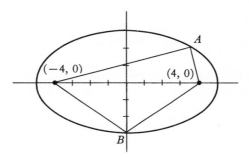

Figure 6.27

can say that the distance from A to $(4, 0)$, plus the distance from A to $(-4, 0)$, is 10; the distance from B to $(4, 0)$ plus the distance from B to $(-4, 0)$ is 10, and so on. If a string of length 10 were placed with one end fixed at $(4, 0)$ and one end fixed at $(-4, 0)$, and if a pencil were held taut inside the string, an ellipse could be traced on the paper. Again, the distance formula may be used to determine the equation of an ellipse, and again the algebraic manipulations are unnecessarily complicated. Therefore, we will only state that the ellipse of figure 6.27 is given by

$$\{(x, y) \mid 9x^2 + 25y^2 = 225\}.$$

Note the characteristics of the relation: both x and y appear squared, but the coefficients of the x^2 and the y^2 terms are different.

Example 6.21. Sketch the graph of the relation

$$\{(x, y) \mid 16x^2 + 9y^2 = 144\}.$$

We know that this relation is an ellipse; after locating a few points that lie on the ellipse we are able to complete the graph. If $x = 0$, then $16(0)^2 + 9y^2 = 144$, and thus $y = 4$ or $y = -4$. Hence $(0, 4)$ and $(0, -4)$ are on the ellipse. Similarly, if $y = 0$ we find that $(3, 0)$ and $(-3, 0)$ lie on the ellipse. In figure 6.28 we plotted these four points and completed the ellipse.

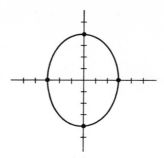

Figure 6.28

Arches are often shaped as half-ellipses; the path of the earth around the sun is an ellipse with the sun as one of the two special points mentioned above.

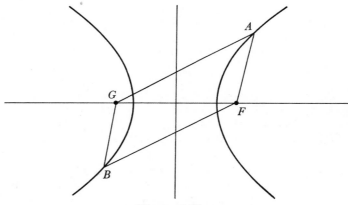

Figure 6.29

The last curve we shall discuss is called a *hyperbola*, which is the set of points in the plane the differences of whose distance from two fixed points is constant. For example, figure 6.29 shows two fixed points, F and G. The distance from A to G, minus the distance from A to F, is the same as the difference between the distance from B to F and the distance from B to G. Typically, the equation of a hyperbola has both variables squared with the coefficients having different signs. (In the problem set we discuss a slightly different type of equation for a hyperbola.)

Example 6.22.   Sketch the graph of the hyperbola

$$\{(x, y) \mid x^2 - y^2 = 16\}.$$

We know the basic shape and must find only a few points of the graph. We cannot have $x = 0$ (why?), but we can let $y = 0$. If $y = 0$, then $x = 4$ or

$x = -4$, which means the points $(4, 0)$ and $(-4, 0)$ belong to the graph. Let $x = 5$, then $5^2 - y^2 = 16$, and $y = 3$ or $y = -3$. Hence the points $(5, 3)$ and $(5, -3)$ belong to the graph. If $x = -5$, we see that $(-5, 3)$ and $(-5, -3)$ belong to the graph, which has been sketched in figure 6.30.

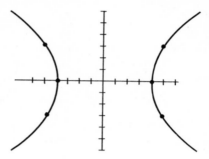

Figure 6.30

Example 6.23.   Sketch the graph of the hyperbola

$$\{(x, y) \mid y^2 - x^2 = 25\}.$$

Here we cannot have $y = 0$. If $x = 0$, then $y = 5$ or $y = -5$; thus $(0, 5)$ and $(0, -5)$ belong to the graph. If $y = 6$, then $x = \sqrt{11}$ or $x = -\sqrt{11}$. As an approximation, $\sqrt{11} = 3.3$, so that $(3.3, 6)$ and $(-3.3, 6)$ belong to the graph, as shown in figure 6.31.

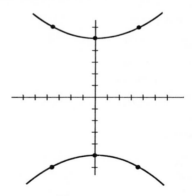

Figure 6.31

We have discussed the circle, ellipse, parabola, and hyperbola. At first glance these graphs seem to have little in common, yet they all may be obtained by cutting a cone with a plane. Look at the cones of figure 6.32. (A cone really has two parts; an ice cream cone is only half a cone.) If a horizontal plane is passed through the cone a circle results, while if the plane is tilted slightly, an ellipse results. If a plane passes through the cone in such a

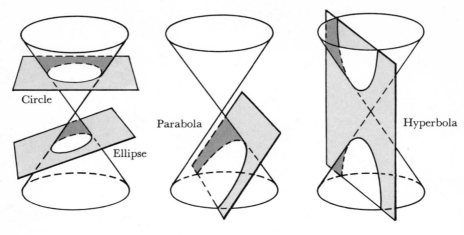

Figure 6.32

way that the plane is parallel to an edge of the cone, a parabola is formed. If a plane cuts both the top and bottom parts of a cone a hyperbola is obtained.

These four *conic sections* may be demonstrated in an average living room using a table lamp with a cylindrical shade. When the light is on, a cone of light is emitted. If both parts of this cone of light (top and bottom) hit the wall a hyperbola will be formed on the wall. If the lamp is tilted so that an edge of the cone of light is parallel to the wall a parabola will be formed. Ellipses and circles may also be formed by the cone of light. This demonstration is always a big hit at parties.

PROBLEMS

Sketch a graph of each of the following relations. Identify each one as either a circle, ellipse, hyperbola, or parabola.

1. $\{(x,y) \mid x = 2y^2\}$.
2. $\{(x,y) \mid 9x^2 + 4y^2 = 36\}$.
3. $\{(x,y) \mid x^2 - y^2 = 36\}$.
4. $\{(x,y) \mid x^2 + y^2 = 36\}$.
5. $\{(x,y) \mid 2x^2 + 2y^2 = 18\}$.
6. $\{(x,y) \mid x = -4y^2\}$.
7. $\{(x,y) \mid x^2 + 2y^2 = 32\}$ Hint: $\sqrt{32}$ is about 5.7, as shown in the appendix.
8. $\{(x,y) \mid 4x^2 + 9y^2 = 36\}$.

Find the intersection of each of the following pairs of relations.

9. $\{(x,y) \mid x^2 + y^2 \le 36\}$, $\{(x,y) \mid 9x^2 + 4y^2 \ge 36\}$.
10. $\{(x,y) \mid x^2 - y^2 \le 8\}$, $\{(x,y) \mid y \ge 4x^2\}$.
11. Consider the relation $\{(x,y) \mid xy = 1\}$. This relation is a hyperbola, but with a different type of equation than that discussed in the text. Complete these ordered pairs,

whenever possible: (0,), (1,), (−1,), (2,), (−2,), (3,), (−3,), ($\frac{1}{2}$,), (−$\frac{1}{2}$,), (, 0). Plot these points and complete the graph.

12. Use the distance formula to calculate the equation of the circle with center at the point $(3, 5)$ and radius 5.

13. Use the distance formula to calculate the equation of the circle with center at $(−5, −2)$ and radius 2.

14. Use the distance formula to calculate the equation of the circle with center at $(−2, 5)$ and radius 3.

15. Use the distance formula to find the equation of the circle with center at (h, k) and radius r.

16. Show how a cone can be cut by a plane in exactly one point. Because of this, a point is sometimes called a *degenerate circle*, or *degenerate ellipse*. Show how a straight line can be called a *degenerate parabola*, while two straight lines, which intersect in one point, can be called a *degenerate hyperbola*. (The theory of degenerates is fascinating, but perhaps too advanced for this course.)

SECTION 7. THREE-DIMENSIONAL ANALYTIC GEOMETRY

Our work in the two dimensions of the plane (called *2-space*) can be extended to three dimensions of space (called *3-space*). Just as 2-space coordinate systems require two perpendicular lines, a 3-space system needs three lines, each perpendicular to the other two, as shown in figure 6.33. Our 2-space coordinate systems have x and y axes; a 3-space system has x, y, and z axes. Ordered pairs (x, y) become *ordered triples* (x, y, z), with points in 3-space located as shown in figure 6.33.

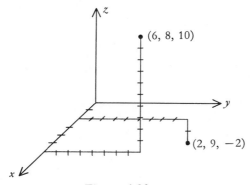

Figure 6.33

Lines such as

$$\{(x, y) \mid ax + by = c\}$$

divide 2-space into two half-planes; similarly

$$\{(x, y, z) \mid ax + by + cz = d\}$$

is a plane, dividing 3-space.

Example 6.24.   Draw the graph of the plane

$$\{(x, y, z) \mid x + y + z = 1\}.$$

Two points are enough to completely determine a line, but three points are needed for a plane. Here, we select any values we like for x and y, and then find the corresponding z values. For example, if $x = 0$ and $y = 0$ we have $z = 1$, so that $(0, 0, 1)$ belongs to the plane. In the same way, the plane contains the points $(0, 1, 0)$ and $(1, 0, 0)$. The graph of part of the plane is shown in figure 6.34.

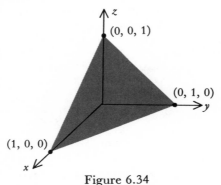

Figure 6.34

Example 6.25.   Draw a graph of the plane

$$\{(x, y, z) \mid y = 6\}.$$

Here x and z can take on any value, but y is fixed at 6. The resulting plane is shown in figure 6.35.

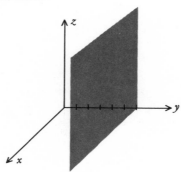

Figure 6.35

If (x_1, y_1, z_1) and (x_2, y_2, z_2) are any two points of 3-space, the distance between them is given by:

$$\sqrt{(x_1 - x_2)^2 + (y_1 - y_2)^2 + (z_1 - z_2)^2}.$$

Using this distance formula we can find the equation of the set of all points 5 units from the origin of the coordinate system: it is a sphere of radius 5, given by:

$$\{(x, y, z) \mid x^2 + y^2 + z^2 = 25\}.$$

Other conic sections also have analogues in 3-space, as shown in figure 6.36.

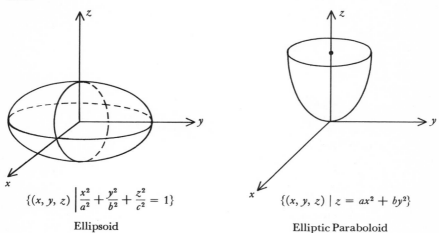

$$\{(x, y, z) \mid \frac{x^2}{a^2} + \frac{y^2}{b^2} + \frac{z^2}{c^2} = 1\}$$

Ellipsoid

$$\{(x, y, z) \mid z = ax^2 + by^2\}$$

Elliptic Paraboloid

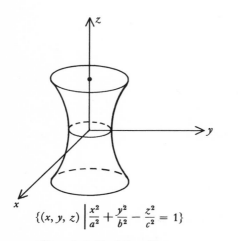
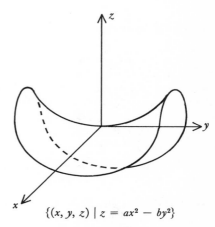

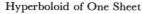
$$\{(x, y, z) \mid \frac{x^2}{a^2} + \frac{y^2}{b^2} - \frac{z^2}{c^2} = 1\}$$

Hyperboloid of One Sheet

$$\{(x, y, z) \mid z = ax^2 - by^2\}$$

Hyperbolic Parabaloid

Figure 6.36

These ideas of 2-space and 3-space can be generalized: *4-space* is the set of all ordered *4-tuples*, (x, y, z, w), and, in general, *n-space* is the set of all ordered *n-tuples* $(x_1, x_2, \ldots, x_n)$. An *n-space hyperplane* is given by:

$$\{(x_1, x_2, \cdots, x_n) \mid a_1 x_1 + a_2 x_2 + \cdots + a_n x_n = b\},$$

while an *n-space hypersphere* with center at the origin and radius r is given by:

$$\{(x_1, x_2, \cdots, x_n) \mid x_1^2 + x_2^2 + \cdots + x_n^2 = r^2\}.$$

The distance between the *n*-space points $(x_1, x_2, \ldots, x_n)$ and $(y_1, y_2, \ldots, y_n)$ is given by:

$$\sqrt{(x_1 - y_1)^2 + (x_2 - y_2)^2 + \cdots + (x_n - y_n)^2}.$$

PROBLEMS

Construct graphs for each of the following
1. $\{(x, y, z) \mid 2x + y + z = 3\}$.
2. $\{(x, y, z) \mid x + y = 4\}$.
3. $\{(x, y, z) \mid x = 3\}$.
4. $\{(x, y, z) \mid y = -4\}$.
5. $\{(x, y, z) \mid x^2 + y^2 = 25\}$.
6. $\{(x, y, z) \mid x^2 + z^2 = 16\}$.
7. $\{(x, y, z) \mid x = y^2 + z^2\}$.
8. $\{(x, y, z) \mid x = y^2 - z^2\}$.
9. $\{(x, y, z) \mid x = y\}$.

FOR FURTHER READING

Campbell, Hugh C. *An Introduction to Matrices, Vectors, and Linear Programming*. New York: Appleton-Century-Crofts, Inc., 1965. This book on linear programming includes a discussion of the "simplex" method of solving more complicated problems.

Leithold, Louis. *Calculus and Analytic Geometry*. New York: Harper and Row, Publishers, Inc., 1968.

Thomas, George B. *Calculus and Analytic Geometry*. Reading, Massachusetts: Addison-Wesley Publishing Company, Inc., 1968.

Calculus books which have "Analytic Geometry" as part of the title, such as the two mentioned above, usually contain a good treatment of the subject.

Taylor, Howard, and Wade, Thomas. *Subsets of the Plane*. New York: John Wiley and Sons, Inc., 1962. This book discusses only analytic geometry.

CHAPTER 7

PROBABILITY

The theory of probability was begun in 1654 with the correspondence between two French mathematicians, Pierre de Fermat (1601–1665) and Blaise Pascal (1623–1662). Their letters discussed a problem which had been posed by the Chevalier de Mére, a gambler and a member of the aristocracy. His question: suppose two people playing a game are forced to quit before the game is finished. How should the pot be divided? Obviously, the player with the greater chance of winning should receive the greater share; Pascal and Fermat formulated the basic methods to determine each player's probability of winning.

Pierre de Fermat was a lawyer and civil servant who studied mathematics as a hobby. He developed analytic geometry independently of Descartes and produced some of the basic ideas of the calculus before Newton. Although he was a co-developer of probability theory, he is perhaps best remembered for his work in the theory of numbers. As an illustration of the type of things he studied, consider the equation

$$x^2 + y^2 = z^2.$$

This equation has integer solutions: for example, $x = 3$, $y = 4$, $z = 5$, or $x = 5$, $y = 12$, $z = 13$. In the margin of one of his books, Fermat wrote that the equation

$$x^n + y^n = z^n$$

has no solution in integers if n is any counting number greater than 2. He also indicated that he had a proof of this fact, but the margin was too small to hold it. Mathematicians since then have been unable to prove or disprove the statement. Did Fermat really have a proof? Some mathematicians say no and offer as evidence the fact that no one has been able to prove the theorem in the three hundred years since Fermat. Others, who say yes, point to the fact that everything Fermat claimed to have proven (except for this one statement) was indeed subsequently proven. The problem is relatively simple to state, and over the years has attracted a countless number of people to attempt proofs. A German professor of mathematics, in 1908, left a prize of 100,000 marks to be awarded to the first person who could solve the problem, but the inflation of the 1920's reduced the value of the prize to a fraction of a cent.

Blaise Pascal was a child prodigy in mathematics, proving some geometrical theorems before ever seeing a geometry book. Before he was sixteen, he had proven what was later to be called Pascal's Theorem (see section 4 of Chapter 11); at sixteen he wrote the *Essay on Conics* which included proofs of over 400 theorems.

He became a firm adherent to the religious sect founded by Cornelius Jansen and published the *Provincial Letters,* an attack on the Jesuits. An interesting reason in support of leading a religious life has come down from Pascal. Expectation is defined as the chance of winning times the amount of winnings, and Pascal rates the eternal happiness of heaven as an infinite winning. He then states that even if the chance that a religious life will lead to heaven is very, very small, the product of this very small chance and an infinite winning is still infinite, and thus it pays to lead a religious life.

Pierre Simon Laplace (1749–1827) completed a great deal of work in probability because he needed it for his masterpiece *Mecanique Celeste,* which appeared in five volumes between 1799 and 1825. In these volumes he attempted to explain the movements of the planets in terms of Newton's theory of gravitation. This book is difficult to comprehend not only because of the nature of the subject matter, but in addition, great gaps in reasoning are simply bridged by the phrase, "thus it is easy to see . . ."; sometimes it took even Laplace several days to reconstruct what supposedly was easy to see. Napoleon is said to have complained because the work contained no mention of God, to which Laplace replied, "Sir, I have no need of that hypothesis." When Napoleon repeated the story to the mathematician Lagrange, he said, "Ah, but that is a fine hypothesis; it explains so many things."

Laplace was an expert at convincing the ruling politicians that he agreed with them: in 1796 a book was dedicated to the Council of Five Hundred; a work in 1802 praised Napoleon, who banished the Council; an 1812 work was dedicated to Napoleon the Great, which was quickly changed in 1814 when Napoleon was out of power (the 1814 book pointed out that an expert in probability could have predicted his downfall). Napoleon had made Laplace a Count; in 1814, Laplace signed a decree banishing his benefactor and was one of the first to fall at the feet of the returning king.

SECTION 1. UNDERSTANDING THE LANGUAGE OF PROBABILITY

People use the rather ordinary words "probability," "random," and "odds" with often only a vague notion of their meaning. Indeed, men who have been most involved in the development of this field have often spent a considerable amount of time and effort ironing out ideas which seemed simple at first glance. Probability usually refers to a particular action or *experiment* which is to be performed and for which there are two or more possible *results* or *outcomes*. A simple case, for example, is the probability of getting heads when tossing a coin. The experiment is tossing the coin, and the possible outcomes, heads or tails (abbreviated *h* and *t*, respectively), are the elements of a set *S*, called the *sample space:*

$$S = \{h, t\}.$$

It seems reasonable to assume that the two possible outcomes, *h* or *t*, are *equally likely;* that is, there is no predictable reason why one should occur rather than the other. We indicate this assumption by saying that the coin is *fair*. Based on this equal likelihood assumption, the probability of the coin landing heads up is the number of outcomes which can be heads divided by the total number of possible outcomes. Hence since there are two possible outcomes and one of them is heads, the probability of tossing heads is $\frac{1}{2}$. (Note that the probability of tails is also $\frac{1}{2}$.)

Even when we know the sample space for an experiment, there is no way of positively predicting which outcome will occur on a given trial. As the experiment is performed time after time, the outcome varies over the entire sample space, and on a given try no possible outcome can be predicted with certainty. Hence the result of such an experiment is called a *random variable*. It has what is called *statistical regularity* since we can predict the approximate *proportion* of times a given outcome will occur, but it is random in the sense that any single outcome is unpredictable. In the experiment of tossing a single coin, "selecting an outcome at random" would be just as likely to result in heads as in tails.

Let's now apply the ideas introduced above to another experiment. If a fair coin is tossed twice, what is the probability that it will land heads once and tails once? The experiment is tossing a coin two times successively. One possible outcome is *hh* (heads both times); the others are *ht*, *th*, and *tt*. The sample space then is

$$S = \{hh, ht, th, tt\}.$$

An *event* is any subset of the sample space. In this case, we are interested in the event of one head and one tail. Of the four possible outcomes, two are "favorable" to the event (are elements of the event), and thus the probability of heads once and tails once is $\frac{2}{4}$ or $\frac{1}{2}$. In general, the probability of an event *E* is the number of possible outcomes favorable to *E* divided by the total number of possible outcomes. The probability of event *E* is often written $P(E)$, so that we have:

$$P(E) = \frac{\text{number of outcomes favorable to } E}{\text{total number of possible outcomes}}.$$

By its very definition, the probability of any event will be a non-negative number less than or equal to 1. If none of the possible outcomes of an experiment is favorable to a given event, then the event has probability 0. If, on the other hand, every outcome is favorable, the probability quotient becomes 1. When E_1 and E_2 are any two disjoint events such that $E_1 \cup E_2 = S$, we have

$$P(E_1) + P(E_2) = P(S) = 1.$$

This fact can be stated in the following more useful forms:

$$P(E_1) = 1 - P(E_2), \quad \text{and} \quad P(E_2) = 1 - P(E_1).$$

If we want to find the probability of an event E_1 and if it is easier to find the probability of its complement E_1', then we simply compute $P(E_1) = 1 - P(E_1')$.

Closely related to the concept of probability is that of *odds*. An example will serve to show the difference between the two ideas. If a coin is tossed twice, the sample space, as we have seen, contains four outcomes (or elements), one of which is *hh*. The probability of getting both heads is $\frac{1}{4}$ (the quotient of favorable outcomes to total outcomes). On the other hand, the *odds in favor* of the outcome *hh* are expressed as the quotient of favorable outcomes to non-favorable outcomes. There is one favorable outcome (*hh*) and three non-favorable ones (*ht, th, tt*) so the odds in favor of getting both heads are 1 to 3. In a case like this where more outcomes are non-favorable than favorable, it is common to speak of the *odds against the event*. The odds here are 3 to 1 against getting both heads.

Example 7.1.   Suppose a single fair die is rolled. Find the probability of getting: (a) 4,   (b) 6,   (c) an even number,   (d) a number greater than 2,   (e) 7.

First determine the sample space. An ordinary die contains the numbers 1 to 6; thus the sample space is

$$S = \{1, 2, 3, 4, 5, 6\}.$$

The result of the experiment, the number showing on the die, is a random variable with six possible values. Let's make the following definitions:

E_1 is the event that 4 is rolled,
E_2 is the event that 6 is rolled,
E_3 is the event that an even number is rolled,
E_4 is the event that a number greater than 2 is rolled,
E_5 is the event that 7 is rolled.

Then we may write the events as

$$E_1 = \{4\},$$
$$E_2 = \{6\},$$
$$E_3 = \{2, 4, 6\},$$
$$E_4 = \{3, 4, 5, 6\},$$
$$E_5 = \{\ \ \}.$$

The probability of rolling 4 is the number of favorable outcomes divided by the total number of outcomes, or $\frac{1}{6}$. Similarly, we may write

$$P(E_2) = \tfrac{1}{6}; \; P(E_3) = \tfrac{3}{6} = \tfrac{1}{2}; \; P(E_4) = \tfrac{4}{6} = \tfrac{2}{3}; \; P(E_5) = \tfrac{0}{6} = 0.$$

Example 7.2.   If a single card is drawn at random from an ordinary 52-card bridge deck, find the probability that it is: (a) an ace,   (b) a face card, (c) a spade,   (d) a spade or a heart.   (e) Find the odds against its being an ace.

Since listing the elements of the sample space would be more trouble than it is worth, we simply note that there are 52 possible outcomes.

(a) There are four aces in the deck, so that

$$P(\text{ace}) = \tfrac{4}{52} = \tfrac{1}{13}.$$

(b) Since there are 12 face cards, we have

$$P(\text{face card}) = \tfrac{12}{52} = \tfrac{3}{13}.$$

(c) Spades make up 13 out of the 52 cards, so that

$$P(\text{spade}) = \tfrac{13}{52} = \tfrac{1}{4}.$$

(d) Half the cards in the deck, or 26, are spades or hearts; thus

$$P(\text{spade or heart}) = \tfrac{26}{52} = \tfrac{1}{2}.$$

(e) Only four cards in the deck are aces, while 48 are not. Hence the odds are 48 to 4, or 12 to 1, against choosing an ace.

PROBLEMS

1. If two fair coins are tossed, find the probability that:
   (a) both come up heads,
   (b) both come up tails,
   (c) they come up one of each.
   (Hint: this problem may be treated as if one coin is tossed twice.)

2. If three fair coins are tossed, find the probability of:
   (a) all three heads,
   (b) two heads and one tail,
   (c) one head and two tails,
   (d) no heads.

3. If a card is drawn at random from an ordinary 52-card bridge deck, find the probability of getting:
   (a) a king,   (e) something greater than 3, but less than 7,
   (b) a heart,   (f) a king or a queen,
   (c) a king or a heart,   (g) a king and a queen,
   (d) a king and a heart,   (h) a diamond or a club.

4. Suppose two dice are rolled. Find the probability of a sum of:

(a) 2   (f) 14

(b) 4   (g) 1

(c) 7   (h) 2 or 12

(d) 11   (i) anything less than 5

(e) 12   (j) anything greater than 5.

(Hint: it will probably pay to start by listing all 36 outcomes in the sample space.)

5. In the same experiment as in problem 4, find the odds against a sum of:

(a) 3   (d) less than 4

(b) 8   (e) greater than 10.

(c) 2 or 12

SECTION 2. COUNTING TECHNIQUES: PERMUTATIONS

In section 1 we established the definition of probability and applied it to a few simple problems. With the ideas of that section as our only tool, most meaningful problems would be very formidable. For example, to find the probabilities of being dealt certain hands in five-card draw poker would require a sample space containing over 300,000,000 outcomes. In this section we shall consider some more sophisticated means of determining the number of possible outcomes and the number of favorable outcomes needed to compute probabilities.

First, let's look at a systematic way to determine sample spaces. Suppose three fair coins are tossed. How many possible outcomes are there? The task (or experiment) of tossing the three coins really consists of three separate tasks, namely, tossing the first, the second, and the third coin. We can illustrate the possible outcomes for each of these tasks in a *tree diagram,* as in figure 7.1.

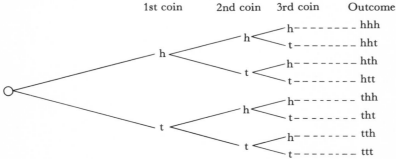

Sample space $S = \{hhh, hht, hth, htt, thh, tht, tth, ttt\}$

Figure 7.1

Starting from the left, we see that the first coin can land either heads or tails up. In either of these two cases, the second coin has two possibilities also, as does the third. Each of these outcomes is listed on the right. Notice that the experiment consists of three tasks, and the number of possible out-comes for each is 2. The total number of outcomes for the experiment is $2^3 = 8$.

Example 7.3.   Consider the following questions:

   (a) How many different three-digit numbers can be formed from the set $\{0, 1, 2, 3, 4, 5, 6, 7, 8, 9\}$?

   (b) How many of these are multiples of 5?

The experiment in part (a) consists of performing three tasks: deter-mining the first digit, the second digit, and the third digit. There are some complicating factors however. Should we allow the first digit to be zero? Actually, the number 058 is the same as 58 and cannot be considered a three-digit number. Therefore the first digit must be non-zero, which means there are just nine choices for the first digit. A tree diagram would have nine branches at this point. What about the second digit? There are no restric-tions here; hence 10 choices. The tree diagram would spread to 9 × 10, or 90 branches. Since there are no restrictions on the third digit either, each branch splits into 10 again for a total of 90 × 10, or 900 possible outcomes (which explains why we are describing the tree diagram rather than actually drawing it.)

Part (b) stipulates that the numbers must be multiples of 5; hence the final digit in each case must be 0 or 5. We have, therefore, only two choices for the third digit, which makes the total number of possible outcomes 9 × 10 × 2, or 180.

The principle used here is the same as with the three coins. It may be reasoned through with the aid of a tree diagram, but once understood it can be applied directly and quickly. The principle is this: when an experiment consists of two or more distinct tasks, the total number of outcomes possible can be found by first determining the number of ways of performing each of the separate tasks and then multiplying these numbers together.

Example 7.4.   Consider the five-member club

$$N = \{\text{Abbot, Babbit, Cynthia, Dillon, Ellen}\}.$$

In how many ways can this club select a president, a vice president, and a secretary (assuming no person can hold more than one office)?

   First task: select a president (5 choices).
   Second task: select a vice president (only 4 choices remaining).
   Third task: select a secretary (3 choices left).

By multiplying the number of choices for the three separate tasks, we have 5 × 4 × 3, or 60 possible ways to select the three officers.

A basic and important difference between examples 7.3 and 7.4 may have already occurred to you. When choosing three-digit numbers, something like 255 or 666 is perfectly acceptable. But when selecting officers for the club, we know that one person is eligible for one office only. *Repetitions are allowed* in the first case but not in the second. Such considerations certainly affect the total number of possible outcomes.

Another point to notice, in both example 7.3 and 7.4, is that the arrangement or order of the elements is important. The number 275, for example, is different from the outcome 752, although the same three digits are used. Similarly, in the selection of club officers, the outcome *A-D-E* (meaning Abbot president, Dillon vice president, and Ellen secretary) is different from the outcome *E-A-D*. Contrast this with a card hand, where ordinarily we would be concerned only with the cards received and not the order in which they are received. In cases like example 7.4, where repetitions are not allowed and where order is important, the total number of outcomes can be computed in a straightforward way. We need to find the number of arrangements of size 3 that can be chosen from a set of size 5. The answer is $5 \times 4 \times 3$, or 60. Ordinarily, this product is referred to as the number of *permutations* (or *arrangements*) *of five things taken three at a time,* and is denoted by $_5P_3$. If the club had eight members and we wanted to select four officers, we would compute the number of permutations of eight things taken four at a time:

$$_8P_4 = 8 \times 7 \times 6 \times 5.$$

The first officer can be chosen in eight different ways, the second in seven, and so on. No matter which officer is considered first, the answer is the same. In general, the number of permutations of n objects taken r at a time (r is never greater than n) is given by:

$$_nP_r = n(n - 1)(n - 2) \cdots (n - r + 1).$$

The factors begin with n and descend until there is a total of r factors.

Example 7.5. Evaluate: (a) $_6P_1$, (b) $_6P_2$, (c) $_6P_3$, (d) $_6P_4$, (e) $_6P_5$, (f) $_6P_6$, and (g) $_6P_0$.

Following the definition stated above, we find that:
(a) $_6P_1 = 6$,
(b) $_6P_2 = 6 \times 5 = 30$,
(c) $_6P_3 = 6 \times 5 \times 4 = 120$,
(d) $_6P_4 = 6 \times 5 \times 4 \times 3 = 360$,
(e) $_6P_5 = 6 \times 5 \times 4 \times 3 \times 2 = 720$,
(f) $_6P_6 = 6 \times 5 \times 4 \times 3 \times 2 \times 1 = 720$.

When the factors run down to 1, as in (f), it is customary to use the term *factorial* for the product. Hence $6 \times 5 \times 4 \times 3 \times 2 \times 1$ is denoted 6! and read "6 factorial." Other examples include $5! = 5 \times 4 \times 3 \times 2 \times 1 = 120$, and $4! = 4 \times 3 \times 2 \times 1 = 24$. We define $0! = 1$.

(g) $_6P_0 = 1$. This may be considered a definition, just as we defined 0!.

Example 7.6. Consider again the Club N of example 7.4. In how many different ways can this club elect a slate of three officers if
   (a) the first two offices must be held by boys and the third by a girl,
   (b) all three must be held by boys,
   (c) there are no restrictions,
   (d) the third one must be held by a girl.

The solutions:
   (a) There are three choices for the first office (Abbot, Babbit, and Dillon), two for the second, and two for the third (Cynthia and Ellen). Hence we have $3 \times 2 \times 2$, or 12 different ways of electing the officers.
   (b) $3 \times 2 \times 1 = 6$.
   (c) $5 \times 4 \times 3 = 60$.
   (d) In this case, the restriction is placed only on the third position. Consider that one first, determining that there are two choices possible. Once the third officer is determined, four choices remain for the first and three for the second. Therefore the total number of possibilities is $2 \times 4 \times 3$, or 24.

PROBLEMS

1. (a) How many different two-digit numbers can be formed using the digits in the set $\{1, 2, 3, 4, 5\}$?
   (b) How many of these numbers are even?
   (c) How many of the even ones do not have a repeating digit? (For example, 55 has a repeating digit.)

2. (a) If Club N is to select a slate of three officers (president, vice president, and secretary), in how many ways can it be done?
   (b) How many of these possibilities will put a girl in the secretary's position?
   (c) If a slate is picked at random, what is the probability that a girl will be secretary?

3. How many outcomes are possible in the experiment of tossing a coin five times?

4. If selective service classifications are specified by a non-zero digit followed by a letter of the alphabet, how many such classifications are possible?

5. How many seven-digit telephone numbers are possible if the first digit cannot be zero and
   (a) only odd digits may be used;
   (b) the number must be a multiple of 10;
   (c) the number must be a multiple of 100;
   (d) the first three digits are 481;
   (e) no repetitions are allowed?

6. Evaluate the following:
   (a) $_3P_2$ (d) $_4P_1$ (g) $_5P_5$ (i) $3!$
   (b) $_5P_2$ (e) $_3P_0$ (h) $5!$ (j) $_3P_3$
   (c) $_6P_4$ (f) $_8P_0$

7. Suppose a license plate always has three letters followed by three digits.
   (a) How many different plates may be made?
   (b) How many can be made if the first digit is not zero?
   (c) How many can be made if no repetition of digits or letters is allowed?
   (d) How many can be made if no repetition of letters is allowed?

8. If a positive two-digit number is chosen at random, what is the probability that:
   (a) it will be even?
   (b) it will be a multiple of five?
   (c) it will have repeating digits?
   (d) it will be between 29 and 50?

9. (a) In how many ways can a program of five musical selections be arranged?
   (b) How many if there are r selections?

SECTION 3. COUNTING TECHNIQUES: COMBINATIONS

Suppose our Club N decides to appoint a committee of three members. In how many different ways can it be done? At first we might try $_5P_3$, the number of permutations of five things taken three at a time. But wait. A committee consisting of Abbot, Dillon, and Ellen is no different from the committee consisting of Ellen, Abbot, and Dillon. When we were designating officers the order was important, but here it is not. What we are really interested in is the number of subsets of size three rather than the number of arrangements of size three. Just as arrangements have been traditionally called permutations, subsets in this new context are called *combinations*. Hence we write $_5C_3$ and ask how many combinations there are of five things taken three at a time.

One possible combination, or subset, is $\{A, D, E\}$. Note: if we were interested in permutations, this single subset would yield the following permutations

$$A\text{-}D\text{-}E, \quad D\text{-}A\text{-}E, \quad E\text{-}A\text{-}D, \quad A\text{-}E\text{-}D, \quad D\text{-}E\text{-}A, \quad E\text{-}D\text{-}A.$$

This illustrates that each combination of size three gives rise to six permutations of size three. Hence there are only one-sixth as many combinations as there are permutations, and we may write:

$$_5C_3 = \frac{_5P_3}{6} = \frac{5 \times 4 \times 3}{6} = \frac{60}{6} = 10.$$

Can we identify a general rule here? To find the number of combinations of size r which are possible from a set of size n ($r \leq n$): first, evaluate $_nP_r$; second, divide by the number of ways each size r subset can be arranged. If you worked problem 9 of the last section, you will recognize that the number of such arrangements can generally be expressed as $_rP_r$, or equivalently as $r!$. Thus, in general,

$$_nC_r = \frac{_nP_r}{r!}.$$

Example 7.7. How many different five-card hands can be dealt from an ordinary 52-card deck?

The order is unimportant since a given hand depends only on the cards dealt; thus we use combinations.

$$_{52}C_5 = \frac{_{52}P_5}{5!} = \frac{52 \times 51 \times 50 \times 49 \times 48}{5 \times 4 \times 3 \times 2 \times 1} = 2{,}598{,}960.$$

Example 7.8. What is the probability of being dealt a hearts flush in five-card poker? A hearts flush is a five-card hand of all hearts.

Since we have already computed in example 7.7 the total number of possible outcomes, we need only find the number of favorable outcomes. There are 13 hearts in the deck; a favorable outcome is simply any combination of five of these 13 cards. But the number of such combinations is

$$_{13}C_5 = \frac{_{13}P_5}{5!}.$$

If E is the event of being dealt a hearts flush, then

$$P(E) = \frac{_{13}C_5}{_{52}C_5} = \frac{\dfrac{_{13}P_5}{5!}}{\dfrac{_{52}P_5}{5!}} = \frac{13 \times 12 \times 11 \times 10 \times 9}{52 \times 51 \times 50 \times 49 \times 48} = \frac{33}{66{,}640}.$$

It is helpful to notice that here the 5! cancelled. The same thing happens whenever we are dealing with the quotient of two combinations in which the second index r is the same. That is, for any values of m and n, we have

$$\frac{_{m}C_r}{_{n}C_r} = \frac{\dfrac{_{m}P_r}{r!}}{\dfrac{_{n}P_r}{r!}} = \frac{_{m}P_r}{_{n}P_r}.$$

Example 7.9. (a) In five-card poker, what is the probability of the event E of being dealt a full house of aces and eights (three aces and two eights)?
(b) What are the odds against such a hand being dealt?

We use combinations here:
(a) A favorable outcome here can be thought of as the completion of two tasks, getting three aces and getting two eights. So we use our product rule for finding the total number of favorable outcomes. Since there are four aces and four eights in the deck, the number of ways of getting three aces is $_4C_3$, and the number of ways of getting two eights is $_4C_2$. Therefore the total number of favorable events is $_4C_3 \times _4C_2$, and

$$P(E) = \frac{_4C_3 \times _4C_2}{_{52}C_5} = \frac{1}{108{,}290}.$$

(b) This example shows a way of finding the odds when the probability is known. Notice first that E and E' (the complement of E) are disjoint events with $E \cup E' = S$ (where S is the set of all possible five-card hands). Hence $P(E) + P(E') = 1$ (as explained earlier), or

$$P(E') = 1 - P(E)$$
$$= \frac{108{,}290}{108{,}290} - \frac{1}{108{,}290}$$
$$= \frac{108{,}289}{108{,}290}.$$

Now in general,

$$P(E) = \frac{\text{number of favorable outcomes}}{\text{number of outcomes}},$$

while

$$P(E') = \frac{\text{number of unfavorable outcomes}}{\text{number of outcomes}}.$$

The ratio of favorable to unfavorable outcomes should be the same as the ratio of $P(E)$ to $P(E')$. Hence in this case, the odds are $\frac{108{,}289}{108{,}290}$ to $\frac{1}{108{,}290}$, or simply 108,289 to 1, against event E.

The procedure for converting from probability to odds can be summarized as follows: if $P(E) = \frac{a}{b}$, then the odds in favor of E are a to $(b - a)$ and the odds against E are $(b - a)$ to a.

PROBLEMS

1. Evaluate:
   (a) $_5C_0$,   (d) $_5C_3$,
   (b) $_5C_1$,   (e) $_5C_4$,
   (c) $_5C_2$,   (f) $_5C_5$.

2. How many subsets does a set of size five have? Use combinations to arrive at the answer. (Hint: see problem 1.)

3. In a club of twelve members, in how many ways can a committee of five be appointed?

4. If a baseball coach has five good hitters and four poor hitters on the bench and chooses three of these at random, what is the probability that he will choose
   (a) all good hitters,
   (b) two good hitters and one poor hitter,
   (c) one good hitter and two poor hitters,
   (d) no good hitters?

5. In problem 4, what are the odds:
   (a) against getting all good hitters,
   (b) against getting all poor hitters,
   (c) in favor of getting at least one of each?

6. If your school offers 400 courses, 20 of which are in mathematics, and your counselor arranges your schedule of four courses by random selection,
   (a) what is the probability that you will not get a math course?
   (b) what are the odds against getting a math course?

7. If five cards are drawn at random from a 52-card deck, what is the probability that:
   (a) they are all queens,
   (b) they are all face cards,
   (c) none of them is a face card,
   (d) two are face cards, and three are not,
   (e) three are face cards, and two are not,
   (f) one is a heart, two are diamonds, and two are clubs?

SECTION 4. SIMULTANEOUS AND SUCCESSIVE EVENTS

Quite often we are interested in determining the probability that two different events are satisfied by a single outcome of an experiment. That is, the outcome is favorable to both events simultaneously. For example, the experiment might be to draw a single card from an ordinary bridge deck, where E_1 is the event of a spade, and E_2 is the event of an ace. In this case, $P(E_1 \text{ and } E_2) = \frac{1}{52}$ since there is only one card in the deck favorable to both events (the ace of spades).

In this same experiment, let E_3 be the event of a heart. Then what about $P(E_1 \text{ and } E_3)$? Because there is no card in the deck that is both a spade and a heart, we conclude $P(E_1 \text{ and } E_3) = 0$. Events E_1 and E_3 are said to be *mutually exclusive;* that is, they cannot both be satisfied simultaneously by a given outcome. Since events are merely subsets of the sample space, we can describe mutually exclusive events by saying that they are disjoint sets. Using set notation for the experiment above then, we have:

$$P(E_1 \cap E_2) = \tfrac{1}{52} \text{ and } P(E_1 \cap E_3) = 0.$$

There is a similar analogy for the union of two events. For the experiment above we have

$$P(E_1 \cup E_3) = P(E_1 \text{ or } E_3) = P(E_1) + P(E_3) = \frac{13}{52} + \frac{13}{52} = \frac{1}{2}.$$

We are saying that 26 out of 52 cards in the deck satisfy the condition of being either a spade or a heart. In this case we add the separate probabilities of E_1 and E_3, but this procedure can only be used when two events are mutually exclusive.

The reason for this is directly related to the fact that, in set theory, the sum of the cardinal numbers of two given finite sets A and B will be the cardinal number of their union only if the two sets are disjoint. If they have a non-empty intersection, then

cardinal number of $A \cup B$ = cardinal number of A
$\qquad\qquad$ + cardinal number of B − cardinal number of $A \cap B$.

In probability theory this same thing is stated for events A and B as follows:

$$P(A \text{ or } B) = P(A) + P(B) - P(A \text{ and } B).$$

For the experiment discussed above,

$$P(E_1 \text{ or } E_2) = P(E_1) + P(E_2) - P(E_1 \text{ and } E_2)$$
$$= \frac{13}{52} + \frac{4}{52} - \frac{1}{52}$$
$$= \frac{16}{52}$$
$$= \frac{4}{13}$$

In a deck of 52 cards, exactly 16 satisfy the condition of being a spade or an ace. Remember that the above formulas should only be applied when a single outcome is being examined with respect to two different events. A different analysis applies to two events which are to be satisfied by two different outcomes successively.

Example 7.10.   Suppose we draw a card from the deck, replace it, and then draw a card again. If E_1, E_2, and E_3 have the same meaning as above, let's use "E_1 and then E_3" to mean "a spade on the first draw, and then a heart on the second." Find the probability of E_1 and then E_3.

We write
$$P(E_1 \text{ and then } E_3) = P(E_1) \cdot P(E_3)$$
$$= \frac{13}{52} \cdot \frac{13}{52}$$
$$= \frac{1}{4} \cdot \frac{1}{4} = \frac{1}{16}.$$

We have simply multiplied the successive probabilities together. Notice that order is important here. We are saying the spade must occur on the first draw, not the second.

In this case, the outcome on the first draw has no effect on the second draw since the first card was returned to the deck. When an event A is not affected by the occurrence or nonoccurrence of an event B, and vice versa, we say that the two events are *independent*. Otherwise they are *dependent*.

Example 7.11.   Evaluate $P(E_1 \text{ and then } E_3)$ in case the first card drawn is not to be returned to the deck (the phrase "without replacement" applies here).

We still multiply the probabilities, but now $P(E_3)$ is $\frac{13}{51}$ since the deck is reduced to size 51 (notice that the first card drawn is assumed to be a spade so that all 13 hearts remain in the deck). We have

$$P(E_1 \text{ and then } E_3) = P(E_1) \cdot P(E_3)$$

$$= \frac{13}{52} \cdot \frac{13}{51}$$

$$= \frac{1}{4} \cdot \frac{13}{51} = \frac{13}{204}.$$

Example 7.12. Recall that E_1 is the event of a spade, and E_2 is the event of an ace. If two cards are drawn without replacement, evaluate $P(E_1$ and then $E_2)$.

As before, $P(E_1) = \frac{1}{4}$. But $P(E_2)$ is now a problem since we do not know if the first card was the ace of spades or some other spade. To overcome the difficulty, divide the event "E_1 and then E_2" into the following two mutually exclusive possibilities:

E_4: the ace of spades on the first draw, and then one of the other aces on the second draw.

E_5: a spade (other than the ace) on the first draw, and then one of the four aces on the second draw.

$$\text{Now } P(E_4) = \frac{1}{52} \cdot \frac{3}{51} = \frac{3}{52 \cdot 51},$$

and

$$P(E_5) = \frac{12}{52} \cdot \frac{4}{51} = \frac{48}{52 \cdot 51},$$

with the desired probability given by the sum of the two:

$$\frac{3}{52 \cdot 51} + \frac{48}{52 \cdot 51} = \frac{51}{52 \cdot 51} = \frac{1}{52}.$$

One advantage (or perhaps disadvantage) of probability theory is that most problems can be solved in a variety of ways. We illustrate this with the next example.

Example 7.13. Suppose that two cards are drawn at random and without replacement from an ordinary 52-card deck. What is the probability of drawing a king and a queen?

Let $E_1 =$ the event of "one king and one queen." Since no particular order was stipulated, either one could be first. If we define

and
$$E_2 = \text{the event of "a king and then a queen,"}$$
$$E_3 = \text{the event of "a queen and then a king,"}$$
then
$$E_1 = E_2 \cup E_3,$$
while
$$E_2 \cap E_3 = \varnothing.$$

Therefore

$$P(E_1) = P(E_2 \text{ or } E_3)$$
$$= P(E_2) + P(E_3)$$
$$= \frac{4}{52} \cdot \frac{4}{51} + \frac{4}{52} \cdot \frac{4}{51}$$
$$= \frac{16}{52 \cdot 51} + \frac{16}{52 \cdot 51}$$
$$= \frac{32}{52 \cdot 51} = \frac{8}{13 \cdot 51}.$$

Looking at the problem in another way, one could say that selecting a king and a queen from the deck really consists of two tasks, selecting the king and selecting the queen. There are four kings in the deck, and $_4C_1$ is the numbr of ways of completing the first task. The second task can also be done in $_4C_1$ ways, since the deck also contains four queens. According to the original product rule, the number of ways of completing both tasks is $_4C_1 \cdot _4C_1$. The total number of ways of drawing two cards without replacement is the same as the number of size 2 subsets of the set of 52 cards; that is, $_{52}C_2$. Hence the probability of one king and one queen is

$$\frac{_4C_1 \cdot _4C_1}{_{52}C_2} = \frac{\dfrac{_4P_1}{1!} \cdot \dfrac{_4P_1}{1!}}{\dfrac{_{52}P_2}{2!}}$$

$$= \frac{\dfrac{4}{1} \cdot \dfrac{4}{1}}{\dfrac{52 \cdot 51}{2 \cdot 1}}$$

$$= \frac{32}{52 \cdot 51} = \frac{8}{13 \cdot 51}.$$

This result is the same as with the first method of solution.

PROBLEMS

1. Suppose a single die is rolled. Find the probability that the result is:
   (a) 3 or 4,
   (b) 5 and greater than 2,
   (c) odd or even,
   (d) even and less than 4,
   (e) even and greater than 3,
   (f) odd or 6.

2. Suppose two dice are rolled successively. Find the probability of:
    (a) two 1's,
    (b) a 1 and then a 2 (why is this different from the probability of rolling a sum of three?),
    (c) an odd and then an even,
    (d) odd and then a 5,
    (e) greater than 2 and then less than 2.

3. If three cards are drawn successively from an ordinary deck (with replacement) find the probability of:
    (a) all three clubs,
    (b) all three sevens,
    (c) all three 7's of clubs,
    (d) a 2, then a 3, then a 4,
    (e) a 2, then a heart, then a club,
    (f) a club, then a face card, then a jack.

4. Repeat problem 3 if the drawing is done without replacement. (Hint: for (e) and (f) refer to the procedure of example 7.12.)

5. If a basket contains five pigeon eggs and three turtle eggs, and if four eggs are drawn at random without replacement, what is the probability of getting:
    (a) all pigeon eggs,
    (b) all turtle eggs,
    (c) two of each,
    (d) one pigeon egg and three turtle eggs,
    (e) three pigeon eggs and one turtle egg,
    (f) more than two pigeon eggs,
    (g) either all pigeon eggs or all turtle eggs,
    (h) fewer than three turtle eggs.

6. If you are dealt a five-card hand from a poker deck, what is the probability of getting:
    (a) a heart flush (all hearts),
    (b) a flush in either hearts or diamonds,
    (c) a flush (in any of the four suits).

7. In a five-card hand, what is the probability of:
    (a) a hearts royal flush (ace, king, queen, jack, and ten of hearts),
    (b) a royal flush (suit not specified).

8. In five-card poker, what is the probability of being dealt a full house? (Hint: first refer to example 7.9 for the probability of an aces and 8's full house. Then decide how many other kinds of full houses are possible.)

SECTION 5. PASCAL'S TRIANGLE

The symbol $_nC_r$ denotes the number of combinations or subsets of size r contained in a set of size n. This number may be computed by the formula:

$$_nC_r = \frac{_nP_r}{r!} = \frac{n(n-1)(n-2) \cdots (n-r+1)}{r(r-1)(r-2) \cdots 2 \times 1}.$$

For example, the number of subsets of size 2 in the set $\{a, b, c, d\}$ is

$$_4C_2 = \frac{_4P_2}{2!} = \frac{4 \times 3}{2 \times 1} = 6.$$

These subsets are $\{a, b\}$, $\{a, d\}$, $\{b, c\}$, $\{b, d\}$, $\{c, d\}$, $\{a, c\}$.

When computing probabilities, it is often necessary to find many such values; therefore a method for eliminating some of the calculations would be handy. Consider the following array:

$$_1C_0 \quad _1C_1$$
$$_2C_0 \quad _2C_1 \quad _2C_2$$
$$_3C_0 \quad _3C_1 \quad _3C_2 \quad _3C_3$$
$$_4C_0 \quad _4C_1 \quad _4C_2 \quad _4C_3 \quad _4C_4$$
$$_5C_0 \quad _5C_1 \quad _5C_2 \quad _5C_3 \quad _5C_4 \quad _5C_5$$

and so on.

If values were entered and the "triangle" continued downward indefinitely, it would enable us to read the number of subsets of any size in a set of any size. For any value of n,

$$_nC_0 = \frac{_nP_0}{0!} = \frac{1}{1} = 1,$$

and

$$_nC_n = \frac{_nP_n}{n!} = \frac{n(n - 1)(n - 2) \cdots 1}{n(n - 1)(n - 2) \cdots 1} = 1;$$

thus the entries at the ends of any row will always be 1. The remaining values may be found, from the top down, by adding any two adjacent values in a row and entering their sum in the position between them in the next row down. In other words, $_{n+1}C_r$ is found by adding $_nC_r$ and $_nC_{r-1}$:

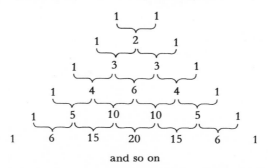

and so on

This array of numbers is called *Pascal's Triangle,* although the Chinese were probably aware of it two or three centuries before Pascal's time. At any rate, it is useful when combinations are being used. To find the value of $_4C_3$ for example, we simply go to the fourth row, then to the fourth entry, which is 4 (remember, the first entry in any row denotes the number of subsets of size 0, which is always 1, the empty set). The following example gives a way of verifying the formula $_{n+1}C_r = {_nC_{r-1}} + {_nC_r}$.

Example 7.14.   Show that

$$_5C_3 = {_4C_3} + {_4C_2}.$$

Consider the set $\{a, b, c, d, e\}$. Its size three subsets are $\{a, b, c\}$, $\{a, b, d\}$, $\{a, b, e\}$, $\{a, c, d\}$, $\{a, c, e\}$, $\{a, d, e\}$, $\{b, c, d\}$, $\{b, c, e\}$, $\{b, d, e\}$, and $\{c, d, e\}$. We can divide these ten subsets into two groups, those not containing the element a, ($\{b, c, d\}$, $\{b, c, e\}$, $\{b, d, e\}$, $\{c, d, e\}$), and those containing the element a. Now, the first group consists of all size three subsets of the set $\{b, c, d, e\}$ so that naturally there are $_4C_3$ in that group. The second group can be formed by taking all possible size two subsets of $\{b, c, d, e\}$ (of which there are $_4C_2$) and then adding a to each of them. Thus the result

$$_5C_3 = {_4C_3} + {_4C_2}$$

seems reasonable.

One of the most common uses of Pascal's Triangle is in studying repeated trials with two equally likely outcomes possible at each step, such as tossing a fair coin. As an example, let us assume that we toss four fair coins. In how many ways can we get exactly three heads? One of the possible outcomes of this experiment would be denoted *htht*. Others would be written similarly. The favorable outcomes are *hhht*, *hhth*, *hthh*, and *thhh* (we wanted exactly three heads). We can consider favorable outcomes as simply four positions listed in order with *h*'s in three of them. Hence the number of favorable outcomes is the same as the number of ways of selecting three of the positions to receive an *h*. But this is simply the number of different size three subsets of the set of four positions, which we recognize as $_4C_3$. This number is 4, read directly from Pascal's Triangle. Notice that inserting *t* in exactly one of the positions is really the same as inserting *h*'s in three of them, which makes it reasonable to say $_4C_3 = {_4C_1}$, which helps explain the horizontal symmetry of the triangle. As a general rule,

$$_nC_r = {_nC_{n-r}}.$$

According to the reasoning above, the entries in row four of Pascal's Triangle give us the number of ways of getting exactly 0, exactly 1, exactly 2, exactly 3, and exactly 4 heads, respectively, when four fair coins are tossed. These are clearly all the possible outcomes, so that the total number of outcomes in the sample space would be

$$_4C_0 + {_4C_1} + {_4C_2} + {_4C_3} + {_4C_4} = 1 + 4 + 6 + 4 + 1 = 16.$$

Since we found above that we could get exactly three heads in four ways, the probability of such an event is $\frac{4}{16} = \frac{1}{4}$.

Example 7.15.   If five fair coins are tossed, what is the probability of getting
   (a) exactly two heads,
   (b) either two heads or four heads,
   (c) more than 3 heads,
   (d) at least 2 heads.

   Row five of Pascal's Triangle is:

$$1 \quad 5 \quad 10 \quad 10 \quad 5 \quad 1$$

From these values we see that the total number of possible outcomes is
$1 + 5 + 10 + 10 + 5 + 1 = 32$, so

   (a) $P(\text{exactly two heads}) = \frac{10}{32} = \frac{5}{16}$. Exactly two heads may be obtained in any of ten different ways, that is, $_5C_2$.

   (b) $P(2 \text{ or } 4 \text{ heads}) = \frac{10}{32} + \frac{5}{32} = \frac{15}{32}$.

   (c) $P(\text{more than } 3 \text{ heads}) = P(4 \text{ or } 5 \text{ heads}) = \frac{5}{32} + \frac{1}{32} = \frac{6}{32} = \frac{3}{16}$.

   (d) $P(\text{at least } 2 \text{ heads}) = P(2, 3, 4, \text{ or } 5 \text{ heads}) = \frac{10}{32} + \frac{10}{32} + \frac{5}{32} +$
$\frac{1}{32} = \frac{26}{32} = \frac{13}{16}$.

   Note that, since for any event E, $P(E) = 1 - P(E')$, part (d) could
have been worked in the following way:

$$P(\text{at least two heads}) = P(\text{more than 1 head})$$
$$= 1 - P(\text{no head or 1 head})$$
$$= 1 - \left(\frac{1}{32} + \frac{5}{32}\right)$$
$$= \frac{26}{32} = \frac{13}{16}.$$

PROBLEMS

1. Construct the first nine rows of Pascal's Triangle.

2. Using the triangle of problem 1, evaluate:
   (a) $_4C_2$,   (d) $_7C_4$,
   (b) $_5C_3$,   (e) $_8C_3$,
   (c) $_6C_5$,   (f) $_9C_6$.

3. Suppose a fair coin is tossed nine times. What is the probability of getting:
   (a) all heads,   (e) exactly seven heads,
   (b) no heads,   (f) at least six heads,
   (c) exactly five heads,   (g) at least six tails.
   (d) exactly four heads,

4. If a bag contains five black, one red, and three yellow jelly beans and you reach
   in and take three without looking, what is the probability of getting:
   (a) all black,   (e) two black, one yellow,
   (b) all red,   (f) two yellow, one black,
   (c) all yellow,   (g) two yellow, one red,
   (d) two black, one red,   (h) one of each color.

5. Recall from section 2 the Club N composed of Abbot, Babbit, Cynthia, Dillon, and Ellen. How many different two-member committees can be selected if
   (a) all club members are eligible,
   (b) both must be girls,
   (c) both must be boys,
   (d) there must be one girl and one boy,
   (e) there cannot be more than one boy,
   (f) there must be at least one boy.

6. Suppose a fisherman has six trout in his creel, and two of them are shorter than the legal size limit. If a game warden picks three fish at random from the creel and measures them, what is the probability that he will detect the violation? (Hint: You might first find the probability of no detection.)

SECTION 6. EXPECTED VALUES; THE LAW OF LARGE NUMBERS

Consider the following game: a player pays one dollar for the privilege of rolling a single fair die once. If he rolls a six, he wins five dollars; otherwise he wins nothing. Would you be willing to play this game? The possibility of a five dollar win might be tempting, but consider that the probability of that win is only $\frac{1}{6}$. We define the *expected value* (or *expectation*) of this game, written $E(\text{game})$, as the probability of rolling a six multiplied by the winnings realized in case a six is rolled, so that:

$$E(\text{game}) = P(6) \times \$5$$
$$= \tfrac{1}{6} \times \$5 = \tfrac{5}{6} \text{ of a dollar.}$$

This, of course, does not mean that you should expect to win $\frac{5}{6}$ of a dollar if you play the game once. It only means that if you were to play a large number of times, you could expect your *average* winnings to approach $\frac{5}{6}$ of a dollar per game. Notice that it costs one dollar to play, so that overall you should expect to lose $\frac{1}{6}$ dollar per game, *on the average*. We say that a game is *fair* if the expected value equals the cost of playing the game. This game is clearly unfair.

Sometimes a game will pay off on several, or even all, of the possible outcomes. For example, suppose you are offered the same game as above, except that now you receive $3 for a six, $2 for a five, and $1 for a four (no winnings for a one, two, or three). To determine the expected value of the new game, we multiply probability times winnings, but now we add the three products that result:

$$E(\text{new game}) = P(4) \times \$1 + P(5) \times \$2 + P(6) \times \$3$$
$$= \tfrac{1}{6} \times \$1 + \tfrac{1}{6} \times \$2 + \tfrac{1}{6} \times \$3$$
$$= \$1.$$

The expected value now equals the cost of playing, and this game is fair. You are not likely to encounter a game that is unfair in your favor unless you devise it yourself. Games in a gambling casino are usually set up so that the player's expected value is slightly less than the cost of playing (see the discussion at the end of this section).

Example 7.16.   If four fair coins are tossed, what is the expected number of heads?

This problem deals with the number of heads on coin tosses, rather than with dollars won, but the treatment is the same as above. From row 4 of Pascal's Triangle, we see that the probabilities of 0, 1, 2, 3, and 4 heads are $\frac{1}{16}$, $\frac{4}{16}$, $\frac{6}{16}$, $\frac{4}{16}$, and $\frac{1}{16}$ respectively. Hence

$$E(\text{number of heads}) = \frac{1}{16} \times 0 + \frac{4}{16} \times 1 + \frac{6}{16} \times 2 + \frac{4}{16} \times 3 + \frac{1}{16} \times 4$$
$$= \frac{4}{16} + \frac{12}{16} + \frac{12}{16} + \frac{4}{16}$$
$$= \frac{32}{16} = 2.$$

This answer seems reasonable. If four coins are tossed over and over again, the average number of heads should approach 2.

It is clear that expected values have very little meaning to a person who plays a game once or twice only. In the above example, a player should not be surprised if he tosses three heads out of four the first time he plays, or even four out of four. However, if he got three heads out of four the second and third times he played, he would probably begin to wonder about the "fairness" of the coins.

This same idea is central to all of probability theory. When we say that the probability of a head on a single toss of a coin is $\frac{1}{2}$ we do not mean that half the tosses will be heads and half tails. Rather we mean that the fraction of coins turning up heads will not be far from $\frac{1}{2}$ if we toss enough coins. One of the authors tossed a (presumably fair) coin 50 times and recorded the following sequence of outcomes:

tthhh   ttthh   hthtt   hhthh   ttthh   thttt   hhthh   ththh   tthhh   hhtht

After two tosses the fraction of heads was 0 (far from $\frac{1}{2}$), and after eight tosses it was $\frac{3}{8}$ (approaching $\frac{1}{2}$). Checking the fraction of heads after each two tosses showed that 16 of these 25 values were $\frac{1}{2}$ exactly. In particular, after 42 tosses the fraction was $\frac{1}{2}$ and even though the next four tosses all came up heads, the fraction after 46 was $\frac{25}{46}$, only $\frac{1}{23}$ higher than $\frac{1}{2}$. The effect here is that the fraction seems to stabilize around $\frac{1}{2}$ as the number of tosses increases. For further discussion of this important concept, known as Bernoulli's Theorem, or the Law of Large Numbers, see James R. Newman, ed., *The World of Mathematics*, (volume 3), p. 1448.

We end this section with a discussion of expectation theory as applied to some common games of chance. Numbers is an ever popular (though definitely illegal) game familiar to viewers of the late movie. In this game, the player selects a three-digit number (guided in his selection, usually, by a dream or a tip from his mother-in-law) and gives the number, with a dollar, to the numbers runner (an elevator operator, newspaperboy, or perhaps his boss). Any three digits are acceptable, such as 008 or 041. A number is selected by the gamblers in some highly honest manner, such as the last three digits of the daily volume of stock transactions. Anyone who selected the correct number receives a payoff of $700. The expected value, then, is

$$\tfrac{1}{1000} \times \$700 = \$.70.$$

Hence the expected loss is 30¢ per play, which adds up to a fantastic profit for those collecting the money.

We assume roulette is played as follows: an ivory ball and a wheel containing thirty-eight compartments are set in motion (by a bearded croupier, no doubt). Eighteen of the compartments are black, eighteen red, one is labeled zero, and one is labeled double zero. It costs $1 to play the game. The player places his money on either red or black. If he picks the correct color of the compartment in which the ball finally lands he is paid $2; otherwise nothing. The expected value of this form of roulette is found as follows

$$\tfrac{18}{38} \times \$2 = \tfrac{36}{38} = \tfrac{18}{19}.$$

Since the game costs $1, the player can expect to lose, on the average, $\tfrac{1}{19}$ dollar, or 5.3 cents per play.

In another form of roulette, a more generous management supplies a wheel having only thirty-seven compartments, with eighteen red, eighteen black, and one zero. In this game the expected value is

$$\tfrac{18}{37} \times \$2 = \tfrac{36}{37}.$$

Here the expected loss per play is only $\tfrac{1}{37}$ dollar, or 2.7 cents. It would take approximately twice as many plays, on the average, to lose a given amount of money at this form of roulette as compared to the roulette containing thirty-eight compartments. (Note: a given amount of money would permit around eleven plays of thirty-seven-compartment-roulette for each play of the numbers racket.)

In keno, the house has a pot containing 80 balls, each marked with a different number from 1 to 80. In a simple version of keno a player buys a ticket for $1 and marks one number on it (from 1 to 80). The management then selects 20 numbers at random (as with numbers, any suspicion of non-random selection causes the take to fall off; for this reason casinos go to great lengths to make sure that the 20 numbers are selected in an unbiased manner). If the number selected by the player is among the 20 selected by the management, the player is paid $3.20. The expected value, then, is found as follows

$$\tfrac{20}{80} \times \$3.20 = \$.80.$$

Thus the expected loss per play is 20 cents.

The authors have heard of a game called 6-spot keno, which is the same as the game above, except that here the player selects 6 numbers on his ticket. In one popular form of the game, the player pays 60 cents for his ticket, with payoffs as follows

3 of the player's numbers among the 20	$ .95
4 of the player's numbers among the 20	2.60
5 of the player's numbers among the 20	60.60
6 of the player's numbers among the 20	1,250.60

The expected value is somewhat difficult to find here, but it can be evaluated using the methods of this chapter

$$E \text{ (6-spot keno)} = \frac{_{20}C_6}{_{80}C_6} \times \$1250.60 + \frac{_{20}C_5 \times {}_{60}C_1}{_{80}C_6} \times \$60.60 +$$

$$\frac{_{20}C_4 \times {}_{60}C_2}{_{80}C_6} \times \$2.60 + \frac{_{20}C_3 \times {}_{60}C_3}{_{80}C_6} \times \$.95$$

$$= (.000129)(\$1250.60) + (.003096)(\$60.60) +$$
$$(.028538)(\$2.60) + (.129819)(\$.95)$$

$$= \$.546.$$

Thus the expected loss is about 5 cents per play, or about 8 cents per dollar.

An article by Andrew Sterrett in *The Mathematics Teacher* for March, 1967,* contains the rules for some games, together with calculations of the expected values of the games. The author uses expected values to find the expected time it would take to lose $1000, playing continuously at the rate of a dollar a minute. Sterrett assumes each play of each game costs $1. His results:

Game	†E(game)	Days	Hours	Minutes
Roulette (with one zero)	− $0.027	25	16	40
Roulette (with a zero and a zero zero)	− $0.053	13	4	40
Chuck-a-luck	− $0.079	8	19	46
Keno (one number)	− $0.200	3	11	20
Numbers	− $0.300	2	7	33
Football Pool (4 winners)	− $0.375	1	20	27
Football Pool (10 winners)	− $0.658	1	1	19

†Note: Sterrett uses a different definition of expected value than the one used in this book. He uses winnings minus cost, which can result in a negative expectation.

PROBLEMS

1. Suppose you pay $1 to roll a die with the understanding that you win $3 for a 1 or a 6 and nothing otherwise.
   (a) What are your expected winnings?
   (b) Is the game fair?

2. A game involves tossing three fair coins, and pays 10¢ for three heads, 5¢ for two heads, and 3¢ for one head. What is a fair price to pay to play this game?

*Table 2 from "Gambling Doesn't Pay!" by Andrew Sterrett, *The Mathematics Teacher*, LX, No. 3 (March 1967). Copyright 1967 by the National Council of Teachers of Mathematics. Reprinted by permission.

3. In a certain game, you pick a single card from an ordinary deck and receive 40¢ for a spade, 40¢ for a heart, 40¢ for a club, 40¢ for a diamond, and 50¢ extra for an ace. If the cost of playing is 45¢, should you play?

4. A game consists of tossing eight fair coins. It costs 10¢ and pays as follows:

> 50¢ for no heads or 8 heads,
> 40¢ for one head or seven heads,
> 20¢ for two heads or six heads,
> 5¢ for three heads or five heads,
> 0 for exactly four heads.

   (a) What is the expected value of the game?
   (b) Is it fair?

5. If a single die is rolled, what is the expected number of spots showing?

6. In a game costing 10¢, two fair dice are rolled with a payoff of 50¢ for a 7 or an 11, nothing otherwise.
   (a) What are the expected winnings
   (b) Is the game fair
   (Hint: see problem 4 of section 1.)

7. Suppose you start tossing a fair coin and toss five heads in a row. What are the odds in favor of tossing heads on the sixth try?

SECTION 7. THE MONTE CARLO METHOD

   We want to find an approximate value for the number $\pi/4$, using a table of random numbers and the Monte Carlo method. A *random number* is one that has been selected at random. For example, a spinner can be set up as in figure 7.2; after the pointer spins it will stop on one of the digits 0, 1, 2, 3, 4, 5, 6, 7, 8, 9. There is no way to predict in advance the number at which the pointer will stop. By spinning the pointer many, many times a table of random numbers can be constructed (see Appendix B). The numbers in Appendix B were obtained on a computer, by a process that can be repeated to produce identical results, unlike the spinner. Therefore the numbers in Appendix B should really be called *pseudo-random numbers*.

   To approximate $\dfrac{\pi}{4}$, we proceed as follows: the diagram of figure 7.3 shows a square one unit on a side, with a quarter circle drawn in. The

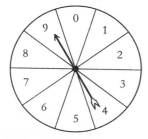

Figure 7.2

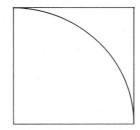

Figure 7.3

formula for the area of a circle is $A = \pi r^2$. Here, $r = 1$, making $A = \pi(1)^2 = \pi$. We have only a quarter circle; thus its area is $\left(\frac{1}{4}\right)\pi = \frac{\pi}{4}$. If we imagine a coordinate system with its origin at the lower left corner of the square, then, as explained in Chapter 6, the set of points inside or on the circle is given by:

$$\{(x,y) \mid x^2 + y^2 \leq 1\}.$$

If points inside the square are selected at random, then the probability that they lie inside the quarter circle is the quotient of the area of the quarter circle and the area of the square; that is, $\dfrac{\frac{\pi}{4}}{1}$, or $\dfrac{\pi}{4}$.

To use the Monte Carlo method, we select a two-digit random number from Appendix B, call it x, and treat it as a decimal between .00 and .99. Next, select another two-digit random number and call it y. Any ordered procedure can be used to select these numbers. For instance, we might pick the first two digits in each entry of column 2, Appendix B, to be x. Then we might let y be the last two digits in each entry of column 1. Any such procedure can be set up.

As discussed in Chapter 6, the x number determines how far over to go in the square from the lower left corner, and the y number determines how far up to go. We then evaluate $x^2 + y^2$. If we find $x^2 + y^2 \leq 1$, then the point (x, y) lies inside or on the circle, otherwise it does not. Because these numbers were selected from a random number table, some of the points will lie inside the circle, with others lying outside. Suppose we select M points (say 100 or 1000) and find that L of them lie inside the circle. As mentioned above, the fraction $\dfrac{L}{M}$ successes divided by total outcomes, should approximate $\dfrac{\pi}{4}$, with a better and better approximation as M becomes larger and larger.

To test this theory, the authors selected 100 points ($M = 100$) and found that 82 fell inside or on the circle ($L = 82$); hence $\dfrac{L}{M} = .82$. The approximation to π is then $4\left(\dfrac{\pi}{4}\right) = 4(.82) = 3.28$, which is as far off as the value for π given in the Bible, $\pi = 3$. To improve the approximation, we let $M = 500$ and found that $L = 396$. Approximately, π is given by 3.17, a number remarkably close to the true value, $\pi = 3.14159$ (to five decimal places). Further accuracy could be obtained by letting M get larger and larger, but we had to quit because it was time to watch "Mission, Impossible."

The Monte Carlo method, developed in 1949, has proven to be of great value in many fields today. Some problems are so complex that standard solutions are either impossible or highly difficult. In such a case, random numbers can be used to represent the variables of the problem. Then, using large computers, it is possible to repeat the process many thousands of times, yielding final results which are usually quite accurate. The Monte Carlo method is often applied to problems in queue theory, "waiting-in-line" theory. For example, given a certain distribution of automobile-arrival-times, a bridge designer can determine how many toll booths are necessary. Telephone companies also utilize applications of the Monte Carlo method when figuring out how large the central office should be in order to have the minimum waiting time on incoming calls consistent with economy.

Another method of approximating the number π was devised in 1777 by Count Buffon. Draw parallel lines two inches apart on a horizontal table top. A needle two inches long is dropped at random on the table. Let M be the total number of times the needle is tossed on the table, and let L be the number of times the needle lands on one of the parallel lines. Count Buffon showed that $\dfrac{L}{M}$ approximates $\dfrac{2}{\pi}$.

PROBLEM

Following the procedure outlined in this section, use the first digit in each entry of column 2, Appendix B, as the x numbers and the last digit in each entry of column 3 as y numbers. Use all 59 rows of entries and determine an approximate value of π.

FOR FURTHER READING

Feller, William. *An Introduction to Probability Theory and Its Applications.* (vol. 1, 2nd edition) New York: John Wiley and Sons, Inc., 1957. This is a classic introductory text which is aimed at a slightly more advanced mathematical level.

Kasner, Edward, and Newman, James. *Mathematics and the Imagination.* New York: Simon and Schuster Publishers, 1940. The chapter of this book entitled "Chance and Chanceability" contains an interesting presentation of many of the ideas of probability, suitable for leisure reading.

Richardson, William H. *Finite Mathematics.* New York: Harper and Row, Publishers, 1968. This text presents (at a level comparable to this book) a somewhat more extensive treatment of counting processes and probability with a little more direct application of set theory.

CHAPTER 8

STATISTICS

The systematic treatment of data, with an attempt to analyze it, probably began with the work of a London shopkeeper, John Graunt (1620–1674), who analyzed the causes of death in London from 1604 to 1661. (It is interesting to note that in 1632 eight people died as a result of jawfaln, thirty-eight of King's-Evil, thirteen of planet, and thirty-four of tissick. Apparently, causes of death come and go in popularity—just as skirt lengths.) Graunt's article is reproduced in *The World of Mathematics*, volume 3, edited by James R. Newman, on page 1420. The studies and findings of Graunt and his successors led to the formation of life insurance companies on a solvent and secure basis.

The *normal curve of error,* a basic idea of statistics, was first developed in 1733 by Abraham de Moivre (1667–1754), but his work went unnoticed. Subsequently, the French mathematician Pierre Laplace (1749–1827) and the German mathematician and physicist Karl Friedrich Gauss (1777–1855), working independently of each other, redeveloped this concept. Gauss is considered by many to be one of the three greatest mathematicians of all time, the others being Isaac Newton and Archimedes. Gauss, a child prodigy in mathematics, displayed evidence of his mathematical ability before he was three years old by correcting errors in a payroll his father was preparing. The school he entered at age seven was best known for the severity of the beatings inflicted upon students, but even here Gauss showed his mathematical ability. His teacher assigned a problem similar to

$$1 + 2 + 3 + \cdots + 98 + 99 + 100,$$

secure in the knowledge that the young students would require considerable time to work it. Surprisingly, almost as soon as the problem was presented, young Gauss had found the answer, 5050. The schoolmaster figured that most young boys (and most old men, for that matter) would work the problem by adding the numbers one at a time. Gauss, however, worked the problem by writing it down twice:

$$
\begin{array}{r}
1 + \quad 2 + \quad 3 + \cdots + \quad 98 + \quad 99 + 100 \\
100 + \quad 99 + \quad 98 + \cdots + \quad 3 + \quad 2 + \quad 1 \\
\hline
101 + 101 + 101 + \cdots + 101 + 101 + 101
\end{array}
$$

and realized that he had 100 sums, each of 101, for a total of 10,100. However, since the problem was written twice, 10,100 must be twice the correct answer. Gauss' remarkable talent came to the attention of the Duke of Brunswick, who guaranteed Gauss a full scholarship. In his doctoral dissertation, Gauss proved the so-called fundamental theorem of algebra; that is, any polynomial equation like

$$2x^4 - 3x^3 + 2x^2 + x - 4 = 0$$

has a solution. (Note: The fundamental theorem of algebra asserts that all such equations have solutions, but does not demonstrate how to find them.)

By the year 1800, seven planets had been discovered. These included the six known to ancient man plus Uranus, discovered by Sir William Herschel in 1781. Astronomers continued to search for more planets, even though the philosopher Hegel assured them the search was in vain since seven is a philosophically satisfying number. However, Ceres, whose orbit is between that of Mars and Jupiter, was discovered early in the nineteenth century. (Although really a planet, today Ceres is referred to as an asteroid.) Gauss became renowned as the leading European mathematician because he succeeded in calculating its orbit. In 1807, Gauss was made director of the observatory at Göttingen University, where he carried on his mathematical studies, along with his work in physics and astronomy. Gauss invented and set up a telegraph system at the university in 1833.

Gauss devoted a large portion of his studies to the Theory of Numbers, a branch of mathematics dealing with integers and their properties. (He spent a lot of time working with mod systems, which are discussed in Chapter 4.) The *prime number theorem* is a good example of the type of work in which he was involved. Prime numbers, such as 2, 3, 5, 7, and 11, are divisible by only themselves and one. They have been studied since the time of Euclid, who first proved that there are infinitely many primes. Primes occur irregularly in the sequence of integers, and, in fact, if k is any counting number, no matter how large, there exists a block of k consecutive counting numbers, none of which is prime. By studying tables of primes, Gauss was able to state the prime number theorem: the total number of primes, less than the counting number k, is approximately given by

$$k/\ln k,$$

with the approximation improving as k increases. (The denominator, $\ln k$, is an abbreviation for "natural logarithm of k." The logarithm of k to the base a is defined as the exponent m, such that $a^m = k$. Consult any college algebra text for details.) Gauss did not prove the prime number theorem, and in fact, a proof was not given until this century.

The nineteenth-century British geologist Charles Lyell (1797–1875), used an essentially statistical argument in his classification of rock strata from Pleistocene (most recent) to Eocene (dawn of the recent). The work of Charles Darwin (1809–1882) on evolution involved much statistics, as did that of Gregor Mendel (1822–1884) on genetics. Karl Pearson (1857–1936) applied mathematics to evolution and produced many new statistical results. Pearson was concerned with large samples, while many other experimenters had, out of necessity, considered small samples. W. S. Gossett (1876–1937), a student of Pearson and an employee of the Guiness brewers, produced some of the first results concerning small samples. He was forced to publish his results under a pseudonym, "Student"; thus his basic finding is today known as "Student's *t*-test."

SECTION 1. THE NATURE OF STATISTICS

Chapter 7 discussed the tossing of a "fair" coin, assuming that heads and tails are equally likely. In the case of rolling a die, each of the six possible outcomes are assumed to be equally likely, so that the probability of each is $\frac{1}{6}$. Historically, the great majority of probability theory has been developed on the basis of the equal likelihood assumption. It is also applicable, however, to situations where such an assumption does not hold. In terms of the law of large numbers, if enough fair coins are tossed, then close to half of them, in the long run, will turn up heads. The actual performance of 50 tosses, recorded in section 6 of Chapter 7, seems to agree with this assumption. Probability theory, then, uses assumed knowledge of the long-term situation to determine likelihoods of certain outcomes or events for an experiment which is to be performed one or a few times. Let us now compare this with the general nature of the closely related field of *statistics*.

Suppose you are in a dice game and suspect the dice of being "loaded." How could you verify your suspicion? A statistician has a very direct approach to this problem. He simply takes a die suspected of being unfair and rolls it a large number of times, say 1000. As the law of large numbers comes into play, the proportion of times each number occurs should begin to approach $\frac{1}{6}$. Suppose he observes, however, that 3 occurs more often than expected, and that in fact as he rolls the die more and more times, the proportion of 3's begins to be stabilizing around $\frac{1}{3}$. After investigating proportions for the other possible outcomes, he could display his results as in figure 8.1.

Outcome	Proportion Approached
1	$\frac{1}{12}$
2	$\frac{1}{12}$
3	$\frac{1}{3}$
4	$\frac{1}{12}$
5	$\frac{1}{12}$
6	$\frac{1}{3}$

Figure 8.1

After a "sampling" of 1000 outcomes, this certainly looks suspicious. Suppose a similar "statistical test" on the second die results in the tendencies shown in figure 8.2. It looks as if this die is loaded to favor 4 and 5, just as the first one favored 3 and 6. A direct result of this unfairness of the dice would be an undue preponderance of the sums 7, 8, 10, and 11. Anyone knowing this fact about the dice would have a clear advantage in the game.

Outcome	Proportion Approached
1	$\frac{1}{8}$
2	$\frac{1}{8}$
3	$\frac{1}{8}$
4	$\frac{1}{4}$
5	$\frac{1}{4}$
6	$\frac{1}{8}$

Figure 8.2

The proportions given in figures 8.1 and 8.2 can be taken as probabilities for the various outcomes. Since they were determined by observing a series of actual outcomes rather than by assuming equal likelihood, they are called *empirical*, or *statistical*, *probabilities*.

There are plenty of cases, of course, where equal likelihood assumptions are valid, and empirical methods are not required. Practically speaking though, statistics and probability theory are intertwined and interdependent to a great degree. Let's examine the above example from a different angle and use it to illustrate the basic nature of statistics. Given either of the loaded dice, it is not known what proportion of rolls would turn up 3 in that die's entire lifetime. But using a sample of 1000 of those rolls, we made a reasonable guess at the long-term proportion, namely $\frac{1}{8}$. All the numbers ever rolled with that die would constitute a *population of values*. We have drawn a conclusion concerning the entire population, based on a sample of 1000 outcomes. With probability theory, we assume knowledge of the population and proceed to make guesses or predictions about specific portions of the population. With statistics, on the other hand, we observe or make actual measurements on portions or samples and proceed to generalize or guess about the nature of the population as a whole. The following sections reveal the kinds of things about which those generalizations are usually made.

SECTION 2. FORMULATING DATA; FREQUENCY DISTRIBUTIONS

A *random variable*, defined in the last chapter, can be thought of as a quantity which can take on any one of a set of values in such a way that we cannot predict which value it will have from one time to the next. The set of possible values is the sample space of the variable. For example, the "value" showing on a tossed coin is a random variable with sample space $\{h, t\}$. The number showing on a rolled die is a random variable with sample space $\{1, 2, 3, 4, 5, 6\}$. If every number rolled on a given die was recorded for say a year, the collection of numbers could be called a *population of values* for that random variable. However, if a year was too long to wait in order to gain certain knowledge about this population, we could take a small *sample,* say 50 values, and then draw some (uncertain) conclusions about the population based upon this limited sample. Let's suppose the values rolled are the following:

```
5 3 6 1 2    6 4 5 5 3    6 2 1 2 1    3 4 1 6 5    4 2 4 2 3
3 4 6 2 4    5 6 6 3 2    3 1 2 1 4    5 5 1 3 2    6 4 1 4 2.
```

   This sequence of numbers is a typical set of "raw data," from which a statistical analysis can be made. An important part of interpreting any collection of data is to present it in a clear and useful way. The first step toward this goal is to tabulate in order of magnitude all the values observed, together with the number of times each value is observed, as in figure 8.3. Formulating

Value	Number of Occurrences
1	8
2	10
3	8
4	9
5	7
6	8

Figure 8.3   Tabulated Data

the data in this way conceals the order in which the values occurred, which we are assuming is unimportant. From the table, we can see the frequency of occurrence of each value observed. To make this information even more readily apparent, we can present it in the form of a *bar graph,* or *histogram;* sometimes a *frequency polygon* is constructed by joining the midpoints of the tops of the bars (see figure 8.4).

   If the die being rolled is fair, we expect that, in the long run, each number would come up as frequently as each of the others. In this case we would say the random variable obeys a *constant frequency distribution.* Since we are dealing with a relatively small sample though, variation in frequencies is not surprising. We can still say that the variable seems to approximately obey a constant distribution.

   The same graphing techniques used here can be applied to all kinds of random variables. For our next example let's consider the number of heads

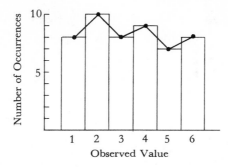

Figure 8.4   Bar Graph and Frequency Polygon

occurring when 5 fair coins are tossed. Suppose we toss the 5 coins 64 different times. By recalling the treatment of sample spaces in Chapter 7, or by using Pascal's triangle, we can make a theoretical prediction as to the number of times each possible value of the random variable will occur. Specifically, row 5 of Pascal's triangle yields the values entered in figure 8.5 (recall we are observing a total of 64 results rather than 32.)

Number of Heads Per 5 Coins	Predicted Number of Occurrences
0	2
1	10
2	20
3	20
4	10
5	2

Figure 8.5

If we performed the experiment of tossing 5 fair coins 64 times and the results ran true to expectation, which is not likely, the bar graph and frequency polygon would appear as in figure 8.6(b). For comparison, the theoretical predictions are also plotted for the cases of (a) 4 coins and (c) 6 coins. They are all examples of what is called the *binomial frequency distribution*, and as with the constant distribution, they are likely to be only approximated by the actual collection of a data sample. The binomial distribution occurs when each trial (for example, tossing a coin) of an experiment can result in either success (heads) or failure (tails), and when the random variable is the number of sucesses for a given number of trials. A binomial graph is symmetric (as in figure 8.6) only if the probabilities of success and failure are equal (that is, both equal to $\frac{1}{2}$).

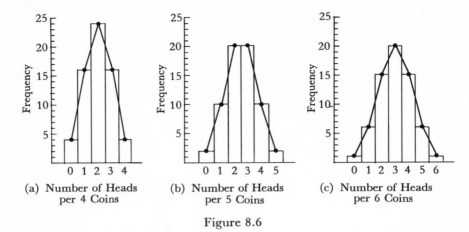

(a) Number of Heads
per 4 Coins

(b) Number of Heads
per 5 Coins

(c) Number of Heads
per 6 Coins

Figure 8.6

Thus far the random variables we have considered have been *discrete-valued;* that is, they could take on only certain isolated values. When a die is rolled, the result must be a counting number less than 7 and when 5 coins are tossed, the number of heads achieved must be a whole number less than 6. Many random variables, however, are not restricted to discrete values. These we classify as *continuous-valued.* Suppose, for example, we are interested in the length of feet of the men students at a certain college. When we take the measurements of a sample of the population, there is clearly no reason to expect only values of whole numbers of inches, or even halves or quarters. For nearly all statistical purposes, it suffices to group the data that is distributed continuously into classes and to record frequencies for each *class interval.* A typical set of data for length of feet is treated in figures 8.7 and 8.8.

Notice that by setting up shorter class intervals, say quarter-inch rather than half-inch, we could have refined the graph, and the polygon would have appeared more like a smooth curve. In fact it is common, especially with continuous-valued variables, to draw a smooth curve rather than a series of

Class Interval Boundaries	Frequency (Number Observed)	Class Interval Boundaries	Frequency
7.0–7.5	2	11.0–11.5	49
7.5–8.0	2	11.5–12.0	40
8.0–8.5	6	12.0–12.5	25
8.5–9.0	12	12.5–13.0	18
9.0–9.5	20	13.0–13.5	5
9.5–10.0	29	13.5–14.0	4
10.0–10.5	47	14.0–14.5	1
10.5–11.0	51		

Figure 8.7   Length of Feet (in inches)

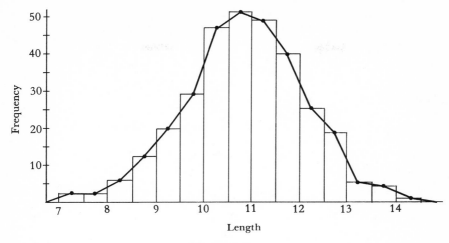

Figure 8. 8

line segments in the form of a polygon. The resulting curve in this case is bell-shaped as in figure 8.9; any set of data which produces such a curve is said to obey a *normal frequency distribution* (often called a Gaussian distribution after the mathematician Gauss).

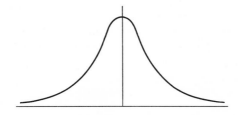

Figure 8.9   Normal Curve

The distinguishing characteristics of a normal distribution are that values near the middle of the distribution occur most often and that values away from the middle decrease in frequency in a symmetric fashion. Of course, most actual samples do not produce a perfect normal curve; but since the discrepancy is only slight for a great many natural phenomena, the normal distribution is very useful in many fields. It is interesting that if the number of coins involved in the experiment of figure 8.6 were increased without bound, the resulting binomial polygons would approach the shape of a perfect normal curve. Hence in many cases a normal curve can be used as an approximation to a binomial distribution.

The constant, binomial, and normal frequency distributions are just three of the simplest and most common in a host of those which have been studied. Some are more suited for discrete-valued variables, some for continuous. A worker in almost any field today needs to have a basic knowledge of certain of these at his disposal for interpreting data, whether it pertains to buying, supply, transportation, genetics, quality control, personality, or any other special area.

PROBLEMS

1. In each part, tabulate the given data in order of magnitude and then construct a histogram and a frequency polygon.
   (a) 1, 2, 4, 6, 2, 3, 2, 2, 1, 4, 3, 4, 5, 3, 4, 2, 1, 3, 4, 5, 4, 3, 2, 4, 6,
   (b) 15, 12, 3, 9, 8, 6, 4, 3, 5, 7, 10, 13, 8, 9, 2, 8, 7, 6, 9, 4, 10, 7, 6, 11, 5.

2. Consider these data: 23, 75, 49, 55, 13, 56, 78, 2, 41, 58, 93, 86, 72, 15, 9, 37, 43, 69, 88, 98, 13, 45, 63, 14, 26, 27, 46, 62, 28, 37.
   (a) Tabulate the given data 3 times using class intervals, first by dividing the range from 0 to 100 into 2 equal class intervals, then into 5, and finally into 10.
   (b) Construct histograms and polygons for all 3 cases in (a).

3. Toss 4 fair coins 64 times, record and tabulate the results, construct a histogram and polygon, and compare with the theoretical binomial distribution in figure 8.6(a).

SECTION 3. MEASURES OF CENTRAL TENDENCY

Regardless of the type of frequency distribution a given population obeys, there are certain basic facts we usually want and standard methods have been developed for deducing them from a set of data. Probably the single most useful bit of information we could have about a collection of values is some kind of an *average*. We present three types of average which are commonly used.

Arithmetic Mean.   The *arithmetic mean* (or simply *mean*), denoted by m, is defined as the sum of the data values divided by the number of values in the set. Hence if the values are $x_1, x_2, x_3, \ldots, x_n$, then

$$m = \frac{x_1 + x_2 + x_3 + \cdots + x_n}{n}.$$

The expression $x_1 + x_2 + x_3 + \cdots + x_n$ indicates the sum of n data values, starting with x_1 and ending with x_n. For such a summation, we commonly use the shortened notation $\sum_{i=1}^{n} x_i$, where the index i takes on all values from 1 to n. For example, $\sum_{i=1}^{5} x_i = x_1 + x_2 + x_3 + x_4 + x_5$. When the summation is over a known set of data, we often omit the subscripts from the notation and simply write Σx. Hence the definition of arithmetic mean becomes

$$m = \frac{\Sigma x}{n}.$$

Example 8.1. Find the arithmetic mean of 1, 4, 5, 4, 9, 4, 8, 5.

According to the definition,

$$m = \frac{\Sigma x}{n} = \frac{1 + 4 + 5 + 4 + 9 + 4 + 8 + 5}{8} = \frac{40}{8} = 5.$$

Instead of writing values repeatedly, we often arrange a table to show the different values occurring, together with their frequencies (the number of times each value occurs), as was done in figure 8.5. The distribution

$$1, 2, 5, 6, 4, 3, 3, 1, 2, 3, 4, 5, 4, 3, 2$$

is presented this way in figure 8.10. In such a case, the mean is calculated according to the formula

$$m = \frac{\Sigma (x \cdot f)}{\Sigma f} = \frac{(x_1 \cdot f_1) + (x_2 \cdot f_2) + \cdots + (x_n \cdot f_n)}{f_1 + f_2 + \cdots + f_n}.$$

Value x	Frequency f
1	2
2	3
3	4
4	3
5	2
6	1

Figure 8.10

For the data in figure 8.10,

$$m = \frac{(1 \cdot 2) + (2 \cdot 3) + (3 \cdot 4) + (4 \cdot 3) + (5 \cdot 2) + (6 \cdot 1)}{2 + 3 + 4 + 3 + 2 + 1}$$

$$= \frac{48}{15}$$

$$= 3.2.$$

When data is treated in terms of class intervals rather than discrete values, we can tabulate in much the same way. To calculate the mean in such a case, instead of using each actual sample value we use the midpoint of that value's class interval. If there are n intervals, and we use t as the midpoint of an interval and f as the frequency, then

$$m = \frac{\Sigma (t \cdot f)}{\Sigma f} = \frac{(t_1 \cdot f_1) + (t_2 \cdot f_2) + \cdots + (t_n \cdot f_n)}{f_1 + f_2 + \cdots + f_n}.$$

Example 8.2.   Compute a mean value for the "length of feet" data of figure 8.7.

According to the above formula,

$$m = \frac{\Sigma (t \cdot f)}{\Sigma f}$$

$$= \frac{(7.25)(2) + (7.75)(2) + (8.25)(6) + \cdots + (14.25)(1)}{2 + 2 + 6 + \cdots + 1}$$

$$= \frac{3374.75}{311}$$

$$= 10.85.$$

Median.   The *median* is defined as the value situated in the middle of the list of data, when the values are arranged in numerical order.

Example 8.3.   Find the median of the values 1, 4, 5, 4, 9, 4, 5, 8.

First arrange the data by magnitude:

$$1, 4, 4, 4, 5, 5, 8, 9.$$

When there is no "middle" value as in this case (due to an even number of data values), we take the median to be the arithmetic mean of the *two* values nearest the middle. In this case the median would be $\frac{4 + 5}{2} = 4.5$.

Mode.   The *mode* is the value that appears most often.

Example 8.4.   Find the mode of the values 1, 4, 5, 4, 9, 4, 5, 8.

Here, 4 is clearly the most frequent value and is the mode.

Quite often, a sample will yield more than a single mode. For example the data set

$$1, 3, 3, 5, 6, 6, 6, 9, 12, 12, 12, 15, 17$$

has both 6 and 12 as modes. In such a case we say the sample is *bimodal*. If we are dealing with class intervals, as in example 8.2, it is possible to get different modes, or even different numbers of modes, by changing the choice of intervals. For this and other reasons, the mode is not usually as reliable or as meaningful as the other indicators of central tendency.

Example 8.5.   Determine the mode of the distribution 20, 10, 30, 50, 30, 80, 90, 90, 10, 100, 10.

The value occurring most often, and hence the mode, is 10. In this case, as in many, the mode does not really indicate much of an "average." In some situations though, it is the best indicator to use. For example, if the values above represent the opinions of the eleven members of an investment club as to how much money to invest in stock Q, the modal response is desirable since it indicates the sum that would please the most members.

Example 8.6. Treat the data of example 8.5 by dividing the range 1–100 into 4 class intervals of equal length.

See figure 8.11 for a summary of the procedure. Notice that this choice of intervals results in two modes, 1–25 and 76–100. (With intervals this large, it can be misleading to take their midpoints as modal values.)

Class Interval Boundaries	Frequency
1–25	4
26–50	3
51–75	0
76–100	4

Figure 8.11

The median and mean also have relative merit and should be used selectively. The median of a distribution is not much affected by the *magnitude* of extreme values but takes into account the *number* of such values. The mean, on the other hand, reflects all values whether or not they are extreme. Also, when repeated samples are taken from a given population, the means of the various samples are generally in more agreement than the medians.

Example 8.7. Find the mean, median, and mode for the distribution of yearly salaries recorded in figure 8.12.

Annual Management Salaries for Company X	
Chairman of the Board	$65,000
President	2,500
1st Vice President	2,000
2nd Vice President	2,000
Personnel Manager	1,900

Figure 8.12

From the data we compute:

$$\text{mean} = \frac{65{,}000 + 2{,}500 + 2{,}000 + 2{,}000 + 1{,}900}{5}$$

$$= \frac{73{,}400}{5}$$

$$= \$14{,}680,$$

$$\text{median} = \$2{,}000, \text{ and}$$

$$\text{mode} = \$2{,}000.$$

The mean, \$14,680, is affected by the magnitude of the one extreme value and hence gives a truer average. But it is clearly not a typical value. The Chairman of the Board might make use of the mean to argue that the salaries, "on the average," are respectable, but the officers would surely oppose that argument by pointing to the median or the mode.

Sometimes the data allows little choice in the kind of average to compute. Consider the values in figure 8.13, for example. There are 47 entries, but we do not know the values of some of them. Hence the mean cannot be computed. But both the median and mode are found to be 12.

Value x	Frequency f
less than 10	3
10	4
11	9
12	16
13	8
14	5
greater than 14	2

Figure 8.13

In some cases, a few extreme values may enter into a sample due to unusual circumstances, and we may want either to disregard those values or to use the median or mode rather than the mean so that their effect is reduced. However, for most applications the arithmetic mean is most reliable. Thus it is used more often than the other measures of central tendency.

PROBLEMS

1. Compute the mean, median, and mode(s) of each of these samples:
   (a) 1, 2, 4, 5, 3, 2, 1, 4, 2, 3, 3,
   (b) 2, 4, 10, 8, 6,
   (c) 15, 19, 32, 16, 43, 81,
   (d) 1431, 1436, 1434, 1434, 1438, 1432, 1436, 1433.

2. Give the mean, median, and mode(s) for each distribution:

(a)

x	f
16	3
17	2
18	1
19	5
20	3
21	4

(b)

x	f
-3	1
-2	2
-1	4
0	8
1	16
2	8
3	4
4	2
5	1

(c)

x	f
500	3
492	5
480	6
465	2
410	9

3. Complete the table given and compute the arithmetic mean for the data shown.

Class Interval Boundaries	Interval Midpoint t	Frequency f
0–2	1	1
2–4		3
4–6		7
6–8		5
8–10		2

Figure 8.14

4. Toss a fair die 20 times recording the results. Repeat the same experiment, thus having two size 20 distributions. For each of the two, find the mean, the median, and the mode. Then compute the difference of the two means, the difference of the two medians, and the difference of the two modes. Arrange these 3 differences in order of magnitude.

5. If 12 workers pick peaches for 8 hours, and if each worker can pick an average (mean) of 10 boxes an hour, how many boxes (total) will they pick?

6. Explain the differences among the 3 formulas:

$$m = \frac{\Sigma x}{n}, \qquad m = \frac{\Sigma (x \cdot f)}{\Sigma f}, \qquad \text{and} \qquad m = \frac{\Sigma (t \cdot f)}{\Sigma f}.$$

SECTION 4. MEASURES OF DISPERSION

The arithmetic mean is a good indication of the average value of a set of data, but it does not give the whole story about the nature of the distribution. The median and mode, as pointed out before, can be even more ambiguous. Consider the two distributions in figure 8.15. They have the same mean and the same median, but beyond that they are quite different.

	1st Sample	2nd Sample
	5	1
	6	2
	7	7
	8	12
	9	13
Mean	7	7
Median	7	7

Figure 8.15

In the first sample, 7 is a fairly typical value whereas in the second, most of the values are quite a bit larger or smaller than 7. What is necessary to describe the difference is some indicator of the degree to which the data is spread out.

Range. The first and simplest of the so-called "measures of dispersion" is the *range*. It is defined as the difference between the largest and smallest data values. In the case of class intervals, we simply subtract the lower boundary of the lowest class from the upper boundary of the highest class. We can differentiate between the two samples in figure 8.15 by saying that the first has a range of 4 while the second has a range of 12. Range can be misleading if it is interpreted unwisely. For example, suppose three judges for a diving contest assign points to Bob and John on five different dives according to the data in figure 8.16. By comparing the range for each contestant, we might be tempted to conclude that Bob is a much more consistent diver than John. However, upon checking more closely, we might decide that John is actually more consistent with the exception of one very poor score, which was probably due to some special circumstance. Notice that John's

	Diver	
Dive	Bob	John
1st	28	27
2nd	22	27
3rd	21	28
4th	26	6
5th	18	27
Mean	23	23
Median	22	27
Range	10	22

Figure 8.16

median score is not unduly affected by the single low score and remains more typical of his performance as a whole than does the mean score. Both divers achieved mean scores of 23, but John's is less "representative" than Bob's because it is pulled down by the one extreme value.

Mean Deviation.   Since the range is governed by extreme values, even if there is only one, other measures of dispersion are often preferable. The *mean deviation* (which we shall denote by m.d.) is defined as the arithmetic mean of all the *magnitudes of deviations from the mean.* The magnitude of a value can be thought of as its size, without regard to whether it is positive or negative. The magnitude of a number x is often spoken of as the *absolute value* of x and is denoted $|x|$. For example, $|7| = 7$, $|-5| = 5$, and $|0| = 0$. Using this notation we have:

$$\text{m.d.} = \frac{\Sigma |x - m|}{n}$$

$$= \frac{|x_1 - m| + |x_2 - m| + \cdots + |x_n - m|}{n}.$$

Columns 1, 2, and 3 of figure 8.17 illustrate the computation of mean deviation for a set of 6 data values. Notice that column 3 contains the absolute values, or magnitudes, of the corresponding values in column 2. Notice also that the sum of all the deviations from the mean (column 2) is 0. This will

1	2	3	4
Data Value x	Deviation from Mean $x - m$	Magnitude of Deviation $|x - m|$	Deviation Squared $(x - m)^2$
15	-5	5	25
17	-3	3	9
19	-1	1	1
21	1	1	1
23	3	3	9
25	5	5	25
Sums: 120	0	18	70

$n = 6$

$$m = \frac{\Sigma x}{n} = \frac{120}{6} = 20$$

$$\text{m.d.} = \frac{\Sigma |x - m|}{n} = \frac{18}{6} = 3$$

$$\text{var} = \frac{\Sigma (x - m)^2}{n} = \frac{70}{6} = 11.67$$

$$\sigma = \sqrt{\text{var}} = \sqrt{11.67} = 3.4$$

Figure 8.17

always be true because of the way the mean was defined. By taking absolute values, we have non-negative quantities whose mean provides some indication of the dispersion of the data.

Variance.   Another way of treating the deviations in column 2 of figure 8.17 is to square each of them (see column 4). This gives a series of positive values which also indicate dispersion. By calculating the arithmetic mean of these squared values, we find what is known as the *variance:*

$$\text{var} = \frac{\Sigma\,(x - m)^2}{n}$$

$$= \frac{(x_1 - m)^2 + (x_2 - m)^2 + \cdots + (x_n - m)^2}{n}.$$

Standard Deviation.   The variance is a popular measure of dispersion, but it is probably used less commonly than the *standard deviation* (denoted σ). This measure is found by simply computing the square root of the variance. Thus it is the square root of the mean of the squared deviations:

$$\sigma = \sqrt{\text{var}}\;.$$

Figure 8.17 shows the computation of mean deviation, variance, and standard deviation. (Appendix A on page 376 can be used for evaluating square roots.) The following example illustrates the computation of mean deviation and variance in the case where class intervals are used rather than discrete values.

Example 8.8.   Compute the mean deviation and variance for a distribution containing 1 value between 0 and 10, 6 between 10 and 20, 8 between 20 and 30, 4 between 30 and 40, and 1 between 40 and 50.

The required computations are shown in figure 8.18. All the values in a given class are treated as if they were at the midpoint of the interval, and the mean is computed on that basis. Deviations are simply the differences between class midpoints and the mean. When adding deviation magnitudes, we must multiply each one by the number of data values in that interval (i.e., the frequency—see column 7). The same applies, of course, for the squares of the deviations (column 9). In this case, since the variance is seen to be 84.9, we have a standard deviation of $\sqrt{84.9}$, or approximately 9.2. Notice that mean deviation and variance both require us to compute the arithmetic mean as an initial step.

Since the bell-shaped normal curve is typical of the distributions of so many natural phenomena, it is useful to see in more detail how measures of central tendency and dispersion apply in that case. Let's take the distribution of scores in a college math class as an example. Most college instructors must get pretty tired of answering the question, "Do you grade on the curve?"

1	2	3	4	5	6	7	8	9
Class Interval Boundaries	Frequency f	Interval Midpoint t	$t \cdot f$	Deviation $t - m$	Magnitude of Deviation $|t - m|$	$|t - m| \cdot f$	$(t - m)^2$	$(t - m)^2 \cdot f$
0–10	1	5	5	-19	19	19	361	361
10–20	6	15	90	-9	9	54	81	486
20–30	8	25	200	1	1	8	1	8
30–40	4	35	140	10	10	40	100	400
40–50	1	45	45	21	21	21	441	441
sums:	$n = 20$		480			142		1696

$$m = \frac{\Sigma(t \cdot f)}{\Sigma f} = \frac{480}{20} = 24$$

$$\text{m.d.} = \frac{\Sigma|t - m| \cdot f}{\Sigma f} = \frac{142}{20} = 7.1$$

$$\text{var} = \frac{\Sigma(t - m)^2 \cdot f}{n} = \frac{1696}{20} = 84.9$$

Figure 8.18

This is mainly because not everyone agrees on just exactly what the question means and on how it applies to a given situation.

The first thing to be aware of is that the distribution of scores in a college class is at best only approximated by a normal curve and that, generally, the smaller the class is, the less accurate the approximation will be. For this reason, "grading on the curve" is not quite as automatic as one might suppose. If, however, the number of data values (scores) is fairly large and if we are sure a normal distribution curve is closely approximated, then a number of conclusions can be drawn with considerable certainty.

First, recall that a normal curve has perfect symmetry (see figure 8.19). Because of this fact, the mean, median, and mode of the distribution will have the same value, namely the value m at the center. With respect to the range of a normal distribution, we should point out that, if the curve is truly normal, there will always be at least some values occurring as far out from the center as you care to look (that is, the curve never actually comes clear down to the axis on either side), and therefore we could not determine a finite range. However, since the frequencies become so small in intervals far from the center, the essential qualities of the normal curve still apply to approximating distributions with a fixed finite range.

The measure of dispersion that is most often applied to normal distributions is the standard deviation. When the mean and the standard deviation are computed, it turns out that approximately 68% of the data values are within 1 standard deviation of the mean, approximately 95% within 2 standard deviations, and approximately 99% within 3 standard deviations (again see figure 8.19). If an instructor wanted to assign certain percentages of A's, B's, etc., and he felt that the assumption of normality was justified in his class, he could use these factors to determine the cut-off points in his grading scheme. A more detailed analysis of normal distribution percentages is presented in the next section.

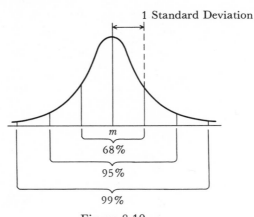

Figure 8.19

Example 8.9. Suppose 300 scores are distributed normally with mean 65 and standard deviation 8. (a) How many scores are between 57 and 73? (b) How many are between 73 and 81? (c) How many are between 2 and 3 standard deviations of the mean?

Using the percentage facts stated above, we can determine the values shown in figure 8.20. (a) Since there are 300 scores involved, the 68% between 57 and 73 is $(300) \cdot (.68)$, or 204. (b) 13.5% are between 73 and 81, that is, about 40 or 41. (c) The portion of the range between 2 and 3 standard deviations of the mean includes 41 to 49 and 81 to 89. These intervals together contain 4%, or 12, of the values.

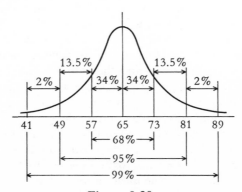

Figure 8.20

PROBLEMS

1. Compute the range, the mean deviation, the variance, and the standard deviation for each of the following sets of data. You might organize the work in a tabular fashion similar to that of figure 8.18. Note, however, that class intervals are not used here.

(a) Value	Frequency	(b) Value	Frequency	(c) Value	Frequency
1	2	1	1	15	2
3	4	2	1	20	4
5	2	3	1	25	3
7	1	4	2	36	2
9	6	5	3	51	1
		6	2	65	3
		7	1		

2. Compute the same quantities as in problem 1. In this case class intervals are used just as in figure 8.18.

(a) Class Interval Boundaries	Frequency	(b) Class Interval Boundaries	Frequency
2–4	1	0–10	5
4–6	3	10–20	15
6–8	1	20–30	4
		30–40	8
		40–50	12

3. Why would the range be a misleading indicator of dispersion for the following set of data?

$$19, 21, 22, 20, 19, 21, 20, 21, 5, 22, 20, 19$$

4. Suppose 100 different chemistry students measure the mass of a sample. Due to human error and to limitations in the accuracy of the balance, they don't all determine the same value, but the results are found to be normally distributed with a mean of 37 grams and a standard deviation of 1 gram.
    (a) How many of the results were greater than 37 grams?
    (b) How many were greater than 36 grams?
    (c) How many were greater than 35 grams?
    (d) How many were greater than 38 grams?
    (e) How many were within 1 gram of the mean?
    (f) How many were further than 2 grams from the mean?

5. (a) Which of the two normal curves below shows the greater standard deviation?
   (b) Which shows the greater mean value?

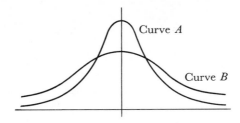

SECTION 5. TESTING HYPOTHESES

Up to this point we have concentrated on measures of central tendency and of dispersion for known data sets. Such considerations are in the realm of what we call *descriptive statistics*. As the opening remarks of this chapter indicated, however, the more important aspect of the subject lies in its ability to let us predict or infer generalities about a population based only upon a limited sample of values from that population. It would be impractical, for example, to poll every prospective voter in the country in order to predict an election winner; so the usual practice is to select a small representative sample upon which to base the prediction. The ideas related to this sampling aspect of statistics belong to what we quite naturally call *sampling statistics* (or *statistical inference*). A multitude of techniques has been developed both for predicting the nature of a population and for estimating any possible error associated with this prediction.

The general procedure used by an experimenter usually involves the following steps:

(1) Propose an hypothesis about some statistical measure of the population.

(2) Gather a data sample from the population.

(3) Either accept or reject the hypothesis according to the degree of consistency between it and the sample.

Various statistical aids, which help in making the required decision, come under the heading of *hypothesis testing*. To illustrate, consider the tossing of a coin; the proposed hypothesis is that the coin is fair. In other words, we propose that if the coin is tossed a very large number of times the proportion of heads occurring would stabilize around $\frac{1}{2}$; hence the probability p of getting heads on a single toss would be $\frac{1}{2}$. Now suppose we obtain a sample by tossing the coin 100 times and observe 56 heads and 44 tails. If x is the number of successes (heads) observed in such an experiment, then the experimental value is $x = 56$. At this point, we must digress for a moment in order to develop the methods of analyzing this result.

We already know that in cases like coin tossing where each trial has two possible outcomes (usually termed success and failure) and where the probability of success (heads in this case) is p, the number of successes per sample of size n is a binomially distributed variable. That is, if we repeated the experiment of tossing the coin 100 times over and over, the number of heads per experiment would obey a binomial distribution (compare figures 8.5 and 8.6). Furthermore, if such an experiment is repeated a great many times, the resulting binomial distribution very closely approximates a normal distribution. As long as the experiment is performed a great number of times, the law of large numbers permits the following important conclusions about the distribution to be drawn:

> If a very large number of samples (consisting of n observations each) are taken and the probability of success on each trial is p, then the variable x (the number of successes per sample) will approximately obey a normal distribution where the mean m is $n \cdot p$ and the standard deviation σ is $\sqrt{n \cdot p \cdot (1 - p)}$. (These formulas are not dependable if $n \cdot p$ is too small, say less than 5.)

These results enable us to ascertain the long-run mean and standard deviation for the distribution of heads per 100 tosses of a coin. Under the assumption that the coin is fair (i.e., $p = \frac{1}{2}$), we would have

$$m = n \cdot p = 100 \cdot (0.5) = 50$$

and $$\sigma = \sqrt{n \cdot p \cdot (1 - p)} = \sqrt{100 \cdot (.5) \cdot (.5)} = \sqrt{25} = 5.$$

Now the question is this: Is our experimental result, $x = 56$, consistent enough with this to allow acceptance of the hypothesis that the coin is fair? Of course, we cannot be sure of making the right decision because 56 heads out of 100 are possible whether the coin is fair or unfair. However, we can usually make a wise choice based upon the following reasoning. Under the assumption of a fair coin, if the observed value (56) is fairly probable, then we should accept the hypothesis. If, on the other hand, 56 heads would be very unlikely if the coin is fair, we should conclude that the hypothesis is false. In order to make the decision, we often refer to the *normal deviate z*, which, for a given observation x from a normal population, is defined as:

$$z = \frac{x - m}{\sigma}.$$

Since $x - m$ is simply x's deviation from the population mean and σ is the population standard deviation, z gives the number of *standard deviation units* x is from the mean. If x is less than m, then z is negative. Clearly, a *z-score* can be computed for every member of a normal population. For our coin-tossing problem above, we have

$$z = \frac{56 - 50}{5} = \frac{6}{5} = 1.2.$$

Figure 8.21 illustrates the relationship between z-scores and the areas under the normal curve. The proportion of population values whose z-scores lie between 0 and 1.2 equals the proportion of area under the curve which is

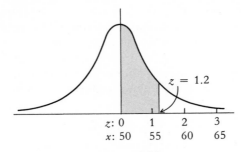

$$z: 0 \quad 1 \quad 2 \quad 3$$
$$x: 50 \quad 55 \quad 60 \quad 65$$

Figure 8.21

shaded. Appendix C on page 378 evaluates such areas for positive z-scores; in particular, for $z = 1.2$ the shaded area is 0.3849 of the total area under the curve. Since half the total population values are to the left of $z = 0$, the proportion of area to the right of $z = 1.2$ is $1 - (.5 + .3849) = 1 - .8849 = .1151$. This means that under the assumption of a fair coin, the probability of observing 56 heads or more out of 100 tosses is 0.1151. A value as far above the mean as we have would occur roughly 11 to 12 per cent of the time if the experiment were repeated a large number of times and if the coin were fair. For example, if the experiment (of tossing a coin 100 times) were performed, say 200 times, we could expect about 23 of these performances to yield 56 or more heads. We might consider this too rare an occurrence to accept the hypothesis or we might not. This is entirely up to us and usually depends upon the risk we are willing to take of being wrong. One of two types of errors is always possible:

Type I: mistaken rejection of a true hypothesis.
Type II: mistaken acceptance of a false hypothesis.

In an experiment, if a Type I error results in more dire consequences than would a Type II error, then it is better to accept rarer occurrences as consistent with the hypothesis. For example, we could decide to accept the fair coin hypothesis above even if the probability of the observed value is only 0.1. Here we are setting up a 0.1 *significance level* for rejection. The probability of 0.1151 is greater than 0.1, and we would accept the hypothesis, thus running the risk of making a Type II error. Most experiments are designed so that it is undesirable to reject the hypothesis unless one is pretty "certain" it is false. Therefore the experimenter commonly sets himself a significance level of 0.05, 0.01, or even lower before beginning to test the hypothesis by sampling.

In the discussion above, the focus of attention is on the probability of observing 56 or more heads out of 100 tosses. Actually, observations which are smaller than the population mean can be just as important as those that are larger. We might just as well have asked for the probability of observing a value 6 units or more away from the mean. The corresponding area is shaded in figure 8.22, and by the symmetry of the normal curve the probability is twice the previous value, or 0.2302. When we use both tails of the curve like this, we are using a *two-tailed test;* when just one is used, it is a *one-tailed test.* As mentioned before, an experimenter usually decides on a significance level before he performs the test.

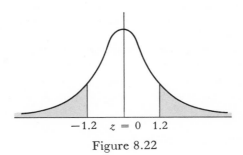

$$-1.2 \quad z = 0 \quad 1.2$$

Figure 8.22

In a one-tailed test on the right where the significance level is set at 0.05, we would reject the hypothesis only if the observed value is in the upper 5% of the population. The rejection region for a two-tailed test at the same significance level includes both the upper 2.5% and the lower 2.5% of the population. Figure 8.23 illustrates both these cases. The critical values of z are determined directly from Appendix C. The upper 5% of the population occurs above the point where area A equals 0.45. We see from the table that the corresponding z-score is about 1.645. The critical z-scores for the two-tailed test are determined by the area value $A = 0.475$.

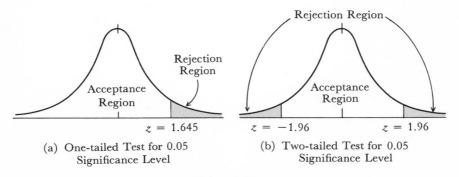

(a) One-tailed Test for 0.05
Significance Level

(b) Two-tailed Test for 0.05
Significance Level

Figure 8.23

PROBLEMS

1. Suppose a coin is tossed 100 times and lands heads up 62 times. Using a one-tailed test with significance level 0.05, determine whether or not to accept the hypothesis that the coin is fair.

2. Apply a two-tailed test at a 0.02 significance level to the hypothesis of problem 1.

3. Happy Hazard, the statistical editor for a college newspaper, interviewed all 8000 girls on campus and found that their heights are normally distributed with a mean of 5 feet 6 inches and standard deviation 3 inches.
   (a) How many of the girls are over 6 feet tall?
   (b) How many are shorter than 5 feet 2 inches?
   (c) How many are between 5 feet 1 inch and 5 feet 8 inches?
   (d) If one girl is chosen at random, what is the probability that she is taller than 6 feet 4 inches?
   (e) If we separated the girls into 4 equal-sized groups according to height, what would be the minimum possible height of a girl in the tallest group?

4. Suppose a die is rolled 90 times, and 5 turns up 20 times. Using a two-tailed test and a 0.05 significance level, test the hypothesis that the die is fair.

SECTION 6. RELATIONSHIPS BETWEEN SETS OF DATA

Statistical Significance. For a sample to be a valid test of an hypothesis about a population, it is important that the sample be chosen randomly. For example, consider the hypothesis that the students of Splash High can swim 25 meters in an average (mean) time of 12 seconds. It makes very little sense to test this hypothesis by timing the members of the swim team and no one else. However in some statistical applications, certain specified samples are chosen intentionally in order to see if they differ significantly from the population as a whole. Some of the ideas from the study of *statistical significance* are illustrated in the following example.

Example 8.10. It is known that the personal annual income in a certain country is normally distributed with a mean of $3700 and a standard deviation of $100. All the residents of a certain town are polled and it is found that their mean annual income is $3950. Take a 0.01 level of significance, and determine whether the value for this town
   (a) is significantly higher than the national average, and
   (b) differs significantly from the national average.

   (a) The z-score for the town's mean value is

$$z = \frac{x - m}{\sigma} = \frac{3950 - 3700}{100} = \frac{250}{100} = 2.5.$$

The population values *significantly higher* than the mean (at the 0.01 level) lie in the shaded region of figure 8.24 (why did we choose $A = 0.49$?). Since the

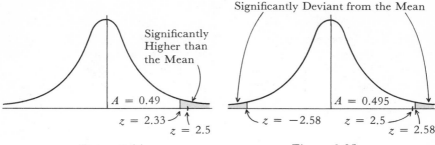

Figure 8.24   Figure 8.25

z-score, 2.5, is greater than 2.33, the result is significantly higher than the national average.

(b) Figure 8.25 shows the regions containing values *significantly different* (or *significantly deviant*) from the mean. Since a two-tailed test applied here, we must use $A = 0.495$ for a 0.01 significance level (why?). The *z*-score of 2.5 is less than 2.58; therefore, the result for the town is not significantly different than the national average.

Regression. In example 8.10 above, personal annual incomes in a given town are compared with those of the country as a whole to determine the extent to which the town is "special" with respect to income. Both sets of values, the national population and the town sample, contain measurements of the same quantity, namely annual income. An entirely different type of comparison occurs when two different quantities are measured and compared. For example, suppose that the person polling the residents of the town discussed above is also recording their ages and that he notices older people seem to have consistently higher incomes. To analyze this observation he might begin by tabulating his data as in figure 8.26 (assume for the moment that the town only has 10 residents). Associating each resident's income with

Resident	Age	Annual Income
Mr. A	19	2150
Mr. B	23	2550
Mr. C	27	3250
Mr. D	31	3150
Mr. E	36	4250
Mr. F	40	4200
Mr. G	44	4350
Mr. H	49	5000
Mr. I	52	4950
Mr. J	54	5650

Figure 8.26

his age results in the set of ordered pairs $\{(19, 2150), (23, 2550), (27, 3250),$ $\ldots, (54, 5650)\}$, which forms a *relation* (see Chapter 6, sections 1 and 2, for a discussion of relations and their graphs). The determination of the type of relationship existing between two quantities (age and income) is called *regression analysis*. The next step in the present example is to graph the ordered pairs on a Cartesian coordinate system (figure 8.27). In statistical work, such a graph is called a *scatter diagram*.

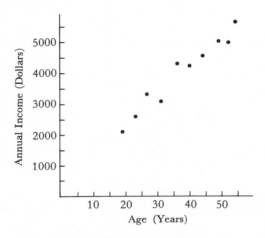

Figure 8.27   Scatter Diagram

Although not all the points in the diagram lie in a perfectly straight line, they are close enough for us to conclude that the relationship is approximately linear and to try and draw a line which "fits" the data in the best possible way. It should be pointed out that there are more precise ways of determining how true a linear relationship is than just looking at a scatter diagram. Various types of *correlation coefficients* can be calculated for a data set, which describe numerically the degree of correlation between the two variables. In many applications the linearity of the relationship is not as obvious as in the above scatter diagram, and it is therefore important to know the correlation coefficient before proceeding with the regression analysis. In our example, where the scatter diagram clearly indicates a linear relationship, the slope of the regression line shows the apparent rate at which income increases as age increases.

On the other hand, it is often true that one measured quantity will decrease (rather than increase) as the other increases, in which case we speak of an *inverse relation*. For example, a certain law in chemistry (*Boyle's Law*) states that the volume of a constant amount of gas at a constant temperature is inversely proportional to the pressure. In other words, as you increase the pressure on a given amount of gas which is being kept at a constant temperature, the volume will decrease proportionally (see figure 8.28).

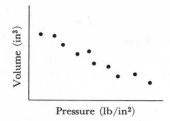

Figure 8.28　Inverse Linear
Relation

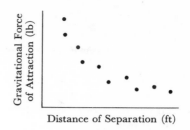

Figure 8.29　Inverse Square
Relation

Relationships between pairs of variables certainly are not always linear. *Newton's Law of Gravitation* is an example of the common *inverse square relation.* It states that the gravitational force of attraction between two bodies decreases at the same rate that the square of the distance between them increases (see figure 8.29).

Plotting scatter diagrams usually gives a rough idea of the kind of relationship, if any, between two variable quantities. But the actual determination of an accurate regression curve requires some calculation. We will treat linear regression only, using age versus income data as an example. In figure 8.30 a tentative line has been drawn. If we let X denote age (on the horizontal axis) and Y denote income (on the vertical axis), then the equation of this line can be written as

$$Y = a + (b \cdot X),$$

where a is the Y value at which the line intersects the vertical axis and b is the slope of the line (again, see Chapter 6 on linear relations). In general, for each X value in the data set, the corresponding Y value differs from the value

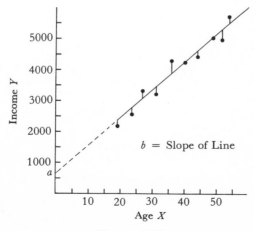

Figure 8.30

it would have if the data point were exactly on the line. These 10 differences are shown in the figure by vertical segments. Choosing a different line would probably make some of these differences greater and some lesser. The most common procedure is to choose the line where the sum of the squares of all these differences is at a minimum; it is therefore called the *method of least squares*. The details of the reasoning behind it involve techniques from differential calculus, but fortunately, the general results can be applied rather easily. If there are n ordered pairs in the set of data and if m_X and m_Y denote the means of the X values and Y values respectively, then the number b can be computed by the formula:

$$b = \frac{\Sigma\,(X \cdot Y) - n \cdot m_X \cdot m_Y}{\Sigma\,(X^2) - n \cdot m_{X^2}}.$$

Once b is found, we compute a according to the formula:

$$a = m_Y - b \cdot m_X.$$

Now, with the numbers a and b determined, we can pick any two X values and use the equation $Y = a + b \cdot X$ to determine the corresponding Y values. This yields two points which determine the regression line.

Example 8.11.   Draw a "least squares" regression line for the scatter diagram of figure 8.27.

In order to compute a and b, refer to the data values in figure 8.26. The determinations of ΣX, ΣY, $\Sigma(X \cdot Y)$, and $\Sigma(X^2)$ are shown in figure 8.31. Using this information, we can find values for a and b:

$$n = 10$$

$$m_X = \frac{\Sigma X}{n} = \frac{375}{10} = 37.5$$

$$m_X^2 = (37.5)^2 = 1406.25$$

$$m_Y = \frac{\Sigma Y}{n} = \frac{39{,}500}{10} = 3950$$

$$b = \frac{1{,}604{,}800 - 10(37.5)(3950)}{15{,}433 - 10(1406.25)} \approx \frac{123{,}550}{1370} \approx 90$$

$$a \approx 3950 - (90)(37.5) = 575.$$

($\approx$ means "approximately equals.")

Hence the equation of the least squares regression line is (approximately)

$$Y = 575 + 90 \cdot X.$$

X	Y	$X \cdot Y$	X^2
19	2150	40,850	361
23	2550	58,650	529
27	3250	87,750	729
31	3150	97,650	961
36	4250	153,000	1296
40	4200	168,000	1600
44	4350	191,400	1936
49	5000	245,000	2401
52	4950	257,400	2704
54	5650	305,100	2916
sums: 375	39,500	1,604,800	15,433

Figure 8.31

Since 575 is the Y value where the line intersects the Y axis, the ordered pair $(0, 575)$ represents one point of the line. To determine another, we let $X = 50$, which yields $Y = 575 + 90 \cdot 50 = 5075$. Thus $(50, 5075)$ represents a second point on the line, and we can draw it as in figure 8.32.

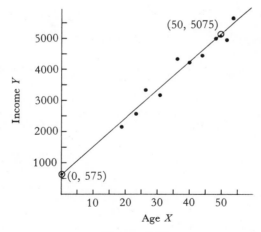

Figure 8.32

PROBLEMS

1. In a certain mathematical aptitude test, the first 10,000 students who took it produced a normal distribution of scores with mean 150 and standard deviation 15. The mean score for one specific class was 190. Is this class significantly higher than the population of 10,000 as a whole (at the 0.01 level)?

2. Explain how, in example 8.10, the mean income for the town could be "significantly higher" but not "significantly different" than the national average at the 0.01 significance level.

3. Refer to example 8.10. (a) How low must the mean annual income for a town be in order to be classified as "significantly lower" than the national average at the 0.01 level? At the 0.05 level? (b) How high or how low must it be to be classified as "significantly different" than the national average at the 0.01 level? At the 0.05 level?

4. Find the values of a and b in the regression line $Y = a + bX$ for the following set of data:

X	Y
1	3.0
2	4.1
3	4.8
4	5.7
5	6.5

5. Use the regression line of problem 4 to predict a Y value corresponding to (a) $X = 6$, (b) $X = 10$, (c) $X = 15$.

6. In problem 5, which of the three Y values would you have the most faith in? The least? Why?

7. The following table gives reading ability scores and I.Q. scores for a group of 10 individuals.
   (a) Plot a scatter diagram with reading on the horizontal axis.
   (b) Find the equation of a regression line.
   (c) Use the regression line equation to estimate the I.Q. of a person with a reading score of 65.

X = reading	Y = I.Q.	X = reading	Y = I.Q.
83	120	90	127
76	104	75	90
75	98	78	110
85	115	95	134
74	87	80	119

8. Two sets of data give rise to the scatter diagrams A and B. Which one would you say exhibits a linear relationship with the most certainty?

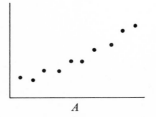

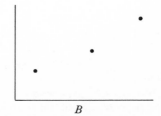

A B

9. Referring again to mean annual income, would you expect smaller towns to be more consistent with the national average or less consistent? List several factors that might affect your answer.

FOR FURTHER READING

Alder, Henry L., and Roessler, Edward B. *Introduction to Probability and Statistics*. San Francisco: W. H. Freeman and Company, 1964.

Carlborg, Frank W. *Introduction to Statistics*. Glenview, Illinois: Scott, Foresman and Company, 1968.

Weinberg, George H., and Schumaker, John A. *Statistics, an Intuitive Approach*. Belmont, California: Wadsworth Publishing Company, 1962.

Statistics is as widely used today as probably any subject in mathematics. Therefore, most students could profit from a more detailed study of this field. The above list contains only a few of many good introductory texts.

CHAPTER 9

MATRIX THEORY

A *matrix* is a rectangular array of numbers enclosed by parentheses. Thus,

$$\begin{pmatrix} 3 & 4 & 2 & -1 \\ 1 & -1 & 0 & 2 \\ -1 & -3 & -2 & -1 \end{pmatrix}$$

is a matrix composed of three rows and four columns. The numbers in the matrix are called the *entries, components,* or *elements* of the matrix. Two matrices are *equal* if the corresponding entries are equal. A matrix whose entries are all zero is called a *zero matrix* and denoted by 0. For the most part we shall discuss *square matrices;* that is, matrices which have the same number of columns as rows.

Matrix theory can be traced to the studies of William Rowan Hamilton (1805–1865), probably Ireland's greatest mathematician. In 1827, at the age of twenty-one, he became Royal Astronomer of Ireland, a position which he held until his death. Hamilton was a neat, precise, and fastidious writer, which may explain why he published so little as compared to the extent of his investigations. As we shall see, matrix multiplication is not commutative; Hamilton was so excited when he discovered this that he carved his discovery into the stone of a Dublin bridge.

The term "matrix" was coined by Arthur Cayley (1821–1895) and James Sylvester (1814–1897). These two good friends, who had entered into an enthusiastic and profitable mathematical partnership, were the first to systematically study matrices. They showed that the behavior of matrices is somewhat similar to that of single real numbers.

Arthur Cayley received a fellowship at Cambridge University, but his refusal to take religious orders, a university requirement at the time, prevented its renewal. He then turned to the study of law and became a prominent London lawyer. In 1863 he was offered a professorship at Cambridge, which he accepted. In addition to his innovations in matrix theory, Cayley also did work in *n*-dimensional space, a study which encompasses spaces of arbitrarily many dimensions.

James Sylvester was not only a mathematician but also a poet, a wit, and one of the greatest creators of new terms in the history of mathematics. Like Cayley, Sylvester attended Cambridge, but because he was a Jew he could not subscribe to the religious test of the Church of England. Therefore the degrees he had earned were not bestowed until many years later, when the requirement was removed. He began working for a London insurance company as an actuary (who prepares life insurance mortality tables), while at night he conducted classes in advanced mathematics; one of his pupils was the famous nurse Florence Nightengale. In 1855 he accepted a position at Woolwich Royal Military Academy, remaining there until 1870, when the administrators forced him to retire.

Sylvester taught in the United States at two different times: he spent one year (1841–1842) at the University of Virginia, but due to his outspoken views on American slavery a longer stay was impractical. During his second stay, as a professor at Johns Hopkins University from 1877 until 1883, he established one of America's first graduate programs in mathematics; with the teaching of Sylvester mathematics began to flourish in the United States. Sylvester worked by inspiration, and all of his work is characterized by powerful imagination and inventiveness.

Matrix theory has been an important tool of the physical sciences since the 1920's. It has found application in many branches of mathematics, astronomy, mechanics, electric circuit theory, nuclear physics, and aerodynamics. However, its use as a tool in business dates only to the late 1940's, when George Dantzig, a mathematician working for the U.S. Air Force, developed the idea of linear programming (elementary examples of which are presented in Chapter 6). Business quickly adopted the ideas of linear programming as an aid in producing the maximum profit and/or minimum cost. Actual problems from business (unlike the ones of Chapter 6) often involve many dozens of variables and are best solved on large computers with the aid of matrices. In this chapter some of the basic ideas of matrix theory are developed, with applications to practical problems presented in the last few sections of the chapter.

SECTION 1. BASIC MATRIX OPERATIONS

The *sum* of two matrices, A and B, is the new matrix $A + B$ that results when the corresponding components of the two matrices are added.

Example 9.1. Let $A = \begin{pmatrix} 2 & 3 & -1 \\ -4 & 2 & 4 \\ 0 & 3 & -2 \end{pmatrix}$, and $B = \begin{pmatrix} 1 & 4 & 3 \\ 6 & -1 & -5 \\ -3 & 4 & 5 \end{pmatrix}$.

Find $A + B$.

Using the definition given above, we find that

$$A + B = \begin{pmatrix} 2 & 3 & -1 \\ -4 & 2 & 4 \\ 0 & 3 & -2 \end{pmatrix} + \begin{pmatrix} 1 & 4 & 3 \\ 6 & -1 & -5 \\ -3 & 4 & 5 \end{pmatrix}$$

$$= \begin{pmatrix} 2+1 & 3+4 & (-1)+3 \\ (-4)+6 & 2+(-1) & 4+(-5) \\ 0+(-3) & 3+4 & (-2)+5 \end{pmatrix}$$

$$= \begin{pmatrix} 3 & 7 & 2 \\ 2 & 1 & -1 \\ -3 & 7 & 3 \end{pmatrix}.$$

Note that two matrices may be added only if they contain the same number of columns and the same number of rows. The *difference of two matrices* is obtained in a similar manner.

Example 9.2. Assume that A and B are the same matrices as in example 9.1. Find $A - B$.

The result:

$$A - B = \begin{pmatrix} 2 & 3 & -1 \\ -4 & 2 & 4 \\ 0 & 3 & -2 \end{pmatrix} - \begin{pmatrix} 1 & 4 & 3 \\ 6 & -1 & -5 \\ -3 & 4 & 5 \end{pmatrix}$$

$$= \begin{pmatrix} 2-1 & 3-4 & -1-3 \\ -4-6 & 2-(-1) & 4-(-5) \\ 0-(-3) & 3-4 & -2-5 \end{pmatrix}$$

$$= \begin{pmatrix} 1 & -1 & -4 \\ -10 & 3 & 9 \\ 3 & -1 & -7 \end{pmatrix}.$$

Multiplication of a matrix A by a real number b, written bA or Ab, is the operation that multiplies every entry of A by the number b.

Example 9.3. Use matrix B from above and find $-3B$.

According to the definition we multiply every entry of B by -3.

$$-3B = \begin{pmatrix} -3(1) & -3(4) & -3(3) \\ -3(6) & -3(-1) & -3(-5) \\ -3(-3) & -3(4) & -3(5) \end{pmatrix} = \begin{pmatrix} -3 & -12 & -9 \\ -18 & 3 & 15 \\ 9 & -12 & -15 \end{pmatrix}.$$

Example 9.4. Using matrices A and B from above, find $3A - 2B$.

Multiply every entry of A by 3, every entry of B by 2, and then subtract. The result:

$$3A - 2B = \begin{pmatrix} 4 & 1 & -9 \\ -24 & 8 & 22 \\ 6 & 1 & -16 \end{pmatrix}.$$

Example 9.5. Decide whether this statement is true: given two matrices A and B, where A and B have the same number of rows and the same number of columns, $A + B = B + A$.

Consider any two matrices A and B of the same size. First, evaluate $A + B$, then $B + A$. Regardless of the matrices chosen, it will be found that $A + B = B + A$. Hence we can consider the statement true.

Now we must look for a reasonable way to multiply two matrices. Consider a point (x, y) in a Cartesian coordinate system. Let us stretch and deform the plane in such a way that the point (x, y) is changed into some new point (x', y'), where (x, y) and (x', y') are related by the stretching equations

$$x' = ax + by$$
$$y' = cx + dy,$$

where a, b, c, and d are real numbers. We would know the essentials of the stretching equations if we had only the matrix

$$\begin{pmatrix} a & b \\ c & d \end{pmatrix}.$$

If we stretch and deform the plane again, we can convert the point (x', y') into a new point (x'', y''), using the stretching equations

$$x'' = ex' + fy'$$
$$y'' = gx' + hy'.$$

Here we obtain the matrix

$$\begin{pmatrix} e & f \\ g & h \end{pmatrix}.$$

What would the stretching equations be if we desired to convert (x, y) directly into (x'', y'')? To find out, we could substitute the first set of stretching equations above into the second, obtaining:

$$x'' = ex' + fy' = e(ax + by) + f(cx + dy) = (ea + fc)x + (eb + fd)y;$$
$$y'' = gx' + hy' = g(ax + by) + h(cx + dy) = (ga + hc)x + (gb + hd)y.$$

The matrix here is

(*)
$$\begin{pmatrix} ea + fc & eb + fd \\ ga + hc & gb + hd \end{pmatrix}.$$

In changing (x, y) into (x', y') we use

$$\begin{pmatrix} a & b \\ c & d \end{pmatrix}.$$

In changing (x', y') into (x'', y'') we use

$$\begin{pmatrix} e & f \\ g & h \end{pmatrix}.$$

Hence to change (x, y) directly into (x'', y'') we need both the matrices above, or

$$\begin{pmatrix} e & f \\ g & h \end{pmatrix} \cdot \begin{pmatrix} a & b \\ c & d \end{pmatrix}.$$

We must define the multiplication of two matrices in such a way that the result is matrix (*) above. The following procedure does just that.

Let's find the product of these matrices:

$$A = \begin{pmatrix} -2 & 3 & -4 \\ 2 & -1 & 3 \\ -6 & -4 & 2 \end{pmatrix} \qquad B = \begin{pmatrix} -1 & -3 & 4 \\ -2 & 2 & 1 \\ 3 & 0 & 2 \end{pmatrix}.$$

To find the entry for row 1, column 1 of the product matrix, consider only row 1 of A and column 1 of B:

$$\begin{pmatrix} -2 & 3 & -4 \\ & & \\ & & \end{pmatrix} \cdot \begin{pmatrix} -1 & & \\ -2 & & \\ 3 & & \end{pmatrix}.$$

(a) Multiply each entry in row 1 of A times the corresponding entry in column 1 of B:

$$(-2) \cdot (-1) = 2$$
$$(3) \cdot (-2) = -6$$
$$(-4) \cdot (3) = -12.$$

(b) Add these three products together:

$$(2) + (-6) + (-12) = -16,$$

which is the entry for row 1, column 1 of the product matrix.

We must complete these two steps for each entry in the product matrix. For example, to obtain the entry in row 3, column 2 of the product matrix, consider only row 3 of A and column 2 of B:

$$\begin{pmatrix} & & \\ & & \\ -6 & -4 & 2 \end{pmatrix} \cdot \begin{pmatrix} & -3 & \\ & 2 & \\ & 0 & \end{pmatrix}.$$

(a) Multiply each entry in row 3 of A times the corresponding entry in column 2 of B:

$$(-6) \cdot (-3) = 18$$
$$(-4) \cdot (2) = -8$$
$$(2) \cdot (0) = 0.$$

(b) Add these three products together:

$$(18) + (-8) + (0) = 10.$$

This is the entry for row 3, column 2 of the product matrix.

By continuing in a similar fashion, we can obtain the entire product matrix:

$$AB = \begin{pmatrix} -16 & 12 & -13 \\ 9 & -8 & 13 \\ 20 & 10 & -24 \end{pmatrix}.$$

In summary, to obtain the product of any two matrices, A and B, multiply the entries in row i of A by the entries in column j of B (where i and j are placeholders for the row and column numbers), then add the resulting products for the one number which is the entry in row i, column j of the product matrix.

Example 9.6. Using matrices A and B above, find BA.

To find the entry for row 2, column 1 of the product matrix, we use row 2 of B and column 1 of A, obtaining:

$$(-2)(-2) + 2(2) + (1)(-6) = 4 + 4 + (-6) = 2.$$

Hence 2 is the entry for row 2, column 1 of the product matrix. The product may be completed in the same way:

$$BA = \begin{pmatrix} -28 & -16 & 3 \\ 2 & -12 & 16 \\ -18 & 1 & -8 \end{pmatrix}.$$

Example 9.7.   Is this statement true: for all matrices A and B, $AB = BA$.

Such a statement is true only if it is true in every case. However, the two matrices A and B of example 9.6 have the property that $AB \neq BA$. Hence the statement is not valid in every case and is false. Matrix multiplication is not commutative.

PROBLEMS

Let $A = \begin{pmatrix} -4 & 0 & 1 \\ 3 & -4 & 2 \\ -1 & 2 & 1 \end{pmatrix}$ and $B = \begin{pmatrix} 2 & -1 & 3 \\ -4 & 0 & 1 \\ 1 & 3 & -3 \end{pmatrix}$.

Evaluate each of the following:

1. $A + B$
2. $A - B$
3. $2A$
4. $B - A$
5. $2B + (-4)A$
6. AB
7. BA
8. $B(AB)$

9. $B(A + B)$
10. $B^2 A^2$
11. $A^2 B^2$
12. $(BA)^2$
13. $(AB)^2$
14. $(-1)A + A$
15. A^3
16. B^4

17. Find a matrix C such that $A + C = B$ and compare with the answer to problem 4.

For each of the following three statements, give an example to show it is false, or else write several examples to verify that the statement is true.

18. For all matrices A, B, and C,

$$(A + B) + C = A + (B + C).$$

19. For all matrices A and B, $A - B = B - A$.
20. For all matrices A and for all real numbers b, $bA = Ab$.

Let $D = \begin{pmatrix} 1 & 0 & 0 & 4 \\ 2 & 2 & -1 & 3 \\ 4 & 0 & 0 & 0 \end{pmatrix}$ while $E = \begin{pmatrix} 3 & 4 & 1 \\ -2 & 0 & 2 \\ 4 & -2 & 0 \\ 1 & 1 & 0 \end{pmatrix}$.

21. Calculate, if possible, ED.
22. Calculate, if possible, DE.
23. Suppose it is desired to multiply two matrices F and G to obtain FG. How must the number of columns of F compare to the number of rows of G? How about the number of rows of F?
24. Write any matrix H containing 4 rows and 6 columns. Then write any matrix J containing 2 columns and 6 rows. It is possible to compute HJ? How about JH?

SECTION 2. THE MULTIPLICATIVE IDENTITY

In Chapter 3, we studied properties of the mathematical system consisting of the set of integers and the operation of multiplication. For example, we found that for every integer a,

$$a \times 1 = 1 \times a = a.$$

Because of this property, 1 is the multiplicative identity for the set of integers. Can we find a similar multiplicative identity for matrices? If

$$A = \begin{pmatrix} -2 & 3 & -4 \\ 2 & -1 & 3 \\ -6 & -4 & 2 \end{pmatrix},$$

can we find a matrix I such that

$$AI = IA = A?$$

Since 1 is the identity element for multiplication, perhaps a matrix containing all 1's is the identity matrix. In order for the matrix containing all 1's to be the identity element, it is necessary that

$$\begin{pmatrix} -2 & 3 & -4 \\ 2 & -1 & 3 \\ -6 & -4 & 2 \end{pmatrix} \cdot \begin{pmatrix} 1 & 1 & 1 \\ 1 & 1 & 1 \\ 1 & 1 & 1 \end{pmatrix}$$

be A again. This means it is necessary to have -2 in the first row, first column of the product (why?). To obtain the entry for row 1, column 1 of the product matrix multiply the entries of row 1 of A by the entries of column 1 of the proposed identity:

$$(-2)(1) + (3)(1) + (-4)(1) = -3 \neq -2.$$

A matrix with all 1's cannot be the identity.

A little strategy. We need to multiply the numbers in row 1 of A by the corresponding entries in column 1 of our sought-for identity I, that is,

$$(-2)\underline{\hspace{1cm}} + 3\underline{\hspace{1cm}} + (-4)\underline{\hspace{1cm}}.$$

We must fill the blanks in such a way that the total is -2. Perhaps 1 in the first blank, and zeroes in the second and third? That would give -2. Then the identity would be, in part

$$\begin{pmatrix} 1 & & \\ 0 & & \\ 0 & & \end{pmatrix}.$$

We must now choose numbers for the boxes of figure 9.1 that will produce 3

$$\begin{pmatrix} -2 & 3 & -4 \\ & & \end{pmatrix} \begin{pmatrix} \Box \\ \Box \\ \Box \end{pmatrix} = \begin{pmatrix} 3 \\ \\ \end{pmatrix}$$

Figure 9.1

in the product matrix. Perhaps a zero in the top and bottom boxes and 1 in the middle. That would give the 3 needed. We can now make a good guess as to what I might be:

$$I = \begin{pmatrix} 1 & 0 & 0 \\ 0 & 1 & 0 \\ 0 & 0 & 1 \end{pmatrix}.$$

Note that $AI = IA = A$, as required.

Example 9.8. Find the multiplicative identity for the set of 2x2 matrices (2 rows, 2 columns).

We can follow the same procedure as above in order to obtain the identity for the 2x2 matrices:

$$\begin{pmatrix} 1 & 0 \\ 0 & 1 \end{pmatrix}.$$

For example,

$$\begin{pmatrix} 2 & -1 \\ -4 & 1 \end{pmatrix} \cdot \begin{pmatrix} 1 & 0 \\ 0 & 1 \end{pmatrix} = \begin{pmatrix} 1 & 0 \\ 0 & 1 \end{pmatrix} \cdot \begin{pmatrix} 2 & -1 \\ -4 & 1 \end{pmatrix} = \begin{pmatrix} 2 & -1 \\ -4 & 1 \end{pmatrix}.$$

This derivation of the identity matrix I is an example of the process a mathematician uses. First, he makes certain that he completely understands the problem: What matrix I can be found so that $AI = IA = A$, for every 3x3 matrix A? He tries analogies to known situations: Since 1 is the multiplicative identity for the integers perhaps the identity matrix is a matrix of all 1's. Relying upon insight from previous problems, he tries various examples. Finally, after a period of trial and error, the solution is ready. The mathematician who solves this problem would merely state:

Let $I = \begin{pmatrix} 1 & 0 & 0 \\ 0 & 1 & 0 \\ 0 & 0 & 1 \end{pmatrix}$. It works. Try it.

He does not describe the blind alleys, the wrong approaches, the frustrations, only the fact that he has solved the problem. Sometimes this presents a problem for the non-mathematician who sees only the solution, free of flaws. The non-mathematician, knowing he could not produce the same work as easily, concludes math is not for him. But behind the solution which proceeds so nicely on the page is a mass of scratch paper and a stack of errors.

Having at last obtained the solution to the problem of finding the identity matrix, the mathematician might have a hard time explaining the thought processes behind his solution. "How did you know to start this way?" or "Why did you take that step?" both seem to be reasonable questions, and yet often they have no answer. There are no rules or automatic methods for problem solving, simply the intuition and experience of the problem solver. To ask a mathematician to describe his methods of thought is much the same as asking Mickey Mantle how he hits a home run. He probably cannot tell you how to do it in such a way that you can go out and do it yourself, but his advice, together with trial and practice on your part, might produce the desired result.

PROBLEMS

In these problems, I is the identity for 3x3 matrices.
1. Find I^4.
2. Does $I^{12} = I$?
3. Find the identity matrix for 4x4 matrices.
4. Let K be the one-row, three-column matrix, $(1 \quad 2 \quad -4)$. Does there exist a matrix I, such that $KI = IK = K$?
5. Try to make a general rule: for a given matrix A, there can exist a matrix I, such that $IA = AI = A$ in case _____ .
6. Find the identity matrix for the addition of 3x3 matrices.
7. Find a matrix Z, such that if A is any 3x3 matrix, $A + Z = A$.
8. Find as many 3x3 matrices D as you can, such that $D = 2D$.
9. Find as many 3x3 matrices D as you can, such that $D^2 = D$.

SECTION 3. DETERMINANTS

With every square matrix, we can associate a certain number called the *determinant* of the matrix. We define the determinant for 2x2 and 3x3 matrices in this section; methods for finding the determinants of larger matrices are given in some of the books mentioned at the end of the chapter. To find the determinant of a 2x2 matrix, first obtain the product of the two numbers circled at the left in figure 9.2: $(3)(-2) = -6$. Then find the product of the

$$\begin{pmatrix} 3 & -4 \\ 5 & -2 \end{pmatrix} \qquad \begin{pmatrix} 3 & -4 \\ 5 & -2 \end{pmatrix}$$

Figure 9.2

two numbers circled at the right: $(5)(-4) = -20$. Subtract the second product from the first: $(-6) - (-20) = 14$, which is the determinant of the matrix. To denote the determinant of a matrix we place straight lines around the entries of the matrix,

$$\begin{vmatrix} 3 & -4 \\ 5 & -2 \end{vmatrix} = 14.$$

Let's find the determinant of a 3x3 matrix,

$$\begin{pmatrix} -2 & 0 & 3 \\ -1 & 4 & 2 \\ 0 & 1 & 5 \end{pmatrix}.$$

Repeat columns 1 and 2 at the right of the matrix, as in figure 9.3. Multiply the numbers connected by arrows pointed down:

$$(-2)(4)(5) = -40$$
$$(0)(2)(0) = 0$$
$$(3)(-1)(1) = -3.$$

Add these three products: $(-40) + 0 + (-3) = -43.$

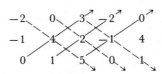

Figure 9.3

Next multiply the numbers connected by arrows pointed up:

$$(0)(4)(3) = 0$$
$$(1)(2)(-2) = -4$$
$$(5)(-1)(0) = 0.$$

Add these three products: $0 + (-4) + 0 = -4.$

Then subtract the second sum from the first sum: $(-43) - (-4) = -39.$ Hence

$$\begin{vmatrix} -2 & 0 & 3 \\ -1 & 4 & 2 \\ 0 & 1 & 5 \end{vmatrix} = -39.$$

Example 9.9.   Find the determinant of the matrix

$$\begin{pmatrix} 2 & 1 & 3 \\ 0 & 4 & 2 \\ -2 & -1 & -3 \end{pmatrix}.$$

Rewrite the matrix repeating the first two columns, as in figure 9.4.

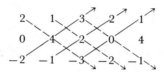

Figure 9.4

Compute the products along the down arrows: $(2)(4)(-3) = -24$; $(1)(2)(-2) = -4$; $(3)(0)(-1) = 0$. Add these products to obtain -28. Then find the products along the arrows going up: $(-2)(4)(3) = -24$; $(-1)(2)(2) = -4$; $(-3)(0)(1) = 0$. Add these, obtaining -28. Subtract this second sum from the first to obtain: $-28 - (-28) = 0$. The determinant of this matrix is 0.

We use the idea of a determinant when looking for the multiplicative inverse of a matrix in the next section.

PROBLEMS

Find the determinant of each matrix.

1. $\begin{pmatrix} 2 & -4 \\ 1 & 3 \end{pmatrix}.$

2. $\begin{pmatrix} -3 & -3 \\ 20 & 10 \end{pmatrix}.$

3. $\begin{pmatrix} -4 & -5 \\ 2 & -\frac{1}{2} \end{pmatrix}.$

4. $\begin{pmatrix} -1 & 0 \\ 0 & -1 \end{pmatrix}.$

5. $\begin{pmatrix} 1 & 0 \\ 0 & 1 \end{pmatrix}.$

6. $\begin{pmatrix} -7 & 8 \\ 80 & 70 \end{pmatrix}.$

7. $\begin{pmatrix} 2 & 3 & 5 \\ 1 & 0 & 1 \\ 2 & 1 & 0 \end{pmatrix}.$

8. $\begin{pmatrix} 2 & -3 & -4 \\ 1 & 0 & -2 \\ 0 & -5 & -6 \end{pmatrix}.$

9. $\begin{pmatrix} 1 & 0 & 2 \\ 3 & 4 & 5 \\ 5 & 6 & 7 \end{pmatrix}.$

10. $\begin{pmatrix} 1 & 0 & 0 \\ 2 & 3 & 5 \\ 4 & 1 & 3 \end{pmatrix}.$

11. $\begin{pmatrix} 1 & 0 & 2 \\ 3 & 0 & 4 \\ 2 & -5 & 1 \end{pmatrix}.$ 12. $\begin{pmatrix} 3 & 4 & 5 \\ 1 & 2 & 3 \\ -2 & 5 & -4 \end{pmatrix}.$

13. $\begin{pmatrix} 2 & 3 & -4 \\ 5 & -6 & 3 \\ 4 & 2 & -3 \end{pmatrix}.$ 14. $\begin{pmatrix} 1 & 4 & 8 \\ -2 & 1 & 5 \\ -3 & 2 & 4 \end{pmatrix}.$

SECTION 4. THE INVERSE OF A MATRIX, PRELIMINARY WORK

The system consisting of the set of all 3x3 matrices and the operation of multiplication has an identity element. Does the system have inverses? That is, given a matrix A, is it possible to find some other matrix, A^{-1}, such that:

$$(A)(A^{-1}) = (A^{-1})(A) = I?$$

The answer is yes—sometimes. We now study a method that can be used to find the multiplicative inverse of a given matrix if it exists. For the rest of this chapter the word inverse will mean multiplicative inverse, unless otherwise stated.

To find the inverse of a matrix it is necessary to manipulate the rows of the matrix according to certain instructions. Three basic instructions are needed:

(a) The interchange of row i and row j of a matrix is denoted by R_j^i.

(b) The multiplication of every entry in row i of the matrix by a non-zero number k is denoted by $R_i(k)$.

(c) The symbol $R_i(k) + R_j$ denotes selecting the entries in row i, multiplying them by the real number k, and adding the results to the entries in row j. Note that row i itself is left unchanged.

Example 9.10. Let $M = \begin{pmatrix} -2 & 0 & 3 \\ -1 & 4 & 2 \\ 0 & 1 & 5 \end{pmatrix}.$

(a) Apply R_1^2 to M.

Interchange the second and first rows of the matrix, giving:

$$\begin{pmatrix} -1 & 4 & 2 \\ -2 & 0 & 3 \\ 0 & 1 & 5 \end{pmatrix}.$$

(b) Apply R_1^3 to the result of (a).

Interchange the third and first rows of the matrix, giving:

$$\begin{pmatrix} 0 & 1 & 5 \\ -2 & 0 & 3 \\ -1 & 4 & 2 \end{pmatrix}.$$

(c) Apply $R_3(-2)$ to M.

Multiply every entry in the third row of M by the real number -2:

$$\begin{pmatrix} -2 & 0 & 3 \\ -1 & 4 & 2 \\ (0)(-2) & (1)(-2) & (5)(-2) \end{pmatrix} = \begin{pmatrix} -2 & 0 & 3 \\ -1 & 4 & 2 \\ 0 & -2 & -10 \end{pmatrix}.$$

(d) Find the result if $R_2(-\frac{1}{2})$ is applied to M.

Multiply every entry of row 2 by $-\frac{1}{2}$.

$$\begin{pmatrix} -2 & 0 & 3 \\ \frac{1}{2} & -2 & -1 \\ 0 & 1 & 5 \end{pmatrix}.$$

(e) Apply $R_2(-2) + R_1$ to M.

Write down all the rows of M except row 1. We must now find the entries for row 1. Multiply the first entry in row 2 by -2: $(-1)(-2) = 2$. Add this answer to -2 of row 1, column 1 of M: $2 + (-2) = 0$, which is the entry for row 1, column 1 of the changed matrix. Repeat the process. Select 4 in the second row, second column of M. Multiply 4 by -2, getting -8. Add this -8 to the 0 in row 1, column 2 of M, obtaining a sum of -8. This number -8 is the entry for row 1, column 2 of the changed matrix. For the third entry in row 1 of the changed matrix we have

$$2(-2) + 3 = -1.$$

Hence if $R_2(-2) + R_1$ is applied to M the result is:

$$\begin{pmatrix} 0 & -8 & -1 \\ -1 & 4 & 2 \\ 0 & 1 & 5 \end{pmatrix}.$$

(f) Apply $R_1(3) + R_3$ to M.

Following the instructions, we select the first entry in row 1 of M, multiply it by 3, and add the product to the first entry in row 3; that is, $(-2)(3) +$

$0 = -6$. Next, $(0)(3) + 1 = 1$, and finally $(3)(3) + 5 = 14$. Therefore if $R_1(3) + R_3$ is applied to M, the result is:

$$\begin{pmatrix} -2 & 0 & 3 \\ -1 & 4 & 2 \\ -6 & 1 & 14 \end{pmatrix}.$$

Row 1 is unaffected by this manipulation; only the entries of row 3 change.

(g) What is the result if $R_2(4) + R_3$ is applied to M?

Following the instructions, we can find the result:

$$\begin{pmatrix} -2 & 0 & 3 \\ -1 & 4 & 2 \\ -4 & 17 & 13 \end{pmatrix}.$$

Each of these three manipulations of the rows of a matrix is an example of a *row transformation* of the matrix. If a finite number of row transformations are applied to a matrix A, resulting in some new matrix B, we say *A is equivalent to B* and write $A \sim B$.

Example 9.11.   Using matrix M from the previous example, apply these row transformations in turn: (a) $R_1(-4)$ (b) $R_2(-2) + R_1$ (c) R_2^3.

Applying (a) to M gives:

$$\begin{pmatrix} -2 & 0 & 3 \\ -1 & 4 & 2 \\ 0 & 1 & 5 \end{pmatrix} \sim \begin{pmatrix} 8 & 0 & -12 \\ -1 & 4 & 2 \\ 0 & 1 & 5 \end{pmatrix}.$$

Now we apply (b) to the result:

$$\begin{pmatrix} 8 & 0 & -12 \\ -1 & 4 & 2 \\ 0 & 1 & 5 \end{pmatrix} \sim \begin{pmatrix} 10 & -8 & -16 \\ -1 & 4 & 2 \\ 0 & 1 & 5 \end{pmatrix}.$$

Applying (c) to this last result gives:

$$\begin{pmatrix} 10 & -8 & -16 \\ -1 & 4 & 2 \\ 0 & 1 & 5 \end{pmatrix} \sim \begin{pmatrix} 10 & -8 & -16 \\ 0 & 1 & 5 \\ -1 & 4 & 2 \end{pmatrix}.$$

Example 9.12.   Let $A = \begin{pmatrix} -2 & 1 \\ 3 & -2 \end{pmatrix}$.

Find a sequence of row transformations that will convert A into the identity matrix $\begin{pmatrix} 1 & 0 \\ 0 & 1 \end{pmatrix}$.

As a practical suggestion, try to get 1 in row 1, column 1. The number -2 is in row 1, column 1, but it can be converted into 1 by applying $R_1(-\frac{1}{2})$. The first step can be written:

$$\begin{pmatrix} -2 & 1 \\ 3 & -2 \end{pmatrix} \underset{R_1(-\frac{1}{2})}{\sim} \begin{pmatrix} 1 & -\frac{1}{2} \\ 3 & -2 \end{pmatrix}.$$

Next try to convert column 1 into all zeros below the 1. To do this we convert 3 into 0 using $R_1(-3) + R_2$.

$$\begin{pmatrix} 1 & -\frac{1}{2} \\ 3 & -2 \end{pmatrix} \underset{R_1(-3) + R_2}{\sim} \begin{pmatrix} 1 & -\frac{1}{2} \\ 0 & -\frac{1}{2} \end{pmatrix}.$$

(How was the $-\frac{1}{2}$ in the second row obtained?) Next, get 1 in the second row, second column, by applying $R_2(-2)$.

$$\begin{pmatrix} 1 & -\frac{1}{2} \\ 0 & -\frac{1}{2} \end{pmatrix} \underset{R_2(-2)}{\sim} \begin{pmatrix} 1 & -\frac{1}{2} \\ 0 & 1 \end{pmatrix}.$$

All that remains is to change $-\frac{1}{2}$ to 0, which we can do by applying $R_2(\frac{1}{2}) + R_1$.

$$\begin{pmatrix} 1 & -\frac{1}{2} \\ 0 & 1 \end{pmatrix} \underset{R_2(\frac{1}{2}) + R_1}{\sim} \begin{pmatrix} 1 & 0 \\ 0 & 1 \end{pmatrix}.$$

In order to change the original matrix A into the identity matrix, we applied in turn, $R_1(-\frac{1}{2})$, $R_1(-3) + R_2$, $R_2(-2)$, and $R_2(\frac{1}{2}) + R_1$. Other such sequences are possible. Is it possible to change any matrix, through a finite sequence of row transformations, into the identity matrix? The next example answers that question.

Example 9.13.   Let $B = \begin{pmatrix} 2 & -4 \\ 2 & -4 \end{pmatrix}$.

Apply row transformations to B to change it into the identity matrix.

As before, try to get 1 in row 1, column 1.

$$\begin{pmatrix} 2 & -4 \\ 2 & -4 \end{pmatrix} \underset{R_1(\frac{1}{2})}{\sim} \begin{pmatrix} 1 & -2 \\ 2 & -4 \end{pmatrix}.$$

Then apply $R_1(-2) + R_2$ to get 0 under the 1.

$$\begin{pmatrix} 1 & -2 \\ 2 & -4 \end{pmatrix} \underset{R_1(-2) + R_2}{\sim} \begin{pmatrix} 1 & -2 \\ 0 & 0 \end{pmatrix}.$$

We cannot go further. We need 1 in row 2, column 2 but we have 0 there. (Why would it not work to use $R_1(-\frac{1}{2}) + R_2$?) It is not possible to convert B into the identity matrix with a sequence of row transformations.

PROBLEMS

Let $A = \begin{pmatrix} -4 & 0 & 1 \\ 3 & -4 & 2 \\ -1 & 2 & 1 \end{pmatrix}$, and $B = \begin{pmatrix} 2 & -1 & 3 \\ -4 & 0 & 1 \\ 1 & 3 & -3 \end{pmatrix}$.

Apply the row transformations as specified.

1. R_3^2 to A
2. R_3^1 to B
3. R_2^3 to $B - A$
4. R_2^1 to $2A - 3B$
5. $R_2(-2)$ to B
6. $R_3(\frac{1}{5})$ to $A + 2B$
7. $R_2(-4)$ to AB

8. $R_2(-1) + R_3$ to B
9. $R_3(\frac{5}{2}) + R_1$ to A
10. $R_1(1) + R_2$ to $A + B$
11. $R_2(-1) + R_3$ to AB
12. $R_3(-3) + R_1$ to $A - B$
13. $R_1(\frac{1}{4}) + R_3$ to B^2
14. $R_1(-\frac{2}{3}) + R_2$ to A^2

15. Which row transformation must be applied to A to obtain:

$$\begin{pmatrix} 3 & -4 & 2 \\ -4 & 0 & 1 \\ -1 & 2 & 1 \end{pmatrix}?$$

16. Which row transformation must be applied to B to obtain:

$$\begin{pmatrix} 3 & 2 & 0 \\ -4 & 0 & 1 \\ 1 & 3 & -3 \end{pmatrix}?$$

17. Which row transformation must be applied to A to obtain:

$$\begin{pmatrix} -4 & 0 & 1 \\ 6 & -8 & 4 \\ -1 & 2 & 1 \end{pmatrix}?$$

18. Which row transformation must be applied to A to obtain:

$$\begin{pmatrix} -4 & 0 & 1 \\ 3 & -4 & 2 \\ \frac{1}{2} & -1 & -\frac{1}{2} \end{pmatrix}?$$

Find a sequence of row transformations that will convert each of the following matrices into the identity matrix, if possible.

19. $\begin{pmatrix} 1 & 2 \\ 0 & -1 \end{pmatrix}$ **20.** $\begin{pmatrix} 2 & 1 \\ 1 & -1 \end{pmatrix}$

21. $\begin{pmatrix} -2 & 2 \\ 4 & 1 \end{pmatrix}$ **22.** $\begin{pmatrix} 0 & -1 \\ -2 & 0 \end{pmatrix}$

23. $\begin{pmatrix} 6 & 3 & 0 \\ 0 & 4 & 0 \\ 0 & 0 & 2 \end{pmatrix}$ **24.** $\begin{pmatrix} -2 & 2 & 0 \\ 0 & 1 & 0 \\ 1 & 1 & 1 \end{pmatrix}$

25. $\begin{pmatrix} 0 & 0 & 1 \\ 1 & 0 & 0 \\ 0 & 1 & 0 \end{pmatrix}$ **26.** $\begin{pmatrix} -1 & 0 & 1 \\ 2 & 0 & 1 \\ 1 & 0 & 2 \end{pmatrix}$

SECTION 5. THE INVERSE OF A MATRIX

Given a matrix A, a matrix A^{-1} is desired such that:

$$(A)(A^{-1}) = (A^{-1})(A) = I.$$

The method we shall use to find A^{-1} is relatively simple to understand, but sometimes involves tedious calculations. Large computers can find the inverse of a matrix very rapidly even if the matrix contains many rows and columns. Since we are not large computers, we shall restrict our attention to 2x2 and 3x3 matrices.

Let's begin by finding the inverse of the matrix:

$$\begin{pmatrix} -1 & 2 \\ 2 & -5 \end{pmatrix}.$$

Write the matrix with the identity next to it:

$$\left(\begin{array}{cc|cc} -1 & 2 & 1 & 0 \\ 2 & -5 & 0 & 1 \end{array} \right).$$

The theory is as follows: If the original matrix is converted into the identity using a sequence of row transformations, the identity will be converted automatically into the inverse. To begin, we try to get 1 in the first row, first column.

$$\left(\begin{array}{cc|cc} -1 & 2 & 1 & 0 \\ 2 & -5 & 0 & 1 \end{array} \right) \underset{R_1(-1)}{\sim} \left(\begin{array}{cc|cc} 1 & -2 & -1 & 0 \\ 2 & -5 & 0 & 1 \end{array} \right).$$

Now try to get 0 under the 1 in the first column.

$$\begin{pmatrix} 1 & -2 & | & -1 & 0 \\ 2 & -5 & | & 0 & 1 \end{pmatrix} \underset{R_1(-2) + R_2}{\sim} \begin{pmatrix} 1 & -2 & | & -1 & 0 \\ 0 & -1 & | & 2 & 1 \end{pmatrix}.$$

Next, get 1 in row 2, column 2.

$$\begin{pmatrix} 1 & -2 & | & -1 & 0 \\ 0 & -1 & | & 2 & 1 \end{pmatrix} \underset{R_2(-1)}{\sim} \begin{pmatrix} 1 & -2 & | & -1 & 0 \\ 0 & 1 & | & -2 & -1 \end{pmatrix}.$$

All that remains is to convert -2 in row 1 into 0.

$$\begin{pmatrix} 1 & -2 & | & -1 & 0 \\ 0 & 1 & | & -2 & -1 \end{pmatrix} \underset{R_2(2) + R_1}{\sim} \begin{pmatrix} 1 & 0 & | & -5 & -2 \\ 0 & 1 & | & -2 & -1 \end{pmatrix}.$$

We have converted the original matrix into the identity element, and the original identity has been converted into the inverse. Check:

$$\begin{pmatrix} -1 & 2 \\ 2 & -5 \end{pmatrix} \cdot \begin{pmatrix} -5 & -2 \\ -2 & -1 \end{pmatrix} = \begin{pmatrix} -5 & -2 \\ -2 & -1 \end{pmatrix} \cdot \begin{pmatrix} -1 & 2 \\ 2 & -5 \end{pmatrix} = \begin{pmatrix} 1 & 0 \\ 0 & 1 \end{pmatrix}.$$

Example 9.14.   Let $B = \begin{pmatrix} 1 & 3 & 3 \\ 1 & 4 & 3 \\ 1 & 3 & 4 \end{pmatrix}$ and find B^{-1}.

The matrix is 3x3, but the procedure is the same. To begin:

$$\begin{pmatrix} 1 & 3 & 3 & | & 1 & 0 & 0 \\ 1 & 4 & 3 & | & 0 & 1 & 0 \\ 1 & 3 & 4 & | & 0 & 0 & 1 \end{pmatrix}.$$

Then proceed as follows:

$$\begin{pmatrix} 1 & 3 & 3 & | & 1 & 0 & 0 \\ 1 & 4 & 3 & | & 0 & 1 & 0 \\ 1 & 3 & 4 & | & 0 & 0 & 1 \end{pmatrix} \underset{R_1(-1) + R_2}{\sim} \begin{pmatrix} 1 & 3 & 3 & | & 1 & 0 & 0 \\ 0 & 1 & 0 & | & -1 & 1 & 0 \\ 1 & 3 & 4 & | & 0 & 0 & 1 \end{pmatrix}.$$

$$\begin{pmatrix} 1 & 3 & 3 & | & 1 & 0 & 0 \\ 0 & 1 & 0 & | & -1 & 1 & 0 \\ 1 & 3 & 4 & | & 0 & 0 & 1 \end{pmatrix} \underset{R_1(-1) + R_3}{\sim} \begin{pmatrix} 1 & 3 & 3 & | & 1 & 0 & 0 \\ 0 & 1 & 0 & | & -1 & 1 & 0 \\ 0 & 0 & 1 & | & -1 & 0 & 1 \end{pmatrix}.$$

$$\begin{pmatrix} 1 & 3 & 3 & | & 1 & 0 & 0 \\ 0 & 1 & 0 & | & -1 & 1 & 0 \\ 0 & 0 & 1 & | & -1 & 0 & 1 \end{pmatrix} \underset{R_2(-3) + R_1}{\sim} \begin{pmatrix} 1 & 0 & 3 & | & 4 & -3 & 0 \\ 0 & 1 & 0 & | & -1 & 1 & 0 \\ 0 & 0 & 1 & | & -1 & 0 & 1 \end{pmatrix}.$$

$$\begin{pmatrix} 1 & 0 & 3 & | & 4 & -3 & 0 \\ 0 & 1 & 0 & | & -1 & 1 & 0 \\ 0 & 0 & 1 & | & -1 & 0 & 1 \end{pmatrix} \underset{R_3(-3) + R_1}{\sim} \begin{pmatrix} 1 & 0 & 0 & | & 7 & -3 & -3 \\ 0 & 1 & 0 & | & -1 & 1 & 0 \\ 0 & 0 & 1 & | & -1 & 0 & 1 \end{pmatrix}.$$

The first three columns have now been converted to the identity matrix, which means the inverse is in the last three columns:

$$B^{-1} = \begin{pmatrix} 7 & -3 & -3 \\ -1 & 1 & 0 \\ -1 & 0 & 1 \end{pmatrix}.$$

To check that we have really found the inverse, evaluate $(B)(B^{-1})$ and $(B^{-1})(B)$.

Example 9.15. Let $D = \begin{pmatrix} 0 & 1 & -1 \\ 4 & -3 & 4 \\ 3 & -3 & 4 \end{pmatrix}$.

Show that D is its own inverse; that is, show $D = D^{-1}$.

Calculate DD; you should find DD $=$ I, which means D is its own inverse. A matrix that is its own inverse is said to be *involutoric*.

Example 9.16. Find the inverse of matrix F:

$$F = \begin{pmatrix} 2 & 1 \\ 6 & 3 \end{pmatrix}.$$

Proceed as before.

$$\begin{pmatrix} 2 & 1 & | & 1 & 0 \\ 6 & 3 & | & 0 & 1 \end{pmatrix} \underset{R_1(\frac{1}{2})}{\sim} \begin{pmatrix} 1 & \frac{1}{2} & | & \frac{1}{2} & 0 \\ 6 & 3 & | & 0 & 1 \end{pmatrix},$$

$$\begin{pmatrix} 1 & \frac{1}{2} & | & \frac{1}{2} & 0 \\ 6 & 3 & | & 0 & 1 \end{pmatrix} \underset{R_1(-6) + R_2}{\sim} \begin{pmatrix} 1 & \frac{1}{2} & | & \frac{1}{2} & 0 \\ 0 & 0 & | & -3 & 1 \end{pmatrix}.$$

It is not possible to obtain the necessary 1 in row 2, column 2 because of the two zeros in the first two columns of the second row. Since we cannot, by a sequence of row transformations, convert the original matrix into the identity, the matrix has no inverse. Check the determinant of matrix F: $6 - 6 = 0$. It can be proven that a matrix has an inverse only if its determinant is not zero; and if its determinant is not zero, it has an inverse. Note the analogy between this result and the corresponding result for real numbers.

PROBLEMS

Find the inverse of each matrix, if it exists.

1. $\begin{pmatrix} 1 & 0 \\ 0 & -1 \end{pmatrix}$.

2. $\begin{pmatrix} 0 & 1 \\ 1 & 0 \end{pmatrix}$.

3. $\begin{pmatrix} 2 & 1 \\ 4 & 3 \end{pmatrix}$.

4. $\begin{pmatrix} -3 & 2 \\ 6 & -5 \end{pmatrix}$.

5. $\begin{pmatrix} 5 & 6 \\ -10 & -13 \end{pmatrix}$.

6. $\begin{pmatrix} 1 & 1 \\ 1 & -1 \end{pmatrix}$.

7. $\begin{pmatrix} 1 & 1 \\ 1 & 1 \end{pmatrix}$.

8. $\begin{pmatrix} -1 & -1 \\ 1 & 1 \end{pmatrix}$.

9. $\begin{pmatrix} 2 & 4 \\ 4 & 6 \end{pmatrix}$.

10. $\begin{pmatrix} 3 & 5 \\ -1 & 2 \end{pmatrix}$.

11. $\begin{pmatrix} 1 & 2 & 0 \\ 0 & 1 & 0 \\ 0 & 1 & 1 \end{pmatrix}$.

12. $\begin{pmatrix} 0 & 1 & 0 \\ 0 & 0 & -2 \\ 1 & -1 & 0 \end{pmatrix}$.

13. $\begin{pmatrix} 4 & 1 & 2 \\ 0 & 3 & 0 \\ -1 & 1 & 0 \end{pmatrix}$.

14. $\begin{pmatrix} -1 & 0 & 2 \\ 3 & 1 & 0 \\ 0 & 2 & -3 \end{pmatrix}$.

15. $\begin{pmatrix} 4 & 3 & 3 \\ -1 & 0 & -1 \\ -4 & -4 & -3 \end{pmatrix}$.

16. $\begin{pmatrix} 1 & 0 & 2 \\ -1 & 0 & -2 \\ 1 & 1 & 1 \end{pmatrix}$.

A matrix A, such that $A^2 = A$, is called *idempotent*. Show that the following matrices are idempotent.

17. $\begin{pmatrix} 2 & -3 & -5 \\ -1 & 4 & 5 \\ 1 & -3 & -4 \end{pmatrix}$.

18. $\begin{pmatrix} -1 & 3 & 5 \\ 1 & -3 & -5 \\ -1 & 3 & 5 \end{pmatrix}$.

SECTION 6. FURTHER PROPERTIES OF MATRICES

Let us now consider the following three properties of real numbers in order to determine whether or not analagous properties hold for matrices.

(1) For all real numbers a and b,

$$(a + b)(a - b) = a^2 - b^2.$$

Recall from algebra that the expression $a^2 - b^2$ may be factored to give the product $(a + b)(a - b)$. Does a similar property hold for matrices? That is, given any two matrices A and B (of the same size), does

$$(A + B)(A - B) = A^2 - B^2?$$

(2) For all real numbers a and b, if $ab = 0$ then $a = 0$ or $b = 0$. By this property, if the product of two numbers is 0, then at least one of the numbers is 0. For example, if we know $3c = 0$, then we are sure $c = 0$. Does an analogous property hold for matrices? If A and B are any two matrices and if $AB = 0$, can we say $A = 0$ or $B = 0$? (When discussing matrices, the symbol 0 represents a matrix with all zeros.)

(3) For all real numbers a, b, and c, if a is not zero and if $ab = ac$, then $b = c$. For example, if we know $3b = 3c$ we may say $b = c$. (Why do we make the restriction $a \neq 0$?) Can we say, in a similar manner: If A, B, and C are any three matrices with $A \neq 0$, and if $AB = AC$, then $B = C$?

Now let's see which, if any, of these properties hold for matrices.

(1) As examples, let $A = \begin{pmatrix} 2 & -1 & 3 \\ 1 & 0 & 2 \\ 0 & 1 & 0 \end{pmatrix}$, and $B = \begin{pmatrix} 1 & 2 & -3 \\ 4 & 0 & 1 \\ 0 & 0 & 1 \end{pmatrix}$.

We want to see if $A^2 - B^2 = (A + B)(A - B)$. First note:

$$A^2 = \begin{pmatrix} 3 & 1 & 4 \\ 2 & 1 & 3 \\ 1 & 0 & 2 \end{pmatrix} \text{ and } B^2 = \begin{pmatrix} 9 & 2 & -4 \\ 4 & 8 & -11 \\ 0 & 0 & 1 \end{pmatrix}.$$

Using these two matrices, we can find $A^2 - B^2$:

$$A^2 - B^2 = \begin{pmatrix} -6 & -1 & 8 \\ -2 & -7 & 14 \\ 1 & 0 & 1 \end{pmatrix}.$$

Next add A and B to obtain $A + B$, then subtract them for $A - B$. Multiply the two results, and you should find:

$$(A + B)(A - B) = \begin{pmatrix} 0 & -9 & 19 \\ 5 & -12 & 27 \\ -3 & 1 & 0 \end{pmatrix},$$

which is not the same as $A^2 - B^2$. Hence statement (1) is not true for matrices.

It is instructive to see why the statement is false for matrices. Note that:

$$(A + B)(A - B) = (A + B)A - (A + B)B$$
$$= A^2 + BA - AB - B^2$$

and since in general $AB \neq BA$, we cannot say that $BA - AB$ is zero. Here we used the distributive property of matrix multiplication over matrix subtraction, which you are asked to verify in the problem set.

What about statement (2)? If A and B are matrices and if $AB = 0$, can we say $A = 0$ or $B = 0$?

$$\text{Let } A = \begin{pmatrix} -1 & 2 & 1 \\ -2 & 4 & 2 \\ -4 & 8 & 4 \end{pmatrix} \text{ and } B = \begin{pmatrix} 2 & 2 & 2 \\ 1 & 1 & 1 \\ 0 & 0 & 0 \end{pmatrix}.$$

Multiply A and B; you should find $AB = 0$. Note that $A \neq 0$ and $B \neq 0$, which means statement (2) is false.

Let's check statement (3). Consider this example:

$$A = \begin{pmatrix} 3 & 0 & 0 \\ 0 & 0 & 0 \\ 0 & 0 & 0 \end{pmatrix} \quad B = \begin{pmatrix} 2 & 1 & 7 \\ 3 & 4 & 6 \\ 2 & 8 & 9 \end{pmatrix} \quad C = \begin{pmatrix} 2 & 1 & 7 \\ 7 & 9 & 8 \\ 2 & 1 & 3 \end{pmatrix}.$$

Note first that $A \neq 0$. Calculate AB and AC. You will find $AB = AC$ even though $B \neq C$. Statement (3) is false.

We are able to produce counter examples (an example proving a statement false) for all the proposed properties. How were these counter examples found? Mainly by trial and error. This is not a very satisfactory answer perhaps, but insight, analogies, past experience, and trial and error all play a part in searching for counter examples. Keep trying various matrices until you either produce a counter example or else convince yourself of the truth of the statement.

PROBLEMS

Are the following statements true?
1. We already know that if a is a real number, and if $a^2 = a$, then $a = 0$ or $a = 1$. Suppose A is a matrix with the property that $A^2 = A$. Then $A = 0$ or $A = I$. (Hint: see the problem set of the last section.)
2. For all matrices A, B, and C, $A(B - C) = AB - AC$.
3. If the determinant of matrix A is 0, then for every matrix B, $AB = 0$.
4. If the determinant of A is 0, and the determinant of B is 0, then the determinant of AB is 0.
5. For all matrices A, B, and C, if the determinant of A is not zero, and if $AB = AC$, then $B = C$. (Hint: If the determinant of A is not zero then the inverse of A exists. Use this inverse to multiply on both sides of $AB = AC$.)
6. For all matrices A and B, $(A + B)^2 = A^2 + 2AB + B^2$.
7. For all matrices A, B, and C, $A(B + C) = (B + C)A$.
8. For all matrices A and B, and for all real numbers c, $c(A + B) = (A + B)c$.

9. For all matrices A and B, where the determinant of A is not 0, and the determinant of B is not 0,

$$(AB)^{-1} = A^{-1}B^{-1}.$$

(Hint: problems 9 and 10 are not the same since matrix multiplication is not commutative. Exactly one of the two statements is true. Use two matrices whose inverses you already know to test the statements.)

10. For all matrices A and B, where the determinant of A is not 0, and the determinant of B is not 0, then

$$(AB)^{-1} = B^{-1}A^{-1}.$$

11. For all matrices A, $(A^2)^{-1} = (A^{-1})^2$.

SECTION 7. GROUPS OF MATRICES

A group, as you recall, is a set of elements S, together with some operation ∘ defined on S. This system must satisfy the following requirements:

(1) Set S is closed under ∘. That is, if $a \in S$ and $b \in S$ then $a \circ b \in S$.

(2) The system composed of S and ∘ has the associative property. If $a \in S$, $b \in S$ and $c \in S$, then we must have:

$$a \circ (b \circ c) = (a \circ b) \circ c.$$

(3) The system must have an identity element. There must exist an element $e \in S$ such that, for every $a \in S$,

$$a \circ e = e \circ a = a.$$

(4) Every element in S must have an inverse in S. For every element $a \in S$ there must exist some element $a^{-1} \in S$ such that:

$$a \circ a^{-1} = a^{-1} \circ a = e,$$

where e is the identity of the system.

Example 9.17.   Does the set of all 3x3 matrices, whose components are real numbers, form a group under the operation of matrix multiplication?

Since we know there is no inverse for the zero matrix, this system cannot be a group. In problem 1 below, you are asked to discuss the case in which the matrices have non-zero determinants.

Example 9.18.   Does the set of all 3x3 matrices, which have real number entries, form a group under the operation of matrix addition?

Check the four requirements: (1) The sum of two 3x3 matrices is a 3x3 matrix. (2) Addition of matrices is associative. (3) The zero matrix is the identity element for the system. (4) The inverse of the matrix A is the matrix $(-1)A$. The four requirements are satisfied and hence the system is a group.

Example 9.19. Is the set of all matrices of the form

$$\begin{pmatrix} 0 & 0 & a \\ 0 & a & 0 \\ a & 0 & 0 \end{pmatrix}$$

a group under the operation of matrix multiplication? (Assume $a \neq 0$.)

Here we consider only those matrices that look like the model, with the same number going up the diagonal and zeros everywhere else. For example,

$$\begin{pmatrix} 0 & 0 & 7 \\ 0 & 7 & 0 \\ 7 & 0 & 0 \end{pmatrix}$$

is in the set of our system, but

$$\begin{pmatrix} 0 & 0 & 7 \\ 0 & -7 & 0 \\ 7 & 0 & 0 \end{pmatrix}$$

is not. Let's check the requirements for a group:
    (1) Closure. Multiply two of the elements of the set of our system:

$$\begin{pmatrix} 0 & 0 & 2 \\ 0 & 2 & 0 \\ 2 & 0 & 0 \end{pmatrix} \cdot \begin{pmatrix} 0 & 0 & -3 \\ 0 & -3 & 0 \\ -3 & 0 & 0 \end{pmatrix} = \begin{pmatrix} -6 & 0 & 0 \\ 0 & -6 & 0 \\ 0 & 0 & -6 \end{pmatrix}.$$

The system is not closed and hence cannot form a group.

PROBLEMS

1. Consider the set of all 3x3 matrices with real number entries that have determinants which are not zero. Is this set a group under the operation of matrix multiplication?
2. Consider the set of all 3x3 matrices that look like

$$\begin{pmatrix} a & 0 & 0 \\ a & 0 & 0 \\ a & 0 & 0 \end{pmatrix},$$

where $a \neq 0$. Is this set a group under the operation of matrix multiplication?

3. Consider the set of all 3x3 matrices of the form

$$\begin{pmatrix} a & 0 & 0 \\ 0 & a & 0 \\ 0 & 0 & a \end{pmatrix},$$

where $a \neq 0$. Is this set a group under the operation of matrix multiplication?

4. In problem 2, replace "multiplication" with "addition," and then answer the question.

5. In problem 3 replace the word "multiplication" with the word "addition" and answer the question.

6. Consider the set of all 3x3 matrices of the form

$$\begin{pmatrix} a & 0 & 0 \\ 0 & b & 0 \\ 0 & 0 & c \end{pmatrix},$$

where a, b, and c are any non-zero numbers. Is this set a group under the operation of matrix multiplication?

7. Consider the set of all *upper triangular matrices*, that is, matrices of the form

$$\begin{pmatrix} a & b & c \\ 0 & d & e \\ 0 & 0 & f \end{pmatrix},$$

where a, b, c, d, e, and f are any numbers. Assume the determinant of the matrix is not zero. Is this set a group under the operation of matrix multiplication?

8. In example 9.19, which group properties do hold?

SECTION 8. A USE OF MATRIX THEORY

In Chapter 6, we discussed some elementary examples of linear programming. The technique requires the point of intersection of linear relations, which are obtained by inspecting the graphs of the relations. Matrix theory can be used to find the intersection of such graphs even when they do not cross in "nice" places. After a short discussion of column matrices, we shall illustrate this method with an example.

So far, we have discussed mostly square matrices. A matrix need not, however, contain the same number of rows as columns. For our purposes, it will be necessary to use a matrix which contains only one column, a so-called *column matrix*. For example,

$$\begin{pmatrix} 2 \\ -1 \\ 3 \end{pmatrix}, \quad \begin{pmatrix} 7 \\ 0 \\ 0 \end{pmatrix}, \text{ and } \begin{pmatrix} 2 \\ 5 \end{pmatrix}$$

are all column matrices.

Example 9.20.   Let $A = \begin{pmatrix} 2 & -1 & 4 \\ 0 & 1 & 3 \\ 2 & 4 & 8 \end{pmatrix}$ and $X = \begin{pmatrix} 1 \\ 3 \\ -8 \end{pmatrix}$. Find AX.

Using the definition of matrix multiplication, we have

$$\begin{pmatrix} 2 & -1 & 4 \\ 0 & 1 & 3 \\ 2 & 4 & 8 \end{pmatrix} \cdot \begin{pmatrix} 1 \\ 3 \\ -8 \end{pmatrix} = \begin{pmatrix} (2)(1) + (-1)(3) + (4)(-8) \\ (0)(1) + (1)(3) + (3)(-8) \\ (2)(1) + (4)(3) + (8)(-8) \end{pmatrix} = \begin{pmatrix} -33 \\ -21 \\ -50 \end{pmatrix}.$$

Note that it is not possible to multiply XA.

Let's find the solution for the set of equations:

$$x + 3y + 3z = 16$$
$$x + 4y + 3z = 18$$
$$x + 3y + 4z = 19.$$

Note here that all the x's are in a column, as are the y's and the z's. The constant terms are on the side of the equals signs opposite the variables. Our goal is to find values for the variables x, y, and z which will satisfy all equations simultaneously.

Recall that the coefficient of x in the term "$3x$" is 3, and the coefficient of x in the term "x" is 1. Also, if a particular variable does not appear in an equation we understand that the coefficient of the variable is 0. For example, the coefficient of z in the expression "$x + 4y$" is 0.

Write down in matrix form the coefficients of the variables of the equation.

$$A = \begin{pmatrix} 1 & 3 & 3 \\ 1 & 4 & 3 \\ 1 & 3 & 4 \end{pmatrix}.$$

Let W be the column matrix of unknowns, that is

$$W = \begin{pmatrix} x \\ y \\ z \end{pmatrix}.$$

Let B be the column matrix of constant terms

$$B = \begin{pmatrix} 16 \\ 18 \\ 19 \end{pmatrix}.$$

Note that the original set of equations can also be written

$$\begin{pmatrix} 1 & 3 & 3 \\ 1 & 4 & 3 \\ 1 & 3 & 4 \end{pmatrix} \cdot \begin{pmatrix} x \\ y \\ z \end{pmatrix} = \begin{pmatrix} 16 \\ 18 \\ 19 \end{pmatrix},$$

or, $AW = B.$

(This is another reason for defining matrix multiplication as we did.)

We want to find numerical values for the variables x, y, and z. If we start with

$$AW = B,$$

and multiply both sides by A^{-1}, we have

$$(A^{-1})(AW) = A^{-1}B,$$

and since $A^{-1}A = I$, we have

$$IW = A^{-1}B.$$

Since $IW = W$, we have:

$$W = A^{-1}B.$$

To find x, y, and z we need to find W, which has x, y, and z as its components. To find W we merely evaluate $A^{-1}B$. Matrix A^{-1} was found in example 9.14:

$$A^{-1} = \begin{pmatrix} 7 & -3 & -3 \\ -1 & 1 & 0 \\ -1 & 0 & 1 \end{pmatrix}.$$

Hence we have

$$A^{-1}B = \begin{pmatrix} 7 & -3 & -3 \\ -1 & 1 & 0 \\ -1 & 0 & 1 \end{pmatrix} \cdot \begin{pmatrix} 16 \\ 18 \\ 19 \end{pmatrix} = \begin{pmatrix} 1 \\ 2 \\ 3 \end{pmatrix} = W,$$

and $x = 1$, $y = 2$, and $z = 3$. We may check these values in the original equations:

$$1 + (3)(2) + (3)(3) = 16$$
$$1 + (4)(2) + (3)(3) = 18$$
$$1 + (3)(2) + (4)(3) = 19.$$

Example 9.21. Solve the system of equations

$$x + y + z = 2$$
$$x \qquad + z = 0$$
$$2x - y \qquad = 2.$$

Here, $A = \begin{pmatrix} 1 & 1 & 1 \\ 1 & 0 & 1 \\ 2 & -1 & 0 \end{pmatrix}$, $W = \begin{pmatrix} x \\ y \\ z \end{pmatrix}$, $B = \begin{pmatrix} 2 \\ 0 \\ 2 \end{pmatrix}$.

Again, we have $AW = B$ and $W = A^{-1}B$. Verify that

$$A^{-1} = \begin{pmatrix} \frac{1}{2} & -\frac{1}{2} & \frac{1}{2} \\ 1 & -1 & 0 \\ -\frac{1}{2} & \frac{3}{2} & -\frac{1}{2} \end{pmatrix}.$$

Also verify that

$$A^{-1}B = \begin{pmatrix} 2 \\ 2 \\ -2 \end{pmatrix}.$$

Hence $x = 2$, $y = 2$, and $z = -2$.

Certain sets of equations either have no solution or infinitely many solutions; see a book on college algebra for the details of the solution of such systems.

Example 9.22.   A psychology laboratory has 17 units of wheat and 24 units of barley available daily. One brown rat eats 2 units of wheat and 3 units of barley each day, and one white rat eats 3 units of wheat and 4 units of barley each day. How many of each type of rat should the laboratory keep if all the food must be eaten each day?

Let x = number of brown rats,
$\quad y$ = number of white rats.

The lab has x brown rats; a total of $2x$ units of wheat and $3x$ units of barley is required by the brown rats each day. The white rats gobble a total of $3y$ units of wheat and $4y$ units of barley daily. Altogether, $2x + 3y$ units of wheat will be needed; the lab has 17 units of wheat a day, thus:

$$2x + 3y = 17.$$

In the same way, the total daily amount of barley needed is composed of the barley needed by the brown rats plus the barley needed by the white rats, or $3x + 4y$. The lab has 24 units of barley available, which means

$$3x + 4y = 24.$$

We must now find the common solution for the two equations. As before, let

$A = \begin{pmatrix} 2 & 3 \\ 3 & 4 \end{pmatrix}$, $W = \begin{pmatrix} x \\ y \end{pmatrix}$, and $B = \begin{pmatrix} 17 \\ 24 \end{pmatrix}$. Again, $AW = B$ so that $W = A^{-1}B$.

Verify that

$$A^{-1} = \begin{pmatrix} -4 & 3 \\ 3 & -2 \end{pmatrix}.$$

We now have

$$A^{-1}B = \begin{pmatrix} -4 & 3 \\ 3 & -2 \end{pmatrix} \cdot \begin{pmatrix} 17 \\ 24 \end{pmatrix} = \begin{pmatrix} 4 \\ 3 \end{pmatrix} = W.$$

The laboratory should have 4 brown rats and 3 white ones. More advanced (and more practical) problems can be solved in similar, but longer, ways.

PROBLEMS

Using the method of this section, solve these sets of equations.

1. $x + 3y = 4.$
    $2x - 2y = 6.$

2. $2x + y = 3.$
    $x - y = 3.$

3. $-2x + y = -2.$
    $3x + 2y = -11.$

4. $x - y = 2.$
    $2x + y = 1.$

5. $2x - y = 2.$
    $x + y = 2.$

6. $-x + 2y = 4.$
    $x + 2y = 4.$

7. $x + 2y + z = 0.$
    $x \qquad + z = 0.$
    $y - z = 3.$

8. $x \qquad + z = 1.$
    $x + y \qquad = 5.$
    $y + z = 2.$

9. The manager of a company is faced with a decision. His factory makes use of two basic machines, A and B. These machines turn out two different products, potrezebies and zotyls. Each zotyl requires 1 hour on machine A and 2 hours on machine B, while each potrezebie needs 1 hour on A and 1 hour on B. Machine A can be operated 8 hours a day, while machine B runs 14 hours a day. How many zotyls and how many potrezebies should the factory make in order to keep its machines running at capacity?

10. A biologist wishes to grow 2 types of algae, types A and B. He has available 15 gallons of nutrient 1 and 26 gallons of nutrient 2. A vat of algae A needs 2 gallons of nutrient 1 and 3 gallons of nutrient 2, while a vat of algae B needs 1 gallon of 1 and 2 gallons of 2. How many vats of each type of algae should the biologist grow in order to use all his nutrients?

11. On the first of May, John bought 2 potrezebies and 3 zotyls, paying $13 for them. One month later he bought one potrezebie and 2 zotyls, paying $7 for them. How much does each item cost?

SECTION 9. CODE THEORY

Code theory, or *cryptography,* offers an interesting application of matrix theory. It is commonly believed that replacing each letter of the alphabet with an obscure symbol, such as

$$
\begin{array}{lll}
a = @ & c = \# & e = + \\
b = \$ & d = (& f = *
\end{array}
\qquad \text{and so on,}
$$

produces a code that is difficult to break. This is perhaps true for very short messages, but as soon as the message begins to contain many words the code becomes relatively simple to break. This is because merely substituting one symbol for another does not affect the relative frequency of occurrence of the symbols. Thus in the substitution of symbols for letters, + would occur more frequently in any reasonably long message simply because + represents e, and e occurs the most often in any reasonably long English message. (We say, "reasonably long message," since in some short messages, such as, "Saw sub, sank same," e might not be the most common letter.) Much research has been done by code-breakers in an attempt to decide this frequency of occurrence of letters. Edgar Allan Poe, in his short story *The Gold Bug,* claims that e is the letter which appears the most often, followed in order by: a o i d h n r s t u y c f g l m w b k p q x z. (No doubt Poe had a good reason for omitting j and v, or perhaps this is the fault of the cheap paperback copy of his story we read.)

Governments thus need to develop more sophisticated methods of coding and decoding messages. We can use matrix theory to illustrate one of these more advanced codes. To begin, we assign numbers to the letters of the alphabet. Since we have nothing particularly secret to encode, we shall simply let a correspond to 1, b to 2, and so on. We shall disregard punctuation and let 27 correspond to a blank space. Break the message into groups of three letters each. Thus:

Mathematics is for the birds.

becomes

Mat hem ati cs— is— for —th e—b ird s—,

where — represents a blank. To each group of three symbols corresponds a column matrix. For example, to the letters Mat we assign the numbers 13, 1, and 20, or

$$
\begin{pmatrix} M \\ a \\ t \end{pmatrix} \leftrightarrow \begin{pmatrix} 13 \\ 1 \\ 20 \end{pmatrix}.
$$

Our message, then, corresponds to the column matrices

$$\begin{pmatrix}13\\1\\20\end{pmatrix}\begin{pmatrix}8\\5\\13\end{pmatrix}\begin{pmatrix}1\\20\\9\end{pmatrix}\begin{pmatrix}3\\19\\27\end{pmatrix}\begin{pmatrix}9\\19\\27\end{pmatrix}\begin{pmatrix}6\\15\\18\end{pmatrix}\begin{pmatrix}27\\20\\8\end{pmatrix}\begin{pmatrix}5\\27\\2\end{pmatrix}\begin{pmatrix}9\\18\\4\end{pmatrix}\begin{pmatrix}19\\27\\27\end{pmatrix}.$$

Now we choose any 3x3 matrix (we must choose one that has an inverse) and find the products of this matrix and the above column matrices. Let us choose the matrix

$$M = \begin{pmatrix}1 & 3 & 3\\1 & 4 & 3\\1 & 3 & 4\end{pmatrix}.$$

If we find the product of M and the column matrices above, we have

$$\begin{pmatrix}76\\77\\96\end{pmatrix}\begin{pmatrix}62\\67\\75\end{pmatrix}\cdots.$$

The entries of these products can then be transmitted as the message.

When the secret agent receives the message, he divides it into groups of three (he learns this by consulting the little black code book so familiar to viewers of spy movies) and converts each group of three into a column matrix. After multiplying each column matrix by the matrix M^{-1}, the message can be read.

Although this code is relatively simple, it is actually difficult to break. Many ramifications are possible: long messages might be placed in groups of 20, thus requiring a 20x20 matrix for coding and decoding.

PROBLEMS

1. Use the methods of the text to encode the message

    Arthur is a tree.

    Break the message into groups of 2 and use the secret spy matrix $\begin{pmatrix}-1 & 2\\2 & -5\end{pmatrix}$

2. Using the secret spy matrix of problem 1, encode the message

    Attack at dawn unless too cold.

3. As a special secret agent, your code book contains the following instruction: "Today's secret matrix is $\begin{pmatrix} -1 & 2 \\ 2 & -5 \end{pmatrix}$; its inverse is $\begin{pmatrix} -5 & -2 \\ -2 & -1 \end{pmatrix}$. Eat this page." With these instructions, decode the following message.

$$\begin{pmatrix} -17 \\ 33 \end{pmatrix} \begin{pmatrix} 26 \\ -72 \end{pmatrix} \begin{pmatrix} 53 \\ -133 \end{pmatrix} \begin{pmatrix} 21 \\ -54 \end{pmatrix} \begin{pmatrix} 41 \\ -103 \end{pmatrix} \begin{pmatrix} 35 \\ -97 \end{pmatrix} \begin{pmatrix} 29 \\ -77 \end{pmatrix} \begin{pmatrix} -15 \\ 24 \end{pmatrix} \begin{pmatrix} 39 \\ -98 \end{pmatrix}.$$

4. Finish encoding the message found in the text.

FOR FURTHER READING

Ayres, Frank Jr. *Theory and Problems of Matrices*. New York: Schaum Publishing Company, 1962. This outline of matrix theory is reasonably good and easily obtainable.

Campbell, Hugh G. *An Introduction to Matrices, Vectors, and Linear Programming*. New York: Appleton-Century-Crofts, Inc., 1965. This text has an excellent general introduction to matrix theory.

Farago, Ladislas. *The Broken Seal*. New York: Random House, Inc., 1967. The United States Government has been reading Japanese secret codes since the early 1920's (and presumably still is). *The Broken Seal* describes part of this "hidden war" which took place before World War II. Note: the historical conclusions are not necessarily correct; judge for yourself.

Poe, Edgar Allan. *The Gold Bug*. Available in a number of editions.

CHAPTER 10

AN INTRODUCTION TO COMPUTERS

It is difficult for the modern person to realize the problems that have arisen throughout history when it has been necessary to work large quantities of common arithmetical calculations. In the early eighteenth century most students learned the multiplication table—up to 2x2. However, the growth of industry and trade, as well as science, increased the need for computation. Logarithms, developed by John Napier (1550–1617) and perfected for ordinary calculations by Henry Briggs (1561–1631), were a boon to the calculator. By means of lengthy tables of numerical values, logarithms reduce problems of multiplication or division to problems of addition or subtraction, respectively, while problems of exponentiation (such as 6.78^{56}) and the extraction of roots (such as $\sqrt[7]{.967}$) are reduced to problems of multiplication and division. Logarithm tables could be constructed in only one way—by dull, deadly hand calculations. Many mathematicians, now long forgotten, spent their entire lifetime calculating logarithms to many decimal places of accuracy. (These early calculators would sometimes purposely introduce minor errors in their work to make it easier to catch plagiarists.) In 1766 the Royal Astronomer of Great Britain began publication of the *Nautical Almanac*, a book of astronomical calculations that can help a sailor determine his position at sea. A tremendous amount of calculation was required to produce this book. Most of the work was done by retired clergymen who did all their work by hand and made many errors; it is known that ships were wrecked due to errors in the *Almanac*.

The first mechanical aid to calculation was the abacus, discussed in Chapter 1. In 1642 Blaise Pascal (see Chapter 7) developed a mechanism for adding and subtracting. (See figure 10.1.) This machine, built by the nineteen-year-old Pascal to help him check long columns of figures for his tax-collector father, had telephone-like dials on which numbers could be entered. A short time later, Leibniz (see Chapter 5) developed a machine that could also multiply, but it was rather unreliable and never became popular.

The British mathematician Charles Babbage (1792–1871) made the next major advances in computing machines. Babbage, who was more than a hundred years ahead of his time, clearly understood the principles inherent in even the most modern electronic computer. In 1812 he began working on the Difference Engine, a machine somewhat similar in principle to a modern desk calculator. (See figure 10.2.) He received help from his government, but the project languished because Babbage's plans were above and beyond the capabilities of the machine shops of the day. Even though Babbage and his assistants developed new ways of working metal, they were unable to produce enough sufficiently precise parts for his machine. He did construct a working model in 1822, but the entire machine was never built. In 1833 Babbage began work on his Analytical Engine, a machine that would compare favorably with today's medium sized computers. The Analytical Engine was designed to store 50,000 decimal digits (that is, it would be possible to place up to 50,000 digits in the machine and retrieve them at some later date) and to have 20-place accuracy. It was to operate on punched cards, just as modern computers, and accept a *program,* a list of instructions to be followed. The Analytical Engine was far too advanced for its day and never materialized. Babbage has been criticized by modern writers because his Analytical Engine was so grandiose; a machine considerably less than half as large

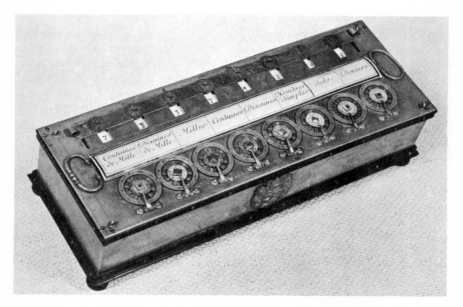

Figure 10.1

Pascal's adding machine was one of the first mechanical computers. It consists of a row of wheels with teeth numbered from 0 to 9. The first wheel represents units; the second, tens; and so on. Numbers are "carried" from one wheel to the next by gears inside the counter. (*Photo Courtesy of International Business Machines Corporation*) would have been much easier to build and would still have revolutionized the computation methods of his time.

Babbage's personal eccentricities made success even more difficult. He was not particularly adept at public relations; he once insulted a committee just as it was deciding whether or not to award him a grant. He harbored a lifelong hatred of organ grinders and initiated a public campaign to run them off the streets. This so incensed the public that children jeered at him in the street, and people came out of their way to blow horns under his window.

Such idiosyncrasies extended even to Babbage's views of poetry; he once sent the following letter to the poet Lord Tennyson:

"Sir,

In your otherwise beautiful poem ("The Vision of Sin") there is a verse which reads—

> 'Every moment dies a man,
> Every moment one is born.'

Figure 10.2

Babbage's "Difference Engine" is often referred to as the first modern mathematical machine. (*Photo Courtesy of International Business Machines*)

It must be manifest that if this were true, the population of the world would be at a standstill. In truth the rate of birth is slightly in excess of that of death. I would suggest that in the next edition of your poem you have it read—

> 'Every moment dies a man,
> Every moment $1\frac{1}{16}$ is born.'

Strictly speaking, this is not correct, the actual figure is so long that I cannot fit it into one line, but I believe that the figure $1\frac{1}{16}$ will be sufficiently accurate for poetry."

Babbage's Analytical Engine was not the first application of punched cards. In 1804 punched cards were used by Joseph Jacquard in his automatic loom, which could produce patterns of great complexity. One design required 24,000 cards to weave a picture of Jacquard himself. Further use of punched cards was made by Herman Hollerith of the U.S. Census Bureau. It had taken seven years hand labor to produce the results of the 1880 census, and because of the population growth, it was estimated that twelve years would be required for the 1890 census. By using punched cards and techniques similar to those of today, Hollerith was able to cut several years off the estimate. Punched cards and modern computers are not a universal cure-all: in 1947 the Thai government conducted a census at the request of the United Nations. The data was put on punched cards and fed to the most modern equipment, but no results were forthcoming. The problem was not hard to locate. At the end of a long row of machines sat one girl, with abacus, checking the work completed by the machines. Her speed was so far behind that of the machines that there was danger the cards would be eaten by white ants.

Babbage's Analytical Engine was all mechanical, with wheels and gears and levers. Modern computers are totally electronic, with transistors and integrated circuits. One of the earliest large computers to combine electrical and mechanical parts was the Mark I, a machine 50 feet long, finished at Harvard in 1944. The first all-electronic computer was ENIAC, built in 1946 for the Army at the University of Pennsylvania. This machine, with 18,000 tubes, filled a space 30 by 50 feet and used enough electricity to power a million transistor radios. ENIAC could do 5000 additions or 350 multiplications per second. It was followed by a large number of other, similar computers. Great changes in computers occurred at the end of the 1950's when transistors began to be used in computer designs. Tremendous reductions could be made in the size and power requirements, with a great increase in reliability.

John von Neumann (1903–1957) was a pioneer in electronic computers. This American mathematician (born in Hungary) did outstanding work in quantum mechanics, helped develop the atomic and hydrogen bombs, and worked in long-range weather forecasting, in addition to his work in computers. The American mathematician Norbert Wiener (1894–1964), referred to as the Father of Automation, worked in control and information theory. The title of his most famous work introduced the word he coined to describe this theory: *Cybernetics, or Control in the Man and the Machine.*

Today commercial computers are built which perform 3,000,000 calculations in one second, and current designers call for computers which will perform 100,000,000 calculations per second. Computers are often interconnected through telephone lines, which enables a small computer at a branch office to have access to a larger machine at company headquarters. *Time-sharing* is one of the fastest growing areas of computer technology. In a typical situation a large computer is connected by phone lines to many small keyboards. Several keyboards can be in use simultaneously with each keyboard operator having the impression he is the only one using the computer. Computer speed enables it to jump from program to program, all the while preserving the illusion to each individual user that it is working on only his program.

Time-sharing is used to a large extent by *computer utilities,* more and more of which are beginning around the country. Typically, such computer utilities consist of a large computer owned by some firm with a modernistic, "space-age" name. The firm rents remote keyboards, which resemble a teletype machine, that are connected to the main computer by telephone lines. The benefit here lies in the fact that the remote keyboard can be any distance from the computer. The user pays a flat charge for the installation of the equipment, along with certain fixed basic charges. The major item of expense is the time used on the computer, which is figured by the minute. Small firms can begin to enjoy the benefits of large computers through such a system, and large firms can afford to provide keyboards for all top employees. The first such computer utility began in 1965.

Computers today are fast enough to be used in *real time* applications; that is, in situations where incoming data is processed so quickly that the output is used to control the current activity. Thus computers receive data from a spacecraft, process it, and use the results to control the craft. Oil refineries are often run by a computer on a real time basis. Large airlines and hotels have real time reservation systems. A person in Sacramento can call a local airline office and receive information on the availability of seats on a flight from Seattle to Vancouver. Members of the highway patrol can radio suspicious license numbers to headquarters to quickly determine whether or not the car is "hot."

Computers are also used for *simulation.* A rocket firing can be simulated by a computer at great savings over an actual firing. All the possible variables are programmed into the computer; then the computer is given a set of data that might actually result from a firing. From this data the machine can predict what might happen to the rocket. By repeating this experiment many times, possible flaws in the rocket design can be detected. Generals and admirals can refine their strategies by playing very realistic war games with the computer, while business executives can decide how best to sell their soap by simulating the possible strategies of competitors on a computer.

Data processing is perhaps the application of computers best known to the public. Through this process, bills are sent to charge account customers, inventories are maintained, and files are kept in order. As a generalization, we can say data processing involves large amounts of data on which relatively few calculations need be made. An oil company may have many thousands of credit card transactions to process in a given month, but essentially the calculations that are made only involve totals, such as totals for each customer and each station. On the other hand, scientific programming involves complicated calculations on relatively little data.

SECTION 1. HOW DOES A COMPUTER WORK?

Let us investigate a little of the mechanism by which a computer operates. Figure 10.3 is a diagram of a typical computer.

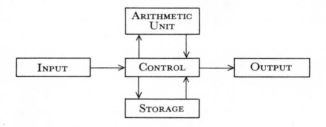

Figure 10.3

The input mechanism is used to enter data and instructions into the machine. This is most commonly done with the familiar punched card of figure 10.4 consisting of eighty columns and twelve rows (only ten of the rows have numbers printed on the cards). The number 6, for example, is represented by a punch in row 6. Letters require two punches in the column directly below them. As shown in figure 10.4, the letter A requires a punch in the top row and in row 1, while W requires punches in row 0 and row 6. Many computers are capable of reading a thousand such cards per minute. Punched cards are prepared on machines called *keypunches* which have typewriter-like keyboards and can produce new cards or duplicate old ones. An organization with a large input of data, such as an insurance company, may have several hundred keypunches and keypunch operators, all preparing punched cards for one computer. *Paper tape* is another common method of inputing information to the computer. Normally somewhat faster than cards, it is able to enter between 80 and 100,000 characters (numbers or letters) per minute. Much faster (and much more expensive) is *magnetic tape* which can be used to enter hundreds of thousands of characters per second.

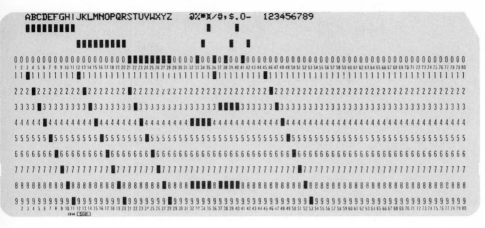

Figure 10.4

    After the information is entered in the computer it is stored until needed. The binary (or base 2) number system is used to store information in a computer. Recall from Chapter 1 that the base 2 number system consists of two digits, 0 and 1. Any number can be expressed using these two digits; for example:

$$2_{10} = 10_2 = (1 \times 2^1) + (0 \times 2^0)$$
$$10_{10} = 1010_2 = (1 \times 2^3) + (0 \times 2^2) + (1 \times 2^1) + (0 \times 2^0)$$
$$31_{10} = 11111_2 = (1 \times 2^4) + (1 \times 2^3) + (1 \times 2^2) + (1 \times 2^1) + (1 \times 2^0).$$

If a switch is turned one way it can represent 0, while turned another way it represents 1. Each 0 or 1 that is stored is called a *bit,* with letters stored as special combinations of bits. Early computers stored these bits with switches, vacuum tubes, tanks of mercury, and cathode ray tubes similar to television picture tubes. Modern computers use a magnetic drum, a magnetic disk, or a magnetic core for storage. A *magnetic drum* is a cylinder coated with magnetic material similar to that on recording tape. When a spot on the drum is magnetized one way, it represents 0; when magnetized another way it represents 1. A *magnetic disk* storage device consists of several disks coated with magnetic material, stacked one on top of another much like records on an automatic changer. Again 0 and 1 are represented by magnetizing certain spots on the disk, and a pickup arm moves back and forth gathering information from the disk. Both disks and drums rotate at high speed when the computer is running, but even so they are very slow when compared to the tremendous speed of the computer. For this reason *magnetic core* storage is often preferred. A magnetic core storage consists of a great number of tiny magnetic doughnuts, called *cores,* which are about the diameter of the head of a straight pin and are strung on wires. Each core can be magnetized to represent 0 or 1. Magnetic core storage offers the advantage of *random access;* that is, any bit can be obtained from storage as easily as any other bit. Magnetic core storage is faster than either drum or disk storage but is also much more expensive. Commonly a machine will have core storage with an auxiliary drum storage. Figure 10.5 pictures these three storage units.

Output can be in the same form as input. Computers can produce output as punched cards, paper tape, magnetic tape, or by typing on paper. Modern printers can produce over a thousand lines of type (each 120 characters long) per minute.

One problem arising in computer usage is that of number scale. Assume a computer is capable of storing numbers up to ten decimal digits. To find the average of 150 nine-digit numbers, we add the 150 numbers and divide the sum by 150. However, the sum of the 150 numbers would be too large a number to store in the computer. To avoid this problem, computer programmers commonly employ *floating point notation*, which is based on the fact that any number can be expressed as the product of a decimal between -1 and $+1$, and a power of ten. Thus

$$150 = .15 \times 10^3,$$
$$15,000 = .15 \times 10^5,$$
$$15 = .15 \times 10^2,$$
$$1,000 = .1 \times 10^4,$$

and so on. We define

$$10^0 = 1,$$
$$10^{-1} = \frac{1}{10} = .1,$$
$$10^{-2} = \frac{1}{10^2} = \frac{1}{100} = .01,$$
$$10^{-3} = \frac{1}{10^3} = \frac{1}{1000} = .001,$$

and so on. Thus

$$.006 = .6 \times 10^{-2},$$
$$.04 = .4 \times 10^{-1},$$
$$.00000004 = .4 \times 10^{-7}.$$

Numbers such as 16,834, -9871, and 611, that are not written in floating point, are said to be in *fixed point* form.

In the next section we investigate the workings of a hypothetical, but typical, computer. Then we investigate compiler languages, which are a relatively simple way for man to communicate with machine.

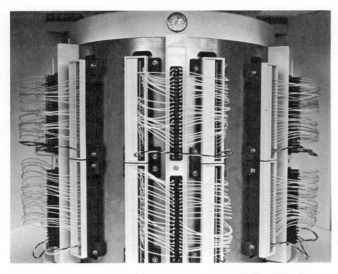

MAGNETIC DRUM
Courtesy
International Business
Machines Corporation.

MAGNETIC DISK
Courtesy
International Business
Machines Corporation.

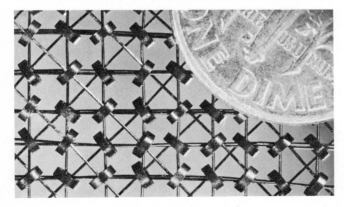

MAGNETIC CORE
Courtesy
General Electric
Corporation.

Figure 10.5   Principal storage units of modern computers.

PROBLEMS:

1. Express in floating point form:
    (a) 648   (d) 913.42
    (b) 1002.83   (e) .668
    (c) .0000412   (f) 3.98

2. Convert to fixed point form:
    (a) $.183 \times 10^5$ (c) $.1 \times 10^1$
    (b) $.12 \times 10^{-4}$ (d) $.8 \times 10^{-7}$

3. Devise a rule for multiplying two numbers in floating point form.

SECTION 2. A TYPICAL COMPUTER

In this section we investigate the workings of the hypothetical, but typical, computer FATCO (Fast and Tremendous Computer, Oh!). FATCO receives information from punched cards, one information statement punched per card, and prints its data on a typewriter. It has 100 storage locations, each capable of storing a fifteen-digit number, and an *accumulator,* a temporary storage for numbers being processed. Each storage location is labeled with an *address* to distinguish it from other storage locations. In FATCO each storage address is a four-digit number starting at 1001; thus the 100 storage locations have addresses 1001, 1002, 1003, ..., 1100. Address 1000 is used for the accumulator.

Each instruction to FATCO takes the following form:

$$10090110461048$$

The digits at the left, 1009, give the address of the storage location in which this instruction will be found. The next two digits, 01, are an *operation code* which tell FATCO what to do with the contents of storage location 1046 (called the *operation address*); the computer then goes to 1048 for its next instruction. FATCO has the following operation codes:

Operation Code	Operation Address	
01	XXXX	Add the number in storage location XXXX to the contents of the accumulator; leave the sum in the accumulator
02	XXXX	Subtract the number in storage location XXXX from the contents of the accumulator; leave the difference in the accumulator

Operation Code	Operation Address	
03	XXXX	Multiply the number in the accumulator by the number in storage location XXXX; leave the product in the accumulator
04	XXXX	Divide the contents of storage location XXXX into the number in the accumulator and leave the quotient in the accumulator
11	XXXX	Transfer the contents of the accumulator to location XXXX
12	XXXX	Transfer the contents of XXXX to the accumulator; the number also remains in storage location XXXX
21	XXXX	If the contents of the accumulator are positive, transfer control to storage location XXXX, otherwise continue
22	XXXX	Same, if negative
23	XXXX	Same, if zero
45	XXXX	Print the contents of XXXX on the typewriter
60	XXXX	Stop; the end of the program has been reached

Thus

$$10081110981002$$

is an instruction stored at address 1008. This instruction tells FATCO to transfer the contents of the accumulator to storage location 1098; the machine is then to go to 1002 for its next instruction. In the same way

$$10512110811009$$

is an instruction for the machine to look at the contents of the accumulator. If the number in the accumulator is positive the machine goes to storage location 1081 for its next instruction; if not FATCO goes to 1009.

Let us now give FATCO a problem to solve: find the sum of the first one hundred counting numbers. We must tell the machine how to do the problem, using only the operation codes mentioned above. The diagram of figure 10.6, called a *flow chart*, shows the procedure to find the sum.

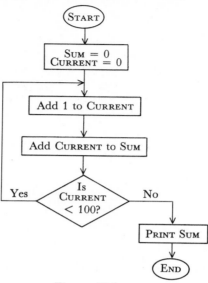

Figure 10.6

Let CURRENT be a variable that keeps track of the number of terms added. To begin, CURRENT equals zero; when CURRENT equals 100 the problem is ended. Let SUM equal zero initially; at the end SUM will be the total of the first hundred counting numbers. Follow the flow chart:

$$\text{SUM} = 0 \qquad \text{CURRENT} = 0$$

Add 1 to CURRENT:

$$\text{SUM} = 0 \qquad \text{CURRENT} = 1$$

Next add CURRENT to SUM:

$$\text{SUM} = 1 \qquad \text{CURRENT} = 1$$

Since CURRENT is less than 100, we proceed. Again add 1 to CURRENT:

$$\text{SUM} = 1 \qquad \text{CURRENT} = 2$$

Add SUM to CURRENT:

$$\text{SUM} = 3 \qquad \text{CURRENT} = 2$$

At the conclusion of the next run through the computer, we have:

$$\text{SUM} = 6 \qquad \text{CURRENT} = 3$$

The program ends with

$$\text{SUM} = 5050 \qquad \text{CURRENT} = 100$$

The computer will print 5050 as the answer. Now let's see what instructions we must give FATCO to produce this result.

Assume the initial value of SUM, zero, is stored at address 1001. CURRENT has an initial value of zero also, which is stored at address 1002. Assume the number 100 is stored at 1004, and the number 1 is stored at 1003. To begin, add 1 to CURRENT, giving a new value of CURRENT. The instruction

10501210021051

tells FATCO to transfer the contents of 1002 to the accumulator (automatically clearing anything there previously). The locations for the instructions of this program (1050, 1051, etc.) are chosen arbitrarily. Next

10510110031052

tells the computer to add the 1 from 1003 to the accumulator, leaving the result in the accumulator. Next return the contents of the accumulator to the CURRENT storage location, 1002:

10521110021053

Now transfer SUM from its storage location, 1001, to the accumulator:

10531210011054

Add SUM and CURRENT to obtain the new value of SUM:

10540110021055

Place the new value of SUM in 1001, the SUM storage location:

10551110011056

Check to see if CURRENT has reached 100 yet. First transfer 100 from 1004 to the accumulator:

10561210041057

Subtract CURRENT from the number 100 in the accumulator:

10570210021058

If the number in the accumulator is positive we should proceed with the summing process by returning to instruction 1050 and repeating the steps. If the number in the accumulator is zero, we are through and need to print the value of SUM.

10582110501059
10594510011060

We then end the program. (The last eight digits are arbitrary.)

10606010001000

The eleven statements 1050–1060 constitute the program that will cause FATCO to find the sum of the first hundred counting numbers.

PROBLEMS

Write FATCO programs for the following problems.
1. Let address 1001 contain the number 12, 1002 contain 16, and 1004 contain 13. Find $(12 + 16)13$ and store the result at 1009.

2. Let a value of x be placed at 1008 and the number 2 at 1009. Find

$$x^2 - 2x + 4$$

and store the result at 1011.
3. Modify the program of the text to produce the sum of the first hundred even counting numbers.

4. (a) First draw a flow chart and then write a program for the following problem: assume x is stored at 1002. Place x at 1004 if it is positive, at 1005 if it is zero, or at 1006 if it is negative.
   (b) Repeat part (a) without using operation code 23.
   (c) Repeat part (a) without using operation codes 22 or 23.

5. Solve the equation $2x + 6 = 11$.

6. Place a at 1001 and b at 1002. Write a program that will place the larger of a and b at 1008, and the smaller at 1007. Assume a and b are unequal. (Hint: $a > b$ means $a - b$ is positive.)

SECTION 3. COMPILER LANGUAGE

The method of program writing presented in the last section, called *machine language programming,* has several disadvantages. It is rather complicated to write since the programmer must keep track of the address of each variable and a long list of operation codes. Also each different computer has a different machine language, so that a program written for one machine might be almost worthless for use on another. Machine language programs do not look very "natural"; that is, it is difficult to get an idea of the meaning of such a program by just reading through it.

To avoid these problems and to produce a language that can be used by large numbers of people, compiler languages were introduced. Compiler language looks like a cross between English and ordinary algebra, thus making it relatively easy to learn and use. For example, the program from the last section could be written in one compiler language as

```
       CURRENT = 0;
       SUM = 0;
LOOP:  CURRENT = CURRENT + 1;
       SUM = SUM + CURRENT;
       IF CURRENT < 100 THEN GO TO LOOP;
       PUT LIST (SUM);
       END;
```

A special machine language program, called a *compiler,* takes the statements above and converts them into machine language for the computer.

In the program above, the first two statements are used to initialize the values of SUM and CURRENT. Note that no numerical label need be assigned the variables because the compiler takes care of that. In this compiler language, called PL/1, a semicolon must be placed at the end of each statement. LOOP in the third statement is a label or name for the statement; any such word may be used as a label. It must be placed at the beginning of the statement and be followed by a colon. In the statement

CURRENT = CURRENT + 1;

the equals sign is used in a manner that seems unusual at first. Here, we instruct the computer to find a new value for CURRENT by taking the old value and adding 1 to it, just as

SUM = SUM + CURRENT;

instructs the machine to determine a new value for SUM by taking the old value and adding CURRENT to it. Thus if SUM = 10 and CURRENT = 5, the machine would add these and let SUM = 15.

The program is designed to add the first hundred counting numbers; CURRENT identifies the number of numbers that have been added, while SUM keeps track of the sum of the numbers added. We want to stop after 100 numbers have been added; this is done by the statement

IF CURRENT < 100 THEN GO TO LOOP;

As long as the value of CURRENT is less than 100, the computer will GO TO LOOP; that is, it will return to the statement labeled LOOP and continue from that point. When the value of CURRENT reaches 100 the machine goes to

PUT LIST (SUM);

which causes the value of SUM to be printed as output. As the program is written the output would be in floating point form. The program would cause the printing of the single number .5050E4, which means the same as $.5050 \times 10^4$.

Note the convenience of the PL/1 program over the machine language program written above. *Debugging,* or error locating, is much easier here. No numbered addresses need be remembered, and no operation codes looked up. In this section we show several examples of PL/1 programs, and then in a later section we compare PL/1 with FORTRAN and BASIC, two other popular compiler languages. We are not aiming at making computer programmers of the readers of this textbook, but we do want to instill a familiarity with the type of instructions given to a computer. Knowing the basic method used to program a computer clarifies the capabilities and limitations of the machine.

In PL/1, + is used for addition, − for subtraction, * for multiplication, and / for division. The expression a^3 is written A**3. The machine makes calculations from inside the parentheses to the outside, just as in algebra.

The operations are arranged in a certain heirarchy. Any exponentiation is done first. Beginning on the left, the computer does any multiplications and/or divisions, in order, as it comes to them. Thus

$$A*B/C*D$$

would be the same as

$$\left(\frac{AB}{C}\right)D,$$

while

$$A*B/(C*D)$$

is the same as

$$\frac{AB}{CD}.$$

Additions and subtractions are then done in order from left to right. To eliminate possible ambiguity, parentheses may be used.

Example 10.1. Write a program to calculate the value of the expression

$$\frac{3x^4 - 4x}{-2x + 3},$$

when $x = -2$.

Here we have two options. We could directly tell the computer the value of x with a statement such as

$$X = -2;$$

or we could tell the computer that a value of x will be supplied. In that case we write

$$GET \ LIST \ (X);$$

and add a card (called a data card) containing only the number -2 at the end of the program. The computer knows from the GET statement that it will find one number on a data card, with this number called x in the program. The advantage is that several data cards can be prepared and placed at the end of the program. In this way the same expression can be evaluated for several different values of x.

Now that the computer knows the value of x, we may write the rest of the program. We use (not very imaginatively) the variable ANSWER to represent the answer:

$$ANSWER = (3*X**4 - 4*X)/(-2*X + 3);$$

We use the following rather fancy statement to print the output.

```
PUT LIST ('IF X =', X, 'THEN THE EXPRESSION EQUALS',
ANSWER );
```

The result of the PUT statement:

IF X = -2 THEN THE EXPRESSION EQUALS 8

Any string of characters can be placed inside apostrophes in a PUT LIST statement, causing them to be printed as output. The program ends with

END;

After END we place any data cards into the program.

Example 10.2. Write a program to find the value of the expression

$$-4x^2 + 1,$$

for all counting number values of x from 1 to 4 inclusive.

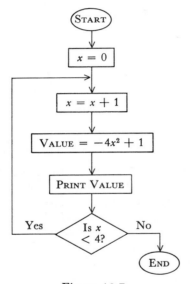

Figure 10.7

We could write a program containing four parts, each similar to the one above. However, there is another, shorter way, as shown in the following program and in the flow chart of figure 10.7 above.

```
       X = 0;
 HARRY:  X = X + 1;
       VALUE = -4*X*X + 1;
       PUT LIST ('WHEN X =', X, 'THE EXPRESSION EQUALS',
       VALUE):
       IF X < 4 THEN GO TO HARRY;
       END;
```

We initialized the value of x at 0. With the statement labeled HARRY, the program beings a *loop,* or string of statements that will be used repeatedly by the machine. To begin the loop, the value of x is increased by 1, and VALUE evaluated. (Note: it is faster for the computer to do x*x than x**2.) The computer then prints the answer. Because of the apostrophes used,

WHEN X = 2 THE EXPRESSION EQUALS −15

is a typical printout. VALUE is to be evaluated for all counting number values of x between 1 and 4 inclusive; the IF statement is used to stop the calculations after x reaches 4. If $x < 4$, the computer returns to the statement labeled HARRY and begins the loop again, increasing the value of x by 1 and proceeding through the program. If x is not less than 4, the machine skips the THEN part of the statement and proceeds to the next statement: END.

It is possible to simplify the program somewhat, using a DO loop:

```
DO X = 1 TO 4 BY 1;
VALUE = −4*X*X + 1;
PUT LIST (VALUE);
END;
```

The DO statement instructs the computer to begin with $x = 1$, work through the statements, increase the value of x by 1, work through the statements again, and so on until x finally has the value 4.

Example 10.3. Find the approximate area of the intersection of the regions:

$$\{(x, y) \mid x \geq 2\}, \{(x, y) \mid y \leq x^2\}, \{(x, y) \mid x \leq 3\}, \{(x, y) \mid y \geq 0\}.$$

A graph of the intersection is shown in figure 10.8. We can approximate the area of the region by drawing a series of small rectangles; the sum of the areas of the rectangles will approximate the desired area. To explain the process used, let's divide the line segment between (2, 0) and (3, 0) into five equal parts. Since the length of the segment is 1, each part has the length $\frac{1}{5} = .2$. The height of the rectangle is the distance from the lower left corner to the upper left corner. The area of the rectangle is given by the formula:

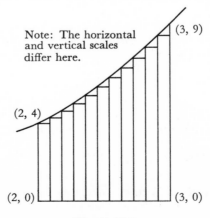

Note: The horizontal and vertical scales differ here.

(3, 9)

(2, 4)

(2, 0)

(3, 0)

Figure 10.8

area = length × width. Figure 10.9 shows the area of the region approximated with five rectangles.

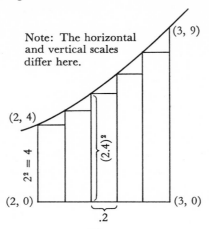

Figure 10.9

The area of, say, the middle rectangle is the product of the length and width, where the length is $[2 + 2(.2)]^2 = (2.4)^2$, and the width is .2. The area then is

$$(.2)(2.4)^2.$$

Similar areas can be found for all five rectangles. It is easier to write a program and let the machine find the areas.

```
TOTAREA = 0;
DO I = 0 TO 4 BY 1;
HEIGHT = (2 + I*(.2))**2;
AREA = (.2)*HEIGHT;
TOTAREA = TOTAREA + AREA;
END;
PUT LIST ('THE APPROXIMATION IS', TOTAREA);
END;
```

Note that each DO loop requires an END statement, as does the program itself. When run through the computer, this statement produces the output

```
THE APPROXIMATION IS    .5840E1
```

To determine a better approximation of the area of the region, we might increase the number of rectangles. If 1000 rectangles are used, the width of each rectangle becomes $1/1000 = .001$. With this in mind we modify the program:

```
TOTAREA = 0;
DO I = 0 TO 999 BY 1;
HEIGHT = (2 + I*(.001))**2;
AREA = (.001)*HEIGHT;
TOTAREA = TOTAREA + AREA;
END;
PUT LIST ('THE APPROXIMATION IS', TOTAREA);
END:
```

Here the output reads

THE APPROXIMATION IS   .6333E1

Anyone who has had a semester of calculus should be able to find the exact area: 19/3 or 6.3333 · · · .

The results of scientific work often produce graphs which are not as simple, and the area under the graph cannot be found readily by methods of elementary calculus. In such cases computer programs similar to those above are used to obtain an approximation to the area. (People in chemistry have been known to find the area of such a region by drawing it on paper, cutting it out, and weighing it. The weight of the region can then be compared to the weight of a known area of paper. Such quaint methods are interesting but do not apply to our discussion of computers.)

Example 10.4. Suppose a firm has 100 employees, each of whom has been assigned a number from 00 to 99. Assume the computer knows the following facts about each employee: his employee number, called EMNO, his total gross salary to date, TGPTD (gross salary is the total amount made by the employee before any deductions), the number of hours worked in the last pay period at the regular rate, REGHRS, his rate per hour for regular work, RATE, the number of overtime hours in the last pay period, OVERHRS, his rate per overtime hour, OVERRATE, the number of dependents claimed, DEPEN, and a union membership code, UNION, which is 0 if the employee does not belong and 1 if he does. Write a program that will produce the payroll for the firm.

We assume that each data card contains all the above information about one employee in the order listed. To begin, we ask the computer to find the data on the first employee.

```
WEASEL : GET LIST (EMNO, TGPTD, REGHRS, RATE, OVERHRS, OVERRATE,
DEPEN, UNION);
```

(WEASEL is a statement label which will be used later.) It is easy to find the gross pay for the last period.

```
GROSS = REGHRS*RATE + OVERHRS*OVERRATE;
PUT LIST ('YOUR GROSS PAY FOR THE PERIOD IS', GROSS);
```

We can also find the total gross pay to date.

```
TGPTD = TGPTD + GROSS;
PUT LIST ('YOUR TOTAL GROSS PAY SO FAR IS', TGPTD);
```

The fun starts when we try to calculate tax deductions. Tax rates change so often that for simplicity we have made up our own. For us, social security taxes are as follows: a tax of 4% on the first $4000 in gross earnings in one year, with a tax of 2% thereafter. Check TGPTD; if it is greater than $4000 tax

GROSS at 2%, otherwise tax at 4%. We have not considered one of the possibilities at this time; it is left as an exercise.

```
      IF TGPTD < 4000 THEN GO TO TOM;
      SOCSEC = .02*GROSS,
      GO TO HARRY;
TOM : SOCSEC = .04*GROSS;
HARRY : PUT LIST ('YOUR SOCIAL SECURITY DEDUCTION IS', SOCSEC);
```

(Note that if TGPTD is less than $4000, then we do not want to execute the next two statements; in order to skip them we use the statement GO TO TOM found in the first line.)

Similar complications arise when we try to calculate income tax withholding. Again we are using imaginary figures: $12.00 of gross pay per dependent is not taxed, but the rest is taxed at 18%.

```
TAXBASE = 12*DEPEN;
DIFF = GROSS - TAXBASE;
```

If DIFF is negative or zero, there is no tax; if DIFF is positive, we deduct 18% of DIFF.

```
      IF DIFF > 0 THEN GO TO GEORGE;
      TAX = 0;
      GO TO HIRAM;
GEORGE:  TAX = .18*DIFF;
 HIRAM:  PUT LIST ('YOUR WITHHOLDING TAX DEDUCTION IS', TAX);
```

Union dues are somewhat easier. If UNION = 1, the employee belongs to the union and pays dues of $2.75; if UNION = 0, he pays nothing.

```
      IF UNION = 0 THEN GO TO TERRY;
      DUES = 2.75;
      PUT LIST ('YOUR UNION DUES ARE 2.75');
      GO TO RICHARD;
TERRY:  DUES = 0;
```

RICHARD is the label of the next statement. Note that nothing will appear in the printout if the employee is not a union member. Now we are ready to find the net pay.

```
RICHARD:  PAYNET = GROSS - SOCSEC - TAX - DUES;
          IF PAYNET <= 0 THEN GO TO CUTHBERT;
          PUT LIST ('YOUR NET PAY IS', PAYNET);
          GO TO TONY;
CUTHBERT:  PUT LIST ('SORRY, YOU GET NO MONEY THIS TIME');
TONY:  IF EMNO < 99 THEN GO TO WEASEL;
       END;
```

The symbols $<=$ mean the same as $\leq$. The statement labeled TONY checks to see if we have evaluated the payroll for all 100 employees; if not we return to statement WEASEL and locate payroll data for another employee. Figure 10.10 (see p. 298) shows a flow chart for this program.

In an actual situation we would probably modify the program so that a card is produced for each employee. The following information would be punched on each one: EMNO, the new value of TGPTD, RATE, OVERRATE,

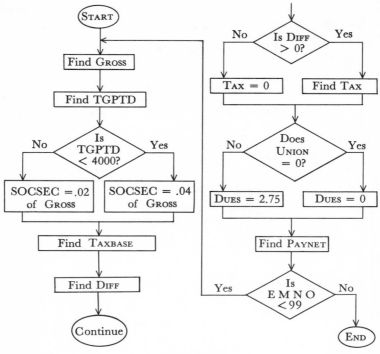

Figure 10.10

DEPEN, and UNION. At the conclusion of the next pay period it would be a simple matter to put these cards in a keypunch and add new values of REGHRS and OVERHRS.

PROBLEMS

1. Let $P = \dfrac{2x^4 + x}{6 + x}$. Write a program that will produce the following output:

   ```
   IF X = 0 THEN P = 0
   ```

2. Let $M = x + y + z$. Write a program to produce the following output:

   ```
   IF X = 2 AND IF Y = 3 AND IF Z = 4 THEN M = 9
   ```

3. What does the following program do?

   ```
   SUM = 0;
   NUM = 0;
   DO I = 1 TO 100 BY 2;
   NUM = NUM + I;
   SUM = SUM + NUM*NUM;
   END;
   END;
   ```

4. Write a program that does the same thing as the program of problem 3, but without the DO statement.

5. Let $P = x + 4$. Write a program to find the value of P as x increases from -2 to 15 in increments of 1.

6. In the payroll program, suppose TGPTD = \$4186.00, REGHRS = 40, RATE = \$6.00, OVERHRS = 8, OVERRATE = \$9.00, DEPEN = 4, and UNION = 0. Write the output that would be produced by the program.

7. The payroll program does not take care of one possibility in calculating SOCSEC. Explain what it is, and how the program might be modified to take care of it.

SECTION 4. SUBSCRIPTED VARIABLES

Many problems, such as those involving matrices, can be handled on a computer more easily if subscripted variables are used. That is, instead of writing variable names as A, B, C, we write A_1, A_2, A_3, (the 1, 2, and 3 are called subscripts); in computer language they are written A(1), A(2), and A(3). For example, if the computer knows the fifteen numbers A(1), A(2), . . . , A(15), we can write a program to find the largest of the numbers. First we construct a flow chart (see figure 10.11).

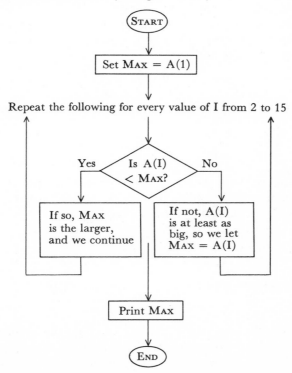

Figure 10.11

Note the procedure used here: the variable MAX is set equal to A(1), and is then compared to A(2); MAX takes the value of the larger of the two. MAX is then compared to A(3) and again takes the larger value. This process continues through the entire list of numbers. The following program can be written from the flow chart:

```
        MAX = A(1);
        DO I = 2 TO 15;
        IF A(I) < MAX THEN GO TO SAM;
        MAX = A(I);
SAM:;
        END;
        PUT LIST ('THE LARGEST NUMBER IS', MAX);
        END;
```

At each step, if A(I) is smaller than MAX, we continue searching for values larger than MAX. This is accomplished by letting SAM be the label of the *null statement* ; which causes the program to continue. The program can be modified so that the subscript of the largest value is printed along with MAX.

Subscripted variables may also be used with matrices. The symbol $A(3, 4)$ denotes the number that is found in row 3, column 4 of matrix A. If the computer knows the components of a 4x4 matrix B and a 4x4 matrix C, we can write a program to find the sum matrix, $S = B + C$. As described in the last chapter, the sum of two matrices is the matrix which is the result of adding corresponding entries. In order to find the entries for the first row of the sum matrix, we must evaluate

$$S(1, J) = B(1, J) + C(1, J),$$

for $J = 1, J = 2, J = 3$, and $J = 4$. We do this with a DO statement.

```
        DO J = 1 TO 4 BY 1;
        S(1,J) = B(1,J) + C(1,J);
        END;
```

We do not want just the entries of the first row; we want the entries of all the rows of the sum matrix. To find all the entries, replace 1 with I and let I take on values 1, 2, 3, and 4, again with a DO loop.

```
        DO I = 1 TO 4 BY 1;
        DO J = 1 TO 4 BY 1;
        S(I,J) = B(I,J) + C(I,J);
```

The computer now contains the values of the sum matrix S.

Example 10.5.   Suppose the computer contains the R numbers A(1), A(2), . . . , A(R), where R is some counting number known to the computer. Write a program to find the average of the numbers.

To find the average we add all the numbers and divide by R.

```
SUM = 0;
DO I = 1 TO R BY 1;
SUM = SUM + A(I);
END;
AVE = SUM/R;
PUT LIST ('THE AVERAGE OF THE', R, 'NUMBERS IS', AVE);
END;
```

Example 10.6. Find the standard deviation of the R numbers of example 10.5.

Recall from Chapter 8 the definition of standard deviation for a set of R numbers: find the average of the numbers, subtract the average from each number of the set, square the results, add the squares, divide this result by R, and take the square root of the result. That is, the standard deviation of the R numbers $A(1)$, $A(2)$, . . . , $A(R)$ is given by

$$\text{STDEV} = \sqrt{\frac{\Sigma(A(I) - AVE)^2}{R}},$$

where Σ means "summation of" and is an instruction to add together all the $(A(I) - AVE)^2$ terms.

Assume we have found AVE. First subtract AVE from each of the $A(I)$:

```
DO I = 1 TO R BY 1;
DIFF(I) = A(I) - AVE;
END;
```

Next square each DIFF(I) and add the results:

```
SUM = 0;
DO I = 1 TO R BY 1;
DIFFSQUARE = DIFF(I)*DIFF(I);
SUM = SUM + DIFFSQUARE;
END;
```

Now divide SUM by R:

```
SUMQUOT = SUM/R;
```

Finally take the square root of SUMQUOT. This fortunately can be done very simply:

```
STDEV = SQRT(SUMQUOT);
```

Here SQRT( ) is used to tell the computer to find the square root of the quantity in parentheses. Similar symbols are available for trigonometric and logarithmic work. To finish the program we could use a PUT statement.

PROBLEMS

1. Using the numbers 3, 4, −2, 1 trace the program at the beginning of the section and write, step by step, what the program does to the numbers. (Change the 15 of the program to 4.)

2. What happens in the first program of the section if two of the numbers are equal?

3. In example 10.5, what would the result be if the numbers − 1, 6, 8, 11, and 1 were placed in the computer?

4. Write a program for linear regression, as explained in Chapter 8, section 6.

5. Write a program to multiply two 3x3 matrices. Assume the machine has the values of $A(I, J)$ and $B(I, J)$ for I and J = 1, 2, 3. Call the product matrix C.

SECTION 5. OTHER COMPILER LANGUAGES

We have been discussing the compiler language PL/1, developed by IBM in the middle 60's. This language is designed to be easy to learn, while at the same time it is powerful enough to work many different types of problems. Many features that we have not discussed are available for more involved problems. FORTRAN, one of the original compiler languages (introduced by IBM in 1957), is designed for mathematical and scientific work. Unlike PL/1, FORTRAN statements require no semicolon; but, on the other hand, they can be punched only one to a card. FORTRAN statements are labeled with numbers containing from 1 to 5 digits, which appear in columns 1-5. If a statement does not fit on one card, it can be continued to another card by punching 1 in column 6.

In FORTRAN variable names must begin with a letter and be 1-6 characters long. Variable names beginning with I, J, K, L, M, or N are reserved for integer variables (variables taking on only integer values), while variable names beginning with other letters are used for floating point numbers. Arithmetic statements in FORTRAN are exactly the same as those in PL/1, except that as a general rule fixed and floating point variables should not be mixed in the same statement. The statement

```
GO TO HARRY;
```

of PL/1 becomes

```
GO TO 1234
```

in FORTRAN. FORTRAN IF statements take the form

```
IF (SOME EXPRESSION) 15, 16, 17
```

If the expression in parentheses is negative, the computer switches to instruction 15. If the quantity is zero it goes to 16, and if it is positive it goes to 17. Two of these numbers can be the same.

```
IF (SOME EXPRESSION) 15, 15, 16
```

tells the computer to go to statement 16 if the quantity in the parentheses is positive, but otherwise go to 15.

DO statements are somewhat different also. The PL/1 DO loop

```
DO I = 1 TO 15 BY 3;
STATEMENT 1;
            .
            .
            .
STATEMENT N;
END;
```

becomes, in FORTRAN,

```
DO 25 I = 1,  15,  3
STATEMENT 1
            .
            .
            .
25 STATEMENT N
```

The last statement of the DO loop is given the number 25; therefore the program works down to and includes statement 25 before starting the loop again.

It is a little harder to print out the results in FORTRAN. For example, suppose the computer contains the following numbers: IAB = 124, ICKR = 102, KBEE = 68, and KR7 = 12360. To have these numbers printed out, we use the following two statements:

```
PRINT 25,  IAB,  ICKR,  KBEE,  KR7
25 FORMAT (4I10)
```

The first statement tells the computer to print the four numbers according to the instructions given in statement 25. In statement 25 the machine is told that four integer numbers will be supplied with ten spaces to be reserved for each. The numbers would be printed as

$$------124-------102---------68------12360$$

(The dashes are not printed.) If, by mistake, 4I4 had been used in the FORMAT statement, the result would have been

$$-124-102--682360$$

The third and fourth numbers run together and also the four-space designation causes only the last four digits of the fourth number to be printed.

BASIC is a compiler language developed at Dartmouth for use in their time-shared computer system. BASIC is designed with beginning students in mind and thus is relatively simple to learn and use. Each statement of a BASIC program must be numbered (unlike PL/1 or FORTRAN), with the numbers written in increasing order. The PL/1 statement

```
GOAT = (X + S)**5;
```

becomes in BASIC,

```
25  LET GOAT = (X + S) ↑ 5
```

where ↑ is used to denote exponentiation. Statements which transfer control, such as:

$$15 \quad \text{GO TO } 25$$

have the same effect in BASIC as in the other languages. IF statements take the following form:

$$60 \quad \text{IF R} > 30 \text{ THEN } 80$$

If the value of the variable R is greater than 30, the machine transfers to statement 80. If R is less than or equal to 30 it proceeds with the next statement. Besides greater than and less than, equals, greater than or equal to, less than or equal to, and not equal ($< >$) can be used. The PL/1 DO loop becomes

```
10 FOR X = 10 TO 20 STEP 2
20    STATEMENT 1
           .
           .
           .
60 NEXT X
```

The computer first sets x = 10 and works through the statements of the loop. When NEXT x is reached, it returns to the top of the loop, increases x by 2, and goes through the loop again. The loop is finished when x = 20.

BASIC provides several special statements:

SQR(x)	Square root of x
INT(x)	Integer part of x
SGN(x)	+1 or −1, depending on whether x is positive or negative
RND(x)	A random number between 0 and 1

Thus SQR(64) is 8, INT(3¼) = 3 (take the largest whole number less than or equal to x), and SGN(3,465,789.234) = 1. If A is a square matrix, writing

$$30 \quad \text{MAT B} = \text{INV(A)}$$

will produce a matrix B which is the inverse of matrix A (compare with the technique presented in Chapter 9). Similarly,

```
30  MAT C = A + B
30  MAT C = A - B
30  MAT C = (K)*A
30  MAT C = A*B
```

are other matrix instructions. (A and B are matrices and K is a number.)

Output statements are easy in BASIC:

`45  PRINT K,  "TONS"`

will produce the following output (if $K = 10$)

`10   TONS`

Input statements take the following form:

`100   READ R,  K,  T`

appears at the beginning of the program; appropriate data values appear at the end, such as

`300 DATA 75,  2.18,  3612`

An END statement appears after the DATA.

Example 10.7. Write a program in BASIC corresponding to the example found in section 7 of Chapter 7.

The example approximated a value for π by randomly selecting numbers in a square one unit on a side. The quotient of the number of points lying inside the quarter-circle of figure 10.12, divided by the total number of points selected, is an approximation to the number $\frac{\pi}{4}$. A random number

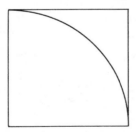

Figure 10.12

between 0 and 1 is selected for X, and a similar number for Y. Using these values, we decide whether or not the corresponding point lies inside the circle. If it does we increase variable M by 1; for every point tried, we increase variable N by 1. After selecting points many times, we form the quotient $\frac{M}{N}$, which approximates $\frac{\pi}{4}$. (The number $\frac{4M}{N}$ approximates π.)

The equation of the circle with center at the origin and radius 1 is

$$x^2 + y^2 = 1;$$

we want to increase M by 1 only when

$$x^2 + y^2 \leq 1.$$

To begin the program, we have

```
10  LET  X  =  RDN(Z)
15  LET  Y  =  RDN(Z)
```

The rest of the program can be completed from the flow chart of figure 10.13.

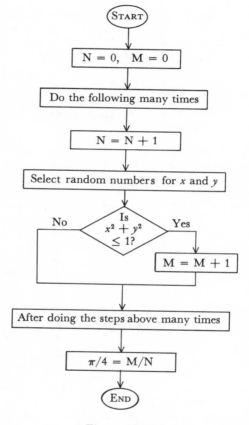

Figure 10.13

Today there are several other compiler languages in use. COBAL was worked out by a committee of computer users and computer designers in 1959–60. It is a language particularly suited to business problems, which often involve large quantities of alphabetic data. ALGOL was developed at a meeting of computer experts in 1958; today it is quite popular in Europe but less so in the United States.

PROBLEMS

1. Work through the following BASIC program. Write the printout that will be produced.

```
10    READ M, N
12    LET K = M + N
15    LET T = K/2
17    PRINT T
18    DATA 7, 9
19    END
```

2. Write a program in BASIC to convert a measurement in inches to one in feet and inches. (Hint: 39 inches = 3 feet, 3 inches, and $\text{INT}(39/12) = 3$.)
3. Write a program in BASIC to find the sum of the squares of the first hundred counting numbers.
4. What would the following FORTRAN statements do?

```
      PRINT 30, ICHY, ICKY, NAN
30 FORMAT (3I9)
```

Assume ICHY = 1348, ICKY = 26, and NAN = 11,461.

FOR FURTHER READING

Bowden, B. V., ed. *Faster Than Thought.* London: Pitman, 1953. This book, although quite outdated in its description of computers, does have a good history of Charles Babbage.

Kemeny, John G., and Kurtz, Thomas E. BASIC *Programming.* New York: John Wiley and Sons, Inc., 1967. A wealth of computer programs are to be found in this book, including ones that play games and write harmony in music.

Saunders, Donald. *Computers In Business, An Introduction.* New York: McGraw-Hill, Inc., 1968. A good introduction to business uses of computers.

Springer, Clifford H., and others. *Statistical Inference.* (*Mathematics for Management Series,* Vol. 3) Homewood, Illinois: Richard D. Irwin, 1966. This four-volume series provides an excellent introduction to mathematics for the manager of a business. Volume 3 includes computer applications. A word of warning: the authors work for a large computer manufacturer; therefore take their claims for the superiority of their machines with at least a grain of salt.

Stark, Peter A. *Digital Computer Programming.* New York: The Macmillan Company, 1967. This is a good general introduction to the modern computer, including a complete introduction to FORTRAN programming.

CHAPTER II

TOPICS FROM GEOMETRY

For the Egyptians living around 1500 B.C., geometry was an important practical tool which they employed extensively. For instance, geometry was necessary in order to construct the pyramids and was also used to measure land. Hence the geometry of the Egyptians was oriented almost exclusively toward practical problems of area and volume with little, if any, concern for derivations or proofs of formulas.

Greek geometry, so different and more far-reaching than that of the Egyptians, supposedly began with the work of a retired olive-oil king, Thales of Miletus, around 600 B.C. Thales made his fortune merely to prove how easy it is to become wealthy; he cornered all the oil presses during a year of an exceptionally large crop. Legend records that Thales studied for a time in Egypt and then introduced geometry to Greece, where he attempted to apply the principles of Greek logic to his newly learned subject. He was the first to attempt to prove theorems of geometry; he is said to have sacrificed a bull in happiness when he proved that any angle inscribed in a semicircle is a right angle. Thales was also an astronomer; one night while looking at the stars he fell in a well, prompting his servant girl to mutter something about people who know what is going on in the heavens but are ignorant about what is happening at their very feet.

Approximately fifty years separated Thales and Pythagoras (572?–500? B.C.) with some authorities claiming that Pythagoras studied under Thales. Pythagoras also studied in Egypt, then returned to Crotona, a Greek city in southern Italy, where he founded the Pythagorean school, a combination school and semireligious fraternity. The Pythagoreans were a close-knit group with secret oaths and observances; one requirement of Pythagoras was that every member should sign Pythagoras' name to all mathematical discoveries. The Pythagoreans were the first to make the distinction between odd and even numbers, calling odd numbers masculine and even numbers feminine (except for 1, which was the generator of all numbers). The number 5 represented marriage since 5 is the sum of the first masculine number (3) and the first feminine number (2). The Pythagoreans discovered an interesting relation between quotients of counting numbers and the theory of music:

if a string produces the note C when plucked, then a string that is $\frac{16}{15}$ as long produces B, one $\frac{6}{5}$ as long produces A, one $\frac{4}{3}$ as long produces G, one $\frac{3}{2}$ as long produces F, one $\frac{8}{5}$ as long produces E, one $\frac{16}{9}$ as long produces D, and one exactly twice as long gives C again but one octave lower. The group was convinced by relationships such as these, that counting numbers rule the universe; they felt that the planets moving through space had a certain counting number harmony, which they called the "music of the spheres."

The belief that all things evolved from the counting numbers provided a basis for the religious studies of the Pythagoreans, so that we can appreciate the horror with which they must have greeted the discovery that $\sqrt{2}$ could not be expressed as the quotient of two counting numbers. The brotherhood tried to keep this finding secret, but one member revealed the discovery; he was thrown overboard from a ship for his troubles.

The Pythagoreans proved theorems in a sequence of steps, each of which followed logically from certain basic assumptions. It became common practice in Greek mathematics to distinguish between *axioms,* or general assumptions (for example, "things equal to the same thing are equal to each other"), and *postulates,* or assumptions referring only to the subject under discussion (for example, "a straight line may be drawn through any two points"). Today these two words are used interchangeably.

Most of the then-current Greek mathematical knowledge was summarized and systematized by Euclid, who lived around 300 B.C. Euclid himself did not produce much in the way of new results, but his textbook on mathematics exerted an important influence. His book, *The Elements,* was used almost unchanged as a standard school textbook well into the middle 1800's. High school geometry even today is almost totally based on work recorded by Euclid. The material of high school geometry is but a small part of his book, which also discusses number theory and proportion.

It is important to remember that Euclid's *Elements* summarized the Greek mathematical knowledge of his time; however, much important work was done for over 100 years after Euclid. Perhaps the two greatest Greek mathematicians after Euclid were Apollonius and Archimedes; Apollonius (260?–200? B.C.) worked mostly with conic sections (which we discussed in Chapter 6), while Archimedes (287–212 B.C.) worked in a large variety of fields, including physics and mathematics. In many ways the work of Archimedes anticipated calculus; many of the ideas of calculus find counterparts in his work. Archimedes is well known for his skill with mechanical devices, especially those he constructed to help defend the city of Syracuse against the Roman legions of Marcellus. He was able to keep the Roman fleet away from the city for three years with assorted catapults, claws, and mirrors of his own design. It was not his fault that the Romans finally took the city—they merely waited until the Greeks became drunk at a religious feast and entered through a weak spot in the city wall.

When Archimedes died during the Roman invasion the golden age of Greek geometry ended. Lesser figures followed, such as Pappus (around

300 A.D.) and Hypatia, (400 A.D.), the woman mathematician who was stoned to death by a Christian mob. It would be over a thousand years after Hypatia before anything of consequence would be done in Western mathematics. (There seems to be some controversy over whether or not Hypatia was beautiful. We prefer to think she was.)

The mathematics that the Greeks studied is today called *synthetic* or *Euclidean* geometry in contrast to other, more recently developed, geometries. Euclidean geometry is used to build bridges or measure land; it is not used to send a spaceship to the moon. In this chapter the authors have assembled several of what we feel are the more interesting topics of Euclidean geometry, together with a brief discussion of projective geometry.

SECTION 1. FIGURE NUMBERS

The Greeks called the numbers 1, 3, 6, 10, 15, 21, . . . *triangular numbers.* The diagram of figure 11.1 illustrates the origin of this name.

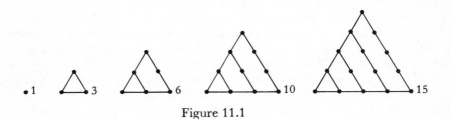

Figure 11.1

On the other hand, 1, 4, 9, 16, 25, . . . were referred to as *square numbers,* as illustrated by figure 11.2.

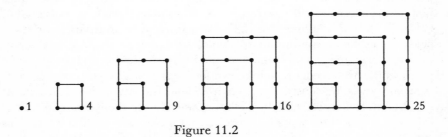

Figure 11.2

Inspection of diagrams such as these demonstrates that every square number greater than one is the sum of two successive triangular numbers, as suggested in figure 11.3.

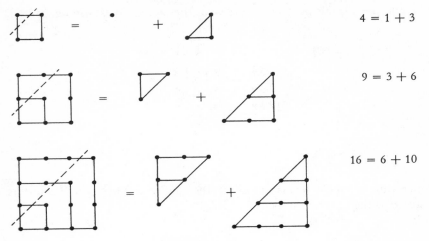

$$4 = 1 + 3$$

$$9 = 3 + 6$$

$$16 = 6 + 10$$

Figure 11.3

As a sample of the type of problem that can be worked using figure numbers, we ask what is the sum of the first 25 odd counting numbers. To find this sum we could write the first 25 odd counting numbers and add them, but that would involve a great deal of work. Let's see if we can discover an easier method. List the first few sums of odd numbers:

$$1 = \ 1.$$
$$3 + 1 = \ 4.$$
$$5 + 3 + 1 = \ 9.$$
$$7 + 5 + 3 + 1 = 16.$$
$$9 + 7 + 5 + 3 + 1 = 25.$$
$$11 + 9 + 7 + 5 + 3 + 1 = 36.$$

A pattern begins to appear: the sum of the first four odd numbers is 16, or 4^2; the sum of the first five odd numbers is 25, or 5^2; and the sum of the first six odd counting numbers is 36, or 6^2. Thus we might predict that the sum of the first 25 odd counting numbers would be 25^2, or 625. In the same way, the sum of the first 40 odd counting numbers should be 40^2, or 1600. We can verify this result by using figure numbers: figure 11.4 demonstrates that the sum of the first five odd counting numbers is 5^2, or 25.

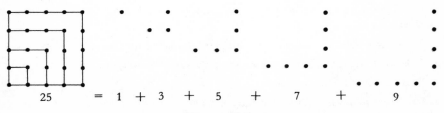

$$25 \quad = \quad 1 \ + \ 3 \ + \ 5 \ + \ 7 \ + \ 9$$

Figure 11.4

We could use a single diagram to arrive at the same result, as in figure 11.5.

Figure 11.5

Hence this statement seems plausible: the sum of the first n odd counting numbers is the square number n^2.

Example 11.1.   Show that when a triangular number is multiplied by 8, and 1 is added, the result is a square number.

Figure 11.6 illustrates this result for the triangular number 6. The number 6 has been used 8 times, 1 added, resulting in a square, 7 on a side. Similar figures could be drawn for other triangular numbers.

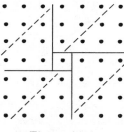

Figure 11.6

PROBLEMS

1. Use figure numbers, as in the text, to show $1 + 3 + 5 + 7 + 9 + 11 + 13 + 15 = 64$.

2. The number 64 is a square number. Find two triangular numbers whose sum is 64.

3. Find two triangular numbers whose sum is the square number 100.

4. Find the ninth triangular number

5. Use figure numbers to show that this statement is plausible: the sum of the first n counting numbers is a triangular number.

Pentagonal numbers are those in the series of figure 11.7.

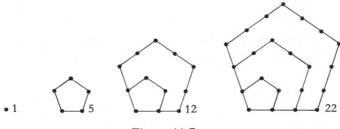

Figure 11.7

6. Find the fifth pentagonal number.

7. Show that the fifth pentagonal number is equal to the sum of three triangular numbers plus five. Do you think a similar result holds in general?

SECTION 2. CONSTRUCTIONS

The Greeks did not study algebra as we do. To them geometry was the highest expression of mathematical science; their geometry was an abstract subject. Any practical application resulting from their work was nice but held no great importance. To the Greeks, a geometrical construction also needed abstract beauty. A construction could not be polluted with such practical instruments as a ruler. The Greeks permitted only two tools in geometrical construction: a compass for drawing circles and arcs of circles, and a straightedge for drawing straight line segments. The straightedge, unlike a ruler, could have no marks on it. It was not permitted to line up points by eye.

Within these restrictions certain things are impossible: for example, trisecting an angle (cutting the angle into three equal parts). We will see methods of angle trisection below, but these methods do not satisfy the restrictions of the Greeks. They are valid, but merely do not meet the criteria of the Greeks.

Let's review four basic constructions which will be used in this section.

Construction 1.   Construct the perpendicular bisector of a given line segment.

Let the segment have endpoints A and B. Adjust the compass for any radius greater than half the length of AB. Place the compass point at A and draw an arc, then draw another arc of the same size at B. The line drawn through the points of intersection of these two arcs is the desired perpendicular bisector. (See figure 11.8 on p. 314.)

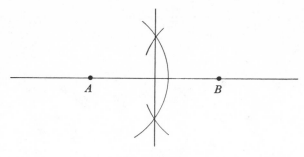

Figure 11.8

Construction 2.   Construct a perpendicular from a point off a line to the line.

(1) Let *A* be the point, *r* the line. Place the compass point at *A* and draw an arc, cutting *r* in two points.

(2) Swing arcs of equal radius from each of the two points on *r* which were constructed in (1). The line drawn through the intersection of the two arcs and point *A* is perpendicular to *r*. (See figure 11.9.)

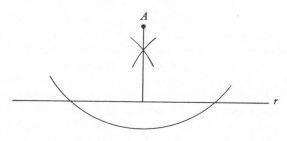

Figure 11.9

Construction 3.   Construct a perpendicular to a line at some given point on the line.

(1) Let *r* be the line and *A* the point. Using any convenient radius on the compass, place the compass point at *A* and swing arcs which cut *r*, as in figure 11.10.

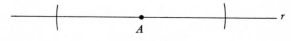

Figure 11.10

(2) Increase the radius of the compass, place the point of the compass on the points obtained in (1) and draw arcs. A line through *A* and the intersection of the two arcs is perpendicular to *r* (see figure 11.11).

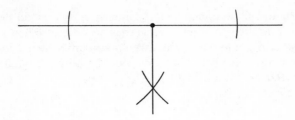

Figure 11.11

Construction 4.   Copy an angle.

(1) In order to copy an angle ABC on line r, place the compass point at B and draw an arc. Then place the compass point on r at some point P and draw the same arc, as in figure 11.12.

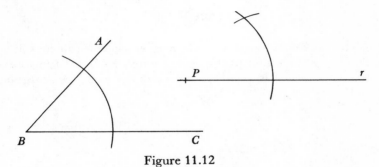

Figure 11.12

(2) Measure, with your compass, the distance between the points where the arc cuts the angle, and transfer this distance, as shown in figure 11.13.

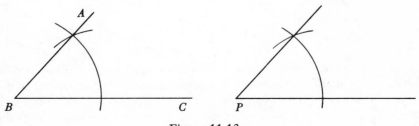

Figure 11.13

Now let's consider some constructions that are a little more advanced.

Construction 5.   Construct a circle that passes through any three non-collinear points.

Let A, B, and C be noncollinear points (points that do not lie on the same line); we want to construct a circle that passes through all three points.

(1) Make a triangle out of the three points by drawing line segments. Using construction 1 from above, construct the perpendicular bisectors of AB, BC, and AC. (See figure 11.14.)

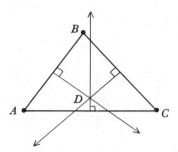

Figure 11.14

(2) The three bisectors should all meet in a point, called D in figure 11.14. Point D is the center of the desired circle. Place the compass point at D, adjust the pencil to point A, and draw the circle, as illustrated by figure 11.15.

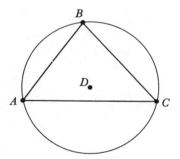

Figure 11.15

Why does this construction work? Recall that any point on the perpendicular bisector of a line segment is equally distant from both ends of the segment. Point D is on the perpendicular bisector of segment AC and thus is equally distant from A and C; hence $AD = CD$. In the same way, D is on the perpendicular bisector of segment AB, so that $AD = BD$. Similarly, $BD = CD$, so that

$$AD = BD = CD.$$

Hence points A, B, and C are each the same distance from D so that a circle with center at D and passing through A will also pass through B and C.

Construction 6.   Divide a given line segment into *n* equal parts, where *n* is a counting number.

As an example, let's divide a segment *AB* into five equal parts.

(1) Draw an angle *BAC* with vertex at *A*. Select any convenient radius on the compass and lay off this radius five times on side *AC*, as shown in figure 11.16.

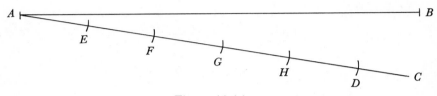

Figure 11.16

(2) Draw a segment connecting *B* and *D*. At points *E*, *F*, *G*, and *H*, copy angle *D* as explained in construction 4. The sides of the angles you draw will cut *AB* into five equal parts. (See figure 11.17.)

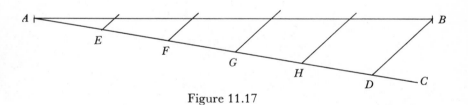

Figure 11.17

To understand why this method works, consider *AB* and *AC* as transversals with the lines drawn from *D*, *E*, *F*, *G*, and *H* a system of parallel lines. Then recall that a system of parallel lines which cuts off equal segments on one transversal does so on every transversal.

Construction 7.   Given two segments, one of length *a* and one of length *b*, and a segment of length 1, construct a segment of length *ab*.

(1) Consider the segments of figure 11.18.

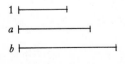

Figure 11.18

(2) Draw an angle *MNP* of any convenient size, as in figure 11.19. From *N*, lay off along *NP* a segment of length 1, while placing a segment of length *a* along *NM*. Starting from *N* again, lay off a segment of length *b* along side *NP* of the angle, as in figure 11.19.

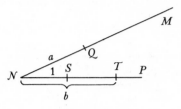

Figure 11.19

(2) Connect *S* and *Q*. Copy angle *NSQ* at *T*; the side you construct will cut *NM* in some point *W*. The length of segment *NW* is *ab*, as desired.

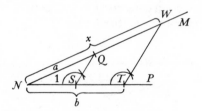

Figure 11.20

Again we ask why the construction works. In figure 11.20 note that triangles *NSQ* and *NTW* are similar (have the same shape). Since similar triangles have their corresponding sides in proportion we can write:

$$\frac{NQ}{NW} = \frac{NS}{NT}.$$

Segment *NQ* has length *a*, *NW* has length *x*, *NS* has length 1, while *NT* has length *b*. Hence

$$\frac{a}{x} = \frac{1}{b}.$$

Upon multiplying both sides by *xb* we have

$$x = ab,$$

which is what we wanted to show.

Construction 8.   Given a segment of length 1, construct segments of length $\sqrt{2}, \sqrt{3}, \sqrt{4}, \sqrt{5}, \sqrt{6}, \ldots$.

(1) First draw any line *r* and select any point *A* on *r*. Using construction 3, construct a perpendicular to *r* at *A*. Call the perpendicular *s*.

(2) Starting at *A*, construct segments of length 1 on both *r* and *s*, as in figure 11.21. Connect the endpoints of these segments; the result is a segment of length $\sqrt{2}$.

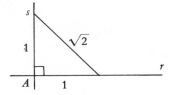

Figure 11.21

Since the triangle of figure 11.21 is a right triangle, the Pythagorean theorem is applicable (see the next section). The legs of the triangle are each 1, and the length of the hypotenuse is thus given by the square root of $1^2 + 1^2$, or $\sqrt{2}$. Now we can construct a segment of length $\sqrt{3}$. As before, select any line *r* and any point *A* on *r* and construct a line *s* perpendicular to *r* at *A*. Place a segment of length 1 on *s* and a segment of length $\sqrt{2}$ on *r* and connect the ends of these segments, as shown in figure 11.22. This new segment is the hypotenuse of a right triangle; its length is given by the square root of $1^2 + (\sqrt{2})^2$, or $\sqrt{3}$.

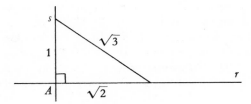

Figure 11.22

This same process may be continued indefinitely, obtaining segments of length $\sqrt{4}, \sqrt{5}, \sqrt{6}, \sqrt{7}, \sqrt{8}, \ldots$. A handy way of performing these constructions is shown in figure 11.23 (see p. 320). As a check on your construction techniques, the segment marked $\sqrt{4}$ should be 2 units long, and the segment marked $\sqrt{9}$ should be 3 units long.

So far our constructions have met the restrictions mentioned at the beginning of the section: we have used only a compass and a straightedge with no marks made on the straightedge. To say we have performed a *Euclidean Construction* is to say we have followed these restrictions; the constructions below, while valid, are not Euclidean.

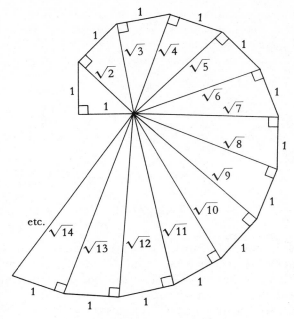

Figure 11.23

Construction 9. Trisect an angle.

(1) Draw a line segment of some handy length on a piece of tracing paper. Divide the segment into three equal parts, as explained in construction 6. Label the segment as in figure 11.24. Construct a perpendicular to the segment at *B*, using construction 3. Place the compass point at *C*, and adjust the radius so that the pencil falls on *D*. Then draw a semicircle, as shown in figure 11.24. The device of figure 11.24, for more or less obvious reasons, is called a tomahawk, and with it we can trisect any angle.

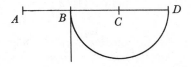

Figure 11.24

(2) Slide the tracing paper containing the tomahawk over the angle until *A* is on one side of the angle, the vertex of the angle is on the perpendicular line drawn from *B*, and the circle just touches the other side of the angle. It may be necessary to extend some of the lines of the figure. Connect

the vertex of the angle to *B* and to *C*, and it is trisected. You can prove in the problems that the tomahawk really trisects the angle.

Construction 9*.   Trisect an angle. The preceding construction can be used to trisect an angle, but requires a piece of tracing paper. No doubt the time will arise when you must trisect an angle but will have no tracing paper; this alternate construction will extricate you from that dilemma.

(1) Label as *B* the vertex of the angle to be trisected. Place point *A* on one side of the angle. From *A*, construct a perpendicular to the opposite side, using construction 2. Let this perpendicular intersect the opposite side at point *C*, as in figure 11.25. Erect a perpendicular to *BC* at *B*, and a perpendicular to *AC* at *A*, forming a rectangle, as shown in figure 11.25.

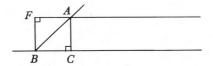

Figure 11.25

(2) Mark a distance equal to twice *AB* on the straightedge, and place the straightedge on *B* and line *FA* extended. Slide the ruler around until the distance between line *AC* and line *FA* extended is equal to twice *AB* (figure 11.26). Let *E* be the point where this line formed by the ruler meets *FA*. Angle *EBC* is one-third of angle *ABC*.

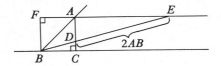

Figure 11.26

Again, the proof of the validity of this construction is included in the following exercises.

PROBLEMS

   1. Prove the validity of construction 1.

   2. Prove the validity of construction 2.

   3. Prove the validity of construction 3.

   4. Prove the validity of construction 4.

In the following problems, the word "draw" permits the use of any desired tools, while "construct" requires the use of the constructions of the text.

5. Draw three points not in a straight line and construct a circle through them. Make a guess as to how many different circles you could find that would go through the three points.

6. What happens if you try four points in construction 5?

7. Is anything wrong with this method of trisecting an angle?
   (a) Select any convenient radius and draw arcs which cut both sides of the angle, as in figure 11.27A.
   (b) Draw a segment connecting the two arcs, and trisect the segment by construction 6, as in figure 11.27B.
   (c) Connect the points of trisection to the vertex, thus trisecting the angle.

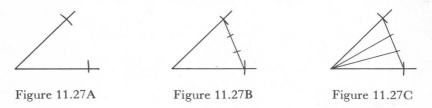

Figure 11.27A   Figure 11.27B   Figure 11.27C

(Hint: Try the method on an angle of 175°.)

8. Draw a segment 6 inches long; divide it into five equal parts by construction 6.

9. Draw a segment of length 9 inches; use two different methods to divide it into four equal parts.

10. Draw a segment of length 5 inches. Divide this segment into seven parts, three of which are one inch each, and four of which are one-half inch each.

11. Draw three segments, one having length 1, one with length $1\frac{1}{2}$, and one with length 2. Using these segments, construct a segment having length 3.

12. Using a segment of length 1, construct a segment of length $\sqrt{5}$.

13. Draw a triangle $A_1A_2A_3$ which has the shape of the triangle in figure 11.28; make the figure large. Perform these constructions in the order listed:

   (a) Construct the perpendicular bisector of side A_2A_3, and name the midpoint M_1. Do the same thing for side A_1A_3; call its midpoint M_2. Let M_3 be the midpoint obtained when the perpendicular bisector of A_1A_2 is constructed. These three perpendicular bisectors will meet in a point, which is called O in figure 11.28.

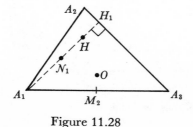

Figure 11.28

(b) Construct a line from A_1 perpendicular to the opposite side. Let H_1 stand for the point of intersection of the side and the perpendicular. In the same way, find H_2 and H_3. If the construction was accurate the segments A_1H_1, A_2H_2, and A_3H_3 will meet in a point. Call this point H.

(c) Bisect the segment A_1H, and call the midpoint N_1 (note: bisect A_1H, not A_1H_1). Bisect A_2H to get N_2, and bisect A_3H to get N_3.

(d) Bisect the segment HO, calling the midpoint N.

(e) Place the point of your compass at N, and adjust the pencil so it falls on M_1, then draw the circle with center at N and radius equal to the length of segment NM_1. This circle will go through the nine points H_1, H_2, H_3, M_1, M_2, M_3, N_1, N_2, N_3. It should not seem strange, therefore, that this circle is called the *nine-point circle*.

14. Give a reason for each step in this proof that the tomahawk really does trisect an angle. Refer to figure 11.29.
   (a) $\angle ABE = \angle EBC = 90°$
   (b) $AB = BC$
   (c) $BE = BE$
   (d) $\triangle ABE \cong \triangle CBE$ (note: $\cong$ denotes congruent—same shape and size.)
   (e) $\angle CFE$ is a right angle (note: CF is a radius of the circle and EF is tangent to the circle at F).
   (f) $BC = CF$
   (g) $CE = CE$
   (h) $\triangle CBE \cong \triangle CFE$
   (i) $\triangle ABE \cong \triangle CBE \cong \triangle CFE$
   (j) $\angle AEB = \angle BEC = \angle CEF$
   (k) $\angle AEF$ has been trisected

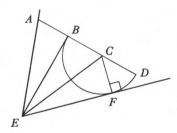

Figure 11.29

15. Draw a diagram illustrating this method of trisecting an angle, which goes back to Archimedes. Does this construction satisfy the restrictions mentioned in the section?
   (a) Select any convenient radius and draw a circle with center at the vertex of the angle you want to trisect. Label the figure so that the center of the circle is O, and let A and B be the points where the circle cuts the angle.
   (b) Extend AO through O, cutting the other side of the circle, and extending past the circle. Call this line r.
   (c) Place your ruler so that it rests on B and the part of line r outside the circle. Adjust the ruler until the distance from line r to the circle equals the radius of the circle. This new angle formed by your ruler and line r is one-third the original angle.

16. Draw a figure illustrating Morley's Theorem: Let ABC be any triangle. Trisect angles A, B, and C. Let a_1 be the trisector of angle A that is adjacent to AC, with a_2 the other trisector of angle A. Let b_1 be the trisector of angle B that is adjacent to AB, with b_2 the other trisector of angle B. Let c_1 be the trisector of angle C that is adjacent to AC, with c_2 the other trisector of angle C. Let a_1 and c_1 intersect at point X, c_2 and b_2 at Y, and a_2 and b_1 at Z. Triangle XYZ is an equilateral triangle.

17. Given a segment of length 1 and a segment of length a, show how to construct a segment of length a^2.

18. Given three segments of lengths a, b, and 1, find a segment of length $\frac{a}{b}$. Hint: find a segment x such that

$$\frac{a}{b} = \frac{x}{1}.$$

19. Construction 9* will only trisect an acute angle. How could this construction be used to trisect an obtuse angle?

20. Give a reason for each step in this proof that construction 9* really does trisect an angle. Refer to figure 11.26.
    (a) Bisect DE to find point G; connect A and G
    (b) Triangle AED is a right triangle
    (c) $AG = DG$ (Hint: The line segment joining the midpoint of the hypotenuse of a right triangle and the vertex of the right angle is equal to half the hypotenuse.)
    (d) $AB = AG = DG = GE$
    (e) $\angle AGB = \angle GAE + \angle GEA$ (Hint: $\angle AGB$ is an exterior angle of triangle AGE.)
    (f) Triangle AGE is isosceles
    (g) $\angle GAE = \angle GEA$
    (h) $\angle AGB = 2 \angle GEA$
    (i) Triangle ABG is isosceles
    (j) $\angle ABG = \angle AGB$
    (k) $\angle ABG = 2 \angle GEA$
    (l) $\angle GEA = \angle EBC$
    (m) $\angle ABG = 2 \angle EBC$
    (n) Angle ABC is trisected by BE.

SECTION 3. DISSECTION THEORY

Another branch of geometry having its origin with the Greeks is *dissection theory,* which involves the cutting of one figure into pieces which can be rearranged to form another figure. Dissection theory has led to some of the most famous puzzles and problems of mathematics; a few of these are reproduced in this section while many others are listed in the references at the end of the chapter. We shall first use dissection theory to prove the Pythagorean theorem.

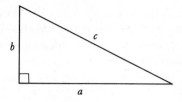

Figure 11.30

The Pythagorean theorem is perhaps the most famous result in all geometry, if not all mathematics. The theorem was known to the Babylonians but was probably first proved by Pythagoras. His theorem asserts that in a right triangle the square of the longest side (hypotenuse) is equal to the sum of the squares of the two shorter sides. In figure 11.30 the hypotenuse is c, and the two shorter sides are a and b. Hence

$$a^2 + b^2 = c^2.$$

Example 11.2. What is the hypotenuse of a right triangle which has short sides of 5 and 12?

Assume $a = 5$ and $b = 12$, so that

$$\begin{aligned} c^2 &= 5^2 + 12^2 \\ &= 25 + 144 \\ &= 169, \\ c &= 13. \end{aligned}$$

To prove the Pythagorean theorem, assume a and b are the two shorter sides of a right triangle, with c the hypotenuse (as in figure 11.30). We want to prove

$$c^2 = a^2 + b^2.$$

(1) We begin with figure 11.31; the squares have sides a and b. The area of the large square is a^2, while the area of the small square is b^2, for a total area $a^2 + b^2$. We want to cut this figure into pieces, and rearrange the pieces, constructing a new square of area c^2.

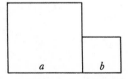

Figure 11.31

(2) Start at the corner marked K in figure 11.32, and lay off length b along KT (KR has length b). Draw segment RM. Note that triangle KRM is congruent (same size and shape) to the original triangle of figure 11.30. (Why?) Since corresponding parts of congruent triangles are equal, the hypotenuse of triangle KRM must be c. The entire length KT is $a + b$, while KR is of length b, leaving length a for RT. Connect R to S; as before, RS has length c. In the problem set below, you are asked to prove that angle MRS is a right angle.

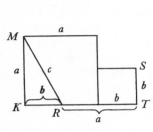

Figure 11.32

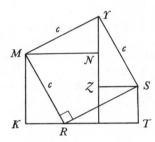

Figure 11.33

(3) Extend ZN upward a length b to point Y, and connect M and Y and S and Y. (See figure 11.33.) As before, the length of segment MY is c, as is the length of segment YS. Angles YMR, MYS, and YSR are each $90°$. Thus $MYSR$ is a square of side c and area c^2.

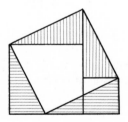

Figure 11.34

(4) The basic idea of the proof is shown in figure 11.34. The two triangles shaded horizontally can be cut out of the original figure, which had area $a^2 + b^2$, and placed where we have the vertically shaded triangles to give a square of area c^2. In conclusion, our original figure of area $a^2 + b^2$ was cut into pieces, and the pieces were rearranged to form a square of area c^2. Hence

$$a^2 + b^2 = c^2,$$

just as we wanted.

Dissection problems require the cutting of one figure into pieces, and the rearrangement of the pieces to produce another figure. In order to do this, it is necessary that the figures have the same area; you could hardly hope to cut a postage stamp into pieces which could be rearranged to form a football field. On the other hand, is this a sufficient condition? That is, if two figures have the same area is it possible to cut one figure into pieces and rearrange the pieces to get the other? The answer is, it depends. For a very important case the answer is yes, as described below. First, however, recall that *polygons* are plane figures made up of straight line segments; examples of polygons are shown in figure 11.35. For our purposes it is unnecessary to give a more precise definition of polygon.

Figure 11.35

We now can state a very important theorem of dissection theory: If two polygons have the same area, it is possible to cut one of them into pieces with a finite number of straight cuts and rearrange the pieces, forming the other polygon. We prove this theorem through the following sequence of steps.

(1) Any triangle can be cut into pieces, and the pieces rearranged to form a rectangle.

(a) Let the triangle be ABC; let R be the midpoint of AC while S is the midpoint of BC. Draw a line through R and S. From A and B draw perpendiculars AT and BU, to line RS. Draw a perpendicular CK from C to line RS. (See figure 11.36.)

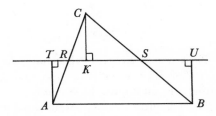

Figure 11.36

(b) It can be proven that triangles CKR and ATR are congruent, as are triangles CKS and SUB. Hence triangle CKR can be placed exactly over triangle ATR, just as triangle CKS can be placed exactly over triangle SUB.

(c) Cut triangle *ABC* along *RS* and then *CK*. Three pieces will be obtained; these pieces can be rearranged to form a rectangle, as shown in figure 11.37.

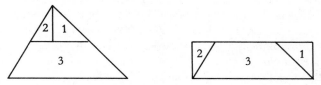

Figure 11.37

(2) If two parallelograms have the same base and altitude, one may be cut into pieces and the pieces rearranged to form the other.

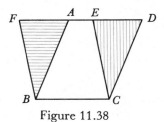

Figure 11.38

(a) Figure 11.38 shows two parallelograms, *BFEC* and *ABCD*. Since triangles *EDC* and *FAB* are congruent (why?), triangle *FAB* may be cut from parallelogram *BFEC* and moved to cover triangle *EDC*.

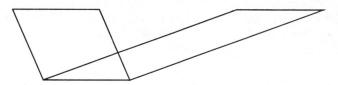

Figure 11.39

(b) Alas, life is not so simple. What happens with the parallelograms of figure 11.39? Try this method. Place one parallelogram next to itself several times, as in figure 11.40, and then include the other parallelogram. The diagram shows where to make the necessary cuts.

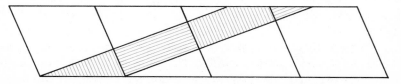

Figure 11.40

(3) If two rectangles have the same area, one of them may be cut into pieces and the pieces rearranged to fit the other.

(a) Assume the two rectangles are labelled as in figure 11.41.

Figure 11.41

(b) Extend sides *XZ* and *PM* of rectangle *PMZX*. Start at point M and measure off, to side *XZ* extended, a segment of length *d*. (See figure 11.42.) Construct a line from *P* parallel to *MR*.

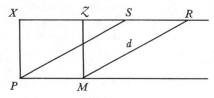

Figure 11.42

(c) Parallelogram *PMRS* has the same area as rectangle *PMZX* since they have the same altitude and base (the base is *PM* and the altitude in both cases has a length equal to the length of *ZM*). Hence the parallelogram has the same area as each of the two rectangles we started with.

(d) Extend *PS* past *S*, and construct *RK* perpendicular to line *PS* extended. Construct *ML* perpendicular to *PS*. (See figure 11.43.)

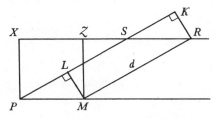

Figure 11.43

Note that parallelogram *PMRS* has the same area as rectangle *LMRK* since they both have the same base (*MR*) and altitude (*LM*). Hence rectangle *LMRK* is congruent to the original rectangle having sides *c* and *d* (they both have *d* as base, and have equal areas).

(e) Take the piece shaded vertically in figure 11.44 and place it over the piece shaded horizontally, converting the thin rectangle into the parallelogram. Part (2) explained how the parallelogram could be cut into pieces which can be rearranged to form rectangle *PMZX*.

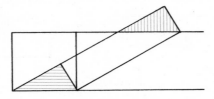

Figure 11.44

(4) A rectangle can be cut into pieces and the pieces rearranged to form a square. Since a square is also a rectangle, make a square having the same area as the rectangle and then follow the instructions of (3).

(5) Two squares can be cut into pieces which can be rearranged to form one new square. This is exactly what was done at the beginning of this section to prove the Pythagorean theorem by dissection.

Many details have been necessary in order to prove our theorem, but now we are ready to summarize all the steps. We begin with two polygons of the same area and divide them into triangles any way we like. (See figure 11.45.) Do not forget the goal: to cut one of the polygons into pieces which may be rearranged to form the other. After drawing the triangles proceed as follows.

I:

II:

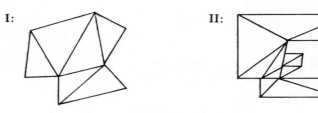

Figure 11.45

(1) Cut each of the triangles of Polygon I into pieces which may be rearranged to form rectangles. At this point we have converted each triangle of the polygon into a rectangle.

(2) Cut the rectangles into pieces which may be rearranged to form squares. Now we have each rectangle converted to a square.

(3) Take any two squares, cut them into pieces, and rearrange the pieces to form one larger square. Cut this new square and one of the others into pieces, rearrange the pieces, and obtain a new larger square. The final result will be one large square formed from all the smaller squares.

Essentially, we have cut Polygon I into little pieces which have been rearranged to form a square having the same area as Polygon I.

(4) Do exactly the same thing with Polygon II; go through all the steps listed above until you have formed one square of the same area as Polygon II. Then place one square over the other and make cuts in one corresponding to the cuts in the other.

In one sentence: cut Polygon I into little pieces which may be rearranged to form a square and then make the pieces of this square fit Polygon II. This process actually works, as we have proven above. If you verify it with two polygons be certain to work where there is no breeze.

Example 11.3.   Figure 11.46 shows a square and an equilateral triangle of the same area. Cut the triangle into pieces which may be rearranged to form the square.

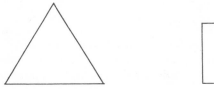

Figure 11.46

(1) Find the midpoints of two sides of the triangle and connect them. Then draw a perpendicular to this midpoint line, as shown in figure 11.47. Cut along the lines drawn in, forming three pieces which can be rearranged to form a rectangle, as shown in figure 11.48.

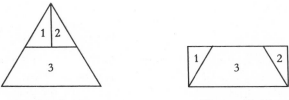

Figure 11.47   **Figure 11.48**

(2) Next convert the rectangle into a square, using the method described above. (See figure 11.49.) Piece 3, which has been shaded in figure 11.49, has been cut into four smaller pieces. Now we are ready to rearrange these six pieces obtained by cutting the triangle; a square is the result. (See figure 11.50 on p. 332.)

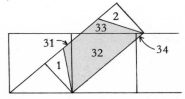

Figure 11.49

By following the method presented in this example, the triangle can be cut into six pieces which may be rearranged to fit the square. It can, however, be done with only four pieces, as explained in the next example.

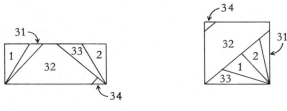

Figure 11.50

Example 11.4. Cut an equilateral triangle into four pieces which may be rearranged to form a square. (See figure 11.46.) This solution was devised by the Englishman Henry Dudeney (1857–1931), a famous creator and solver of puzzles.

Figure 11.51

(1) Label the triangle as in figure 11.51; let D be the midpoint of AC with E the midpoint of BC. From E draw a segment whose length equals a side of the square, to a point F on AB. From F, lay off (on AB) a segment equal to BE, to point G.

(2) From D and G draw perpendiculars to FE, as in figure 11.52A. The pieces of the triangle may be rearranged, as in figure 11.52B, to form the square. If hinges are placed at points D, E, and G, the pieces could swing from the square to the triangle. This would make a great coffee table.

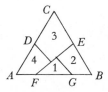

Figure 11.52A

Figure 11.52B

PROBLEMS

For problems 1 and 2 below, assume that the area of a rectangle is equal to its base times its height.

1. Prove, by dissection, that the area of a triangle is equal to one half the base times the height. (Hint: A line cutting the midpoint of two sides of a triangle also cuts the corresponding altitude in half.)

2. Prove, by dissection, that the area of a parallelogram is the base times the height.

3. Draw any triangle whose base is 4 and altitude 2, with an area of $\frac{1}{2}(4)(2) = 4$. Draw a rectangle whose base is 4 and height 1, for an area of $4(1) = 4$. Cut the rectangle into pieces which may be rearranged to fit the triangle.

4. Draw a square of side 1, which also has area 1, and then draw a rectangle which has a base of $\frac{3}{2}$ and a height of $\frac{2}{3}$, which also has an area 1. Cut the square into pieces which may be rearranged to fit the rectangle.

5. Cut the star of figure 11.53 into pieces which can be rearranged to form a rectangle. (Assume that the triangles forming the points of the star are all congruent.)

Figure 11.53

6. Consider the octagon of figure 11.54. Cut the figure as indicated and rearrange the pieces to form a square.

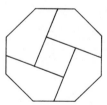

Figure 11.54

7. Consider the octagons of figure 11.55. Show that in each case the octagon can be cut into pieces, and the pieces rearranged to form rectangles.

Figure 11.55A

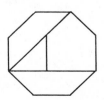

Figure 11.55B

8. Figure 11.56A shows a square 8 units on a side, and hence of total area 8^2, or 64. The square can be cut as indicated, and the pieces rearranged, forming the rectangle of figure 11.56B, which has length 13, height 5, and area $5(13) = 65$. Where did the extra unit of area come from?

Figure 11.56A

Figure 11.56B

9. Explain how the diagram of figure 11.57 might be used to prove the Pythagorean theorem.

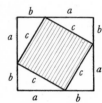

Figure 11.57

10. An original proof of the Pythagorean theorem was discovered by President Garfield. Explain his proof using figure 11.58. (Hint: The area of the trapezoid equals the sum of the areas of the three triangles. The area of a trapezoid is half the product of the altitude and the sum of the bases.)

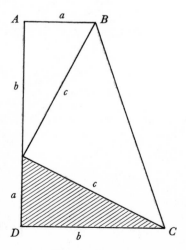

Figure 11.58

11. Three Navajo women are sitting around the campfire. One woman is sitting on a hippopotamus hide; she weighs 300 pounds. The second lady is sitting on a horse hide; she has a son who weighs 160 pounds. The last lady, who is sitting on a sheepskin, has a son who weighs 140 pounds. What famous theorem of geometry does this illustrate?

12. Prove that ∠MRS (figure 11.33) is a right angle.

SECTION 4. PROJECTIVE GEOMETRY

Two lines are parallel if they lie in the same plane and do not meet, no matter how far extended. There are many examples of parallel lines in everyday life: railroad tracks, for example, never meet no matter how far extended, and yet if we look at railroad tracks they appear to meet off in the distance. This can cause problems for an artist, who looks around at a world composed of circles, squares, parallel lines, cylinders, spheres, cones, and the like, and who must take this world and transcribe it onto a flat piece of canvas. But, for example, how can he draw a scene with railroad tracks leading off to the horizon? He could not place the tracks an equal distance apart on the canvas since then they would not look right to the eye. His past experience tells him that he must make the tracks appear to converge at a point. Only in this way can he make his picture real. In the same way, a circle viewed from an angle does not look like a circle anymore, but rather like an ellipse. The artists of the fifteenth century, led by Leonardo da Vinci and Albrecht Durer, began a study of the problem of reducing a three-dimensional scene to a two-dimensional canvas. Certainly the concept of distance could play no major role in their studies since a tree one foot high but a hundred feet away, for example, would not look the same on canvas as a tree one foot high but four feet away. Also, parallel lines could play no role; to the artist there are no parallel lines going off to infinity.

This study was carried into other fields by draftsmen, mapmakers, and mathematicians. Today the subject is considered as two topics: *descriptive geometry* deals with the practical details of putting a picture of a solid object on a flat piece of paper, while *projective geometry* deals with the more mathematical aspects of this world in which distance is meaningless and any two lines will meet, sooner or later. In projective geometry, two parallel lines are said to meet at an *ideal point,* or *point at infinity;* two ideal points determine an *ideal line.*

Since projective geometry has no concept of distance there can be no distance formula and no triangle congruence. The Pythagorean theorem involves distance and hence must be discarded in the study of projective geometry. What then is left to study? The theorems below provide a brief introduction to the topics studied in projective geometry; at no time is the concept of distance used.

The Theorem of Desargues in a Plane.   In a plane, if two triangles are placed so that lines joining corresponding vertices meet in a point, then the corresponding sides, when extended, will meet in three collinear points.

In figure 11.59 we have lines through A and A', B and B', and C and C'.

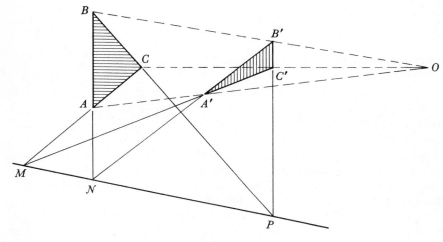

Figure 11.59

All three of these lines meet at point O. Sides AC and $A'C'$, when extended, meet at point M; sides BC and $B'C'$, when extended, meet at P; sides AB and $A'B'$, when extended, meet at N. Note that M, N, and P, as the theorem asserts, are collinear. A proof of this theorem can be found on page 187 of *What is Mathematics?* by Courant and Robbins.

The Theorem of Desargues was one of the earliest results to come from the study of projective geometry; it is named for the French engineer and architect Gerard Desargues (1593–1662).

The Theorem of Desargues in Space.   If two triangles ABC and $A'B'C'$ are on two non-parallel planes, and if the lines AA', BB', and CC' meet in a point, then the extensions of the corresponding sides will meet in three points, all of which lie on the same line. (Note: The theorem is also valid if the triangles lie on parallel planes; in that case corresponding sides are parallel and intersect in ideal points, with these ideal points collinear on an ideal line.) (See figure 11.60.)

Unlike the Theorem of Desargues in the plane, the result in space is relatively easy to prove if we recognize the fact that if two planes intersect, they intersect to form a straight line. You can supply the details of this proof in one of the problems.

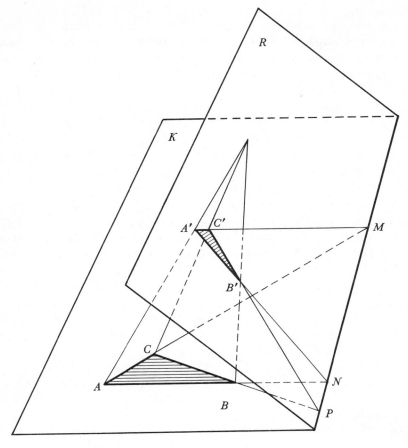

Figure 11.60

Let's inspect a new definition of an old word: a *hexagon* is any six lines in a plane, no three of which meet in the same point. Figure 11.61 shows three hexagons. Numbers are used to label the vertices of the hexagon; assume 1-2

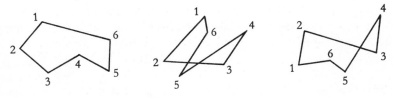

Figure 11.61

represents the line passing through vertices 1 and 2. By looking at the common garden-variety hexagon of figure 11.62, we see that it is reasonable to call 1-2 and 4-5 *opposite sides* of the hexagon, as are 2-3 and 5-6, and 3-4 and 6-1. A hexagon is *inscribed* in a figure when the vertices of the hexagon lie on the figure. We use these words in the next theorem.

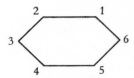

Figure 11.62

The Theorem of Pappus.   If a hexagon is inscribed in two intersecting straight lines and if the opposite sides of the hexagon are extended, the three points of intersection of the opposite sides are collinear. (Again, if two of the sides of the hexagon are parallel, the same result holds by considering ideal points and ideal lines.)

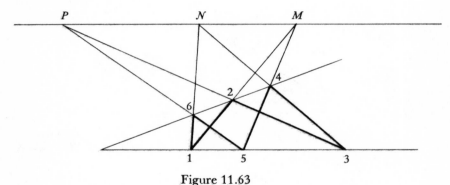

Figure 11.63

In figure 11.63, opposite sides 1-2 and 4-5 have been extended to meet at *M*, 2-3 and 5-6 to meet at *P*, and 3-4 and 6-1 to meet at *N*; *M*, *N*, and *P* are collinear. A proof of this theorem is given on page 188 of the book by Courant and Robbins. Pappus, mentioned at the beginning of this chapter, was one of the last great Greek mathematicians.

A cone exists in projective geometry since a cone can be obtained without the use of parallel lines or distance; the cone can still be cut with a plane to obtain conic sections: parabola, ellipse, hyperbola, (these curves were discussed in Chapter 6). A result similar to the Theorem of Pappus is valid for conic sections.

The Theorem of Pascal.   If a hexagon is inscribed in a conic section and if the opposite sides are extended, the three points of intersection of the opposite sides are collinear.

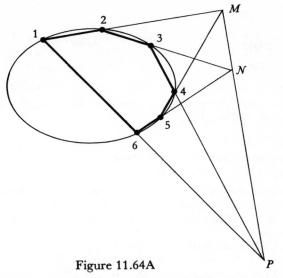

Figure 11.64A

In each diagram of figure 11.64, sides 1-2 and 4-5 have been extended to meet in M, 2-3 and 5-6 to meet in N, while 3-4 and 6-1 meet in P. In each case, points M, N, and P are collinear.

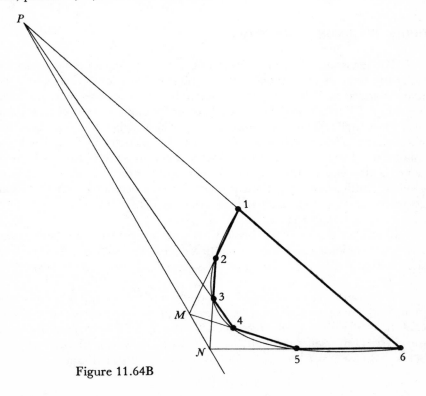

Figure 11.64B

PROBLEMS

1. Refer to figure 6.25, which shows a parabola. Trace that graph, place 6 points on it, label them 1, 2, 3, 4, 5, 6, and verify the Theorem of Pascal. It may take some adjustment of the position of the points to find a figure that fits on paper.

2. Draw a circle and place six points on it. Verify the Theorem of Pascal.

3. Draw a right angle; label it AOB. Place three points, 1, 3, and 5 on OA, and three points 2, 4, 6 on OB. Verify the Theorem of Pappus.

4. Repeat problem 3 for an angle of $120°$.

5. State the converse of the Theorem of Desargues in the plane; in space. Does the converse seem valid? (Converse is discussed in Chapter 5.)

6. Supply a reason for each step in this proof of the Theorem of Desargues in space:
   (a) Let K be the plane that contains triangle ABC, while R is the plane that contains triangle $A'B'C'$. These planes are non-parallel and hence intersect to form a straight line.
   (b) Points A, B, A', and B' all lie in a plane.
   (c) Lines AB and $A'B'$ lie in the same plane.
   (d) Hence the point of intersection of lines AB and $A'B'$ (called N) must be in both plane K and plane R.
   (e) N is on the line formed by the intersection of K and R.
   (f) P and M are in the intersection of K and R. Hence M, N, and P are collinear.

SECTION 5. INVERSION IN THE PLANE

The ideas taught in most beginning geometry courses today are essentially the same as those taught 2000 years ago. Notations change, and sets may be added to make the course modern, but the basic theorems and ideas are those of Euclid's day. This is perhaps unfortunate since it gives the student the idea that geometry is dead, a body of knowledge that is constant and unchanging. This idea is false. The synthetic geometry of Euclid is but a small part of the subject called geometry. Look in some of the books mentioned at the end of this chapter and you will see such words as projective geometry, affine geometry, finite geometry, metric geometry, non-Euclidean geometry, and topology. Each of these is a large field of study in its own right, ever growing and changing.

In the last section of this book, we discuss a topic from synthetic geometry not commonly encountered in a first course; we will consider the inversion transformation, an idea that was developed some 2000 years after Euclid.

The *inversion transformation* gives a method of transforming points of the plane into other points, as described here: Begin with a circle of radius 1 unit. Call the center of the circle O. Select any other point P inside, outside, or on the circle. Draw a line through O and P. Using a ruler, or the construction below, find a point P' (on the line through O and P) such that

$$(OP)(OP') = 1.$$

This point P' should be on the same side of O as P. Points P and P' are called *inverses* of each other. The inverse of point O is an ideal point (figure 11.65).

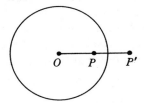

Figure 11.65

Example 11.5. Point P is $\frac{1}{2}$ inch from the center of a circle of radius 1 inch. Where is the inverse point P'?

We want to find a point P' such that $(OP)(OP') = 1$; $OP = \frac{1}{2}$ so that $OP' = 2$. Hence P' must be 2 inches from O, as shown in figure 11.66. Inverse points may also be obtained by construction.

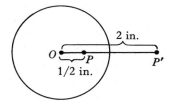

Figure 11.66

Construction 10. Construct the inverse of a given point P.

Consider this construction as two cases.

(1) Point P is inside the circle.
Draw OP extended, then construct a perpendicular to OP at point P. Let M be one of the points where the perpendicular cuts the circle. Draw radius OM. Construct a perpendicular to OM at M. Extend this perpendicular until it cuts line OP extended. Let P' be the point where this perpendicular cuts OP; then P' is the inverse of P. (See figure 11.67.) The problem set gives you an opportunity to prove this result.

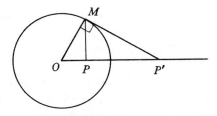

Figure 11.67

(2) Point P is outside the circle.

Connect O and P. Place the compass point at P and adjust the radius of the compass until the pencil falls on O; draw an arc with this setting. Let this arc cut the circle in points M and N. Place the compass point at M and adjust the pencil until it falls on O. Draw an arc with this setting; this arc should cut OP to determine the inverse point P'. (See figure 11.68.) The proof of this construction is also included in the problems.

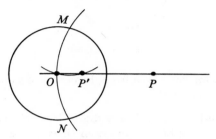

Figure 11.68

Consider figure 11.69; it shows a circle and a line. If the inverse of each point on the line is obtained, what sort of figure will be formed by these inverse points? In figure 11.69 several points on the line were selected, and the inverse of each obtained by construction. It appears that all the inverse points obtained lie on a circle that goes through O. This result is an example of one of the basic theorems concerning the inversion transformation: If a line is outside the circle used for the inversion transformation, and if the inverse of each point on the line is found, all these inverse points will lie on a circle which goes through the center of the circle used for the transformation. The problem set gives you an opportunity to obtain similar results.

PROBLEMS

All problems refer to a circle of radius 1 and center O.

1. What is the inverse point of a point on the circle?

Complete the following statements:

2. If a line is drawn through O, and the inverse of each point on the line found, then . . . .

3. If a line is drawn cutting the circle in two points, but not going through O, and if the inverse of each point on the line is found, then . . . .

4. If a circle is drawn that goes through O, and if the inverse of each point on the circle (except O) is found, then . . . .

5. If a circle is drawn that does not go through O, and if the inverse of each point on the circle is found, then . . . .

6. If two parallel lines are drawn, each cutting the circle in two points, and neither going through O, and if the inverse of each point on the lines is found, then . . . .

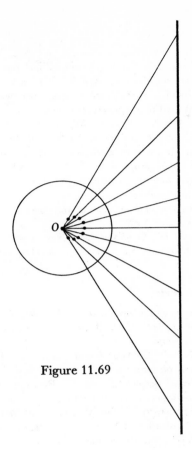

Figure 11.69

7. Give a reason for each step in this proof that construction 10(1) really works. Refer to figure 11.67.

(a) $\angle MPO = 90°$

(b) $\angle OMP' = 90°$

(c) $\angle MPO = \angle OMP'$

(d) $\angle O = \angle O$

(e) $\triangle OMP'$ is similar to $\triangle OPM$

(f) the length of OM is 1 unit

(g) $\dfrac{OP}{1} = \dfrac{1}{OP'}$

(h) $(OP)(OP') = 1$

(i) P' is the inverse of P.

8. Give a reason for each step in this proof that construction 10(2) really works. Refer to figure 11.68.

(a) $PM = PO$

(b) $\triangle PMO$ is isosceles

(c) $\angle MOP = \angle PMO$

(d) $MO = MP'$

(e) $\triangle MOP'$ is isosceles

(f) $\angle MOP = \angle MP'O$

(g) $\triangle MOP'$ is similar to $\triangle PMO$

(h) $\dfrac{OP}{OM} = \dfrac{OM}{OP'}$

(i) $OM = 1$

(j) $\dfrac{OP}{1} = \dfrac{1}{OP'}$

(k) $(OP)(OP') = 1$

(l) P' is the inverse of P

9. How can a mathematician catch a lion?

FOR FURTHER READING

Courant, R., and Robbins, H. *What Is Mathematics?*. New York: Oxford University Press, 1941. This is one of the leading "semipopular" mathematics books.

Coxeter, H. M. S. *Introduction to Geometry*. New York: John Wiley and Sons, Inc., 1961. The author of this book is perhaps the foremost geometer alive today. His book gives a general treatment of advanced geometry.

Crowdis, David G., and Wheeler, Brandon W. *Introduction to Mathematical Ideas*. New York: McGraw-Hill Book Company, 1969. See this text for a brief discussion of *axiomatics*, which has been a more traditional approach to geometry.

Eves, Howard. *A Survey of Geometry,* volume 1. Boston: Allyn and Bacon, Inc., 1965. Eves' book contains a wealth of historical material, plus information concerning the ideas discussed in this chapter.

Gardner, Martin. *The Scientific American Book of Mathematical Puzzles and Diversions.* New York: Simon and Schuster, 1959.

——— . (ed.) *Mathematical Puzzles of Sam Loyd.* New York: Dover Publications, Inc., 1959. These two books on mathematical puzzles include some material on dissections.

More specialized books include:

Golos, Ellery B. *Foundations of Euclidean and Non-Euclidean Geometry.* New York: Holt, Rinehart, and Winston, Inc., 1968. A good treatment of geometry, including a discussion of axiom systems.

Heath, Sir Thomas. *A Manual of Greek Mathematics.* New York: Dover Publications, Inc., 1963. The classic book on Greek mathematics.

Meserve, Bruce. *Fundamental Concepts of Geometry.* Reading, Massachusetts: Addison-Wesley, 1955. Covers projective geometry in detail.

Young, John W. *Projective Geometry.* (Carus Mathematical Monograph Number Four.) The Mathematical Association of America and Open Court Publishing Company, 1930. A classic work on projective geometry.

ANSWERS
TO SELECTED PROBLEMS

CHAPTER 1

Section 1

1. (a) thirty-one, cardinal   (c) seven, cardinal   (e) two, ordinal

3. (a) simple grouping, 36   (c) positional, 14   (e) simple grouping, 627
   (g) multiplicative grouping, 23   (i) simple grouping, 781   (k) multiplicative
   grouping, 80   (m) simple grouping, 100   (o) positional, 390   (q) simple
   grouping, 16,375   (s) multiplicative grouping, 2375   (u) positional, 2930
   (w) positional, 24,336

4. (a) M   (c) NNNN   (e) NNN
   (g) MMMMMMMMNNNII   (i) MMMMNNNMMMM

5. (a) ⊙M   (c) ⊙N   (e) ⊙NN⊙N   (g) ⊙MM⊙M⊙N⊙I
   (i) ⊙MM⊙N⊙M

6. (a) ⊙○○○   (c) ⊙○○   (e) ⊙○⊙○○   (g) ⊙○⊙⊙○⊙
   (i) ⊙⊙⊕○○○

7. (a) 327   8. (a) ⊙M⊙N   9. 117,649

11. (a) 114   (c) 2451   12. (a) ⊙⊕⊙   (c) ⊙○○⊙⊕⊙

Section 2

1. (a) 231   (c) 2,000,030   (e) 2,030,405   2. (a) 135   (c) 872

3. (a) |||, 三   (c) ∩∩∩∩|||| 七
      ∩∩∩∩ |||, 千
                 七

   (e) 999 ∩∩ ||| 五   (g) 𝟈𝟈999 ∩∩|||| 二   (i) 𝟈𝟈𝟈𝟈 ∩∩∩ 七
        99 ∩∩∩ ||, 百   ∩∩||||, 千   𝟈𝟈𝟈 ∩∩∩, 千
                   五   六   九
                   十   百   十
                   五   四
                                           十
                                           九

5. (a) Mayan, 4456   (c) Roman, 74   (e) Greek, 39   (g) Babylonian, 40,271
(i) Roman, 10,911   (k) Babylonian, 1933

6. (a) XVII, $\iota\zeta$, ⟨ɾɾɾɾɾɾɾ, ≝
(c) MMMMDCXCV, $\delta\chi\text{?}\epsilon$, ɾ⟨ɾɾɾɾɾɾɾɾ⟨ɾɾɾɾ, ⊜

Section 3

2. (a) [Egyptian numeral symbols]

3. (a) [Egyptian numeral symbols]

4. (a)

1	27
2	54
4	108
→ 8	216 ←
8	216

(c)

→ 1	43 ←
2	86
4	172
8	344
→ 16	688 ←
17	731

5. (a) DCCCXXXVI   (c) MCCLXIV

6. (a) DCLXXXII   (c) CDLVI

Section 4

1. (a) 101   (c) 1000   (e) 3111

2. (a) 101   (c) 4443   (e) 220143

3. (a) 123   (c) 4   (e) 123

4. (a) 4   (c) 102   (e) 12

5. 1, 2, 3, 4, 5, 6, 10, 11, 12, 13, 14, 15, 16, 20, 21, 22, 23, 24, 25, 26, 30, 31, 32, 33, 34, 35, 36, 40, 41, 42, 43, 44, 45, 46, 50, 51, 52, 53, 54, 55, 56, 60, 61, 62, 63, 64, 65, 66, 100, 101

Section 5

1. 254   **3.** 21023_4 **5.** 121333_4 **7.** 100110_2 **9.** $23e_{12}$

11. (a) 785   (c) 1342

12. (a) 93   (c) 406

13. (a) 111   (c) 10000   (e) 100000

15. (a) 1100   (c) 1010   (e) 1010100

17. (a) 100   (c) 11001   (e) 1

18. (a) 110   (c) 111

Section 6

1. Take all of group 1.

3. Insist that he take the first move.

CHAPTER 2

Section 1

1. false   **3.** false   **5.** true   **7.** false   **9.** false

11. true   **13.** true   **15.** true   **17.** true   **19.** true

21. false   **23.** false   **25.** false   **27.** true   **29.** false

31. The set contains no elements.   **33.** The set contains no elements.

35. $\{11, 13, 15, \ldots\}$ **37.** no   **39.** no   **41.** yes   **43.** 63

45. {Tom, Dick, Harry}, {Tom}, {Dick}, {Harry}, {Tom, Dick}, {Tom, Harry}, {Dick, Harry}, $\varnothing$; 8

47. E = F   **49.** finite   **51.** infinite   **53.** finite

55. 8   **57.** 16

Section 2

1. $\{3, 5\}$ **3.** $\{2, 4\}$ **5.** $\{2, 4\}$ **7.** $\{2, 3, 4, 5, 7, 9\}$

9. $\{2, 3, 4, 5\}$ **11.** $\{1, 6, 7, 8, 9, 10\}$ **13.** $\{1, 6, 8, 10\}$

15.

17.

19. $\varnothing$

21.

23.

25.

27. $\varnothing$

29.

31.

33.

35.

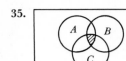

37.

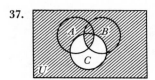

39.

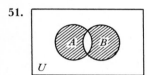

41.

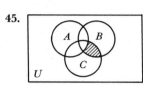

43.

45.

47. true

49. {2, 6, 8, 12}

51.

53.

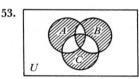

55.

57. When *A* and *B* are disjoint.

59. no

61. no

Section 3

1. (a) 12   (c) 6   (e) 48   **2.** (a) 0   (c) 3   (e) 6

3. Her data are inconsistent. For example, she claims only 103 like to bake cakes, but her other data indicate at least 104 like to.

4. (a) 8   (c) 27   **5.** (a) 54   (c) 10

Section 4

Note: problems 1–7 can each be done in several ways, even though we show only one method per problem.

1. $\{1, 3, 5, 7, 9, 11, \ldots, 2n - 1, \ldots\}$
$\updownarrow \updownarrow \updownarrow \updownarrow \updownarrow \updownarrow \qquad \updownarrow$
$\{1, 5, 9, 13, 17, 21, \ldots, 4n - 3, \ldots\}$

3. $\{1/2, 2/2, 3/2, 4/2, 5/2, \ldots, n/2, \ldots\}$
$\quad\updownarrow \quad \updownarrow \quad \updownarrow \quad \updownarrow \quad \updownarrow \qquad \updownarrow$
$\{\ 1, \quad 2, \quad 3, \quad 4, \quad 5, \ \ldots, \ n, \ \ldots\}$

5. $\{1/3, 2/3, 3/3, 4/3, 5/3, 6/3, \ldots, n/3, \ldots\}$
$\quad\updownarrow \quad \updownarrow \quad \updownarrow \quad \updownarrow \quad \updownarrow \quad \updownarrow \qquad \updownarrow$
$\{\ 1, \quad 2, \quad 3, \quad 4, \quad 5, \quad 6, \ \ldots, \ n, \ \ldots\}$

7. $\{-7/1, \ -7/2, \ -7/3, \ -7/4, \ -7/5, \ \ldots, \ -7/n, \ldots\}$
$\quad\ \ \updownarrow \qquad\ \updownarrow \qquad \updownarrow \qquad\ \updownarrow \qquad\ \updownarrow \qquad\qquad \updownarrow$
$\{-7/7, \ -7/14, \ -7/21, \ -7/28, \ -7/35, \ \ldots, \ -7/7n, \ldots\}$

9. Yes; then the statement becomes true.

11. $\{(1, 1), (1, 8), (7, 1), (7, 8), (9, 1), (9, 8), (12, 1), (12, 8)\}$

13. $\{(2, 1), (2, 3), (2, 5), (4, 1), (4, 3), (4, 5)\}$, no

15. $\{(1, 2), (1, 8), (2, 2), (2, 8), (3, 2), (3, 8), \ldots\}$

17. $\{(1, 1), (2, 1), (3, 1), (4, 1), \ldots\}$

19. $A \times B$ is infinite unless B is the empty set.

21. yes   **23.** no

Section 5

1. If he is telling the truth, then he is lying.

3. If the father guessed correctly, then the child will be returned, and he guessed incorrectly. If he guesses incorrectly then the child will not be returned and he guessed correctly.

5. Since only nonresident hippies can live in the new city, its official hippie can not live there. However, if he lives outside the new city he is a nonresident hippie and must live in the new city.

CHAPTER 3

Section 1

1. (a) $5\frac{1}{2}$ (c) -3 (e) $1\frac{1}{2}$ (g) 10 (i) -7 (k) 1 (m) 49 (o) 49 (q) 2
(s) $\frac{1}{2}$ (u) -3

2. (a) $6\frac{1}{2}$ (c) 30 (e) 3 (g) $\frac{49}{4}$ or $12\frac{1}{4}$ (i) 3249 (k) 0 (m) 2

3. (a) 1 (c) 4   **4.** (a) 0 (c) 25   **5.** (a) 3 (c) 2

6. (a) 2 (c) 0   **7.** $a \mathbf{G} b = a + ab$ **9.** $a \mathbf{M} b = 2a - b$

10. (a) true (c) true (e) true (g) true (i) true

Section 2

1. (a) no   (c) no   (e) no
2. (a) $(100 \div 20) \div 5 = 1$ (c) $(360 \div 18) \div 4 = 5$
3. no

Section 3

1. (a) no   (c) no   (e) yes   3. yes

Section 4

1. yes   3. yes   5. no   7. yes; yes   9. no   11. yes
13. $\{0, 1\}, \{0\}, \{1\}, \{0, 1, -1\}, \{1, -1\}$

Section 5

1. yes; 1   3. yes; 1   5. yes; 0   7. yes; 1   9. yes; 0   11. no
13. no; although, for example, $b \ \mathsf{T} \ a = b$, notice that $a \ \mathsf{T} \ b = c$.

Section 6

1. no   3. yes   5. no; no identity   7. yes

Section 7

1. yes   3. no   5. no

Section 8

1. yes   3. associative, commutative, identity element (U), closed
5. yes   7. commutative, closed
9. all except distributive   11. all except distributive
12. (a) commutative property of addition   (c) associative property of multiplication
   (e) commutative property of multiplication   (g) closure
   (i) inverse

Section 9

1. (a) $.\overline{052631578947368421}$ (c) $6.\overline{6}$ (e) $4.\overline{5}$ (g) $.250\overline{0}$ (i) $1.\overline{571428}$
2. (a) $\frac{35}{99}$ (c) $\frac{70}{99}$ (e) $\frac{11}{111}$ (g) $\frac{3}{20}$ (i) $\frac{137}{110}$ 3. no
4. (a) $.1_2$ (c) $.01_2$ (e) $.\overline{10}_2$

Section 10

1. (We list a reason for each step, in order.) Multiply both sides of the previous equation by b^2; any number which is a multiple of 2 is an even number; $a^2 =$ an even number; the square of an odd number is odd, so a can not be odd; since $(2c)^2 = 4c^2$; divide both sides by 2; any number which is a multiple of 2 is even; b^2 is even since $b^2 =$ an even number, and thus b is even; we know both a and b are even, and yet we said $\dfrac{a}{b}$ was in lowest terms; since (i) leads to a contradiction.

3. We begin as in problem 1: $\dfrac{a}{b} = \sqrt{4}$; so $\dfrac{a^2}{b^2} = 4$; and $a^2 = 4b^2$; thus a^2 is a multiple of 4, but it does not follow that a is also. ($6^2 = 36$ is a multiple of 4, but 6 is not.)

5. i 7. $-i$ 9. $4i$ or $-4i$ 11. $10i$ or $-10i$

13.   Complex
      $\diagup$ $\diagdown$
   Imaginary   Real

Section 11

(We present only one possible answer for each problem.)

1. $\{0, 5, -5, 10, -10, 15, -15, 20, -20, \ldots\}$
   $\{1, 2,\ \ 5,\ 4,\ \ \ 5,\ 6,\ \ \ 7,\ 8,\ \ \ 9, \ldots\}$

3. $\{0, 2, -2, 4, -4, 6, -6, 8, -8, \ldots\}$
   $\{1, 2,\ \ 3, 4,\ \ 5, 6,\ \ 7, 8,\ \ 9, \ldots\}$

5. $\{1, -1, 3, -3, 5, -5, 7, -7, 9, -9, \ldots\}$
   $\{1,\ \ \ 2, 3,\ \ \ 4, 5,\ \ \ 6, 7,\ \ \ 8, 9,\ \ 10, \ldots\}$

7. $\{-1, -2, -3, -4, -5, \ldots\}$
   $\{\ \ 1,\ \ \ 2,\ \ \ 3,\ \ \ 4,\ \ \ 5, \ldots\}$

9.

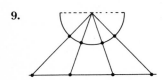

CHAPTER 4

Section 1

1. E   3. B   5. A   7. D

9. D   11. D   13. yes   15. yes, inverse for A is B, while C is its own inverse.

Section 2

1.

	M	N	P	Q	R	S	T	V
M	N	P	Q	M	V	T	R	S
N	P	Q	M	N	S	R	V	T
P	Q	M	N	P	T	V	S	R
Q	M	N	P	Q	R	S	T	V
R	T	S	V	R	Q	N	M	P
S	V	R	T	S	N	Q	P	M
T	S	V	R	T	P	M	Q	N
V	R	T	S	V	M	P	N	Q

3. yes to all parts

5. MP = PM = Q; NN = Q; QQ = Q;   RR = Q; SS = Q; TT = Q; VV = Q

7. yes   9. no; no identity   11. no; no inverses

13. yes   15. no; division by zero is not permitted

17. no; not closed   19. no; not closed

Section 3

1.

	A*	B*	C*	D*	E*	F*
A*	E*	D*	A*	F*	C*	B*
B*	F*	C*	B*	E*	D*	A*
C*	A*	B*	C*	D*	E*	F*
D*	B*	A*	D*	C*	F*	E*
E*	C*	F*	E*	B*	A*	D*
F*	D*	E*	F*	A*	B*	C*

3. yes   5. yes   7. yes, A   9. yes

11. yes   13. no; not closed, for example, MD = N.

Section 4

1. (c), (d), (e), (f), (g), and (h) are true

3.

	1	2	3	4	5	6
1	1	2	3	4	5	6
2	2	4	6	1	3	5
3	3	6	2	5	1	4
4	4	1	5	2	6	3
5	5	3	1	6	4	2
6	6	5	4	3	2	1

5. usually 100,000

7. yes   **9.** no; no identity

11. yes   **13.** true

Section 5

1. $\{2, 5, 8, 11, 14, 17, \ldots\}$ **3.** $\{3, 12, 21, \ldots\}$

5. no solution   **7.** 161   **9.** 43   **11.** 86

Section 6

1. $U^1 = U$; $U^2 = T$; $U^3 = J$; $U^4 = A$ **3.** no   **5.** yes; no

Section 7

1. yes   **3.** yes   **5.** yes   **7.** use any set of multiples of a counting number

9. use, for example, $\{Q, R\}$ from problem 3 above; let $Q \leftrightarrow 1$ and $R \leftrightarrow 2$. (By the way, any two groups, each of which contains only two elements, are isomorphic.)

11. The group from problem 1 above is not isomorphic to the subgroup $\{A, B, G, H\}$ of the rearrangements on four symbols. To see this, note that each element of the second group is its own inverse, which is not true in the first group. (Any group containing exactly four elements is isomorphic to one or the other of these two groups.)

13. Label the triangle so that 4 replaces 1′, 5 replaces 2′ and 6 replaces 3′. Then the desired correspondence is

$$A \leftrightarrow \frac{1\text{-}2\text{-}3\text{-}4\text{-}5\text{-}6}{2\text{-}3\text{-}1\text{-}5\text{-}6\text{-}4} \qquad C \leftrightarrow \frac{1\text{-}2\text{-}3\text{-}4\text{-}5\text{-}6}{4\text{-}6\text{-}5\text{-}1\text{-}3\text{-}2} \qquad E \leftrightarrow \frac{1\text{-}2\text{-}3\text{-}4\text{-}5\text{-}6}{6\text{-}5\text{-}4\text{-}3\text{-}2\text{-}1}$$

$$B \leftrightarrow \frac{1\text{-}2\text{-}3\text{-}4\text{-}5\text{-}6}{3\text{-}1\text{-}2\text{-}6\text{-}4\text{-}5} \qquad D \leftrightarrow \frac{1\text{-}2\text{-}3\text{-}4\text{-}5\text{-}6}{5\text{-}4\text{-}6\text{-}2\text{-}1\text{-}3} \qquad F \leftrightarrow \frac{1\text{-}2\text{-}3\text{-}4\text{-}5\text{-}6}{1\text{-}2\text{-}3\text{-}4\text{-}5\text{-}6}$$

CHAPTER 5

Section 1

1. (a) sentence   (c) neither   (e) sentence   (g) sentence   (i) neither
(k) open sentence   (m) sentence   (o) open sentence

2. (a) compound; or   (c) compound; or   (e) simple

3. one or the other, but not both

4. (a) I am a nice boy and I like girls.
(c) I am a nice boy and I don't like girls.
(e) I am not a nice boy or I like girls.
(g) I am not a nice boy or I do not like girls.

5. (a) $p \wedge q$ (c) $\sim p \wedge \sim q$ (e) $(p \vee q) \wedge \sim (p \wedge q)$ (g) $\sim p \wedge \sim q$

6. (a) F (c) F (e) T

7. (b), (d), (e), (f) are true

9. (a) His mother is not tall.
    (c) Some dew forms in the desert.
    (e) No men eat pancakes.
    (g) Not all rioters riot.

Section 2

1. (a) If it flies then it's a bird.
    (c) If it's Saturday then he goes to town.
    (e) If it's a dog then it has fleas.
    (g) If it's a dog then it's not a cat.

2. (a) If I study hard then I pass this lousy course.
    (c) It is not true that if I study hard then I won't pass.
    (e) I will pass unless I study hard.
    (g) If I don't pass then I study hard.
    (i) Either I study hard or I pass.

3. (a) $q \rightarrow \sim p$ (c) p unless q (e) $p \wedge q$ (g) (either q or p) unless $(q \wedge \sim p)$

5. (a) T (c) T (e) T   Note: There are several correct answers for (g).

7.

p	q	p because q
T	T	T
T	F	T
F	T	F
F	F	T

8. (a) p: he will do it; q: I will go to town; either $\sim p$, or q (c) p: I will go; q: George will stay; r: Alicia buys a coat; s: Sam will go; [(neither p nor q) unless $\sim r$] $\wedge \sim s$ (e) p: Hortense will go; q: I like raisins; $\sim p$ because q (Note: several answers are possible.)

9. $p \vee q$ is the same as $\sim(\sim p \wedge \sim q)$; $p \rightarrow q$ is the same as $\sim(p \wedge \sim q)$

11. (a) $\sim p$ (c) $p \wedge q$ **12.** (a) $\sim p$ (c) $p \wedge q$

13. Show that the expression on the right has the same truth table as the expression on the left.

Section 3

p	q	$\sim p \vee \sim q$
T	T	F
T	F	T
F	T	T
F	F	T

1.

p	q	$\sim p \rightarrow \sim q$
T	T	T
T	F	T
F	T	F
F	F	T

3.

p	q	either $\sim p$ or q
T	T	T
T	F	F
F	T	F
F	F	T

5.

7.

p	q	$(\sim p \vee \sim q) \wedge (\sim p \to \sim q)$
T	T	F
T	F	T
F	T	F
F	F	T

9.

p	q	$(\sim p \to \sim q) \to (q \to p)$
T	T	T
T	F	T tautology
F	T	T
F	F	T

11.

p	q	$(p \vee q) \to (q \vee p)$
T	T	T
T	F	T tautology
F	T	T
F	F	T

13.

p	q	r	$[(r \vee p) \wedge \sim q] \to p$
T	T	T	T
T	T	F	T
T	F	T	T
T	F	F	T
F	T	T	T
F	T	F	T
F	F	T	F
F	F	F	T

15.

p	q	r	s	$(\sim r \to s) \vee (p \to \sim q)$
T	T	T	T	T
T	T	T	F	T
T	T	F	T	T
T	T	F	F	F
T	F	T	T	T
T	F	T	F	T
T	F	F	T	T
T	F	F	F	T
F	T	T	T	T
F	T	T	F	T
F	T	F	T	T
F	T	F	F	T
F	F	T	T	T
F	F	T	F	T
F	F	F	T	T
F	F	F	F	T

17. 128

19. The operation may be defined as follows.

$\vee$	T	F
T	T	T
F	T	F

The identity element is F. There is no inverse for T: Thus the system is not a group.

Section 4

1. If it rains then I'll go to town.

3. If I pass the class then I did the homework.

5. If I drive fast then my father is the traffic judge.

7. If I cut the lawn then I have long grass.

9. If the temperature goes over 100° then it is summer.

11. If I feel bad then I lost on the slot machine.

13. Converse: If you endanger your health then you smoke cigarettes.
    Inverse: If you don't smoke then you don't endanger your health.
    Contrapositive: If you don't endanger your health then you don't smoke.

15. Converse: If it's not gold then it glitters.
    Inverse: If it does not glitter then it is gold.
    Contrapositive: If it is gold then it does not glitter; no

17. Converse: If you are rich then you live in a mansion.
    Inverse: If you don't live in a mansion then you're not rich.
    Contrapositive: If you're not rich then you don't live in a mansion.

19. F   21. F   23. consistent   25. contrary

27. By *cp*, we mean take the converse of a statement, then take the contrapositive of the result; this is the same as taking only the inverse of the original statement.

29. Make a chart of combinations:

	d	p
d	d	p
p	p	d

The system is closed and associative; d is the identity and each element is its own inverse.

31. Yes; p is the generator: $p^1 = p$, and $p^2 = d$.

33. Yes; see the group of problem 7, section 2, Chapter 4.

Section 5

1. valid   3. invalid   5. valid   7. valid   9. valid   11. invalid

13. valid   15. invalid

17. (a) invalid   (c) valid   (e) valid

18. (a) invalid   (c) valid   (e) invalid   (g) invalid

Section 6

1. My poultry are not officers.

3. Jenkins is inexperienced.

5. No name in this list is unmelodious.

7. No pawnbroker is dishonest.

9. No heavy fish is unkind to children.

CHAPTER 6

Section 1

1.

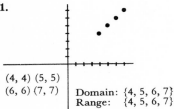

(4, 4) (5, 5)
(6, 6) (7, 7) | Domain: {4, 5, 6, 7}
Range: {4, 5, 6, 7}

A FUNCTION

3.

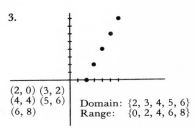

(2, 0) (3, 2)
(4, 4) (5, 6)
(6, 8) | Domain: {2, 3, 4, 5, 6}
Range: {0, 2, 4, 6, 8}

A FUNCTION

5.

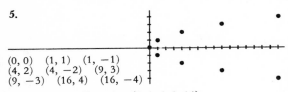

(0, 0) (1, 1) (1, −1)
(4, 2) (4, −2) (9, 3)
(9, −3) (16, 4) (16, −4)

Domain: {0, 1, 4, 9, 16}
Range: {0, 1, −1, 2, −2, 3, −3, 4, −4}

NOT A FUNCTION

7.

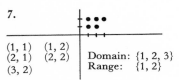

(1, 1) (1, 2)
(2, 1) (2, 2)
(3, 2) | Domain: {1, 2, 3}
Range: {1, 2}

NOT A FUNCTION

9.

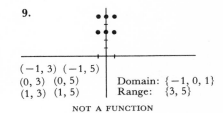

(−1, 3) (−1, 5)
(0, 3) (0, 5)
(1, 3) (1, 5) | Domain: {−1, 0, 1}
Range: {3, 5}

NOT A FUNCTION

11.

(−4, −3)
(−3, −3)
(0, −3)
(1, −3) (6, −3) | Domain: {−4, −3, 0, 1, 6}
Range: {−3}

A FUNCTION

13. equivalence relation

15. not an equivalence relation; not transitive

17. equivalence relation

19. Whenever a vertical line cuts the graph in more than one point, we have one x value but more than one y value.

20. The symmetric property says "*If* $(r, s) \in R$ then $(s, r) \in R$," while the transitive property says "*If* $(x, y) \in R$ and $(y, z) \in R$ then $(x, z) \in R$." The reflexive property, on the other hand, requires that (r, r) be in R for every element r. The proof in the text merely shows that if $(r, s) \in R$ then $(r, r) \in R$; not that $(r, r) \in R$ for every element r.

Section 2

1.

3.
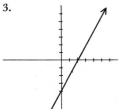

5.

7.
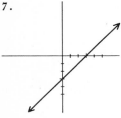

9.
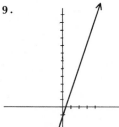

11.
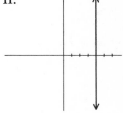

13. 1   15. 2   17. 1   19. 0

21.
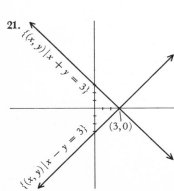

$\{(x, y) \mid x + y = 3\}$

$\{(x, y) \mid x - y = 3\}$

(3,0)

23.
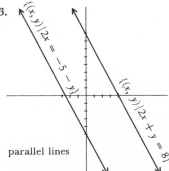

$\{(x, y) \mid 2x = -5 - y\}$

$\{(x, y) \mid 2x + y = 8\}$

parallel lines

25.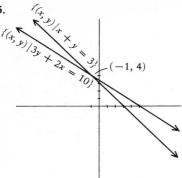

27. $\frac{5}{4}$; -3

28. (a)

(c)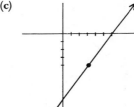

(e)

Section 3

1.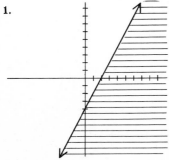

3.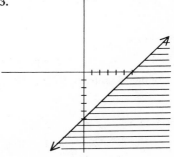

5.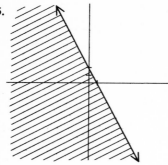

7.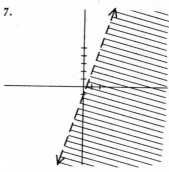

9.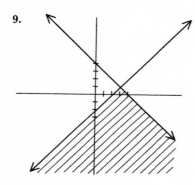

11.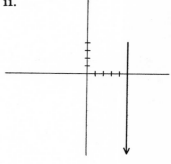

13.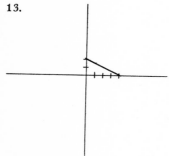

15. a circle, a square, a triangle   **17.** yes

Section 4

1. 12   **3.** \$112, with 4 pigs, 12 geese.   **5.** 8 of #1, 3 of #2

7. either 6 ashtrays, 3 cufflinks or $7\frac{1}{2}$ ashtrays only.

Section 5

1. 5   **3.** $\sqrt{29}$ **5.** 1

7. The distance between $(1, 3)$ and $(5, 6)$ is 5, between $(5, 6)$ and $(9, 9)$ is 5, and between $(1, 3)$ and $(9, 9)$ is 10. Since $5 + 5 = 10$, the 3 points cannot be the vertices of a triangle and must be on the same line.

Section 6

1.

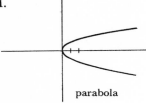

parabola

3.

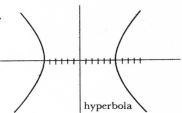

hyperbola

5.

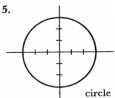

circle

7.

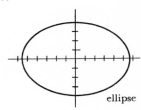

ellipse

9.

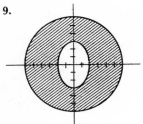

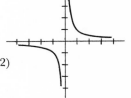

11. $(0, \ )$—impossible;
$(1, 1), (-1, -1), (2, \frac{1}{2}), (-2, -\frac{1}{2}), (3, \frac{1}{3}), (-3, -\frac{1}{3}), (\frac{1}{2}, 2)$
$(-\frac{1}{2}, -2)$;
$(\ , 0)$—impossible

13. $(x + 5)^2 + (y + 2)^2 = 4$ **15.** $(x - h)^2 + (y - k)^2 = r^2$

16.

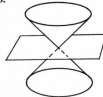

plane cutting cone to form one line

degenerate circle

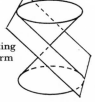

plane cutting cone to form two intersecting straight lines

degenerate parabola

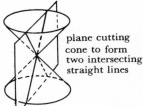

degenerate hyperbola

Section 7

1.

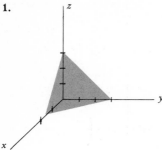

3.

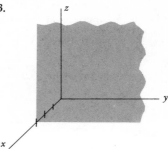

5.

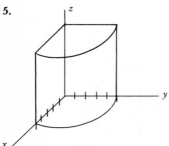

7. This graph is an elliptic paraboloid. See figure 6.36.

9.

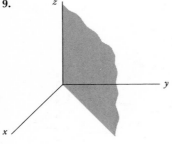

Note: we show only those portions of the graphs where x, y, and z are all positive.

CHAPTER 7

Section 1

1. (a) $\frac{1}{4}$ (c) $\frac{1}{2}$

2. (a) $\frac{1}{8}$ (c) $\frac{3}{8}$

3. (a) $\frac{1}{13}$ (c) $\frac{4}{13}$ (e) $\frac{3}{13}$ (g) 0

4. (a) $\frac{1}{36}$ (c) $\frac{1}{6}$ (e) $\frac{1}{36}$ (g) 0 (i) $\frac{1}{6}$

5. (a) 17 to 1 (c) 17 to 1 (e) 11 to 1

Section 2

1. (a) 25   (c) 8

2. (a) 60   (c) $\frac{2}{5}$

3. 32

5. (a) $5^7 = 78,125$ (c) $9 \cdot 10^4 \cdot 1^2 = 90,000$ (e) $9 \cdot 9 \cdot 8 \cdot 7 \cdot 6 \cdot 5 \cdot 4 = 544,320$

6. (a) 6   (c) 360   (e) 1   (g) 120   (i) 6

7. (a) $26^3 \cdot 10^3 = 17,576,000$ (c) $26 \cdot 25 \cdot 24 \cdot 10 \cdot 9 \cdot 8 = 11,232,000$

8. (a) $\frac{1}{2}$ (c) $\frac{1}{10}$

9. (a) $5! = 120$

Section 3

1. (a) 1   (c) 10   (e) 5

3. $_{12}C_5 = 792$

4. (a) $\dfrac{_5C_3}{_9C_3} = \dfrac{5}{42}$ (c) $\dfrac{_5C_1 \cdot _4C_2}{_9C_3} = \dfrac{5}{14}$

5. (a) 37 to 5   (c) 5 to 1

6. (a) $\dfrac{_{380}C_4}{_{400}C_4}$

7. (a) 0   (c) $\dfrac{_{40}C_5}{_{52}C_5} = \dfrac{2109}{8330}$ (e) $\dfrac{_{12}C_3 \cdot _{40}C_2}{_{52}C_5} = \dfrac{55}{833}$

Section 4

1. (a) $\frac{1}{3}$ (c) 1   (e) $\frac{1}{3}$

2. (a) $\frac{1}{36}$ (c) $\frac{1}{4}$ (e) $\frac{1}{9}$

3. (a) $\frac{1}{64}$ (c) $\frac{1}{140,608}$ (e) $\frac{1}{208}$

4. (a) $\frac{11}{850}$ (c) 0   (e) $\frac{1}{204}$

5. (a) $\dfrac{_5C_4}{_8C_4} = \dfrac{1}{14}$ (c) $\dfrac{_5C_2 \cdot _3C_2}{_8C_4} = \dfrac{3}{7}$ (e) $\dfrac{_5C_3 \cdot _3C_1}{_8C_4} = \dfrac{3}{7}$ (g) $\dfrac{_5C_4}{_8C_4} = \dfrac{1}{14}$

6. (a) $\dfrac{_{13}C_5}{_{52}C_5} = \dfrac{33}{66,640}$ (c) $4 \cdot \dfrac{_{13}C_5}{_{52}C_5} = \dfrac{33}{16,660}$

7. (a) $\dfrac{_5C_5}{_{52}C_5} = \dfrac{1}{_{52}C_5} = \dfrac{1}{2,598,960}$

Section 5

1.
```
                                        1       1
                                    1       2       1
                                1       3       3       1
                            1       4       6       4       1
                        1       5      10      10       5       1
                    1       6      15      20      15       6       1
                1       7      21      35      35      21       7       1
            1       8      28      56      70      56      28       8       1
        1       9      36      84     126     126      84      36       9       1
```

2. (a) 6   (c) 6   (e) 56

3. (a) $\frac{1}{512}$ (c) $\frac{63}{256}$ (e) $\frac{9}{128}$ (g) $\frac{65}{256}$

4. (a) $\frac{5}{42}$ (c) $\frac{1}{84}$ (e) $\frac{5}{14}$ (g) $\frac{1}{28}$

5. (a) $_5C_2 = 10$ (c) $_3C_2 = 3$ (e) 7

Section 6

1. (a) $1

3. no

4. (a) 9.45¢   (b) no

5. $3\frac{1}{2}$

6. (a) 11.1¢   (b) no

7. 1 to 1

Section 7

3.39

CHAPTER 8

Section 2

1. (a)

Value	Number of Occurrences
1	3
2	6
3	5
4	7
5	2
6	2

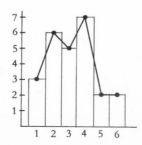

2. Two equal class intervals:

(a)

Class Interval Boundaries	Frequency
0–50	17
50–100	13

(b)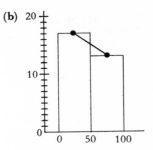

Five equal class intervals:

(a)

Class Interval Boundaries	Frequency
0–20	6
20–40	6
40–60	8
60–80	6
80–100	4

(b)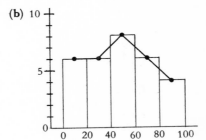

Section 3

1. (a) mean = 2.727; median = 3; modes are 2 and 3
(c) mean = 34.33; median = 25.5; all six values are modes

2. (a) mean = 18.8; median = 19; mode = 19
(c) mean = 458.4; median = 480; mode = 410

3. mean = 5.44

5. 960 boxes

Section 4

1. (a) range = 8; mean deviation = 2.84; variance = 9.42; standard deviation = 3.07
(c) range = 50; mean deviation = 15.57; variance = 328.38; standard deviation = 18.1

2. (a) range = 6; mean deviation = 0.8; variance = 1.6; standard deviation = 1.26

3. Because there is a single extreme value, 5

4. (a) 50   (c) 97 or 98   (e) 68

5. (a) curve *B*   (b) both the same

Section 5

1. Should not accept fair coin hypothesis [$z = 2.4$, well up in the rejection region shown in figure 8.23(a)]

3. (a) 200   (c) 5609   (e) 5 feet 8 inches

Section 6

1. yes; the probability of a result that high is only about 0.004

3. (a) 0.01 level: \$3467; 0.05 level: \$3535
    (b) 0.01 level: less than \$3443 or more than \$3957;
        0.05 level: less than \$3504 or more than \$3896

4. $b = 0.86$; $a = 2.24$

5. (a) 7.40   (c) 15.14

7. (a)

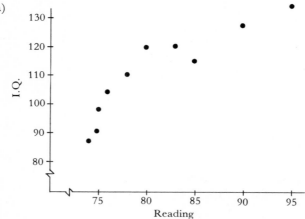

   (b) $Y = -51 + 2X$
   (c) 79

9. probably less consistent

CHAPTER 9

Section 1

1. $\begin{pmatrix} -2 & -1 & 4 \\ -1 & -4 & 3 \\ 0 & 5 & -2 \end{pmatrix}$ **3.** $\begin{pmatrix} -8 & 0 & 2 \\ 6 & -8 & 4 \\ -2 & 4 & 2 \end{pmatrix}$ **5.** $\begin{pmatrix} 20 & -2 & 2 \\ -20 & 16 & -6 \\ 6 & -2 & -10 \end{pmatrix}$

7. $\begin{pmatrix} -14 & 10 & 3 \\ 15 & 2 & -3 \\ 8 & -18 & 4 \end{pmatrix}$ **9.** $\begin{pmatrix} -3 & 17 & -1 \\ 8 & 9 & -18 \\ -5 & -28 & 19 \end{pmatrix}$ **11.** $\begin{pmatrix} 190 & 149 & -135 \\ -387 & -12 & -241 \\ 89 & -19 & 114 \end{pmatrix}$

13.
$$\begin{pmatrix} 352 & -88 & 158 \\ -87 & 173 & -359 \\ 195 & -67 & 147 \end{pmatrix}$$

15.
$$\begin{pmatrix} -51 & -14 & 16 \\ 167 & -86 & 11 \\ -58 & 32 & 1 \end{pmatrix}$$

17.
$$\begin{pmatrix} 6 & -1 & 2 \\ -7 & 4 & -1 \\ 2 & 1 & -4 \end{pmatrix}$$

19. not always true

21.
$$\begin{pmatrix} 15 & 8 & -4 & 24 \\ 6 & 0 & 0 & -8 \\ 0 & -4 & 2 & 10 \\ 3 & 2 & -1 & 7 \end{pmatrix}$$

23. Same: doesn't matter

Section 2

1. $I^4 = I$

3.
$$\begin{pmatrix} 1 & 0 & 0 & 0 \\ 0 & 1 & 0 & 0 \\ 0 & 0 & 1 & 0 \\ 0 & 0 & 0 & 1 \end{pmatrix}$$

5. A is a square matrix

7. A 3x3 matrix containing all zeros

9. The only real numbers m such that $m^2 = m$ are 1 and 0; however, the situation is different with matrices. See problems 17 and 18 of section 5.

Section 3

1. 10   **3.** 12   **5.** 1   **7.** 9   **9.** -6 **11.** -10 **13.** -31

Section 4

1.
$$\begin{pmatrix} -4 & 0 & 1 \\ -1 & 2 & 1 \\ 3 & -4 & 2 \end{pmatrix}$$

3.
$$\begin{pmatrix} 6 & -1 & 2 \\ 2 & 1 & -4 \\ -7 & 4 & -1 \end{pmatrix}$$

5.
$$\begin{pmatrix} 2 & -1 & 3 \\ 8 & 0 & -2 \\ 1 & 3 & -3 \end{pmatrix}$$

7.
$$\begin{pmatrix} -7 & 7 & -15 \\ -96 & -12 & 4 \\ -9 & 4 & -4 \end{pmatrix}$$

9.
$$\begin{pmatrix} -\frac{13}{2} & 5 & \frac{7}{2} \\ 3 & -4 & 2 \\ -1 & 2 & 1 \end{pmatrix}$$

11.
$$\begin{pmatrix} -7 & 7 & -15 \\ 24 & 3 & -1 \\ -33 & 1 & -3 \end{pmatrix}$$

13.
$$\begin{pmatrix} 11 & 7 & -4 \\ -7 & 7 & -15 \\ -\frac{41}{4} & -\frac{33}{4} & 14 \end{pmatrix}$$

15. $R_{\frac{1}{2}}$ **17.** $R_2(2)$

Note: more than one sequence may be possible in the problems below.

19. $R_2(-1)$, $R_2(-2) + R_1$

21. $R_1(-\frac{1}{2})$, $R_1(-4) + R_2$, $R_2(\frac{1}{5})$, $R_2(+1) + R_1$

23. $R_1(\frac{1}{6})$, $R_2(\frac{1}{4})$, $R_3(\frac{1}{2})$, $R_2(-\frac{1}{2}) + R_1$

25. R_2^1, R_3^2

Section 5

1. $\begin{pmatrix} 1 & 0 \\ 0 & -1 \end{pmatrix}$ **3.** $\begin{pmatrix} \frac{3}{2} & -\frac{1}{2} \\ -2 & 1 \end{pmatrix}$ **5.** $\begin{pmatrix} \frac{13}{5} & \frac{6}{5} \\ -2 & -1 \end{pmatrix}$ **7.** no inverse

9. $\begin{pmatrix} -\frac{3}{2} & 1 \\ 1 & -\frac{1}{2} \end{pmatrix}$ **11.** $\begin{pmatrix} 1 & -2 & 0 \\ 0 & 1 & 0 \\ 0 & -1 & 1 \end{pmatrix}$ **13.** $\begin{pmatrix} 0 & \frac{1}{3} & -1 \\ 0 & \frac{1}{3} & 0 \\ \frac{1}{2} & -\frac{5}{6} & 2 \end{pmatrix}$

15. The matrix is its own inverse.

17. The square of the matrix equals the matrix

Section 6

1. no   **3.** no   **5.** yes   **7.** no   **9.** no   **11.** yes

Section 7

1. yes   **3.** yes   **5.** no; no identity   **7.** yes

Section 8

1. $x = 3\frac{1}{4}, y = \frac{1}{4}$ **3.** $x = -1, y = -4$ **5.** $x = \frac{4}{3}, y = \frac{2}{3}$

7. $x = 3, y = 0, z = -3$ **9.** 2 potrezebies, 6 zotyls

11. each potrezebie cost \$5, each zotyl costs \$1

Section 9

1. $\begin{pmatrix} 35 \\ -88 \end{pmatrix}$ $\begin{pmatrix} -4 \\ 0 \end{pmatrix}$ $\begin{pmatrix} 15 \\ -48 \end{pmatrix}$ $\begin{pmatrix} -9 \\ 9 \end{pmatrix}$ $\begin{pmatrix} 35 \\ -97 \end{pmatrix}$ $\begin{pmatrix} 53 \\ -133 \end{pmatrix}$ $\begin{pmatrix} 16 \\ -50 \end{pmatrix}$ $\begin{pmatrix} 5 \\ -15 \end{pmatrix}$

3. Santa Claus is fat.

CHAPTER 10

Section 1

1. (a) $.648 \times 10^3$ (c) $.412 \times 10^{-4}$ (e) $.668 \times 10^0$

2. (a) 18,300   (c) 1

3. Multiply numerical parts, and add the exponents.

Section 2

Note: Normally there are several ways to write a given computer program; therefore the answers presented here should not be considered the only ones possible.

1.
10401210011041	transfer 12 to the accumulator
10410110021042	add 16 to the contents of the accumulator
10420310041043	multiply the contents of the accumulator by 13
10431110091044	transfer the number in the accumulator to 1009
10446010011001	end

3. Assume 2 is stored at location 1003, with 200 stored at location 1004. With these modifications the program will produce the sum of the first 100 even counting numbers.

5. Assume that 2 is stored at 1001, 6 at 1002, and 11 at 1003. Then go through the following steps:

10041210031005	transfer 11 to the accumulator
10050210021006	subtract 6 from the number in the accumulator
10060410011007	divide 2 into the number in the accumulator
10071110091008	transfer the contents of the accumulator to 1009
10084510091010	print the answer
10106010111011	end

Section 3

1.
```
X = 0;
P = (2*X**4 + X)/(6 + X);
PUT LIST ('IF X = ', X, 'THEN P = ', P);
END;
```

3. Find the sum of the squares of the first fifty squares of counting numbers, or add the fourth powers of the first fifty counting numbers.

5. One solution:
```
DO I = −2 TO 15 BY 1;
P = I + 4;
PUT LIST ('WHEN X = ', I, 'THEN P = ', P);
END;
END;
```

7. If the old value of TGPTD is less than $4000, but the new value is more than $4000, then the program of the text does not properly tax the employee. It should be modified as follows.

> Change the first computer display on page 297 to read:
> IF TGPTD $<$ = 4000 THEN GO TO TOM;
> IF (TGPTD − GROSS) $<$ 4000 THEN GO TO EEK;
> SOCSEC = .02*GROSS;
> GO TO HARRY;
> EEK: SOCSEC = .02*(TGPTD − 4000) + .04*(4000 − (TGPTD − GROSS));
>   GO TO HARRY;
> TOM: SOCSEC = .04*GROSS;
> HARRY: Continue

Section 4

1. Begin: A(1) = 3, A(2) = 4, A(3) = −2, A(4) = 1. MAX = A(1), so here MAX = 3. Now, let I = 2. Since A(2) is not less than MAX we know A(2) is at least as large as MAX, so we let MAX = A(2); thus MAX = 4. Now, increase I by 1 to 3. Since A(3) = −2 is less than MAX we proceed. Increase I to 4 and compare MAX and A(4). Since A(4) is smaller, MAX = 4 is the largest of the numbers, and the computer prints

THE LARGEST NUMBER IS 4

3. The computer will find the average: 5.

5. Entry $C(I, J)$ of the product matrix is obtained by multiplying the entries of row I of A by those of column J of B, and adding the results. The following program will do this:

> C(I, J) = 0; (see below)
> DO I = 1 TO 3 BY 1;
> DO J = 1 TO 3 BY 1;
> DO K = 1 TO 3 BY 1;
> C(I, J) = C(I, J) + A(I, K)*B(K, J);

To finish the program we need END statements for each DO loop and for the entire program. We have assumed here that at the beginning of the program $C(I, J) = 0$ for every value of I and J.

Section 5

1. 8

3. 10   LET S = 0
   12   FOR X = 1 TO 100 STEP 1
   14   LET S = S + X*X
   16   NEXT X
   18   PRINT S
   20   END

CHAPTER 11

Section 1

1.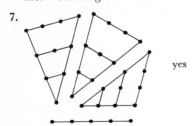

3. $45 + 55 = 100$

5. The sum of the first five counting numbers is represented by

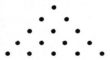

This is the triangular number 15. A similar thing can be done for the sum of the first *n* counting numbers.

7.

yes

Section 2

1. In the figure $AC = BC$, $AE = BE$, and $CE = CE$. Thus triangles ACE and BCE are congruent (by side-side-side). Therefore, angles ACE and BCE are equal. Since

$AC = BC$ and $CD = CD$, we can say triangles ACD and CDB are congruent (by side-angle-side). Thus $AD = DB$ and angles ADC and CDB are equal supplementary angles and hence are right angles.

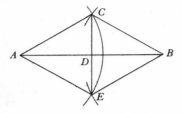

3. We know, by construction, that $BA = AC$ and $BD = CD$. Since $AD = AD$ we have triangles ABD and ADC congruent by side-side-side. Thus, angles BAD and CAD are equal supplementary angles and hence right angles.

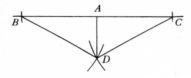

5. Just one.

7. The method doesn't work on an angle of $175°$:

9. Use construction 6 as one method; bisect the segment and bisect each resulting part as the other method.

11. Use construction 7.

13.

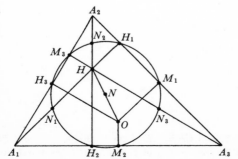

15. 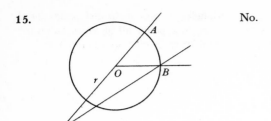   No.

17. Use construction 7, with the two segments having a length equal to *a*.

19. First bisect the angle, and then trisect each half.

Section 3

1. Use figure 11.36. The area of rectangle *TABU* is given by the product of its base (*AB*) and height. However, by the hint for this problem, the height of the rectangle is half the altitude of the triangle. Since the area of the triangle equals the area of the rectangle, we have the area of the triangle given by one-half the product of its base and altitude.

3. Follow the steps leading to figure 11.37.

5.

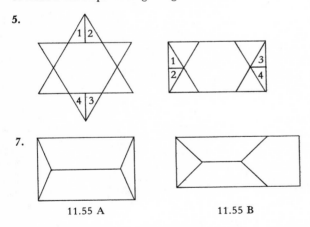

7.

11.55 A   11.55 B

9. The shaded area in the left figure is a square of area c^2, while the shaded portion on the right has area $a^2 + b^2$.

11. The squaw on the hippopotamus equals the sons of the squaws on the other two hides.

Section 4

5. In a plane, if two triangles are placed so that lines joining corresponding sides, when extended, meet in three collinear points, then lines joining corresponding

vertices meet in a point. In space, if two triangles are on nonparallel planes and if the extensions of corresponding sides meet in three points all of which lie on the same line, then the lines joining corresponding vertices meet in a point. Yes.

Section 5

1. A point on the circle is its own inverse.

3. The inverse points lie on the circle going through 0 and the points of intersection of the line and the circle of inversion.

5. The inverse points lie on a circle that does not go through 0.

7. (a) by construction   (b) by construction   (c) both right angles   (d) reflexive property   (e) two angles of one equal to two angles of the other   (f) given as the radius   (g) corresponding sides of similar triangles are proportional   (h) multiply both sides of the equation of (g) by OP' (i) the definition of inverse point.

9. Build a circular cage and stand inside it. Upon performing an inversion transformation the mathematician is transformed to the outside of the cage and the lion to the inside.

APPENDIX

Table A. SQUARE ROOTS

n	$\sqrt{n}$	$\sqrt{10n}$	n	$\sqrt{n}$	$\sqrt{10n}$	n	$\sqrt{n}$	$\sqrt{10n}$
1	1.000	3.16	41	6.403	20.25	81	9.000	28.46
2	1.414	4.47	42	6.481	20.49	82	9.005	28.64
3	1.732	5.48	43	6.557	20.74	83	9.110	28.81
4	2.000	6.32	44	6.633	20.98	84	9.165	28.98
5	2.236	7.07	45	6.708	21.21	85	9.220	29.16
6	2.449	7.75	46	6.782	21.45	86	9.274	29.33
7	2.646	8.37	47	6.856	21.70	87	9.327	29.40
8	2.828	8.94	48	6.928	21.91	88	9.381	29.66
9	3.000	9.49	49	7.000	22.14	89	9.434	29.83
10	3.162	10.00	50	7.071	22.36	90	9.487	30.00
11	3.317	10.49	51	7.141	22.58	91	9.539	30.17
12	3.464	10.95	52	7.211	22.80	92	9.592	30.33
13	3.606	11.40	53	7.280	23.02	93	9.644	30.50
14	3.742	11.83	54	7.348	23.24	94	9.695	30.66
15	3.873	12.25	55	7.416	23.45	95	9.747	30.82
16	4.000	12.65	56	7.483	23.66	96	9.798	30.98
17	4.123	13.04	57	7.550	23.87	97	9.849	31.14
18	4.243	13.42	58	7.616	24.08	98	9.899	31.30
19	4.359	13.78	59	7.681	24.29	99	9.950	31.46
20	4.472	14.14	60	7.746	24.49	100	10.000	31.62
21	4.583	14.49	61	7.810	24.70			
22	4.690	14.83	62	7.874	24.90			
23	4.796	15.17	63	7.937	25.10			
24	4.899	15.49	64	8.000	25.30			
25	5.000	15.81	65	8.062	25.50			
26	5.099	16.12	66	8.124	25.69			
27	5.196	16.43	67	8.185	25.88			
28	5.292	16.73	68	8.246	26.08			
29	5.385	17.03	69	8.307	26.27			
30	5.477	17.32	70	8.367	26.46			
31	5.568	17.61	71	8.426	26.65			
32	5.657	17.89	72	8.485	26.83			
33	5.745	18.17	73	8.544	27.02			
34	5.831	18.44	74	8.602	27.20			
35	5.916	18.71	75	8.660	27.39			
36	6.000	18.97	76	8.718	27.57			
37	6.083	19.24	77	8.775	27.75			
38	6.164	19.49	78	8.832	27.93			
39	6.245	19.75	79	8.888	28.11			
40	6.325	20.00	80	8.944	28.28			

Table B. RANDOM NUMBERS

51592	05409	48616	49258	84927	01554
77876	36431	94419	29477	78788	31695
36500	16309	52572	02856	28538	57056
40571	28158	71378	18714	11569	44233
04822	70116	43810	55522	43178	34029
53033	98859	69766	57888	00973	60015
92080	88676	25517	72875	30828	62619
01587	93663	76384	86829	16623	58748
36006	24654	80874	00479	62213	54986
63698	25989	99467	96968	37390	91503
17297	29748	25189	13665	56708	56670
22841	01089	33603	24044	70973	86582
91979	25875	89630	62756	45088	26202
96480	41199	44064	52832	21637	49681
74949	05575	94715	88114	14510	33243
76896	73132	08119	41041	65825	37687
47588	63242	69260	72805	79518	40142
45521	63906	56355	22969	05621	90714
02472	14355	11644	50844	93285	64798
55184	39661	92318	97487	95679	19687
40177	89610	53965	83173	68849	53643
84861	54344	58346	60375	09052	12522
36937	56274	71269	51583	80762	26142
20931	42679	55328	02893	68408	76415
22454	17567	43731	70143	36321	07382
73219	65549	65754	63897	33788	69213
55707	65723	42297	14516	89035	12067
48007	20246	43460	72654	28217	13454
65191	87395	43015	18635	40455	90529
06772	31033	03161	00209	50808	52852
94928	55741	89567	19017	01305	04104
15709	31249	71893	77692	98133	41084
39922	82319	86717	95969	76687	88813
96365	09359	09523	58728	65729	18593
14655	78731	66736	55810	20876	36062
65587	18804	79856	41850	66923	78530
76905	58230	92671	69291	00607	89199
12369	38927	10794	35132	20576	39688
54219	04606	55713	95137	13924	92141
89329	42553	54727	66731	88300	19874
90060	55470	28445	41086	17323	25103
06975	06250	92544	74277	71219	83337
05050	01132	45005	44925	01550	34514
69774	51403	33654	20204	86261	22628
78351	39635	00471	90516	57471	54520
11464	20344	39253	96317	84067	95365
84086	09843	35827	80337	48123	00244
51497	73378	28420	13622	56041	27958
12307	44437	09304	31129	12593	36101
68009	39674	02746	53208	22212	62471
39687	42846	76228	82338	68431	94605
45062	81641	62544	93418	73479	04950
43752	84131	37249	39415	93918	25039
05477	88906	43198	28929	48957	78845
28636	52109	80957	90112	87141	84641
44070	58436	38175	30222	22592	58977
77653	86333	09237	99926	95099	77856
39931	88249	79358	73938	15818	81452
04744	37991	53313	10649	93971	51981

Table C. AREAS UNDER THE STANDARD NORMAL CURVE

The column under A gives the proportion of the area under the entire curve which is between $z = 0$ and a positive value of z.

z	A	z	A	z	A	z	A
.00	.0000	.53	.2019	1.06	.3554	1.59	.4441
.01	.0040	.54	.2054	1.07	.3577	1.60	.4452
.02	.0080	.55	.2088	1.08	.3599	1.61	.4463
.03	.0120	.56	.2123	1.09	.3621	1.62	.4474
.04	.0160	.57	.2157	1.10	.3643	1.63	.4485
.05	.0199	.58	.2190	1.11	.3665	1.64	.4495
.06	.0239	.59	.2224	1.12	.3686	1.65	.4505
.07	.0279	.60	.2258	1.13	.3708	1.66	.4515
.08	.0319	.61	.2291	1.14	.3729	1.67	.4525
.09	.0359	.62	.2324	1.15	.3749	1.68	.4535
.10	.0398	.63	.2357	1.16	.3770	1.69	.4545
.11	.0438	.64	.2389	1.17	.3790	1.70	.4554
.12	.0478	.65	.2422	1.18	.3810	1.71	.4564
.13	.0517	.66	.2454	1.19	.3830	1.72	.4573
.14	.0557	.67	.2486	1.20	.3849	1.73	.4582
.15	.0596	.68	.2518	1.21	.3869	1.74	.4591
.16	.0636	.69	.2549	1.22	.3888	1.75	.4599
.17	.0675	.70	.2580	1.23	.3907	1.76	.4608
.18	.0714	.71	.2612	1.24	.3925	1.77	.4616
.19	.0754	.72	.2642	1.25	.3944	1.78	.4625
.20	.0793	.73	.2673	1.26	.3962	1.79	.4633
.21	.0832	.74	.2704	1.27	.3980	1.80	.4641
.22	.0871	.75	.2734	1.28	.3997	1.81	.4649
.23	.0910	.76	.2764	1.29	.4015	1.82	.4656
.24	.0948	.77	.2794	1.30	.4032	1.83	.4664
.25	.0987	.78	.2823	1.31	.4049	1.84	.4671
.26	.1026	.79	.2852	1.32	.4066	1.85	.4678
.27	.1064	.80	.2881	1.33	.4082	1.86	.4686
.28	.1103	.81	.2910	1.34	.4099	1.87	.4693
.29	.1141	.82	.2939	1.35	.4115	1.88	.4700
.30	.1179	.83	.2967	1.36	.4131	1.89	.4706
.31	.1217	.84	.2996	1.37	.4147	1.90	.4713
.32	.1255	.85	.3023	1.38	.4162	1.91	.4719
.33	.1293	.86	.3051	1.39	.4177	1.92	.4726
.34	.1331	.87	.3079	1.40	.4192	1.93	.4732
.35	.1368	.88	.3106	1.41	.4207	1.94	.4738
.36	.1406	.89	.3133	1.42	.4222	1.95	.4744
.37	.1443	.90	.3159	1.43	.4236	1.96	.4750
.38	.1480	.91	.3186	1.44	.4251	1.97	.4756
.39	.1517	.92	.3212	1.45	.4265	1.98	.4762
.40	.1554	.93	.3238	1.46	.4279	1.99	.4767
.41	.1591	.94	.3264	1.47	.4292	2.00	.4773
.42	.1628	.95	.3289	1.48	.4306	2.01	.4778
.43	.1664	.96	.3315	1.49	.4319	2.02	.4783
.44	.1700	.97	.3340	1.50	.4332	2.03	.4788
.45	.1736	.98	.3365	1.51	.4345	2.04	.4793
.46	.1772	.99	.3389	1.52	.4357	2.05	.4798
.47	.1808	1.00	.3413	1.53	.4370	2.06	.4803
.48	.1844	1.01	.3438	1.54	.4382	2.07	.4808
.49	.1879	1.02	.3461	1.55	.4394	2.08	.4812
.50	.1915	1.03	.3485	1.56	.4406	2.09	.4817
.51	.1950	1.04	.3508	1.57	.4418	2.10	.4821
.52	.1985	1.05	.3531	1.58	.4430	2.11	.4826

Table C. AREAS UNDER THE STANDARD NORMAL CURVE (Cont.)

z	A	z	A	z	A	z	A
2.12	.4830	2.57	.4949	3.02	.4987	3.46	.4997
2.13	.4834	2.58	.4951	3.03	.4988	3.47	.4997
2.14	.4838	2.59	.4952	3.04	.4988	3.48	.4998
2.15	.4842	2.60	.4953	3.05	.4989	3.49	.4998
2.16	.4846	2.61	.4955	3.06	.4989	3.50	.4998
2.17	.4850	2.62	.4956	3.07	.4989	3.51	.4998
2.18	.4854	2.63	.4957	3.08	.4990	3.52	.4998
2.19	.4857	2.64	.4959	3.09	.4990	3.53	.4998
2.20	.4861	2.65	.4960	3.10	.4990	3.54	.4998
2.21	.4865	2.66	.4961	3.11	.4991	3.55	.4998
2.22	.4868	2.67	.4962	3.12	.4991	3.56	.4998
2.23	.4871	2.68	.4963	3.13	.4991	3.57	.4998
2.24	.4875	2.69	.4964	3.14	.4992	3.58	.4998
2.25	.4878	2.70	.4965	3.15	.4992	3.59	.4998
2.26	.4881	2.71	.4966	3.16	.4992	3.60	.4998
2.27	.4884	2.72	.4967	3.17	.4992	3.61	.4999
2.28	.4887	2.73	.4968	3.18	.4993	3.62	.4999
2.29	.4890	2.74	.4969	3.19	.4993	3.63	.4999
2.30	.4893	2.75	.4970	3.20	.4993	3.64	.4999
2.31	.4896	2.76	.4971	3.21	.4993	3.65	.4999
2.32	.4898	2.77	.4972	3.22	.4994	3.66	.4999
2.33	.4901	2.78	.4973	3.23	.4994	3.67	.4999
2.34	.4904	2.79	.4974	3.24	.4994	3.68	.4999
2.35	.4906	2.80	.4974	3.25	.4994	3.69	.4999
2.36	.4909	2.81	.4975	3.26	.4994	3.70	.4999
2.37	.4911	2.82	.4976	3.27	.4995	3.71	.4999
2.38	.4913	2.83	.4977	3.28	.4995	3.72	.4999
2.39	.4916	2.84	.4977	3.29	.4995	3.73	.4999
2.40	.4918	2.85	.4978	3.30	.4995	3.74	.4999
2.41	.4920	2.86	.4979	3.31	.4995	3.75	.4999
2.42	.4922	2.87	.4980	3.32	.4996	3.76	.4999
2.43	.4925	2.88	.4980	3.33	.4996	3.77	.4999
2.44	.4927	2.89	.4981	3.34	.4996	3.78	.4999
2.45	.4929	2.90	.4981	3.35	.4996	3.79	.4999
2.46	.4931	2.91	.4982	3.36	.4996	3.80	.4999
2.47	.4932	2.92	.4983	3.37	.4996	3.81	.4999
2.48	.4934	2.93	.4983	3.38	.4996	3.82	.4999
2.49	.4936	2.94	.4984	3.39	.4997	3.83	.4999
2.50	.4938	2.95	.4984	3.40	.4997	3.84	.4999
2.51	.4940	2.96	.4985	3.41	.4997	3.85	.4999
2.52	.4941	2.97	.4985	3.42	.4997	3.86	.4999
2.53	.4943	2.98	.4986	3.43	.4997	3.87	.5000
2.54	.4945	2.99	.4986	3.44	.4997	3.88	.5000
2.55	.4946	3.00	.4987	3.45	.4997	3.89	.5000
2.56	.4948	3.01	.4987				

INDEX